UNDERSTANDING PSYCHOTIC SPEECH:
BEYOND FREUD AND CHOMSKY

UNDERSTANDING PSYCHOTIC SPEECH:
BEYOND FREUD AND CHOMSKY

By

ELAINE OSTRACH CHAIKA, PH.D.

Providence College
Providence, Rhode Island

CHARLES C THOMAS • PUBLISHER
Springfield • Illinois • U.S.A.

...istributed Throughout the World by

CHARLES C THOMAS • PUBLISHER
2600 South First Street
Springfield, Illinois 62794-9265

© *1990 by* CHARLES C THOMAS • PUBLISHER

ISBN 0-398-05648-X

Library of Congress Catalog Card Number: 89-20437

With THOMAS BOOKS *careful attention is given to all details of manufacturing
and design. It is the Publisher's desire to present books that are satisfactory as to their
physical qualities and artistic possibilities and appropriate for their particular use.*
THOMAS BOOKS *will be true to those laws of quality that assure a good name
and good will.*

Printed in the United States of America
SC-R-3

Library of Congress Cataloging-in-Publication Data

Chaika, Elaine, 1934-
    Understanding psychotic speech : beyond Freud and Chomsky / by
Elaine Ostrach Chaika.
        p.   cm.
    Includes bibliographical references.
    ISBN 0-398-05648-X
    1. Psychoses—Patients—Language.   2. Schizophrenics—Language.
3. Psycholinguistics.   I. Title.
    [DNLM: 1. Psycholinguistics. 2. Schizophrenic Language. WM 203
C434u]
RC530.C4   1990
616.89′82—dc20
DNLM/DLC
for Library of Congress
                                                                                              89-20437
                                                                                                  CIP

To Benjamin, Jonathan, and Rebecca
Keepers of the Flame

PREFACE

This book was born as a treatise on what is often termed *schizophrenic* speech, but, increasingly, it has become clear that such speech also can occur in manics and other patients. Therefore, it is more accurate to speak of psychotic speech. This does not mean that there is no difference between schizophrenic and other psychotic speech. As this book shows, there is, but it is a difference in degree rather than one in kind. The argumentation over terminology that so delights scholars will be addressed in the body of this book, so I shall leave it now and briefly discuss my own role in the field as a linguist, one versed in *scienta linguarum*, the science of language.

What special value does a linguistic analysis have? For one thing, the linguist focuses on language itself, on interpreting data in light of what we know of how people learn and use language, spoken or written. Then those analyses are compared to the situations which evoke them. Unlike those of other fields who simply take language as a given, without examining it in its own right, the linguist always takes language as something to be analyzed in its own right.

Much of the argumentation in the literature over whether or not schizophrenics suffer from thought disorder or whether or not their speech is ungrammatical, whether or not it is deliberate, and certainly, disagreements over what it means are artifacts of not understanding what language is and how it is normally produced and understood. Every psychological test in some way depends upon language, even when it doesn't purport to. For instance, directions are given and understood—or misunderstood—via the medium of language. All psychoanalysis, all therapeutic situations, in fact, are mediated by language, but, often, the therapist has not looked at language in its own right, has never asked questions like, "How do I know X is implying that?" "Why do I feel that this speech is strange?" "What exactly is it to be tangential?" "What does it mean to keep to a topic? What is telling me that this person is or is not keeping to one?" "Why am I so sure that this patient is using a metaphor, and really means something quite different from what he says?"

That, then, is the business of this book. In it, I show what the features of schizophrenic speech are, how they deviate from normal speech, and what accounts for our feeling that it is, after all, crazy talk. I distinguish between speech of schizophrenics which is structurally deviant and that which is not. The relation of speech to thought is also explored. It is vital that those concerned with the mentally ill understand the differences between language and thought and understand as well how languages are structured. To some degree, this can be described as a quickie course in linguistic concepts, but, **at no time is any concept of linguistics presented unless it is immediately applied to psychotic speech.**

This is true as well of the chapters of discourse analysis presented here. What is metaphor, how do we know when one has been made and how do we know how to interpret it so as to garner the meaning intended? What is intention and how is it signalled in speech? What are the laws, so to speak, of implication. What is the difference between poesy and schizophrenic speech? What constitutes a valid experimental procedure to uncover any deficits in linguistic production? How is speech made relevant?

This book is not only about a linguist's contribution to schizophrenia, however. Linguists are as contentious a lot as scholars in any other field are, and I have to admit that my 17 year career studying psychotic language has certainly shaped my own views about normal language and linguistic theory itself. To be most accurate, this is a book by one linguist, one who falls into the camps of those who believe in a context-dependent model of language, not a context-free one. There is a reason that this is called "Beyond Chomsky" as well as "Beyond Freud."

I have avoided technical talk as much as possible, but one matter must be touched upon: the matter of phonetic symbols. The only ones used in this book are

[ǰ] for the <j> in *judge*

[č], for the <ch> in *child*

[D] for the <tt> in *betting* and the <dd> in *bedding*

[θ] for the <th> in *thing*

[ɔ], for the vowel in *talk* as pronounced in British and New York City English (and a few other places as well).

[æ] for the vowel in *cat*

[I] for the vowel in *is*

[ʊ] for the vowel in *put*

[ə] for last vowel in *sofa*

Brackets with special meaning are:

[ ] = phonetic symbol for actually pronounced sound

/ / = phoneme, sound hearer thinks has been made

< > = conventional spelling

Additionally, first mention of any technical term is in small caps and is included in the index so that the reader can easily go back to its first mention in the text.

ACKNOWLEDGMENTS

I am indebted to Patricia Strauss for her reading of and copious commenting on every phase of this book, from the first foggy notes to the finish. To have found time for me despite the demands of her students, children, professors, and cats was truly generous. That she classified it as "having fun" was amazing.

Thanks are due to my colleague Richard A. Lambe for his help in designing and carrying out the statistical analyses of The Ice Cream Stories. He also collaborated with me on earlier versions of Chapters 3 and 6. Although they are hard to measure in the numbers of which he is so fond, his lengthy discussions with me on all the material in this book certainly contributed a great deal to it, as has his pithy commenting on my prose.

I have often been grateful that I have the mother I do, but yet more thanks are due her for her reading and rereading this entire manuscript, patiently finding errors and infelicities for me.

If, despite all this help, there are errors in this book, the fault is all mine.

Permission to reproduce material from the following is also gratefully acknowledged:

Bertram D. Cohen for the speech samples from "Referent communication disturbances in schizophrenia" originally published in *Language and Cognition in Schizophrenia*, edited by Steven Schwartz. Copyright © by Lawrence Erlbaum Associates, Inc. 1978

Mary Seeman and Howard Cole for passages from "The effect of increasing personal contact in schizophrenia." 1977. *Comprehensive Psychiatry.* 18:283–292 Copyright © Grune and Stratton, Inc.

William Labov and David Fanshel. *Therapeutic Discourse: Psychoanalysis as Conversation.* Copyright © by Academic Press, Inc.

Edward M. Hallowell and Henry F. Smith. 1983. Communication through poetry in the therapy of a schizophrenic. *Journal of the American Academy of Psychoanalysis.* Copyright © by the American Academy of Psychoanalysis.

CONTENTS

Chapter 3
Language and Thought

Chapter 4
The Levels of Language

Chapter 5
Syntax, Semantics, and Metaphor: Beyond Chomsky

Chapter 6
Cohesion and Coherence

Chapter 7
Pragmatics, Intention, and Implication

Chapter 8
The Ice Cream Stories: A Study of Narrations

Chapter 9
Relevance

Chapter 10
Topic

UNDERSTANDING PSYCHOTIC SPEECH: BEYOND FREUD AND CHOMSKY

Chapter One

THE FEATURES OF PSYCHOTIC SPEECH

The strange speech of some psychotics has baffled clinicians and laypersons alike, exciting all kinds of extraordinary interpretations. Some even have assumed that there is nothing wrong with schizophrenic speech, claiming that it is deliberate. An analysis of the linguistic forms of such speech demonstrate that it is definably different from normal speech, and the many kinds of deviations evinced are all disruptions of normal speech processes. This chapter demonstrates the kinds of disruptions responsible for psychotic speech.

[1] The Value of a Linguistic Analysis.

Caplan (1980, p. 235) sums up the value of linguistic analysis of aberrant speech production:

> ...it utilizes psycholinguistic and linguistic constructs derived from scientific studies of language structure and processing rather than intuitive taxonomies and analyses. As a result, it achieves...specificity in the description of the linguistic and psychological deficits...

Such an analysis bears heavily on the question of whether or not schizophrenic speech shows structural deviation, as well as the nature of any deviation. It can be shown that such speech can be deviant although not all is. Furthermore, the kinds of deviation manifested in schizophrenic speech must be taken in account in any interpretation of it.

[2] The Cyclic Nature of Schizophrenic Speech.

One of the most baffling characteristics of the kinds of speech that is associated with schizophrenia (henceforth SD) is that it is intermittent. Not all schizophrenics speak this way, and those who do, do so at some times and not at others. It is not only schizophrenics who are likely to speak this way. Manics do, and so do some with schizoaffective disorders.

3

For this reason, the term *psychotic speech* is more accurate than *schizophrenic*. Unless findings show that only schizophrenics manifest certain features of speech, and there are some that do, the former term will be used. Because some psychotics show no structural deviations in their speech, those who do will be termed SD, speech disordered speakers, as opposed to NSD, nonspeech disordered. A major problem in research has been that investigators have not ensured that they were testing only SD psychotics so that, often, studies seem to contradict each other because like populations have not been compared with each other.

Because of its intermittent character, many observers have assumed that it is deliberate and that the patient can speak differently if he or she so wishes. Laffal (1965), for instance, assumes that one of his patients resorted to deviant speech because he wished to avoid the therapeutic situation. Forrest (1965, 1976) maintains that SD patients are trying to say what it is to be schizophrenic, but that ordinary language is not sufficient for this task. It will subsequently be argued that as attractive as these positions are, they are untenable.

Bateson (1972, pp. 202–217) advanced the interesting theory that schizophrenics were caught in a double bind as children because they had unloving parents. When the child accused the parent of being unloving, he or she was punished and the parent denied lack of love. Hence, Bateson posited, the child did not learn to communicate properly.[1] Bateson offered no observational proof of this theory, nor has anybody else done so. There is no case history proof that all schizophrenics or even most schizophrenics were ever caught in such a bind. Nor is there any evidence that normals have not been caught in such a double bind. The intermittent character of SD speech negates the double-bind theory. It cannot be the case that schizophrenics haven't learned how to communicate, because there are times when their communication is normal in structure. Another point of information relevant to the double-bind theory is that children learn language as much from peers and other adults as from their parents. In fact, sociolinguistic studies have determined again and again that the peer group is the primary source of a child's language, not the parent. Peer learning is one reason that language changes in every generation. In contrast, even when schizophrenic speech is displayed, it coincides with psychotic bouts. Most likely, then, it is psychosis which causes the speech, not failures in early language learning.

The cyclic character of SD speech must be explained, as well as the particular deviations. SD patients might evince difficulty in a different stratum of linguistic production at different times, even in the same discourse. That is, at one time, a patient might have intact syntax but evince word-creation difficulty; yet, at another time, might show disordered syntax although words used seem to be usual words in the language (Chaika 1974; Rochester and Martin, 1979, pp. 177–178).

That I here and earlier (Chaika 1974, 1977, 1982a) present a list of the kinds of speech disruptions associated with schizophrenics does not mean that these are a "checklist" of symptoms as Herbert and Waltensperger (1982, p. 244) claim. No one patient may display all of the deviations reported in conjunction with a diagnosis of schizophrenia, nor will any particular deviation occur in all patients, both circumstances that I have always stressed. Even though no one patient may have evinced them all, many patients have evinced some of them, some patients have evinced them all, and, of course, some patients have evinced none of them, all circumstances which must be accounted for in any discussion of psychotic speech. All of the deviations presented here have been reported again and again as occurring in some schizophrenic patients at least some of the time. These are the deviations that have long excited comment, and those who evaluate psychotic patients rely on these symptoms for diagnostic purposes.

Still, researchers like Maher (1972), Fromkin (1975), Cohen (1978), and Herbert and Waltensperger (1980, 1982) claim that there is nothing structurally wrong with schizophrenic speech. Maher (1972, p. 13) says, "What seems to be most clear is that . . . perhaps most of the disturbances of language found amongst schizophrenic patients do not involve syntactic errors . . ." With the exception of Fromkin, none of these are linguists so that their evaluations are essentially lay evaluations. Fromkin asserts that schizophrenic speech is normal creative language, and Cohen (1978, p. 1) stated that " . . . as cryptic or disorganized as schizophrenic speech may sound, it rarely (if ever) includes hard instances of agrammatism or word-finding deficits." Yet word salads, outright gibberish, and other severe syntactic errors have long been reported in the literature. Hard instances of agrammatism have long been noted in the literature and are quite easy to find, as we shall see.

Lecours and Vanier-Clement (1976) assert that schizophrenics do not suffer from semantic errors or word-finding differences, although they do admit that schizophrenics make unusual, abstract, and bizarre word choices. This in itself, as they note, is not a sign of linguistic dysfunction.

Unusual word choices abound in witticisms, good prose, and artistic language, but these are quite different from schizophrenic unusual word choices. Witticisms, good prose, and artistic language in some way elucidate a message in a memorable or aesthetic manner. In contrast, schizophrenic "unusual" word choices rarely have any such relevance. Similarly, the "abstract speech" of schizophrenics differs from normal abstract speech. Any scholar indulges in the latter, but the abstraction is in aid of presentation of intellectual constructs and the abstract language in which such presentation is embedded is relevant to the points being made. Moreover, the scholars can bring it up again, discuss its import, rephrase it. In contrast, schizophrenic abstractions show no coherence to any point, nor can they usually be discussed, much less rephrased and refined. Paraphrasability is a hallmark of normal speech production. It is part of the essential character of language. Every normal utterance can be paraphrased. The paraphrase may not be as beautiful as the original or as succint, but it can convey the same meaning. All psychotic utterances cannot be paraphrased. Here, and in subsequent chapters, we will see distinct definable and testable differences between the most creative of normal speech and psychotic speech itself.

Lecours and Vaniers-Clement do acknowledge schizophrenic gibberish but attempt to distinguish it from those in aphasic productions by claiming that schizophrenics reemploy their **nonwords.** However, there is no support in the literature to substantiate such a claim beyond the fact that, occasionally, within one stretch of speech, the same nonword might be repeated. There is presently no hard evidence that such reemployments last beyond that one interaction. My own study of psychotic narrative, The Ice Cream Stories, henceforth referred to as ICS (Chaika 1982e, 1983b; Chaika and Alexander 1986; Chapter 8), did yield some gibberish, but, the next week when patients were asked to recall their stories, they never reemployed the gibberish, nor did they even in the first telling. In addition, as the next chapter shows, apart from repetitions of a given word or nonword in one speech situation, there may be many other kinds of perseveration (Chaika 1982a; Manschrek, Maher, Hoover, and Ames 1985). It is the sum of repetitions and perseverations which must be accounted for.

Gibberish and neologisms are clear instances of word-finding deficits, and they, too, are easy to find. ICS yielded both syntactic and lexical deficits as well as deviations in global narrative structure. These lexical deficits included circumlocution reminiscent of mild anomic aphasia in which the meaning is inappropriately spread over too many words (Chapter 8).

Schizophrenic utterances have been likened to poetry, sleeptalking, and the aphasias (e.g., Forrest 1965, 1976; Sullivan 1964 [originally published 1944]; Brown 1977; Chapman 1966; Benson 1963; Chaika 1974a, 1977; Buckingham 1974 [personal communication]). These comparisons are apt, and that they can be made at all is, in itself, revealing. There may well not be any single deviation which can't be found in other speech pathologies, or even in normal creativity and error. What characterizes speech as being particularly schizophrenic is some combination of errors depicted below, occurring cyclically, intermittently, but, in a given interaction, persistently.

[3] The Features of Psychotic Speech.

Clinicians themselves have long considered the speech disruptions illustrated below as pathognomic of positive symptom schizophrenia. Andreasen's (1979a, 1979b) widely used diagnostic guidelines actually center on these kinds of speech disruptions although her terminology differs from mine (Chapters 2, 10, and 11) reflecting our mutually different backgrounds, but the characteristics she cites seem to accord with mine—or mine accord with hers.

Viewed in comparison with the levels of normal language, the features of schizophrenic speech are:

- gibberish
- neologisms
- opposite speech and other erroneous retrievals of words
- glossomania
- rhyme and alliteration inappropriate for the context
- intrusive errors
- word salad and other syntactic disruptions
- perseveration and other repetitions.

Any interpretation of schizophrenic speech and any hypothesis of its provenance must take these into account.

[4] Gibberish and Neologizing.

The first kinds of speech disruption are perhaps the most disruptive of all and seem to occur more rarely than the others

[I] Gibberish:

1A.   ... gao, itivare ... ovede (Forrest 1976)
1B. [speaking about a pet] He still had *fooch* [fUč] with *taykrimez* [tʰeⁱkraⁱmz] I'll be willin' to betcha.   (Chaika 1974)

Assuming that Forrest spelled his examples of nonwords as accurately as the orthographic system of English allows, then his examples of gibberish conform to the phonetic rules of English. Naive spellings, spellings which are used by those unversed in phonetic transcription, are frequently an accurate index to pronunciation. Most of our information about Colonial American English, for instance, derives from the study of semiliterate spelling errors. Of course, I am not calling Forrest semiliterate. Forrest is a sensitive psychiatrist, but the principle is the same. If one does not know a standard spelling for a word, then one will substitute letters from the ordinary orthography that would usually spell the sounds in question.

Fortunately, I was able to transcribe the gibberish I present, so I can attest to the fact that both the sounds used and their combinations are allowable in English. This is both interesting and significant as it suggests, but of course does not prove, that the speaker intended to utter an actual word in the language. The patient who uttered *taykrimez* above, for instance, aspirated the initial [t] as is required by English phonetic rules. Although these productions are gibberish, they seem to be gibberish in English. Phonologically and phonotactically, the only things wrong with any of these nonwords is that they do not happen to be words in the language, and a perusal of the venerable OED reveals that they never were.

[II]. Neologizing

2A ... you have to have a *plausity* of amendments to go through for the children's code, and it's no mental disturbance of *puterience,* it is an *amorition* law. (Vetter 1968, p. 189)
2B. ... with syndicates organized and *subsicates* in the way that look for a civil war ... (Herbert and Waltensperger 1982)
2C. I'm don't like the way I'm *puped* today in thought ... because of

the slash of my wrist like I'm was *puped* to do. I'm be *puped* tall
letter I'm write to you . . . (Herbert and Waltensperger 1980)

As with the gibberish, all of this neologizing forms distinctly English
nonwords, using unremarkable English roots and morphemes. *Plausity*
has what appears to be the same root as the *plaus* in *plausible*, and the
-erience in *puterience* occurs in words like *experience*. Similarly, *subsicates*
is formed out of the common morphemes *sub-* and *-icate*. Since neither
Vetter nor Herbert and Waltensperger provide IPA transcription, we
can't know whether or not the *put-* is pronounced like *putrid* or like
the verb *put*. For the same reason, we can not determine how the <u> in
puped was pronounced. I would assume that it was not the <oo> in
pooped or they would have spelled it that way. I also have to assume that
the other morphemes were pronounced as American speakers usually
pronounce syllables spelled that way, for untrained ears typically adhere
to spellings commonly used for given syllables. That is, if the patient
pronounced *-ity, -erience,* and *-ition* normally, then the naive transcriber
is most likely to spell those as he always does. In contrast, a linguist
would use IPA and spell *plaus-* with a [z] not an <s>, *-erience* with an [s],
not a <c>, and *-ition* with an [s] rather than a <ti>. Vetter and Herbert
and Waltensperger also do not indicate meaning, presumably because
the patient did not, and the context did not provide clues.

The gibberish and neologizing above are two halves of the same coin.
Their only substantive difference is that gibberish is composed of sounds
that do not form any recognizable word or morpheme. Neologisms, on
the other hand, while still not forming words now in the language, do
contain recognizable morphemes or other nonmorphemic parts of words.
They are alike, however, in that neither results in recognizable lexical
items in the language, **nonwords**.[2] Furthermore, the patient who utters
either does not or cannot say what it is that they have said. Robertson
and Shamsie (1958) claim that the gibberish they observed in a multilingual belonged to different languages although they don't say how they
determined this and, of course, they provide no phonetic transcription
as a check. They admit that although the patient uttered a great deal of
such gibberish, he wasn't "prepared" to explain what he said.

There are two logical reasons for this circumstance. One is the one
Robertson and Shamsie presuppose: that the patient simply did not want
to explain it. The other is that the schizophrenic intended to say something,
but it would only come out as gibberish. In point of fact, if SD patients

do not explain what their gibberish means, there is no basis for the assumption that their gibberish is intentional. Gibberish is gibberish because no meaning can be extracted from it, just as neologisms are discerned as such because they convey no meaning.[3] Therefore, all we can do is compare it to normal language and to other features of SD productions; thereby finding a consistent, rational and verifiable analysis for all of them.

[5] Explaining Gibberish and Neologisms.

Chapman (1966) and Chaika (1974a, 1977, 1982a), albeit on somewhat different grounds, argue that gibberish and neologizing are indicative of word finding difficulties. Considering that human languages are so constructed that new words can be made up and old words can be used in new ways to effect new meaning, it is not likely that neologizing and gibberish are a sign of creativity (LaFerriere 1977; Forrest 1976; Fromkin 1975). That is, there is usually a recognizable difference between normal creativity and unusual schizophrenic usages, although some find that link tenuous at best. For instance, Nancy Andreasen (1973), a psychiatrist with the rare qualification of also having earned a Ph.D. in literature, questions the artistry in James Joyce's *Finnegan's Wake*, claiming that much of it is merely schizophrenic speech, and that portions of this were rated as schizophrenic by raters, a claim sure to be contested by some Joyce scholars.

The gibberish and neologizing noted above occur within sentences with otherwise recognizable words, lending credence to the belief that the patient is trying to convey an actual message, but is undergoing problems in retrieval of words. Because anybody can use a new word in such a way that another can understand it, we have to count this as a real deficit since the patients seem not to be able to provide enough context for this to happen.

Over the years, those who would explain psychotic speech have imputed intention to such incomprehensible speech, claiming that it is deliberate. However, it is the very production of gibberish and neologizing which must be explained, not what it means, for it may mean nothing and even if the patient intended a meaning, we cannot always derive it. Trying to derive intent from grossly disordered speech is akin to an English speaker's making an interpretation of a Populucan sentence if she were dropped into the remote corner of Mexico in which that language is spoken. If natives used graphic enough gestures, she might get some meaning and determine intention from them, but on the basis of their words, she could not impute intention because she can't understand the meaning of their utterances. It is true that we derive meaning partially — indeed largely — on the basis of what we perceive the intent of the speaker to be, but this is done by matching the words and syntax to the context of utterance and to the conventions of the social group in which it was uttered (Chaika 1989, pp. 114–115, and Chapter 7).

Moreover, we can never get away from the incontrovertible fact that a person who is having difficulty explaining an experience does not suddenly launch into gibberish or spout unexplained neologisms to do this. That is why schizophrenic speech has been labeled as schizophrenic and it is why psychiatrists and other researchers have devoted so much time and effort to explain it.

This does not mean that I think all psychotic speech is uninterpretable, as Hoffman and Sledge (1984, p. 153) strangely claim. They assert that I have said that "schizophrenic irregularity is identified according to its nondecodability." Chaika (1974, 1977, 1981, 1982a,c,d,e, 1983a,b) has shown the contrary. One can't decode gibberish. That's why it has been called gibberish. Nor, frequently, can one decode word salads. That's why they have been called word salads. But many other less disrupted utterances of schizophrenics can be decoded very sensibly by reference to what we know of normal linguistic production and normal decoding strategies. By using such tactics, I have even been able to show that some schizophrenic discourse can be understood by our usual strategies, and, in fact, is quite normal (Chaika 1981). It is part of the beauty of our natural linguistic abilities that we can decode imperfect speech. If we couldn't, then we would never be able to understand toddlers, foreign speakers, and those with various speech impediments. It is only the most highly disrupted speech which we cannot understand by usual means. Some schizophrenic speech is comprehensible. Some is not. Some comprehensible schizophrenic speech may still be definably bizarre or "schizophrenic" in the sense that term has long been used.

[6] Slips of the Tongue, Neologizing and Gibberish.

The relationship between neologisms and gibberish is that both may be caused by a failure in retrieving an intended word from the mental lexicon. They appear to be severe instances of what in normals are called slips of the tongue.

Fromkin (1975) asserted that such schizophrenic errors were no more abnormal than normal slips of the tongue, providing as instances of normal slips:

3A. Soul hecond path

3B Slee throwed sloth

She says that if one did not know the context or the reference . . . "soul hecond path" for "whole second half," or "slee throwed toth" for "three toed sloth," these would seem to be gibberish as much as the schizophrenic "He still had fooch with teykrimez." (X reported in Chaika 1974). In this evaluation Fromkin ignores a crucial difference between normal slips and psychotic ones. Normal slips show distinct patterns and are in a sense orderly as one can retrieve the speaker's intended words quite easily. For instance, one need only isolate the consonant phonemes in each phrase Fromkin mentions and move them to corresponding positions in other items in the phrase until the apparently intended words appear. For "soul hecond," only the initial consonants need be transposed. *Path* can be explained easily on the grounds of similarity of phonetic features. Both the intended lexical item and its substitute contain acoustically similar consonants initially and finally,[4] and have the same vowel sound. Furthermore, confusion of $/\theta/$ for $/f/$ is a common cross-dialectal and child language phenomenon as when *mouth* is pronounced "mouf." "Slee throwed toth" is correctable by moving the initial consonants to their proper places. This is a typical anticipatory slip in which the /sl/ of *sloth* replaced the initial consonant cluster of *three;* then the initial cluster of *three* replaced the initial cluster of *toed;* finally, the initial consonant of *toed* replaced the initial cluster of *sloth,* so that the error constitutes a retrievable round robin.

This is not possible with the gibberish reported in Chaika (1974a). Transposition of phonemes does not correct "[fUč] 'fooch' with [tʰekraⁱmz] 'teykrimez' " or [sɔwəndan] 'sawendon' saw [tʰ₃ rč]'turch' [fɔ]'faw' [juə ri] 'juerie" (Chaika 1974a, p. 260). These schizophrenic errors are not orderly as are those presented by Fromkin (1971, 1975). Like a child's errors or a foreigner's, a normal slip can usually be understood by regular human decoding ability. Psychotic gibberish can't be.

[7] Synonyms and Glossomania.

GLOSSOMANIA, also known as ASSOCIATIONAL CHAINING, is often cited as a particularly schizophrenic verbal display (Werner et al. 1975; Lecours and Vanier-Clement 1976). It is related to SYNONYMY. It seems to me that glossomania is related to the fact that synonyms are never complete. Even when two or more words share some meaning, typically they do not share them all, and even when they do share meaning, they often cannot be used in the same contexts. That is, synonyms typically have different COLLOCATIONS, words they may co-occur with. They are synonyms only to the extent that they share a common meaning.

For instance, note the differences in the semantically almost identical words *roast* and *bake:*

- *Roast* the peppers and the beef.
- *Roast* the pork.
- *Bake* the ham.
- *Bake* the cake or the cookies.
- *Bake* the potatoes.
- *Roast* the potatoes.

The kind of potatoes referred to changes according to the verb selected. Although both *roast* and *bake* refer to cooking in an oven, *roast potatoes* are peeled and cooked with a roasted meat, but *baked potatoes* are cooked with jackets on, often apart from any other foodstuffs in the oven. Synonyms, even very close ones, can allude to quite different things in certain contexts. Despite their shared semantic features, they often don't easily substitute for each other.

Glossomania is a chaining in which shared meanings of words progress linearly, so to speak, from one phrase to another, getting progressively further and further away from whatever meaning was apparently intended as in the following excerpts:

4A. Did that show up on the X-rays?
You'll see it tonight
I've been drinking phosphate.
You'll see it in the dark (inaudible)
Glows.
We all glow as we're glowworms. (Patient X reported on in Chaika 1974.)

Here, the mention of X-rays appears to have triggered the mention of phosphate, which triggered the statement that something will be seen in the dark, which triggered the word *glows*, which triggered the statement about *glowworms*.

> 4B. My mother's name was Bill.
> (low pitch, as in an aside, but with marked rising question intonation)
> . . . And coo?
> St. Valentine's Day is the official startin' of the breedin' season of the birds.
> All buzzards can coo.
> I like to see it pronounced buzzards rightly.
> They work hard.
> So do parakeets. (Patient X reported on in Chaika 1974)

In the above, the name *Bill* reminded X of the now almost archaic expression *bill and coo*, which is a reference to lovebirds. Hence, St. Valentine's Day, the holiday of love, is mentioned, followed by comments about birds, including another repetition of *coo*, this time attributed to buzzards. Expressions like "they work hard" are common short phrases of the sort that are often spoken in full almost as automatic responses. In fact, it is such bizarre couplings, here of buzzards and working hard, that are especially indicative of the automatic nature of glossomanic chaining. Phrases and words related to each other in some way elicit each other, although they are inappropriate.

The following samples of glossomania were elicited by Bertram Cohen (1978) from first admission acute schizophrenic males describing Farnsworth-Munsell color disc #2, a salmon pink:[5]

> 5A. A fish swims. *You* call it a salmon. You cook it. You put it in a can. You open the can. You look at it in this color. Salmon fish.

Here, the color reminds the speaker of the color of a fish, a salmon. Salmon is typically eaten after it has been cooked and canned, hence the allusions to this process. What is especially interesting in this response is that the very first statement of identification is the generic "a fish swims," even before the color is identified. The swimming has nothing to do with the color naming task, but fish swim and the color reminded him of a fish.

> 5B. Pancake make-up. You put it on your face and they think guys run after you. Wait a second! I don't put them on my face and guys don't run after me. Girls put it on them. (Cohen 1978, p. 29)

In this, Cohen's subject apparently correctly identified the discourse as being the color of pancake make-up which goes on the face and which is something identified with girls who want to attract guys. This leads to the comment that the speaker doesn't use it, so that guys don't run after him which is followed by the avowal that girls use pancake make-up.

The following were all elicited from Disc #35

> 5C. How blue I am (singing). If I were blue, I'd like to be this green instead, I really like it. You could put it in a salad and eat. (Cohen, p. 28)

Here the green color chip apparently reminds the patient of a commonly sung or spoken phrase involving the color blue which is related to green, and like green has a special metaphorical sense. *Blue* is associated with melancholy in English, and *green* with youth or innocence.[6] Both can appear syntactically after the verb *be* to indicate the state mentioned, as in "I am blue/green" or "She is blue/green." The mention of the target word *green* triggers the food that is usually green, salads, and that, in turn, elicits *eat.*

> 5D. Green (SHOUTS) Hold on, the other is too! In the garden such a green is unlikely. Too synthetic! The other is more gardenreal [Cohen's spelling as one word], piecemeal, oatmeal green, greenreal, filmreal, greenreal. (Cohen, p. 28)

This shows still other kinds of associations. Green is evocative of gardens, but the speaker feels that this particular green is not the green of gardens. It is synthetic. *Synthetic* is the opposite of *real,* so the speaker combines into one word repetitions of both *garden* and *real.* This evokes the rhyming association of *piecemeal,* which leads to another compound word with *meal,* then the *green* is picked up again, this time wholly inappropriately as oatmeal is not really green. Then both *green* and *real* are triggered, this time in a new compounding. Cohen gives the spelling of *real* in *filmreal,* but the association could very well have been *reel* of film. The homophony of *real* and *reel* could have triggered the word *film.* As will be shown shortly, glossomanic chaining may also occur because of other kinds of similarity between words such as their rhyming or alliteration, and then we have to see the differences caused by antonymy.

In all of the above passages, chains of utterances are related to each other on the basis of partial semantic similarity of immediately prior statements. As Vonnegut (1976) wrote of his own schizophrenic episode, the schizophrenic pays too much attention to everything at once. Irrelevant associations which are normally suppressed come to the fore inappropriately, leading the SD speaker to hop from one to the next without relating them to a topic. Many of these synonymous chains also have common expressions like "they work hard," "I am blue," and "picnic on the green" interlarded with the semantically triggered retrievals.

Such output indicates a lack of control of normal speech processes in which such phrases and lexical associations do not usually figure. That this can happen even in relatively constrained environments is amply shown in Cohen's study.

[8] Morphemic Glossomania.

Glossomania can also be triggered by chance repetition of morphemes with or without shared meanings:

> 6. . . . Das ist vom Kaiserhaus, sie haben es von dem Voreltern, von der Vorwelt, von der Urwelt, Frankfurt-am-Main, das sind die Franken, die Frankfurter Wurschtchen, Frankenthal, Frankenstein . . . (Maher 1972, p. 9)

Besides the semantic connection of the *Kaiserhaus* with the *Voreltern*, ancestors, there is the repetition of the morpheme *Vor-* in *Vorwelt*, and the *-welt* in *Urwelt*, and, of course, the *Urwelt* is literally the *Vorwelt* as well. Since the Kaisers were descended from the Franks, there is a semantic connection between *Kaiserhaus* and *Franken*. The city Frankfurt-am-Main was named for the Franks, therefore eliciting mention of *die Franken*. *Frankfurter Wurschtchen*, little sausages made in Frankfurt, repeats the morpheme *Frank*, as does the name of the city *Frankenthal* and, of course, *Frankenstein*. We certainly have no difficulty seeing the connections between the phrases in 6 above, but we still feel its bizarreness. In addition to the repetition of morphemes, this passage also displays alliteration. In German, a word initial *V* as in *Vorwelt* and *von* and the *F* in Frank are both pronounced as [f]. This chance alliteration might also have prompted the mention of these words.

This passage consists of words that are especially tightly related both morphemically and semantically in certain features. It is, nevertheless, incoherent and recognizably schizophrenic because it is not subordinated to a topic. Each phrase is glued to others by inherent features in the lexicon of German. The phrases in which some of the words are embedded are themselves trite phrasing serving as a vehicle to present the words.

[9] Rhyming and Alliterating.

Glossomania may also be triggered by chance phonological features of words, resulting in rhymes and alliterative strings inappropriate to the topic or occasion of discourse, as in:

> 7. [in response to Farnsworth-Munsell disc #2]: Looks like clay. Sounds like gray. Take you for a roll in the hay. Hay day. May day. Help! I just can't. Need help. May day.   (Cohen 1978, p. 29)
> 8. [in response to statement "Hello, anyone here want some coffee?"]: Head, heart, hands, health. (Chaika, 1974a)

The alliterative chain "head, heart, hands, health" appeared to have been prompted by an exceptionally strong aspiration on "**Hello** . . . **here** . . .** " the *h*'s elicited the "four H's" (of the young farmers' organization). This is virtually a clang response. Clark (1970) comments that this kind of response occurs in word association testing, especially if subjects are forced to respond rapidly, although 8 did not result from any limit on response time.

The following two were produced in the ICS:

> 9A. Little girl in candy store. Mommy and Daddy away [pause] that day. . . .
> 9B. Little girl in candy store. [pause] Runnin' free. Her parents did not really care. So she just gets up and takes to the air.

The last two, 9A and B, were produced by the same person one week apart. In both instances, the patient uttered these with a strong repetitive beat, and paused before the rhyming line just as if he were reciting poems in grade school.

[10] Intrusive Matters.

At times, psychotics may start talking on a topic and suddenly slip into another. This differs from glossomania because there is no chaining on the basis of morphemic or phonological similarity. Rather while speaking of one thing, the patient suddenly starts to recount another. The following narrative was elicited by asking a patient to describe the ICS videotaped sequence. The videotape showed no boys, nor did it have anything to do with anybody looking out for anybody else, or anybody getting blamed for anything or anything about men using other people. The narrator here did mention that the video brought back memories, but there was no elucidation of "that area" or what it is that people will do every time. There seems to be a general mixing up of various ideas and memories of actual events:

> 10 . . . I was watching a film of a girl and um s bring back memories of things that happened to people around me that affected me during the time I was living in that area and she just went to the store for a candy bar and by the time oooh of course her brother who was supposed to be watching wasn't paying much attention he was blamed for and I did not think that was fair the way the way they did that either so that's why I'm just asking yah could we just get together and try to work it out all together for one big party or something ezz hey if it we'd all in which is in not they've been here so why you just now discovering it. You know they they've been men will try to use you every time for everything he wants so ain't no need and you trying to get upset for it. That's all. That's all.

Harrow, Lanin-Kettering, Prosen, and Miller (1983) employ the terminology "intermingling and loss of set" for such speech. They use this terminology for glossomanic chaining as well (Chaika and Lambe 1985). Their terminology just labels the behavior. It does not explain it in any way. In what ways does it intermingle? How is this different from normal recollection of the "Oh, that reminds me . . ." variety? As we shall see, changes of topic, hence "loss of set" is a normal and usual phenomenon. Yet, 10 above is typical of psychotic speech. How does it differ from normal changes of topic and what can have caused it?

[11] Automatic and Controlled Processes.

Comparing psychotic glossomanic productions to normal ones subordinated to the topic or nature of the social interaction makes manifest the difference between controlled and automatic retrieval of linguistic forms. Glossomania sets off a round of synonyms, rhymes, alliterations, or personal memories not germane to the matter at hand. This seems to be an automatic process. Normal speech is controlled, subordinated to both the social situation and the intent of the speaker. There is no such control in glossomanic chaining and related intrusions.

[12] Antonomy, Opposite Speech, and Semantic Feature.

Schizophrenics also have been reported to use an antonym of an appropriate word or to otherwise select the wrong word for what apparently would be the correct meaning.

11A.   Dr. Dean, **come** here.
 Pt.   What, you said **go** already.
 Dr.   **No, I** didn't say go. I wanted to sit down **near you** Dean.

(Patient leaves room, and doctor follows)

 Dr. Mr. Redfield, come on, I want to talk to **you.**
 Pt. You want to talk to **him?** (pointing to another patient)
 Dr. No, I want to talk to you. Laffal (1965, P. 84)
 11B. [the patient said] *yes* for *no, always* for *never, I do know* for *I don't know.* (Laffal, 1965, pp. 31–35).
 11C. I seen a little **girl** lookin' in the window 'n ah say wan' some ice cream so but didn't have money to get it so she asked **her** mother 'n **her** mother said not now because it's near suppertime uh the kid was put down so **he** goes to the father 'n the father say ch-told where to go gave **him** the money so **she** could buy ice cream . . . **she** was sittin' there . . .

Laffal believes that the patient used opposite speech in order to avoid the therapeutic situation. It is entirely possible, however, that the patient was having difficulties in discriminating between words which share semantic features. 11A, for instance, was produced after a stretch of gibberish. The patient who produced 11C was telling me what he had seen in a video I had presented the week before. He confused masculine and feminine pronouns, and the *sittin' there* referred to the girl's standing there. It is surely not without significance that the substitutions seen here parallel the kinds of error prevalent in normal slips of the tongue. Fromkin (1971, p. 46) says

> The literature and my own data attest the fact that, besides the phonological similarity in substituted words, errors often involve semantic features in common or substitution of antonyms, i.e., words having the same features with opposite values.

She gives as examples of antonymous slips:

- I really like to—hate to get up in the morning
- It's at the bottom—I mean—top of the stack of books
- This room is too damn hot—cold
- The oral—written part of the exam.

Normal slips of the tongue commonly consist of antonyms or other words in sets so that people say *up* for *down, more* for *less, big* for *little,* or *stove* for *refrigerator.* Children typically use one-half of an antonymous set to stand for each, for instance saying *up* when they are in your lap and want to go down. Additionally, in word association testing, antonyms are the most common response, even more likely than synonyms. The reason for this is that antonyms are actually more alike than synonyms are. They typically can appear in the same linguistic environments and share all features of meaning save the one that distinguishes between them. For instance,

- This elevator goes *up*/ This elevator goes *down.*
- I want *more*/ I want *less.*
- He's so *big*/ He's so *little.*
- Put it in the *stove*/Put it in the *refrigerator.*

Antonyms and related words in sets, unlike synonyms, are easily substitutable for each other, which explains why they are more likely to be given in word association tests than synonyms are. This is true of words that belong in the same semantic sets, such as color words. Such responses are called *paradigmatic associations* (Clark and Clark 1977, pp. 477–483). It is generally conceded that testing of word associations gives us a picture of the probable organization of the mental lexicon. It is important, therefore, to note that schizophrenic errors implicate word sets that are common responses in word association testing.

There is corroborating evidence for the position that opposite speech and other confusions of semantic features on words are not deliberate. A patient, here called Y, presented me with what appeared to be some interesting confounding of closely related words. Consequently, I devised a simple test to see if he could distinguish whether or not certain sentences and words meant the same thing or not (Chaika 1977). During our first interview, Y commented:

12. I think you can [help me]. You're an open system.
    I'm an open system.

Knowing that the verbs *have* and *be* (Chapter 5) have the same meaning in certain paraphrases, I suspected that he might have meant 'You **have** an open system. **I have** an open system.' In 12, the verb *be* is inappropriate. Humans usually can't be systems. However, in certain sentences, those involving locations, *have* and *be* alternate depending upon the subject of the sentence. If a location is the subject of a sentence, a form of the verb *have* must be used, but a synonymous sentence with the location postponed to the end of the sentence would require *be,* as in

- The box **has** toys.
- The garden **has** roses.

Here, the box is the location of the toys, and the garden is the location of the roses. Because the locative noun is in subject position, it does not take a preposition, although speakers know that the subject is the location. If the location appears at the end of the sentence, then the preposition must be stated and the verb is a form of *be,*[7] as in

- Toys **are** in the box.
- Roses **are** in the garden.

One can't say *Toys have in the box.

Because Y told me that he was a cookware salesman, in the same conversation I asked whether he gave discounts. **He** replied

13. Yes, I'm 75%, 50%.

This makes sense only if one assumes that Y meant 'Yes, **I give** 75%, 50%. This again appears to be a confusion between two words with shared semantic features.

As Bendix (1966) showed, a componential analysis of English verbs reveals that there is a large set of verbs which share a great many semantic features, and, like antonymous pairs, differ from each other only by one value. Although the verb *take* is not the issue here, it will be used to illustrate componential analysis of semantic features. *Give* and *take* share the meaning of "be in possession of." These are reciprocal verbs, indicating the same action. They differ in that the source of one action is the object of the other. If Jack gives me something, then I took it from him. There is also a feature of time involved. To *take* is to *be* in possession at the time one is speaking of; that is, it is to *have* possession. To *give* is not to *be* in possession at that time; that is, it is not to *have* possession. *Give* (and its reciprocal *take*) contain both the features of *be* and of *have.* Notice the four-way synonymy of the following:

- I **gave** him arms.
- He **took** arms.
- He **was** armed.
- He **had** arms.

If Y had a disruption in his ability to assign semantic features to lexical items, he could easily confuse *have, give,* and *be.* The disruption need not be permanent. It coincided with his psychosis at the time of the interviews. To test this hypothesis, I devised a simple test. After receiving informed consent, Y was asked to tell whether two short sentences differentiated only by antonyms were alike or different. These were presented orally with the verbs in different persons and tenses and the order of presentation was randomized. Typical sentence pairs were:

- I have an open system/I am an open system.
- You are 75%/ You give 75%.
- John brought books/John took books.
- Henry lost his watch/Henry found his watch.

He said that each pair above was the same. His incorrect judgment on the first two pairs coincided with his incorrect production of 12 and 13 above. He did confuse the pairs of verbs *have* and *be,* and *be* and *give,* saying they meant the same thing in contexts in which they didn't. Thus, as Fromkin noted in slips of the tongue, he substituted words with semantic features in common. He also substituted antonyms, words having the same features with opposite values, such as *brought* and *took,* and *lost* and *found.*

Y did not have complete inability to judge antonyms[8] for he correctly identified the following pairs as being different.

- I became 40/I am 40.
- Jack is tall/Jack is short.
- I take 75%/I give 75%.

He was then tested on sets of words, some of which differ in their morphological structure, notably affixes, and some of which are antonyms. He had no difficulty in distinguishing the following pairs as being different.

- lie-liar
- lie-truth
- tall-short
- trap-trapper

- hypnotize-hypnotist
- tall-taller-tallest

However, again, he judged the following as being the same when given as individual words.

- is-has

He also rated as being alike:

- getting into-getting off.

Both the opposite speech presented by Laffal and patient H's twin difficulties with antonymy and synonymy match Fromkin's slip of the tongue data.

Kaplan (1957) claimed that "opposite speech," the use of the antonym of a target word, comes from "a relatively lower stratum in the development of linguistic thought organization." That is, it represents a step prior to the selection of an intended word. Jason Brown (1977), speaking more broadly, says, "Even pathological speech forms can be thought of as a preliminary level in normal language that pathology has brought to the fore." That is, the word actually uttered is not the one intended, but one related to it in one or more different ways. Such a view explains the correlation of opposite speech with slips of the tongue and responses in word association testing, as noted above. It also explains the occurrence of opposite speech in schizophrenia. That, too, can be seen as an instance of retrieval of words semantically related to target words. In a sense, opposite speech and other such retrievals are severe and persistent examples of the slip of the tongue phenomena.

Although he interprets these data differently from me, Laffal (1965) demonstrates that the words in opposite speech are antonymous to those appropriate for the context. "I do know" vs "I don't know" is an antonymy at the level of syntax as well as of semantics, as the language encodes that meaning onto a grammar rule operating at the level of the clause.

[13] Effects of Synonymy, Antonomy, and Phonology on Schizophrenic Speech.

Interestingly, errors caused by retrieval of antonyms of apparently target words do not seem to be implicated in the kinds of verbal chaining that are strongly associated with psychotic speech. The reason for this might be that the antonymic set is completed with two words or phrases, the two opposites, whereas synonyms, rhymes, and alliterative sets are far longer and more complex. There are typically several synonyms and paraphrases for any given word or phrase, there are potentially many rhymes, and, of course, many words start with the same sound. Therefore, once a synonymic, rhyming, or alliterative chain is accessed, it can literally go further than an antonymic set. There is not so much of a natural brake for these as there is for antonyms which can be considered chains with only two links.

[14] Word Salad and Other Disruptions in Syntax.

The picturesque term WORD SALAD was coined to describe an odd jumble of words which sound like connected discourse, but are lacking the syntactic markers to subordinate them to syntactic structures. This, of course, leads to incomprehensibility even when the words themselves are quite ordinary and usual, as we see in:

> 14. After John Black has recovered in special neutral form of life the honest bring back to doctor's agents must take John Black out through making up design meaning straight neutral underworld shadow tunnel. (Lorenz, 1961)

Allied to word salads are stretches of discourse which, for the most part, conform to normal sentence structures but in which some syntactic markings are, nevertheless, missing. As in the following, it is often possible to decode these simply by adding the missing syntactic cues. In 15A, for instance, the verb and noun suffices -*ing* and -*ion* are missing, and in 15B, verb tense and possessive endings are missing as indicated in the boldfaced words, as is -*ize* on *memory*. Also, such syntactic markers as the use of the auxiliary *do* in "I still not have . . . " is omitted:

> 15A . . . succeeded in the *pull* of a perfect crime . . . framed by the artificial *inseminate* Detroit Michigan is in danger of *have* of World War III site Russia and Israel is *try* to drive me to approve of war against Canada. (Herbert and Waltensperger, 1980, p. 85)
>
> 15B. I am being help with the food and the **medicate** . . . to speak and think in a **lord** tongue . . . the **memory** knowledge . . . **I still not have** the thought pattern. . . . (courtesy of Dr. Bonnie Spring)

The above show clear instances of errors in sentence syntax and certainly falls into the category of *agrammatism.* Syntactic markers such as the *-ing* morpheme to indicate gerunds, the *-ion* morpheme to change a verb to a noun, and the *-ing* indicating the present progressive of *try* are all missing.

[15] Perseverations.

Besides missing syntactic markers, the larger discourse in which 15B was embedded also showed perseveration beyond the requirements of the discourse (Chapter 7, 9, 10, 11), resulting in the repetition of words and phrases such as *the food and the medicate.* The pathological nature of this perseveration can be appreciated only by seeing the entire. There can be no explanation for psychotic speech without also taking into account such perseverations

> 16. well I want to work for god[9] in the mission and to work for god in the mission you have to be able to speak and think in a lord tongue in my opinion now to speak and think in a lord tongue you have to be able to memory the process memory the parle- the process in the bible the thought pattern the brain wave and your thought process must be healthy enough and your legs must be healthy enough to when you want to study and and from when you want to study and progress in the way of the lord you should you should read the bible and as you read the bible you should if you are in good shape physical and mental and mental good shape and physical good shape you should be able to with your thought process your mental process and your brain wave you should be able to acquire the memory knowledge necessary as to study the bible to speak and think in a lord tongue you should be able to memory all the knowledge down on down on the page in the bible book to work for god in the mission now in the position I am in now with the medicate andwith the hospital program I am being helped but at the same time that I am being help with the food and the medicate and the the food and medicate and the ah same process that I am being help by the food and medicate and the and the ah rest I feel that I still do not have this I still not have the thought pattern and the mental process and the brain wave necessary top open up a page open up the old testament and start to memory it the old te- the old new testament page of the bible start to have me-memory knowledge necessary to speak to think in the lo- speak and think in the lord's

tongue while you study while you study the bible while you study the bible the memory the knowledge necessary to go to work for god in the mission so when your thought problem your brain wave and your mental process is quick enough you will be able to memory the knowledge in in the old testament and new testament bible and from memory knowledge in the old testament and new testament bible you are able to memory the knowledge necessary to to memory the knowledge necessary necessary to think and speak in the lord's tongue and go to work for god in the mission. (Data courtesy of Dr. Bonnie Spring)[10]

Rutter (1985) claims that psychotic speech emanates from a social dysfunction, that the speaker fails to take into account the needs of the listener. The kinds of anomaly laid out in this chapter make manifest the difficulty with such an interpretation. We have seen disruption at every level of language, from word formation to discourse.

We all at least sometimes fail to take into account the needs of our listeners. Bores frequently do, as do the overly taciturn, but such failure does not take the form of gibberish, word salads and the kinds of circular discourse we have just seen. These all indicate a larger problem.

The next chapter will attempt to give a unified explanation of this almost bewildering variety of linguistic dysfunction, exploring as well what schizophrenics have said about their own condition.

Notes

[1] Using participant observations, researchers can devise a wide variety of tasks, e.g. asking for directions, both during an SD patient's psychotic bout and when in remission.

[2] Robertson and Shamsie (1958) do claim that a multilingual patient was speaking different languages in gibberish, but they offer no proof that this was actually so and none of the gibberish I have ever heard or seen mentioned in the literature supports their conclusion.

[3] When new words are coined, they typically are not heard as neologisms, but as slang or metaphor. For instance, whoever coined the metaphor *uptight* in the 1960s would not have been perceived as uttering a neologism as it was understandable by normal means of decoding.

[4] For the uninitiated, both [f] and [θ] (*th*) are made by forcing air between the lips and upper teeth (for the [f]) and the tongue held behind the teeth (for [θ]). Because friction is produced, these are both called *fricatives*. Additionally, both are produced with the vocal cords spread apart so that a hissing sound is produced. This results in

voiceless sounds. Both are voiceless fricatives. When sounds are so similar they often are involved in slips of the tongue. (Voiced sounds occur when the vocal cords are relaxed and air pushed through them vibrates, as in making a [v]).

[5]Cohen's interpretation of these data did not agree with mine, however, and he is in no way responsible for my interpretation.

[6]Notice that other primary colors like red, orange, or white cannot be used alone to indicate some other state.

[7]Actually, other verbs could also be substituted for *be* with slight differences in connotation, such as "The toys are lying in the box" and "Roses are growing in the garden." This does not affect the analysis here, however, since the alternation between *have* and *be* still holds, so that a confusion between them still can occur.

[8]The reader may disagree that *be* and *become* are true antonyms. They pattern with antonyms because they can be inserted in the same environments in most instances.

[9]The transcript of this monologue capitalized the first person pronoun and nothing else. I have adhered to this practice.

[10]Dr. Spring does not necessarily endorse my interpretations of these data, however.

Chapter Two

THE NATURE OF DEVIATION
IN PSYCHOTIC SPEECH

The variety of deviations associated with schizophrenic speech can be seen to arise from a deficit in speech production, one probably related to other known deficits in schizophrenics and their relatives, such as those revealed in studies of eyetracking. Viewing schizophrenic deviations in terms of path control allows us to see an underlying unity in what appears to be a bewildering variety of deviations. The kinds of deviations long classified as being schizophrenic differ from normal errors. Even such matters as clichés arise from different conditions in the two populations.

[1] Out of Many One.

As one looks at the apparently bewildering variety of SD productions, it is easy to see the reasons for the many conflicting theories about what causes it and what it can mean. It is also easy to see why so many different kinds of experimental protocols have been attempted, each designed to test for some apparent feature of such speech. Insofar as these rested upon simplistic views about what language is, their results were flawed. A corollary problem has been an incomplete understanding of what psychotic language is. This, too, has foiled attempts at an adequate understanding of the problem.

It bears repeating that any explanation also must account for the variability in the degree of deviance manifested in the speech of schizophrenics, especially in terms of linguistic structure (e.g., Brown 1973; Cohen 1978; Rochester, Martin, and Thurston 1977; Cromwell 1984; Fraser, King, Thomas, and Kendell 1986; Andreasen and Grove 1986). It must also explain why only a subset of patients diagnosed "schizophrenic" produce structurally deviant speech, and why those that do produce it do so intermittently (e.g., Maher, McKeon, & McLaughlin 1966; Reilley, Harrow, & Tucker 1973; Benson 1973; Chaika 1974a,b,

28

1977; Lecours & Vanier-Clement 1976). In evaluating any study, we must ensure that the researchers have selected their subjects from among those who are SD (Chapter 8). DiSimone, D'arley, and Aronson (1977), for instance, say that schizophrenics did not perform like aphasics on an aphasia test battery, but they nowhere indicate that they have selected an SD population. Even if they had, it is entirely possible that SD psychotic speech proceeds from different underlying sources than does aphasic speech.

The explanation offered here uses as its empirical base all of the kinds of speech data that have been reported as pathognomic to schizophrenics. Most important, perhaps, the power of the explanation presented here is that it takes a set of ostensibly confusing data and shows that they make sense when looked at in a certain way. In the words of Morton (1979, p. 109) "Inasmuch as . . . the model accounts for data and generates further understanding, it fulfills its purpose as a psychological model."

As disparate as the features of schizophrenic speech seem on the surface, closer inspection suggests that all of these deviations may actually be different manifestations of two underlying dysfunctions: lack of control over selection of linguistic material combined with inappropriate perseverations (Chaika 1982a). Actually, even inappropriate perseverations can be seen as a process of getting stuck, which is also a problem in controlling one's speech.

As we have seen, the lack of control leads to the word finding difficulties revealed by gibberish, neologizing, opposite speech, and other erroneous word retrieval. It also manifests itself by morphological and syntactic errors ranging from relatively transparent failures to attach noun or verb morphemes appropriately to speech so disordered that it creates a word salad in which individual words are recognizable but their syntactic frames are not. Then there are problems at the discourse level, such as intrusive material not germane to the task at hand or the general context. These are so called because the resultant output is as if incidental or unintentionally produced material has intruded. Intrusions actually occur on the level of word selection as well as that of discourse itself. Glossomanic chaining is as much an intrusion as the wandering narrative in which someone starts talking about events or ideas having no relevance to the matter at hand. Lack of control leads to intrusions because unwanted or unintended material has intruded into target utterances as a byproduct of problems in speech production.

There is evidence to suggest strongly that at least some SD speakers themselves are aware that they are not controlling their speech processes. Chapman (1966) interviewed schizophrenics after they recovered from a psychotic episode. They told him that they were trying to talk but what was coming out of their mouths was not what they intended to say, and they could not correct themselves. Similarly, in my own studies, many patients apologized for their speech, saying, for instance, that they stuttered or couldn't speak correctly. One patient I observed whose speech was larded with gibberish, after seeing himself in a videotaped interview, commented "No wonder people don't understand me. I heard myself on tape before but I thought the tape was distorted."

This same patient said a chipmunk brought him his special language in seeds. As is well known, other patients complain that a spirit or some other being has taken over their minds or supplied them with a new language. Such delusions can possibly arise from their feelings of lack of control, of not being able to control what they want to say. People are always trying to explain their behavior, especially if they feel that it is inappropriate or outlandish. I am not offering this suggestion as God's Truth, but as a hypothesis which explains both the weird language of some psychotics, and their own consequent belief that they can no longer control their speech and other mental activities, including perceptions.

Such feelings may also be the origin of the intense interest in religion evinced so many schizophrenics. They may ascribe the auditory and visual hallucinations to their being inhabited by spirits or to special messages brought to them by Jesus or a saint or other spirit. In support of my speculation here there is independent corroboration of the psychotic's awareness. Chapman (1966) also showed that schizophrenics reported distorted vision as well as a lack of control over their speech.[1] Therefore, they assume that they are being controlled by other spirits, and that their inability to control their speech is because spirits, good or bad, have taken it over. They know that strange things had happened to their very perceptions as well as to their ability to speak. Maher (1983, p. 154) gives a number of first person accounts of schizophrenics. In these, they say they cannot control what they notice. This suggestion as to the genesis of schizophrenic claims of being possessed may very well also explain paranoia. If one no longer can control what's coming out of one's mouth—or what one hears as in auditory hallucination—it must be very frightening, and the sufferer might well suspect that some ones or some things have taken adverse possession or want to do that.

[2] The Cycle of Speech as a Symptom.

The analysis presented here not only accounts for all of the kinds of deviant speech data reported in the literature, but for the cyclicity of their occurrence. Schizophrenic speech disruption is frequently cyclic in that a given patient might evince difficulty in a different stratum of linguistic production at different times, even in the same discourse. That is, at one time, a patient might have intact syntax but evince word-creation difficulty; yet, at another time, might show disordered syntax although words used seem to be usual words in the language (Chaika 1974; Rochester and Martin 1979, pp. 177–178).

As Brown (1977, p. 4) noted, "a symptom is a scientific datum no less than a sine wave or a synaptic cleft." Structurally deviant speech is a symptom in and of itself and, as such, must be analyzed in its own right. This necessarily entails examining speech without reference to the thought behind it. The relationship between language and thought will be discussed in Chapter 3. Even if one's scientific or philosophic principles, or both, allow one to deduce thought disorder from speech disorder, the exact nature of the speech disorder still must be characterized in and of itself. If one is basing an assumption of thought disorder on speech disorder, then the disordered thought still has to be related to the disordered speech.

Often, patients have deviations interspersed between otherwise normal discourse. This circumstance also must be taken into account in any explanation. As Kean (1980, p. 242) emphasizes, "deviant linguistic behavior arises as a consequence of an interaction between impaired and intact components of the language faculty." In all that follows, this must not be forgotten.

[3] Punning.

There are, to be sure, occasions for producing normal speech according to chance associations as in a punning situation. This occurs if there is some way that both meanings of a word can be forced into the topic at hand, e.g., *read* vs *red*, as in "What's black and white and read all over?" Even here, topic and social situation constrain whether or not the chance association is appropriate. In recent years, American advertising has been characterized by a fit of punning. These puns have to be carefully constructed so that readers or viewers will stop a millisecond or so to decode the double meaning. Such puns have got to be clever enough to catch the ear and eye and to imply good things about the product. For example, a face lotion advertising that it is pH balanced, advertised "A balancing act for your skin."

In contrast, Maher (1972) gives an example of what appears to be punning gone wild. Phonological shapes of words cause the puns, which seem clever enough at the outset, but degenerate into a punning glossomania:

1. To Wise and Company,

If you think that you are being wise to send me a bill for money I have already paid, I am in nowise going to do so unless I get the whys and wherefores from you to me. But where fours have been then fives will be and other numbers and calculations and accounts to your no-account no-bill noble nothing.

We see here intricate puns on *wise* and *whys,* including *nowise,* and the association of the common expression *whys and wherefores* all of which seem related to the complaint to the company, but the pun on *-fores* and *fours,* like other kinds of glossomania start veering off the topic. The number word *five* seems to be an intrusion of the number after four, just as the words *calculations* and *accounts* seem to have been triggered by the mention of numbers and of bills. Since accounts are bills, the writer then makes another pun, this one on the negative evaluation of a person, a *no-count,* which leads to *no-bill* which reminds the person of *noble.* Given the tightness of these associations and our love for puns, this passage seems enormously clever, but the irrelevant punning and the chaining character of each successive pun puts it squarely in the camp of glossomanic chaining. Once in a while, such chaining can be felicitous. Usually it is just baffling and strange.

Note that none of these perseverations involve unusual or "strong" association per use, contrary to Chapman et al. (1964) and Chapman et al. (1976). For instance, the relationship between *wise, nowise, no bill* and *noble* is quite unusual, so much so that the chaining is startling. Nor does such glossomanic perseveration show "weakening of constructs" (Bannister 1960, 1962). Indeed, the bond of meaning that causes associational chaining is, if anything, stronger than in normals since the chaining is based upon accidental sharing of morphemes, accidental rhyming and alliterating, and accidental sharing of partial meanings. In normal speech words and phrases are chosen to advance a topic, not because their structures are similar.

[4] Word Finding and Creativity.

Chapman (1966) and Chaika (1974), albeit on somewhat different grounds, argue that errors like gibberish and neologizing are indicative of a word finding difficulty. Considering that human languages are so constructed that new words can be made up and old words can be used in new ways to effect new meaning, it is not likely that incomprehensible neologizing and gibberish are a sign of creativity (Forrest 1976; Fromkin 1975). When new words or new meanings on old words are created normally, they are subordinated to a target meaning. Moreover, they can be utilized again by speakers or writers, and admit of discussion by their creators. None of these conditions seem to apply to psychotic neologizing.

There is usually a recognizable difference between normal creativity and schizophrenic novel usages although, as we have seen, in instances such as James Joyce's *Finnegan's Wake,* there may be question (Andreasen, 1973). It is not without significance, however, that Joyce like other artists of his day was experimenting with presenting the reader with the protagonist's stream of consciousness, that interior dialogue usually hidden from public view. This explanation does not depend upon the question of whether or not Joyce or any other stream-of-consciousness artists actually studied Freud, but psychoanalytic constructs were exhilarating to the intelligentsia and the works of many artists were stimulated by him whether or not they actually read him. Freud's belief in the inner reality of a well-developed unconscious had an undeniable effect on 20th century artists who then tried to explore the unconscious in their works.

As opaque as many such artistic works may be, if the artist develops them, refines them, works on them over and over, and can discuss his or her productions, we can still count them as art, in the sense of deliberate working of linguistic material. Joyce, for instance, is said to have worked painstakingly on *Finnegan's Wake* for 17 years. Joyce scholars claim that he reworked older sections in accordance with newer ones. His highly intricate verbal and mythic motifs definitely showed an artist's control. This is all in great contrast to the random output of psychotics, output that is rarely repeated on two consecutive days, if even in two consecutive conversations. All the evidence that I have been able to garner from the psychiatric literature and my own contacts with SD schizophrenics shows a random associational course usually dependent on what their first sentence or phrase was, then in response to someone else or not. SD nonce-productions, then, are random, show no development, and show no working-over of material, nor do they show the relationship between the parts of a discourse to the whole (see Chapter 9). Genius often consists in being able to forge connections between new and disparate phenomena, but this forging is controlled. In contrast, psychotic slippage causes phrases, both usual and bizarre, to be juxtaposed with no control and usually with no further development, and this is true even when we can point to the presence of overtly stated cohesive devices (see Chapter 6).

[5] Perseverations.

We have seen several kinds of perseveration: repetitions of morphemes like -*welt* and *Frank-* or of phonological shapes like *whys, wise, no-bill* and *noble.* Sometimes the perseverations simply repeat words, as in

> 2A . . . Send it to me, Joseph Nemo, in care of Joseph Nemo, and me who answers by the name of Joseph Nemo and will care for it myself. Thanks everlasting and Merry New Year to Mentholatum Company for my nose, for my nose, for my nose, for my nose, for my nose. (Maher 1968, p. 30)

In word association testing, Clark and Clark (1977, pp. 477–483) also speak of syntagmatic associations, words that commonly precede or follow another word. These figure in responses in word association tests, such as *whistle* eliciting *stop* or *long* eliciting *fellow.* In schizophrenics, syntagmatic responses also occur, but, besides such usual ones shared by many speakers of a language, apparently idiosyncratic syntagmatic responses may occur, as in the connections between the parts shown below, such as the questions about Paradise or the comments about liking the families on Mill Avenue:

> 2B. **Mill Avenue is a** house in between avenues U and avenue T I live **on Mill Avenue** for a period of for now a period of maybe fifteen year for around approximate fifteen years **I like it the fam**—I like every **family on Mill Avenue I like** every **family** in the world **I like** every **family** in **The United State of America I like** every **family on on Mill Avenue I** like **Mill Avenue is a** is a block with that is busy cars always pass by all the time I always look out the window of

my front porch front porch at time when I s- when I'm not sure if it's possible about the way I think I could read people mind about people's society attitude plot and spirit so I think I could read their mind as they drive by in the car sh- will I see Paradise will I not see Paradise should I answer should I not answer I not answer w- their thought of how I read think I could read their mind about when they pass by in the car in the house pass by in the car from my house I just correct for them for having me feel better about myself not answer will I should I answer should I not answer will I see Paradise will I not see Paradise I just correct them to have me feel better about myself about the way I think I can hear their mind r- about the way I think I could read their mind as they pass by the house Mill Avenue is also Mill Avenue is also a place of great event for all the families that live on Mill Avenue always eht- receive world wide attention and I am o- I am just one of the families live on Mill Avenue that always receive world wide attention so therefore [unintelligible] to receive world wide attention is receive world wide attention is some some you should be proud of you should be proud of world wide attention (unintelligible) there's the family are just too out in the open not to have world wide attention so they all have world wide attention by the cars pa—that pass in the front cars that pass by all the time so therefore Mill Avenue is also a a I like a quiet residential n- block like a quiet residential block with a Italian people talk outside by the fence discuss their feelings their attitudes their opinions opinion about any story feeling concept idea or sentence that they may have and once again when I look outside the window because I think I could read people's minds about people's society attitude plot and spirit w- should I answer should I not answer will I see Paradise will I not see Paradise I not answer correct them have me feel about better about myself like I said before I'm not sure if it's possible about the way I think I could read people mind about people's society attitude plot and spirit so I not answer them I just correct them have me feel better about myself Mill Avenue is also a place where people gather in back yards to have people gather in back yards to have a barbecue in the back yard to have relative over to have friend over to talk in the back yard to be merry with each other. (data courtesy of Dr. Bonnie Spring)[2]

Even where phrases are repeated such as the "should I answer should I

not answer . . . Will I see Paradise will I not see Paradise . . . " the repetitions serve none of the usual purposes. They are reminiscent of **refrains,**
but they fail as true refrains for four reasons. First, they do not come at
predictable points as a true refrain does. Second, they do not function to
strengthen some message or to create cohesion. Third, all the repetitious
phrases in this passage are not repeated entirely and in the exact way as
true refrains are. Rather, they seem to be randomly accessed sometimes
after the start of a word which is then broken off. Fourth, the repetitions
often seem to be broken off willy-nilly again in the middle of a phrase.
The effect is that of a broken record in which the needle keeps getting
stuck at certain points as well as skitters over tracks, accessing parts of
refrains.

Both the glossomanic chaining and the pseudo-refrains are perseverations. In the case of the chaining, accidental similarities of morphemes or of meanings of words cause the chaining. It is as if the patient
accesses one word or morpheme, and then, instead of ignoring its affiliates,
so to speak, simply continues accessing other words connected to the first
in some structural manner. In contrast, one normally accesses the word
or phrase one wishes in order to express an idea or to otherwise give
information, but then one goes to the next item which will advance one's
topic, all the while avoiding those which do not do that regardless of
whether or not they show some structural similarity to a word just
expressed. To do otherwise is to lose what Werner et al. (1975) termed
"path control" in fashioning utterances.

The inappropriate rhyming and alliterating associated with psychotic
speech are also manifestations of inappropriate perseverative chaining.
In these instances, chaining is on the basis of repeated final syllables
(rhymes) or first sounds (alliteration), or both. Perseverations may be on
several planes all at once, not simply one of rhymes or of morphemes.

The intricacy and intertwining of perseveration is beautifully illustrated in the sequence mentioned earlier "Looks like clay. Sounds like
gray. Take you for a roll in the hay. Hay day. May Day. Help!" Cohen
(1978, p. 29). This started out as an appropriate response to the color
naming task which evoked this sequence. Besides the perseverating of
the *-ay* in making the rhyme of "*clay* and *gray,* the two first sentences
share the paradigmatic "looks like" and "sounds like," both part of the set
of two-part verbs used for describing the senses. Since "sounds like" is
wholly inappropriate here, it can be seen both as an intrusion of a
member of a set, but also as a perseveration of the construction [verb of

sense] + *like*. Additionally, the color *gray* seems to have been mentioned because it is a color and this was a color-naming task, as well as because of its chance phonological association with *clay*.

Although clearly the initial motivation for saying "mayday" may have been the rhyme, the end of the sequence, "Mayday . . . Help! I just cannot. Need help." are semantically related. Even without positing that the patient really wanted help, which is entirely possible, the round-about way of asking for it is peculiarly schizophrenic, arising as it does at the end of a rhyming sequence. This passage, so notable for its rhyming and its ultimate semantic chaining, also shows syntactic chaining. Its first three sentences are all [Verb + Object] without overt subjects. That is, "Looks like clay," "Sounds like gray," and "Take you for a roll in the hay" and, later "Need help" all show the same basic syntactic frame. Then, too, *looks like* and *sounds like* are part of a paradigm of verbs + *like* that are used for describing experiences of the senses. Intrusions, then, are irrelevant but structurally similar items, and perseverations continue down what may have originated as an intrusive pathway.

The richness of the possible perseverations and intrusions in psychotic speech is matched by the richness of the associations of words in our brains which range from phonological, syntactic, semantic, cultural, and personal connections (Miller 1978; Forster, 1978; Morton 1979; Clark 1970; Deese 1965; Clark and Clark 1977, pp. 411–414; Foss and Hakes 1978, pp. 105–110, 122–124. Lieberman (1984, p. 47), for instance, lays out the way words in memory form associational networks in which phonetic representations serve as addresses to semantic readings. For his purposes, he considers initial sounds, positing a dictionary-like mental lexicon. The data from SD speech suggests that these phonetic addresses are even more complex, including final syllables, for instance, so that words are also connected to those that rhyme with them. Lieberman's model of "associative distributive neural models" is certainly consistent with the interpretation presented here for glossomania. Every word in the lexicon is associated with many others. Further, each word is associated in many ways: according to shared sounds, number of syllables, shared meanings, shared registers, shared derivations, shared topics likely to elicit them, and the like (Miller 1978). Given this richness, the apparent diversity of psychotic speech is explicable. The underlying process of impaired retrieval itself can be quite simple, but because this process can tap into an intricate and extensive set of networks, the output seems bafflingly varied.

Whatever factors that lead normals to screen out irrelevant associations and to control their output somehow fail for SD schizophrenics. As Rose (1976) said of free associating

> Once the brain has "chanced upon" a particular state, perhaps as a result of random or spontaneous firing, as in dreaming, the ensuing states will follow almost by necessity. (p. 262)

[6] Failures in Subordinating.

There is an alternate way of looking at the same data, that of failing to subordinate at different levels of linguistic processing. Neologisms and gibberish can also be seen as failure to subordinate sounds to appropriated word shapes, just as word salads show a failure to subordinate words to sentences. Failure to use appropriate inflectional markers is also a failure in subordination, as is failing to use appropriate syntactic markers like *-ize, -tion,* or *-s'* Intrusive matters not pertaining to any discernible topic, as in glossomania, are also failure of subordination.

Topic is to discourse what sentence is to word and what word is to sound. The question of *topic* itself and its role both in producing discourse and understanding it merits a chapter in itself (Chapter 10). For now we note that language forms a hierarchy of subordinating structures. Failing to subordinate any level in this hierarchy into its appropriate higher structures leads to deviations.

These failures are major disruptions in speech production. In normal discourse, sounds and morphemes (such as *Vor-* or *pup*) are always subordinated to word shapes. Words have to be subordinated both to the syntactic requirements of the sentence and to the topic at hand. If a given word reminds the normal speaker/hearer of another topic, a signal is given announcing that. For instance, one says, "Ooh-that reminds me," or "not to change the topic, but . . . " In some way, change of topic is announced, and subsequent utterances become subordinated to the new topic. By contrast, SD schizophrenics flit from one associated word or phrase to another, often with far fewer and shorter pauses than normal speakers (Rochester et al. 1977b; Silverman 1973). This last suggests a lack of planning in their productions.

Speech often considered most pathognomic of schizophrenia typically is not controlled by any discernible topic (Lecours and Vanier-Clement 1975; Werner et al. 1975). As already noted, even if the utterance starts out with a phrase relevant to the context and topic at hand, it quickly veers away from it. Grice (1975, pp. 51–55) and Van Dijk (1977, p. 109) consider mention of matters extraneous to the topic at hand a far more serious failure in discourse than omissions of what might be considered relevant. Part of our normal decoding strategy is to figure out what has been left out. Adding too much detail actually makes discourse less interpretable for two reasons. One is obviously the load of remembering so much. The other is that if someone does mention something that can be figured out, the hearer assumes that there has been a special reason for doing so and then has to try to figure out that reason. If the point of the discourse is not germane to the overdetailed presentation, its entire point is soon lost.

VanDijk (1980, pp. 29–50) convincingly shows that meaning and coherence are dependent on the macrostructure of discourse and the subordination of microstructures, such as phrases and sentences, to that macrostructure. Furthermore, he emphasizes that normal discourse has a discernible macrostructure, what is often idiomatically called "the point" and "the gist," as well as "the theme" or "the topic." It is this macrostructure that seems to be missing from much of the discourse presented in the literature as "schizophrenic," even that in which the individual words and syntax are not deviant. The importance of a topic as a determinant of meaning will be explored later (Chapter 10).

It is the schizophrenic's failure to subordinate to macrostructure that leads to the impairment of communicability found by researchers like Salzinger et al. (1978). They used the Cloze procedure on schizophrenic discourse. That procedure asks subjects to guess what deletions have been made in a given discourse. When decoding normal speech, one guesses at parts left out or not heard by referring to what is being talked about. Since SD schizophrenics veer off the topic erratically, it is much more difficult to guess what they have left out. All the Cloze procedure does is show the result of such veering. It is another way of saying that SD speech is not controlled and subordinated to a topic. There is a similar difference between schizophrenic rhyme and alliteration and that of artists. The former is random, caused by intrusions and perseverations whereas the latter adheres to a larger topic (Chaika 1977; LaFerriere, 1977).

Like normal discourse SD schizophrenic output often seems to start out motivated by context and purpose. However, subsequent utterances may not be so motivated. Rather, unlike normal production, the rest of the SD production may travel through associated words, cycling through them with no checking back to context or purpose, resulting in a cycling through associated words, referring back to syntax to put those words into a syntactic frame. In the case of complete word salads there is no reference back to syntax. In other instances, in fact, in glossomanic strings very frequently the syntactic frame of a previous utterance is perseverated.

Neologizing, gibberish, and wrong word, including opposite speech, are explained by the same circumstance. In these instances, the target word is not hit. Rather, as when normals are fatigued or excited, a word related to the target is retrieved. With neologizing and gibberish, the purposeless course of speech production interferes with the process of matching lexicon to proper phonology. If at least some morphemes are matched up, then neologisms result. If not, then gibberish does.

Punning, rhyming, alliterating, or other kinds of repeated words are also perseverations. If the perseveration cycles through the same syntax and words, then repeated phrases or sentences will occur, sometimes but not always as a refrain. All perseverations may be interspersed with apparently uninhibited "firings" of associated words.

This explanation accounts for one phenomenon that Reilly, Harrow, Tucker, Quinlan, and Siegel's (1975) describe in schizophrenic speech. They believe that

> . . . a certain portion of schizophrenics who show marked looseness during the acute phase may have always been somewhat vague . . . tend[ing] to grasp at the jargon of the moment . . . by virtue of the fact that this form of speaking does not give away . . . the speaker's fundamental disorganization, confusion, vagueness, or lack of comprehension.

A more likely explanation, and one which has the merit of referring to observable data, is that clichés are accessed just as individual words are accessed. In Chapter 8, we will see such accessing of clichés interspersed throughout psychotic narratives.

[7] The Relative Rarity of Agrammatism.

There are two possible reasons that there seems to be less agrammatism than associative chaining. First, as Bradley et al. (1980) point out, grammatical function words are treated differently psychologically than the far larger class of lexical words with referential meaning. Disruption in grammar, then, is not necessarily mirrored by disruption in word usage, and vice versa.

Second, there are fewer possible choices in syntax than in lexicon. This suggestion is borne out by the observation of Maher et al. (1966) that speech disruption in schizophrenics most frequently occurs at the ends of sentences. Under conditions of relatively free speech, speech unconstrained by experimental tasks, for instance, in English and most European languages, new information typically comes at the end of sentences. New information requires the most heavily modified phrases. Hence, there are more choices to be made at the ends of sentences, so that more mistakes can be made.

Because of the many ways words can be associated in the mental lexicon, and because of the complexity of language in general, the surface results of such firing appear to be great, resulting in deviations such as those presented in deviations 1-8 above.

[8] The Explanatory Value of This Explanation.

It should be noted that the explanation given here accounts for all data and does not posit steps in speech production for which we have no evidence, e.g., Cohen's (1978) model. He, for instance, explains glossomanic chaining in terms of sampling responses and rejecting them for fear of punishment. Yet, in all of his examples, it is clear that the first response is almost always correct, with each subsequent utterance becoming more and more "punishable," in behavioral terms because it becomes more and more bizarre for the context. Furthermore, there is no proof that such sampling for punishable responses takes place in production of speech, normal or not. Nor does the explanation tendered here ascribe putative motivations to the speakers, motivations which cannot be checked. One does not get very far asking an SD psychotic what he or she meant by what was just said.

The explanation offered here accounts for all of the aberrations considered typical of SD psychotic speech, including the differing degrees of incoherence. The intensity of the inhibitory dysfunction in each patient at varying times determines the degree of speech disorder, accounting for relatively minor intrusions as well as the most severe.

It also explains the often noted similarity between schizophrenic speech and poetic speech. What the poet does deliberately, subordinating to intended meaning, is to find new and unusual connections between words. The schizophrenic chances upon such connections, although he/she cannot control them (LaFerriere, 1977, pp. 33–37). Some claim that schizophrenics are being creative, noticing new connections when they utter strings as in 5(a) above (Forrest 1976). Sometimes patients may even claim that they are noticing new relation between words. Other patients complain, however, that what got uttered is not what they intended to say (Chapman 1966). While I was doing an experiment at Butler Hospital, one SD patient listened to a tape recording of his speech made during a psychotic episode. He wonderingly commented that it was no wonder that no one understood him, and that he had heard himself on tape before, but he assumed that the tape was distorted.

Even if the patient feels as if he or she is noticing new connections, as noted above, the kinds of rhymes one finds in schizophrenic associative chaining are usually quite ordinary, about the level one hears from young children first experimenting with end rhyme.

Finally, the explanation offered here also shows why speech during psychotic episodes is more disorganized than at other times. Our inhibitory mechanisms do vary according to our mental states. During excitement and times of stress, for instance, "path control" is often lessened even for normals, and intrusions and slips increase. At these times, but to a lesser degree than SD schizophrenics, normals produce some of the same kinds of errors.

[9] Confirmation From Other Research.

Shimkunas (1978, p. 211) claims that schizophrenics show excessive verbal-temporal activation as compared with normal controls. Studies have shown that "Heightened general arousal, as indicated by skin-conductance levels, appears to be primarily mediated by the left hemi-spheres of acute . . . schizophrenics." That is, the language hemisphere shows the kinds of overactivation that could lead to the kinds of intrusions discussed above. Rochester and Martin (1979, pp. 192–193) agree that "it is necessary to suppose *some* impairment in the left-hemisphere processes of schizophrenic patients."

[10] Automatic and Controlled Processes.

Comparing psychotic glossomanic productions to normal speech sub-ordinated to the topic or nature of the social interaction makes manifest the difference between controlled and automatic retrieval of linguistic forms. Glossomania sets off a round of synonyms, rhymes, alliterations, or personal memories not germane to the matter at hand. This seems to be an automatic process. Normal speech is controlled, subordinated to both the social situation and the intent of the speaker. There is no such control in glossomanic chaining.

Stilling, Feinstein, Garfield, Rissland, Rosenbaum, Weisler, and Baker-Ward (1987, pp. 55–60) in quite a different context discuss several studies of automated processes and how they can interfere with controlled processes, the latter being any goal-directed behavior. Typically, in such studies subjects first are trained to learn an automatic procedure. Once they have, they then are asked to do the controlled tasks. Researchers have found that the automatic processes can interfere with the task at hand if they they redirect attention from it. Although none of these studies seem to have dealt with a psychotic population, they nevertheless predict incoherence arising from a state in which automatic processes dominate conscious controlled behavior.

> Optimal skilled performance seems to balance the speed and high capacity of automatic processes with the goal-directedness and flexibility of controlled processes. A system that acted only by allowing the currently most active automatic procedure to carry through to completion without any influence by goals **would be incoherently impulsive without consciousness as we know it.** [boldface mine] (Stillings et al. pp. 59–60)

Glossomania in any of its forms provides perfect examples of the takeover of automatic processes, as do word salads and even gibberish.[3] The lack of control seen in these productions is certainly as if word and syntactic selection has gone on automatic pilot, so to speak. This is probably why gibberish seems to conform to the phonotactics of the language, but doesn't happen to form words. Wandering narratives in which personal memories are interspersed, memories which are not subordinated to what the patient is supposed to be narrating are also examples of automatic processes.

[11] Eyetracking Dysfunction.

That the above analysis is essentially correct is suggested by a quite different study by Holzman et al. (1978). This research provides some interesting parallels to SD verbal output. Briefly, Holzman et al. found that 65 to 85 percent of schizophrenic patients, in contrast to only 6 percent of normals, show disordered eye pursuit movements. In order to pay attention to the swinging pendulum in such studies, subjects must be willing participants, but once they look at the pendulum, the pursuit system is triggered, so that the eyes follow the pendulum. This kind of eyetracking is involuntary attention, unaffected by motivation (Holzman et al. 1978, p. 297).

There are two kinds of eyetracking dysfunction. The first character-ized by short, fast movements, sacades, of the type used to focus, repre-sents failure to turn on the pursuit system. In the second, "spiky" type, the pursuit movement starts, but is interrupted by brief, frequent eye arrests. It is as if other interferences do not switch off (Holzman et al. 1978, p. 300). Not surprisingly, the latter seems to be prevalent in schizo-phrenics and their relatives.

The speech data presented here are consistent with such spiky-type eye movements. The perseverations of syntactic frames or words and phrases are like the arrests in spiky-type pursuit. Random travel along associative networks of linguistic material is like the spikes. The triggering of associated words not relevant to the context seems to be another instance of interferences, here previously uttered words, not switching off.

It must be emphasized, however, that even if the eyetracking studies did not exist, the speech data would still admit of the explanation given above, of random triggering of linguistic material (i.e., intrusions) com-bined with unmotivated perseverations along any of the language networks. Both phenomena suggest problems in neurotransmissions affecting the speech production capability of some schizophrenics.

[12] Parallels to Other Populations.

Holzman et al. (1978, p. 304) note that eyetracking dysfunction is not specific to schizophrenia. Nonspecificity is a help in the understanding of dysfunction in schizophrenia. When we see similar effects with known or better understood causes, we may extrapolate to the less well known. For this reason, with speech data, reference is often made to those normal states which most approximate the SD states. Eyetracking becomes impaired with age. The older the person, the greater number of eye arrests. Besides that found in old age, spiky-type tracking has been described in patients who have Parkinson's disease, multiple sclerosis, brain stem and hemispheric lesions, as well as alcohol or barbiturate intoxication, all indicative of CNS involvement.

Holzman et al. (1978) point out that the movements in spiky-type tracking suggests that random, asynchronous neural firing is occurring. So do the linguistic data from SD patients. Since the tracking dysfunction occurs

> ... in degenerating conditions, including aging, it would be likely that the high speed, asynchronous firing reflects not an increased activity of some parts of the nervous system, but a failure of inhibiting, modulating, or integrating control ... to assume that failure of such central nervous system inhibitory activities also accompanies schizophrenic conditions. (p. 305)

This explanation holds for the language data as well. The mention of words inappropriate to the speech situation, but related phonologically, morphologically, semantically, or syntactically, seems to represent lack of inhibition of matters extraneous to the context. Maher (1972) made a similar observation, positing some sort of attentional dysfunction in schizophrenia. Inability to "pay attention" and to subordinate speech output may be caused by failure of inhibitory mechanisms. Indeed, since normals do not evince inattention by uttering gibberish, random alliterating and rhyming, or making gross syntactic errors, the special quality of schizophrenic inattention must be delineated. Dysfunction in inhibitory mechanisms seems to discriminate between normal and SD schizophrenic inattention.

Brown (1980, p. 294) notes that neologistic jargons are a disorder of elderly aphasics. Recalling that the aged also show the kind of eyetracking abnormality of schizophrenics, it is reasonable to assume that the degeneration of CNS of inhibitory function might also be responsible here, as well as for the neologistic jargon of SD schizophrenics.

Green (1985) as a result of dichotic listening testing shows that acute schizophrenics could not focus attention on one ear in the presence of competing stimulus to another. This, too, is evidence of CNS dysfunction.

[13] Why Some Schizophrenics Are Not SD.

Viewing SD psychotic speech production in this light may help explain why all schizophrenics do not evince structurally impaired speech. Traditionally, those who do have been termed "thought disordered," whereas those who do not are termed "nonthought disordered." This terminology implies that some who are diagnosed as schizophrenic have unimpaired thinking (Chapter 3).

If schizophrenia causes a dysfunction in neurotransmission however, then the SD patient can be viewed as one in which the difficulty has affected the speech production areas of the brain. Those who do not evince SD symptoms, but do have other schizophrenic symptoms, including hallucinations and systematic delusions, are affected in other areas of the brain, including those that store visual imagery. Some patients may be affected in different areas at the same time, or at different times. Note that this explanation, although not identical, is accordance to Shimkunas (1978, pp. 225, 227–228), for both assume CNS involvement and both assume that the schizophrenic is affected by internal stimuli more than normal.

Allen and Allen (1985) disagree that schizophrenics suffer from a "general loss of control in producing speech" as outlined here. They do not offer any actual samples of schizophrenic speech to verify their position, nor do they analyze any of the disordered speech easily gathered from the literature, including that presented here and in Chaika (1974, 1982a; Chaika and Alexander 1986) to show how and why such speech is not disordered. If, indeed, their experiment did not yield evidence of weakness in linguistic path control, such evidence is not lacking in other studies and still must be accounted for. In other words, if they can refute the long-standing assumption that schizophrenics do not suffer from problems in path control, then they must show that the data presented in defense of that position can be explained in another way. This is especially important since glossomanic speech has so long been considered particularly pathognomic of this illness. How do they explain the speech in 2B above, for instance?

The task upon which Allen and Allen base their conclusions, the *Thematic Apperception Test* gave each patient only 2 minutes to describe each of 4 pictures. It has repeatedly been shown that the more bounded the task, the less psychotic speech disintegrates. This was one of the earliest points made by Maher, for instance. As we saw above, glossomanic chaining often starts out fine, but as the speech event continues it becomes more and more bizarre (also see Cozzolino 1983, p. 121). Within the confines of a 2-minute output constrained by a picture, we would not expect loss of path control. It is vital that researchers use comparable tasks to compare results. Allen and Allen also consistently interchange the word *ideas* with words for linguistic structures, as in:

At a local level this involves connecting elements in the previous or immediately following part of the discourse. It is this which distinguishes meaningfully integrated ideas from collections of unrelated ideas. (p. 75)

As the next chapter shows, terms like *ideas* are poorly defined. What is an idea? How does it correspond to speech? To date there is no firm correlation between any linguistic structure and ideas or thoughts. The very polysemy of language makes it unlikely that there ever will be. The most we can do is to correlate speech structures with meanings, and meanings with possible speech structures. That is how languages work.

[14] What This Explanation Explains.

This has attempted to explain the diverse speech phenomena long associated with those schizophrenics who evince structurally abnormal verbalizations. In words of Shimkunas (1978):

> Given the complex psychobiological problem that schizophrenia represents, broad, structurally oriented theorizing appears to be a necessary step in the ultimate construct validation of the phenomenon. (p. 228)

The analysis presented here is also consistent with a wide variety of findings of attentional and filtering deficits in schizophrenia (e.g., Hemsley 1976, 1977; Oltmanns 1978; Maher 1972; Schwartz 1978) but goes further in offering an explanation for all of the peculiarities of "schizophrenic" speech, especially in the combinations in which it is manifested.

It also accords with findings of hemispheric asymmetry in schizophrenics (e.g., Flor-Henry 1976; Shimkunas 1978. Rochester and Martin 1979, p. 192) as well as with first person accounts of schizophrenic experiences (Chapman 1966; Vonnegut 1976).

It also correlates with at least one other aspect of schizophrenic behavior: the eyetracking studies. Furthermore, it does not seem to be inconsistent with studies explaining the effects of antipsychotic medication on schizophrenics (Snyder 1978; Sachar et al. 1978; Davis 1978; Matthysse 1978). These claim that such medication inhibits the action of biochemicals associated with facilitated neurotransmission. In other words, they slow down mental functions. The speech data indicate that SD psychotics can use such slowing down.

[15] Academic Disciplines and Point of View.

One problem in studies of psychotic populations is that researchers come from diverse academic backgrounds, each with his or her own set of constructs into which any data are fit. We are all creatures of our training. Linguists have been trained to view language objectively as a system of interrelated levels; hence, they are often struck by the disruption in levels of language evinced by schizophrenic patients. My earliest papers had noticed that speech pathognomic of this population could be described in terms of disintegration in each of these levels. The well-known linguistic scholar Eugene Nida, after listening to one of my papers, independently observed to me about a schizophrenic friend:

> Observation of pathology is first evident in discourse, second in syntax, third in morphology, and lastly in phonology. I could almost predict the number of days he had refused to take his medication by the degree of disintegration.

Clinical psychologists and psychiatrists, more used to thinking of language holistically, and, furthermore, used to equating language with the thought behind it rather than as a structure in and of itself, have come to different conclusions. For instance, Lanin-Kettering and Harrow (1985, p. 3) cite the well-known characteristic of schizophrenic speech, its failure to maintain a topic. They refer to this as "an intermingling of personal material into speech when it does not fit neatly with the external context of the conversation." They see this as a "mixing of ideas related to conflicts and issues of personal concern to the patient."

This same phenomenon, as we have just seen, can more simply be explained by random triggering of interlocking semantic networks. The latter explanation requires no assumptions about the patient's inner conflicts, conflicts for which we often have no evidence. This is not to say that such conflicts don't lead to intrusions. They can and do, but that is not the same thing as saying that all digressions represent a patient's inner conflicts. For instance, the following excerpt from a monologue by X, reported on in Chaika (1974) shows such a digression:

3. Did that show up on the X-rays?
>
>   You'll see it tonight.
>   I've been drinking phosphate.
>   You'll see it in the dark (inaudible)
>   Glows.
>   We all glow as we're glowworms.

Aside from the veracity of the claim that she was drinking phosphate, a claim prompted apparently because of the mention of X-rays, not out of any conflict over phosphate, there is the peculiar statement that "we all glow as we're glowworms." This is semantically related to phosphate, which has the property of glowing. In order to validate Lanin-Kettering and Harrow's claim about schizophrenic digressions, we would have to try to find some personal conflict related to glowworms. Since X fails to mention glowworms elsewhere and her psychiatrist could report no other evidence of a concern with glowworms, we can only validate the semantic connection between the lexical items in the monologue. That is, we can't correlate it with the speaker's "conflicts and issues of personal concern." In short, we can explain the digression in terms of the lexical structure of English, but we ourselves have to digress from the data in order to explain them in terms of thought. The entire question of the allowable degree of creativity in extrapolating meaning will be deferred until Chapter 11.

Notes

[1]The schizophrenic preoccupation with religion has frequently been commented upon. Many samples of schizophrenic speech over the years have religious material in them. Many, many patients whom I interviewed easily derailed onto all sorts of religious matters: a concern with salvation, interest in Hinduism, Buddhism, and other Eastern religions, claims of communicating with Jesus or Mary or the like. Why this should be so has never been explained in the literature, at least so far as I can determine.

[2]I repeat that Dr. Spring does not necessarily endorse my interpretations of these data.

[3]Some Pentecostals and Charismatic Catholics are insulted by terming such gibberish "glossolalia" as that term refers also to "speaking in tongues" in a religious setting. For that reason, I have chosen the lay term *gibberish* to indicate this behavior. However, it is not surprising that the output of both states, schizophrenic and religious, are so alike since both proceed from rising above ego constraints.

Chapter Three

LANGUAGE AND THOUGHT

Because language is used to encode thoughts, many believe that thought and language are the same. Frequently, this is an unexamined assumption, one held by scholars, clinicians and laypersons alike. There are many problems with such an assumption, however. The position defended here, a position dependent upon language data, is that thought and language are separate entities. Although we often convey thought by language, this does not mean that language and thought are the same.

[1] The Interface between Thought and Language.

Until we are forced to examine their relationship, we assume that language and thought are one and the same. Before embarking on any discussion of psychotic speech, it is essential to separate the concept of language as opposed to thought. As a linguist, one oriented to pragmatics and discourse analysis, my position has been and still is that one analyzes discourse according to verifiable constructs and, from those analyses, one proceeds to the thoughts behind the discourse (Chaika 1974, 1981, 1982a, d, e; Chaika and Lambe 1985). Such an insistence on the separation of language from thought has excited much debate, but it has been gratifying to see that others have begun to see the value of such an approach (Andreasen 1982a; Neale, Oltmanns, and Harvey 1985). Harvey and Neale (1983, p. 165) remind us that Bleuler (1950) himself made the point that thought and language are not one and the same. Still, the issue is clouded for many.

Lanin-Kettering and Harrow (1985, p. 1) claim that my position is that "we often see disordered speech in patients who have adequate underlying thoughts and ideas." Not only have I never made any such claim, I do not even see how such a claim can be made at all at this time or in the foreseeable future. Not only are there as yet no infallible instruments for measuring the adequacy of underlying thoughts, but there has certainly

50

been no widespread cognitive testing of speech disordered patients. What I have said is that we must first consider in what ways schizophrenic speech is disordered and then determine what mechanisms must have gone awry to produce such speech. Then, perhaps, speech data can be correlated with thinking.

I have also insisted that any explanation for schizophrenic speech must be based upon all the data as elaborated in Chapters 1 and 2. Certainly, some schizophrenics show no structural deviation in their speech and even those who do, do not necessarily do so all of the time. If we do not insist upon the separation of thought and language, then we would be in the odd position of claiming that schizophrenics with structurally intact speech have no thought disorder. Thought disorder is not necessarily accompanied by any of the speech disorders discussed in the previous chapters, nor, so far as we know, does it necessarily indicate disordered thought (sec. 5).

Andreasen and Scott (1982) and Andreasen (1982b) have revived the concept of negative versus positive schizophrenia with the latter including hallucinations, delusions, and TD but the former showing flattened affect and paucity of speech. Their specification of negative and positive symptoms provides a welcome distinction between the terms TD and SD, and yet unites them on a scale. As the last chapter showed, hallucinations and delusions are related to speech dysfunction even if they are not one and the same. As with SD, not all patients have hallucinations and delusions and those who do, do not always have them.

[2] Schizophrenic Speech or Language?

Holzman, Shenton, and Solovay (1986, p. 361) argue that the term *thought disorder* (*TD*) should be retained rather than adopting *speech disorder* (*SD*), because schizophrenics do not share a language or even a dialect. This, of course, is very true. In some measure, I myself may have contributed to their criticism of the term SD. Chaika (1974) made the tactical error of referring to "schizophrenic" language. All language is polysemous. The word *language* can mean either the system that is a separate language or it can refer to a specific kind of language within one language. For instance, if we hear profanity, we could say, "such **language**," or "strong **language**" as in movie ratings. Neither of these is referred to as *speech.*' More recently, in his impressive review of the subject, Cozzolino (1983) many times speaks of schizophrenic *language* as I did, as in entitling a section *The Importance of Language Analysis for Diagnosis* (p. 105.) Since I erred in that 1974 article by referring to an **intermittent aphasia,** many scholars devoted themselves to arguing about whether or not schizophrenics were aphasic in the sense of the term meaning organic impairment. I had used *aphasia* in its generic sense of speech dysfunction.

The position here is that there is schizophrenic **speech,** but not a schizophrenic language. As already demonstrated, there is a constellation of errors in speaking performance which is associated with some schizophrenics, but, to date, there is no solid proof that the underlying language system is impaired. To the contrary, Grove and Andreasen (1983) have shown that psychotics can process speech, but that their output is dysfunctional[1] (p. 32). The fact that their processing shows no deficit certainly argues for an intact underlying system.

The most compelling evidence that SD psychotics are suffering from a speech disorder is that they manifest the same symptoms whether or not they have ever even been in contact with other schizophrenics. Non SD patients do not necessarily themselves become SD even if they are hospitalized together.[2] There are many kinds of speech dysfunction, ranging from childhood aphasics to stutterers to severe pathologies preventing clear pronunciation to that caused by physical damage to parts of the brain. Disordered psychotic speech is another of those pathologies.

In support of this contention, it has often been reported that there is high interrater reliability in discriminating between normal and schizophrenic speech and that lay judges can discriminate between such speech and that of normals as well as psychiatrists can (Andreasen 1979a; Kertesz 1982; Maher, McKeon, & McLaughlin 1966; Rochester, Martin, & Thurston 1977). Andreasen's *Scale for the Assessment of Thought, Language, and Communication,* henceforth *TLC,* is a widely used scale which engenders high interjudge rater reliability. Allen (1985) shows that "a clinician's acumen" can reliably discriminate between SD schizophrenic speech and normal speech. This concurs both with previous studies and with the contention by linguists that, by and large, native speakers of a language can judge if it is being used deviantly without any particular training. Gleitman, Gleitman, and Shipley (1972) found that young children could make such judgements.

Allen (1985) also makes the interesting claim that "the speech of all schizophrenics does indeed differ from that of normals but in as yet unspecified ways." Given the large literature on the characteristics of schizophrenic speech, this is a startling conclusion. In contrast to Allen, Fraser, King, Thomas, and Kendell (1986) made a linguistic analysis of schizophrenic speech and found that schizophrenics did produce syntactically simpler sentences with more errors than did manic and control populations. The judgements of deviance have to proceed from actual deviations in the message given.

[3] Thought Disorder or Speech Disorder?

Some clinicians characterize the population of schizophrenics as being either TD (thought disordered) or NTD (non-thought disordered). Rochester and Martin (1979, pp. 4–6, 169) argue convincingly that the diagnosis of TD is circular since it depends on the patient's speech. In their words, "The clinician proceeds from a personal experience of confusion to infer that the patient is confused." Despite the fact that they see the circularity of this concept, still they use the terminology throughout their work, a study of cohesive ties in narratives.

Several investigations have shown that *thought disorder,* or what is called thought disorder does not distinguish between patient populations. Simpson and Davis (1985) found that manics were more likely to be TD than were schizophrenics. Harvey, Earle-Boyer, and Wielgus (1984) using the TLC found it reliable for discriminating schizophrenics from manics, but they also found that the concept of TD was not useful for discriminating between the groups. Although TD was present at the outset, "the majority of the differences between the two groups were apparently due to verbal productivity and not other aspects of "thought disorder (p. 462)." Their results vis à vis manic and schizophrenic TD were different from Simpson and Davis." Harvey et al. found that TD somewhat was more stable in schizophrenics than in manics.

Andreasen (1982) herself makes some compelling arguments that the term *thought disorder* should be revised, also noting its circularity, by virtue of its being inferred from speech. She also comments on the vagueness of that term. She (p. 296) demonstrates that

> Thought is a philosophical term rather than a medical or scientific one and therefore should probably be avoided in scientific writing. When the concept of thought is invoked, thought process should be distinguished from thought content.

She suggests that either the term *dysphasia* or *dyslogia* be substituted, a suggestion apparently not followed. Some investigators have adopted SD, a nomenclature I suggested as it is parallel to the already entrenched TD (Chaika 1982d) Andreasen and Grove (1986), revive *thought disorder* in a discussion of the reliability of the TLC. However, they do reiterate that a diagnosis of thought disorder is inferred from speech; thus, is circular. It is undeniable that the TLC does work as a diagnostic tool. Notice that this doesn't mean that it reliably measures thought or speech. What it does is to allow clinicians to diagnose schizophrenics and manics reliably. Andreasen and Grove (p. 356) conclude that " 'thought disorder' should not be considered to be pathognomic of schizophrenia or diagnostic of it." They found that mild abnormalities in language behavior even occur in normals, as did Rochester and Martin (1979) and Chaika (1982e, 1983b; Chaika and Alexander 1986. See Chapter 8).

Harvey and Neale (1983, p. 175) maintain that " . . . the term *thought disorder* in its present use is misleading and should be split into two categories . . . discourse failure . . . deviant cognitive processes that relate to discourse failure. They (p. 160) show that " . . . a simple designation of a patient as thought disordered or not on the basis of a clinical evaluation of speech is not a useful diagnostic sign."

[4] Is Language Is Based on Thought?

Simpson and Davis (1985) say that "Disordered thought structure **results** . . . from abnormalities in the pattern of speech such as . . . word salad . . . " (boldface mine). It is not clear how word salad, which is a collection of words lacking syntactic markers, causes thought disorder. The term *word salad* refers to an agrammatical collection of words. It is not clear how these can change the structure of thought, especially since all humans have collections of words in their mental lexicons, but few are psychotic.

More likely, syntactic rules have been violated in word salad, or haven't been brought into play, but anthropological and cognitive linguistics have repeatedly shown that syntax itself does not affect thoughts (Kay and Kempton 1984; Scribner 1977; Macnamara 1977; Bickhard 1987). Rosch (1977, p. 519) insists: . . . it has not been established that the categorizations provided by the grammar of the language actually correspond to the linguistic units." Macnamara (1977) says that it is not likely that we will find a physical resemblance between language and thought. McNeill (1979, p. 294) puts it well when he says that grammars describe a language, but do not describe "...(however ideally or abstractly) the cognitive functioning of individual users." Kreckel (1981, pp. 37–38) emphasizes "the predominance of cognitive categories over linguistic expressions...the predominance of principles of organizing knowledge-...over the way of expressing this knowlege. In other words, thought and language are not the same, and it is thought that motivates language, not the reverse.

Aha! I can almost see the scholarly thrust to the jugular. If thought does direct language, then doesn't that mean that disordered thought produces disordered speech? No. There is no evidence at all from cognitive or social science studies that there is such an equation. The one thing we can say with assurance is that **language does not control thought,** but we cannot say that thought always controls speech. Commonsensically, we can think one thing and say another. We need not say anything at all about what we are really thinking. Casual chit-chat and other forms of phatic communication often has little to do with conveying thoughts.

[5] The Disjunction Between Thought and Language.

Although it is thought that determines what language forms we select, there is still no one-to-one correspondence between the two. Many scholars disagree. Holzman (1978, p. 373) declares "Speech is, after all, spoken thought," an idea reiterated in Holzman et al. (1986). Even though speech is **often** spoken thought, it does not follow that all speech directly reflects an individual's thoughts, nor that all thought is accompanied by speech, nor that all deviant speech proceeds from deviant thought processes. People can be crazy in quite ordinary speech (sec 6).

Chaika (1974, 1982d) and Chaika and Lambe (1985) have consistently maintained that there is a fatal circularity in claiming that speech is thought because thought is encoded in speech. In response, Lanin-Kettering and Harrow disclaim that

> ...the inference that strange speech suggests strange thinking is *not* circular since the schizophrenic patient's strange speech can fit into a construct about his disordered thinking that is grounded in a larger nomological net...

In other words, strange speech is caused by strange thinking because the strange thinking is grounded in the net of nomology (the laws of the mind). Not only does this fail to prove causation, it fails to prove correlation between strange speech and disordered thinking. Thought is expressed through the medium of language, but it does not follow that language is a direct expression of thought. That is a logical fallacy. Structurally deviant speech can contain logical thoughts that are appropriate for the matter at hand. For instance,

> In temperance due I don't see any reason why two men can't proceed as popular as ever both in themselves as a duocratic and as a democratic premise. I mean the God-given greatness of this country, and I hope there are no more triangular conflicts in a two-party government. (reported in Laffal, 1965, p. 133)

As one raised on the premise that two-party systems are essential to our democracy, but that a three-party one would weaken it, I find this patient's plea for temperance, the ideation expressed, far from bizarre, although the deviations in expression are evident as they are in the following from the nonproficient writing of aostensibly normal college freshman.

> Generalizations have no place in terms of different opinions insofar as the discussions of heroes or any other topic.

Again the ideation here is perfectly normal. The student was simply trying to say that we cannot make generalizations about heroes or related topics. As I was the professor for whom this was written, I was able to verify what it was the student meant. This kind of fractured writing is not at all unusual from the pens of incompetent writers. The point is that the kinds of deviance we see in incompetent normal writers may occur as well in psychotic speech and writing. The incompetence in deviant sentences in each group arises from different underlying causes. Whatever causes the incompetence, however, the result is the same. In neither instance, is it possible to correlate thought structures with language structures.

Another kind of evidence for the separation of language and thought comes from Curtiss (1977). She studied the tragic case of Genie, a girl tied to a bedpost with no human companionship until she was pubescent. Despite intensive training, and a willingness and enthusiasm on her part, Genie's speech remained syntactically like a two year old's but her cognitive processes, including solving problems, were far beyond that of a child whose syntax was as rudimentary as hers.

Kuczaj (1983) has also studied the child's self-learning strategies. As a result, he affirms that children are far more sophisticated in language learning than in any other cognitive sphere at the same age, pointing out that children have to deduce such things as abstract form classes and rules for manipulating them. The enormous literature on first language acquisition has demonstrated time and again that nobody could teach children to do what they do when learning to speak (e.g., Menyuk 1971; Brown 1983; Bickerton 1981; Wanner and Gleitman 1982). They analyze language and show evidence of abstraction and logical deductions from their analysis before their second year. There is a great disjunction between speech and other cognitive processes in childhood. This argues that speech and thought are separate and develop separately.

[6] What Is a Thought?

The very concept "thought" is ill-defined. Cummins (1983) has summarized the difficulty psychology has had in defining thought in any general way. Thought remains an undefined entity. How then can we correlate speech with a concept so nebulous as thought? If we cannot make such a correlation, then we cannot define thought in terms of speech or vice versa. Nor can we readily determine the interface between them.

Is a thought equivalent to a word, a phrase, or a sentence? Traditional grammar equates thoughts with sentences, as in the well-known definition of a sentence as a complete thought. There are many problems with this formulation. The first deals with the problem of subordinate clauses. Since sentences with subordinate clauses can be broken down into several sentences, does each clause contain one thought, or does the entire structure punctuated as a sentence represent the thought? Consider the following:

1. The boy who dated Griselda before he dated Maria went to his prom with Zelda who used to date Oscar.

This can broken down into four sentences: (1) the boy went to his prom with Zelda, (2) the boy dated Griselda before, (3) the boy dated Maria, (4) Zelda used to date Oscar. How many thoughts are contained in 1 then? One or four? If one claims that language and thought are identical and that disruption in speech is the same as disruption in thought, then one must be able to correlate thought with speech structures.

A second problem concerns the ubiquity of ambiguity and paraphrases. In themselves, these show that language and thought are not identical.

One statement such as "exciting women can be dangerous" can mean two very different things like:

2A. Women who are exciting are dangerous.
2B. If you excite women, that is dangerous

If one can get two entirely different thoughts from an identical sentence, then language and thought cannot be the same. Similarly, if one can give the same thought in divergent ways, then, too, language and thought cannot be the same, as in

3A. Despite years of trying, nobody has ever been able to prove that language and thought are the same.
3B. Scholars have not demonstrated that linguistic functioning and cognitive activities are identical although they have tried to do so for a long stretch of time, years, in fact.

Other problems with assuming an identity of thought and language structure is that normals frequently make slips of the tongue and other errors in speech production. If speech and thought were one and the same, these would always indicate disruptions in thought processes, a conclusion few would care to make. Rather, it is usually assumed that such errors proceed from momentary lapses in retrieving correct words or sounds, or lapses in self-monitoring (Fromkin 1971.)

Those patients who do produce abnormal speech during psychotic bouts may themselves verify that such speech does not reflect their actual thoughts. Chapman (1966) presents several such comments from patients, and the patient mentioned in Chapter 2 who was surprised at his speech when he saw himself on video is another.

Thoughts cannot be directly observed although speech can (Chaika 1982d; Chaika and Lambe 1985). If speech shows structural deviance, that does not constitute proof that thought does. It is possible for normals to create nonsense words and sentences although their thinking processes may be intact. The classic example is Lewis Carroll's *Jabberwocky*, which is structurally normal but has words which do not happen to appear in the language. So far as we know, the ability to produce this kind of nonsense is part of one's natural linguistic ability. Conversely, one can create structurally abnormal sentences from known words such as "am girl yesterday went come boy." One can produce total gibberish as Sid Caesar and Danny Kaye did in their comedy routines. They went one better. They produced gibberish that sounded like different languages.

None of these kinds of deviant productions, not even the gibberish, derives from any dysfunction in thought. There is also religious GLOSSO-LALIA in which people utter concatenations of sounds and others in the congregation interpret these as meaning something. Lee (1982) reports on two intellectual (his term) glossolalists who claim to remember their glossolalic utterances and what they meant. Upon observation, "... it was observed that the form of their utterance changed and did not correspond to the given interpretation in a consistent way" (p. 552). As much as one might disagree with Pentecostal Christianity's belief in speaking in tongues, one certainly cannot say that those who do this are necessarily demented in any way. Many very brilliant people, highly intellectual and productive, who seem normal in every way, engage in this activity. No researcher into this population has ever found evidence that they are thought disordered.

The opposite may also be true. A patient might utter structurally normal sentences which indicate impaired cognition. One complained to me, "That tape recorder is reaching out and destroying my brain cells." Another asked me if I was still talking. When I said, "no?" He said, "That's not you talking?" He was having auditory hallucinations and we were in a private room alone with no person in earshot. I had not said a word. Such comments and questions indicate either hallucinations, grossly impaired ability to deduce cause and effect, or failure to discriminate between animate and inanimate objects, all of which impinge directly on thought. Yet there was no disruption of language itself.

[7] Language-less Thought.

Most telling, perhaps, is that there are several cognitive tasks for which language is of little or no value, although they certainly seem to demand thinking. Language is notoriously poor for describing how to use tools or how to construct something. For this reason, descriptions of mechanical devices typically contain copious diagrams. The best way to teach someone how to sew or to use any kind of tool is to demonstrate it physically. No language is needed at all. Anyone who has to put together a complicated toy from verbal directions knows how little good verbosity is for a guide in this sphere. It is with good reason that trade schools emphasize hands-on experience. Yet, certainly, figuring out what one needs to do to achieve certain ends with tools involves problem-solving skills as well as other thought processes.

One sees this disjunction in academic pursuits. Richard Lambe provides the example of teaching statistics. Many concepts in the text become comprehensible to the student only after he or she has begun to put the techniques to practice when solving statistical problems. Similarly, many teachers have had the experience of difficulty in verbalizing abstract material when they have had to teach it, although they were able to solve complex problems using the same principles when they were students themselves.

Neisser (1976) cites the complex mental imagery involved in the orienteering of the Puluwat as they travel hundreds of miles over the open seas in their canoes. He shows that their orienting schemata accept visual information and direct action with no necessary interface of verbalization. Similarly, city dwellers have recursive cognitive maps upon which they act daily, but do not necessarily—indeed, frequently cannot—verbalize the landmarks upon which they base their actions.

Note that all of the above disjunctions between language and cognition involve very different kinds of thinking: verbal, mechanical, mathematical, concrete, abstract, orienteering. What constitutes "thoughtness" of all these kinds of thinking?

[8] Confusion Between Language and Thought.

There is an essential distinction between speech, an overt behavior, and thought, a cognitive process inferred on the basis of many different overt behaviors including speech. The fundamental importance of this distinction requires the fullest possible analysis of psychotic speech qua speech since no inference can be more secure than its base in observation.

We have first to explain the observable linguistic behavior and not confuse the issue by talking about thought disordered (TD) vs non-thought disordered (NTD) speakers. Indeed, if one is using structural deviation as the basis of dividing schizophrenic patients into TD vs. NTD, then one is in the peculiar position of claiming that some schizophrenic patients, those with structurally normal speech, are not thought disordered. Why then do we consider them schizophrenic? One would assume that all psychotic patients suffer from an impairment in thinking, but structural deviations in speech in and of themselves are not the proof of that nor are they proof of the nature of the impairment.

Lanin-Kettering and Harrow (1985, p. 4) provide an example of the problems attending undifferentiated constructs of language and thought.

They argue that "a flexible boundary should be maintained concerning what is considered a problem in thought versus what is considered a problem in language." Such a procedure obviates all science. One cannot push the boundaries of analysis around willy-nilly. One needs principled reasons for establishing, changing, and maintaining boundaries. The alternative is to advance *ad hoc* explanations. By definition, this is the stuff of fable and prejudice, not medicine or science.

They ask, "When we discover stretches of discourse that show problems in cohesion, should we attribute them simply to a speech-language dysfunction independent of and subsequent to thought?" As Chapter 6 shows, cohesion in discourse is effected by syntactic means. It is not at all unusual for speakers to fail to apply the appropriate means in speech or in writing. Effecting cohesion for one's listeners/readers is an ongoing problem even in the most ordinary of interactions. Hence, comments like, "I don't follow" or "Run that by me again" or even "Huh?" If language were one with thought, such promptings would not be necessary.

Following Chaika and Lambe (1985), the position here is that we must first unearth the nature of schizophrenic speech behaviors in and of themselves, and then we must correlate those with other cognitive and problem-solving tasks. We are in a poor position to use speech as an inferential base for claims about thought until we understand more clearly the interface between speech and thought in normal as well as well as nonnormal populations.

If we seek to explain speech in terms of cognition, then the underlying cognitive skills for which we are testing must be those known to figure in speech production. This, of course, forms the basis to my objections about word association testing as a way to determine dysfunction in speech. Since speech is never normally produced on the basis of associations between semantically or phonologically-related words, results of word association tests do not explain production. Even if people give weird word associations to words given in isolation, that doesn't explain weird sentences or discourses because sentences aren't formed on the basis of word associations. Similarly, theories like faulty pigeonholing do not explain speech dysfunction because speech is not produced on the basis of pigeonholing.

[9] Inference from Performance Versus Evidence.

There is a difference between what we infer or suppose or imagine and what we observe. For instance, Lanin-Kettering and Harrow say that we may justifiably deduce from the outward facial expression of a frown that someone is depressed. However, such an inference is justifiable only after specific neuromuscular pathology has been ruled out such as tardive dyskinesia. Moreover, a frown does not only indicate depression. It may indicate intense concentration or it may be only a pretended frown assumed for purposes of discipline or humor.

In defense of their equation of thought with language, Lanin-Kettering and Harrow (1985, p. 2) make the interesting claim that "we do not understand all of the details about many of our best constructs...[but] they can still be useful and valuable even before we have gained complete understanding of them" and then "prove" this by saying that intelligence is one such construct, "e.g., highly intelligent people perform better on intellectual tasks than less intelligent people." This is a classic example of circular reasoning. If you define intelligence as what is measured by certain tests, then obviously those who do well on those tests are intelligent, but that doesn't mean that *intelligence* is a valid construct, or a construct at all, or that people who do well on those tests are genuinely more intelligent than those who do not.

Their second example of a poorly understood construct is that of the "concept of the gene which was at the level of construct for many years until recent advances provided strong evidence for the physical existence of genes." The problem here, counters Richard Lambe, is that as these advances were made, in observation as well as inference, the entire concept of what a gene is itself changed as well, so that the original constructs were modified or altogether abandoned. In sum, utilizing the construct of *thought* in the absence of hard data about it is as likely to yield fallacious correlations with speech as it is to yield valid ones.

[10] Discriminating Between Competence and Performance.

Lanin-Kettering and Harrow argue for discriminating between competence and performance, what deSaussure long ago termed *la langue* versus *la parole*. Although Chaika (1974) did assume a deficit in competence, subsequent research has indicated that this was putting the cart before the horse. Chaika, like previous authors, was attempting a characterization of performance, extrapolating from that a characterization of competence.

The entire question of competence vs performance when applied to research in a linguistically impaired population is a can of worms. Neither de Saussure nor Chomsky derived their theories from mucking about with real people. Chomsky himself has repeatedly warned that his theories are not necessarily applicable to the real world. He has on several occasions specifically disavowed any practical applications of transformational grammars to teaching or psychology. This is not to say that they cannot be so used. It is just that he claims no necessary psychological or pedagogical validity for them.

The problem with questions of underlying competence rests largely on the problem of deciding what constitutes competence in the first place. For instance, some aphasics with known lesions do know that their utterances are faulty. Does this mean that their competence is all right, but their performance is not? Recall also that Chapman (1966) interviewed schizophrenic patients after psychotic episodes. He reports that they complained that while they were psychotic they were not able to say what they intended. They recognized the deviation in their speech but at that time were not able to correct it. Can we say that their competence is diminished because they can't say what they want? Or do we say that it is only a performance error? If they recognized the deviation, then that argues for intact competence, but if they cannot produce structurally nondeviant speech, is not that a matter of competence as well? Or is it performance?

If upon release, a patient evinces surprise at a tape recording of his disrupted speech during a psychotic bout, does that mean that he was not linguistically competent before the viewing, but he was after? Or did he simply have performance problems before? In a subsequent hospitalization, should we consider his performance but not his competence impaired just because he was able to judge his speech as deviant during a prior hospitalization?

Consider also patients who claim to be possessed by spirits or other outside agencies and that this accounts for their garbled speech. What does this mean in terms of competence vs performance? It may be that such an explanation derives from the patient's desire to explain what he or she perceives as deviant speech. If so, does this argue that the patient suffers only from a deficit in performance? Given a patient whose speech is so disintegrated that he or she descends into uninterpretable gibberish, can we really say that competence is not affected at least during the time of the disordered performance? It is incumbent on any scholar to describe how they distinguish between competence and performance if they wish to use that distinction in their explanations.

[11] The Lexicon Has Fixed Concepts.

The strange associational chaining seen in schizophrenia is evidence of lexical storage with interlocking networks between lexical items. As Chaika (1982a; Chapter 2) observes, the triggering in these chains often seems to be "thought-less" although the individual lexical items in other contexts would communicate thoughts. What makes these chains so strange is that although we can figure out why one lexical item is triggered by another on the basis of semantic or phonological features, there is no meaningful connection in terms of the communicative situation. That is, we know why the chaining occurred but we can't derive meaning from it.

Lanin-Kettering and Harrow employ a static conception of language. They assume that "language provides an intricate system of concepts that is the foundation and instrument of conceptual activity." For language itself to be the foundation of concepts, the meaning of lexical items would have to be fixed. However, a crash course in the *Oxford English Dictionary* quickly reveals just how drastically meanings change over time, and they do because lexical items do not have fixed meanings, constructs, or concepts. Nor do speakers and writers have to redefine a word used in a somewhat new context. They need only be skillful enough to use it so that a hearer can figure out its meaning in a given context. Hence, some years ago, an innovative use of *rip off* resulted in a meaning of "steal" added to the original one of "tearing something off of something" and *gay* has pretty much lost its earlier meaning of "lighthearted fun."

Meanings of words are the most changeable part of a language. Unless we assume that our "foundation . . . of conceptual activity" changes every time someone uses a word in a new way, then there must be some differences between the words and the thoughts behind their selection. **Also, the very fact that any concept may be conveyed by many different words and sentences, that is, can be paraphrased, indicates that language may be the instrument of thoughts, but words are hardly a static system of concepts.**

[12] Strange Speech Is an Undifferentiated Given.

Unfortunately, many of Lanin-Kettering and Harrow's arguments are weakened by imprecise terminology. For instance, they repeatedly refer to "strange speech." Do they mean "strange in the sense of structural strangeness," or "strange in the sense of bizarre imagery or claims?"

Content and form in speech are two very different things, constituting situations that may well take very different explanations. Paraphrases often take very different forms even when they mean the same thing. By definition, paraphrase must be in a different structure and use different words than the item paraphrased. As the next chapter will show, the very selection of a synonymous verb may result in a very different sentence form. It would be difficult to the point of impossible to figure how many possible paraphrases any given sentence might engender, even one quite semantically simple. The problem is that any speaker can be skillful enough to employ an old word in a new sense. Therefore, even though one person might finally hit a point beyond which his or her ingenuity can think up a new paraphrase, another person might be able to come up new ones. There is no fixedness of form in language.

[13] Explanation of the Data.

Any explanation for schizophrenic speech must account for all of the data observed. We cannot sweep data embarrassing to our personal scientific constructs under the rug. In addition, any explanation must accord with what we know of the structure of normal language and speech, how it is acquired, how perceived, and how performed. We know that speakers do make slips of the tongue and have other temporary, even transient, problems with encoding their thoughts, such as not being able to explain to another exactly what one means in a given instance. Whether in writing or in speech, "the right words" may be a long time coming.

A behavioral explanation for schizophrenic speech would have to show how one class of people was stimulated to respond linguistically with the peculiar combination of features of SD speech, and, at that, only during psychotic bouts. Even in a family with a history of schizophrenia, all children do not become schizophrenic and even of those that do, not all evince archetypal schizophrenic speech. Berenbaum, Oltmanns and Gottesman (1985) showed that twins do not necessarily both evince formal thought disorder. Berenbaum et al are careful to say (p. 4) that by thought disorder they mean speech disorder, "—such as derailment, incoherent speech, and non sequitor responses to questions—and not as an inference of underlying pathology in cognitive processes." Moreover, there are also SD patients who do come from families with no other schizophrenics surrounding them, SD or not. How could they have "trained" to speak this way?

Behavioral explanations for schizophrenic speech have been advanced since Bleuler (1950) because of the "associational" character of glossomanic chaining. Behavioral psychologists study the ways that one event is associated with another. The problem in schizophrenic speech is that normal speech is never produced by chance associations of shared semantic, phonological, or syntactic relations of one word with another. What makes such speech deviant is the fact of the chaining itself.

Rutter's (1985) theory that schizophrenics fail in communication because they don't take into concern the needs of the listener fails on similar grounds. He is correct. However, it is a usual thing in discourse for people to fail to take into account the needs of listeners. These include bores, nags, long-winded pests, professors whose lectures are "over the heads" of their students. However, none of these break into word salads, gibberish, neologizing, and glossomanic strings. What requires explanation is why one class of people, psychotics, behave linguistically in a manner perceived to be bizarre by laypersons and scholars alike. Rutter's theory begs the question.

[14] Vygotsky.

Vygotsky's (1934a,b[3]) *Thought and Language* has taken on fresh importance in recent years partly because of his early insistence on the cultural origins of language learning (Hickman 1986; Lee 1987; Paprotte and Sinha 1987; Lucy and Wertsch 1987; Holzman and Newman 1987), and partly because of his discussions of word associations and, as we shall see, of his formulation of the concept of INNER SPEECH, a form of speech completely unlike overt speech. The latter two domains of inquiry have been attractive to clinicians as well (Harrow and Quinlan 1985; Kozulin 1986).

By inner speech, Vygotsky does not mean the internal dialogues and monologues which we all regularly indulge in. These are in our normal everyday tongue, using our regular vocabulary and syntax.

These differ from outer speech only in that we utter these inaudibly or not at all. However, if we did utter them, we would be using our normal pronunciations. Grumet (1985, p. 185) quotes research which shows that such internal dialogues are accompanied by sensorimotor excitation in the larynx, tongue, and lower lip measurable by electromyographic impulses. It is not unusual to notice normal people moving their lips and tongue while actively engaging themselves in such self-speech. However, this kind of internal speech is subauditory normal speech, not the kind of speech which has its own laws.

We can pay tribute to Vygotsky's brilliance, but still acknowledge that many of his ideas have been superceded in the half century since his death. Vygotsky's theorizing about schizophrenia forms a very small part of his work. He believed (1934b, p. 129) that schizophrenics can only think concretely, a position with which Kozulin (1986, p. xxxiii) and Harrow and Quinlan (1985, p. 159) concur. Vygotsky bases this belief on the erroneous one that primitive people think concretely, a view no longer held. We have come to realize that such judgments derived from the inability of anthropologists to come up with tests that elicited the mental operations being investigated. We still don't know how to test unerringly for cognitive skills. As Scribner (1977) pointed out, in her studies of the Kpelle in Liberia, she regularly saw them using cognitive skills in daily life although in formal testing they couldn't seem to use them. Similarly, many of Vygotsky's pronouncements on how children think have to be modified in view of more recent research.

Perhaps Vygotsky's greatest appeal to clinicians is because of his conception of inner speech. He[4] (1934b, p. 30–32) posited that children first accompany their activities with EGOCENTRIC speech (pp. 30–34) and that this develops into inner speech (pp. 225–235). He conceives of this inner speech as originating in truncated external speech. In time, it develops into everything preceding speaking, except thought itself (p. 249). Moreover,

> . . . it is a specific formation with its own laws and complex relations to the other forms of speech activity . . . the opposite of external speech. The latter is the turning of thoughts into words . . . With inner speech, the process is reversed, going from outside to inside. Overt speech sublimates into thoughts. (p. 225–230)

Nowhere does Vygotsky describe this formation, give us any of its laws, nor tell us how he knows what these relations are. He also (1934a, p. 135; 1934b, p. 230) claims that his formulation of inner speech unfolding inwards, so to speak from egocentric speech, is " . . . a fact and facts are notoriously hard to refute." Kozulin (1986) sums up Vygotsky's position as

> . . . the predominance of sense over meaning, of sentence over word, and of context over sentence are rules of inner speech. While meaning stands for socialized discourse, sense represents an interface between one's individual (*and thus incommunicable*) [italics mine] thinking and verbal thought comprehensible to others . . . in inner speech words must sublimate in order to bring forth a thought. In inner speech, two important processes are interwoven: the transition from external communication to inner dialogue and the expression of intimate thoughts in linguistic form, thus making them communicative. (p. xxxviii)

Kozulin says that inner speech is incommunicable. If it can't be conveyed to someone else then we know neither what it is nor how it relates to outer speech. If it is incommunicable, then we can't know anything about it. Nobody can observe it. Nobody can communicate it. What, then, is inner speech? Vygotsky (1934b, p. 225) denies Kurt Goldstein's formulation of it as the preverbal stage, the stage in which ordinary language does not figure, that shadowy area of motive and "the whole interior aspect of any speech activity." Vygotsky especially descries such "inarticulate inner experience" because it "dissolves" separate structural planes. The construct of inner speech can be tempting. Psychiatrically, for instance, one could assume that the strange verbalizations of SD schizophrenics is inner speech breaking through. The problem is that, despite Vygotsky's claims, what he describes, the very development of inner speech in the child and the existence of inner speech itself, are not facts.

By his own definition, Vygotsky's definition of inner speech is unobservable, unknowable, and untestable, hence, unscientific. Even so uncritical a pair of reviewers as Lucy and Wertsch (1987, p. 81) demur that Vygotsky "did not sufficiently account for the differentiation of the egocentric function from the social function of speech." Vygotsky died long before the significant research into linguistics, cognition, and language acquisition that we have today. Research methodology has become more sophisticated, as has the uses of statistical measures. None of my arguments mean that there is no inner speech. I cannot prove that it does not exist any more than Vygotsky proved that it does. Like Freudian and Chomskyan interpretation, this one aspect of Vygotsky's work remains a matter of faith.

Because they impinge on questions of schizophrenia, Vygotsky's views on language learning also require some mention. Vygotsky died long before the explosion of research into language acquisition and linguistics that we can draw upon today. In part, his conceptions rested unavoidably upon an inadequate view of the complexity of the task. For instance, he (1934b, p. 219) thinks that children start out expressing single words because their thought is "an amorphous whole" and that as they develop inner speech, they learn to map their thoughts onto larger structures.

Intensive study into language acquisition has confirmed that the mapping actually goes in the other direction. The toddler frequently uses single words to indicate sentential communication before he or she has had a chance to learn syntactic rules. We now know that the reason that children start out with one word utterances is that it is not possible simply to imitate language (Ervin 1964; Chaika 1989[5], pp. 17–18). At the time of the one-word stage, children haven't figured out the complexity of rules for word formation, much less for syntax and discourse, but this doesn't mean that their thinking is so limited. Gleitman, Gleitman, and Shipley (1972) showed that children under the age of 4 use adult standards to make grammatical judgments about the well-formedness of speech, even though the children themselves are still making the errors in their own productions that they detect in others.

Their knowledge is in advance of their actual linguistic skills. For instance, children confuse most sets of antonyms and other words in sets, such as *wife, mother,* and *sister* (Donaldson and Wales 1970; Clark 1971, 1972, 1973)[6] for the same reasons that adults have so many slips-of-the-tongue involving them (Chaika 1974, 1977). Antonyms are used in the same syntactic environments and share a good many semantic features with each other. The child may confuse the words *big* and *small,* but this does not mean that he or she doesn't distinguish between a big piece of cake and a small one.

More recently, Slobin (1982), who has studied language acquisition in children learning languages as diverse as Turkish, Serbo-Croatian, and Italian, warns against assuming that a child's immature syntax mirrors similarly immature thinking. He suggests the metaphor of a waiting room. Children make use of the linguistic means at their disposal to express what they wish "while 'waiting' to master the adult forms (p. 168)." Lois Bloom (1970) even earlier made the point that even when the child was limited to a two-word utterance, like "Mommy sock," he or she would use that utterance for a variety of meanings, such as "this is

Mommy's sock," "Mommy, put on the sock," "the doll has on Mommy's sock," or "let's find Mommy's sock." The child certainly knows the difference between these meanings, but has to use what is at his or her disposal, depending on the adult to match the utterance to the context to get the right meaning.

Vygotsky's conclusion (1934b, p. 231) is unwarranted that a child's egocentric speech derives from "insufficient individualization of primary social speech," such that children do not separate it from social speech and is "a correlate of the insufficient isolation of the child's individual consciousness from the social whole" (p. 232).

To the contrary, study after study on child language acquisition has given us a picture of the child as an active investigator, controlling his or her input, setting up his or her own practice drills, deciding what he or she will learn (e.g., Brown 1973; Menyuk 1969; Kuczaj 1983). A particularly American experience illustrates. Children of European immigrants have regularly failed to learn their parents' native language despite being raised in homes in which it was spoken regularly. The United States provides us with a virtual laboratory of the baby's sense of autonomy from social speech as represented by the languages spoken in its home. A very common occurrence in immigrant homes was—and is—that children as young as 2 years old make no attempt to imitate or practice a language spoken by grandparents, or even parents.[7] The fate of bilingualism in America shows clearly that toddlers have already separated their individual goals from their families'. The family language constitutes the first social speech of the child.

In quite a different context, Cook-Gumperz and Green (1984) show the dangers in assuming that egocentricity[8] in speech causes a child's speech productions, such as narrating a story in what appears to be a highly idiosyncratic way. What they found was that apparent deviations in such narrations actually represented a first step, so to speak, in relating stories. They examined books written for young children to see what effect these books might have on narration, finding that children include in their verbalizations representations of the pictures which accompanied the stories. Stories by children which researchers thought had no form actually do have the form of the books read to them including the graphic forms and their pictorial representations.

How Vygotsky's formulations would have changed had he lived we do not know. His conception of inner speech depended upon his beliefs about how children learn language and he claimed that these were based upon experiments. Unfortunately, he did not describe them in any detail, nor did he show explicitly how his conclusions related to his results. In fact, he considered poems and passages from novels adequate proof and it is these which he specifically cites in defense of his opinions.

Vygotsky (p. 213) does remain fresh in his conception of the cultural origins of learning and how these are mediated by language learning. That is, as the child learns language, he or she does learn strategies for understanding as well as for speaking. For instance, Scollon and Scollon (1981) show how Athabaskan children learn how to abstract themes from stories as part of the child rearing practices in their culture. Ochs (1987), based on her study of Samoan children, demonstrates that even when one understands words in nonnative culture, one may not understand the point of those words. She claims that even though children may display egocentric speech, it means different things in different cultures, going so far as to suggest that Piaget's and Vygotsky's sharply differing views on egocentricity of early speech may have been because of the differences between Russian and Swiss societies.

[15] Common Sense and the Thought-Language Distinction.

Finally, common sense must prevail. If thought does not exist prior to language, then how does the speaker or writer know which LEXICAL ITEMS (what are commonly called "words)" to choose? If, indeed, thought and language are one and the same, we have no way to account for the words and syntax that are selected by the speaker. Since the speaker has many choices for any given thought or thoughts, it cannot be that the language is prior. There has to be a step previous to selection of language forms.

Notes

[1]They attribute this deficit to a short term memory loss.

[2]This is actually a question of some interest. There are tales of people learning to "speak schizophrenic" either because of being hospitalized for long periods with them, or because they were nurses or orderlies. However, I can find no longitudinal studies which confirm this. Nowadays, few patients remain in a hospital setting for very long, so the opportunities for observing such a phenomenon may no longer be present.

[3]Rather than entering these by the dates of the translations, I have opted for this perhaps unconventional dating for the two versions. Kozulin's translation is substantively different from Hanfmann and Vakar's; he has revised the text; and has

provided his own extensive notes and preface. This preface, "Vygotsky in Context," and the endnotes constitute another interpretation of Vygotsky's work. What I have done is listed Kozulin's lengthy prefatory essay as a separate work, which indeed it is. This was done in order to lessen confusion between the Kozulin preface and notes and the Vygotsky translations themselves.

[4]Actually, Vygotsky and Piaget both dealt with this issue. Vygotsky disagreed with Piaget's formulations of inner speech.

[5]The literature is literally loaded with examples of children's inability even to know what an adult is getting at. One of my favorites provided by Fromkin and Rodman (1983, p. 333) is:

Child: Want other one spoon, Daddy.
Father: You mean, you want *the other spoon?*
Child: Yes, I want other one spoon, please, Daddy.
Father: Can you say "the other spoon"?
Child: Other . . . one . . . spoon.
Father: Say . . . other.
Child: Other.
Father: Spoon.
Child: Spoon.
Father: Other . . . spoon.
Child: Other . . . spoon. Now give me other one spoon?

[6]It is often said that autistic children do not distinguish their ego boundaries because they confuse the words *you* and *me.* All children confuse words used in sets like these. How they ever learn *you* and *me* correctly is a wonder. The children are always referred to as *you* and the other person always refers to him or herself as *I.* The child somehow has to learn to reverse these references despite the fact that they never hear them that way. Autistic children notoriously have language learning difficulties. We should expect that their problem with the words for first and second reference persist longer than in other children.

[7]A friend of mine recently told me that he and his twin visited their grandmother every single day of their childhood, but, since she spoke no English, they never had any conversations with her and they really know nothing about her except for her baking prowess. They never learned her language at all. Similarly, a Cuban emigré acquaintance told me of the problems his son had with his father, the child's grandfather. It seems that the father speaks no English, and the child knows no Spanish. When I asked why the child never learned Spanish which is spoken in the home, the answer I got was classic, "He's American."

[8]They do not discuss this in the Vygotsian context, nor do they speak specifically of *egocentric* speech. However, the deviant narrations they are investigating seem to qualify.

Chapter Four

THE LEVELS OF LANGUAGE

Laypersons typically confuse the written and spoken language, assuming that the former is true language. This is a fallacy. Spoken language is both prior to and different from writing. Language is actually composed of interrelated levels, each with its own rules, but each of which leaks into the other, so to speak. Language has fuzzy borders between levels, a fact that has to be considered in all explanations for how we use it. Here we shall see the unsuspected complexity of even the simplest part of language, the sound system. The problems of defining what a word is has relevance for a great deal of research which depends upon its results by assuming that words are self-evident entities. Although we know a good deal about how words are created, a definition of what a word actually is, has proven to be elusive.

[1] Message and Meaning.

Human language is not an isomorphic system. That is, there is no one-to-one correspondence between meaning and message. A human message can equal more or less than its meaning. A speaker need overtly say only enough for a hearer to deduce the message. In addition, any meaning can be given in a variety of ways. That is, all language is paraphrasable. To illustrate, the preceding sentences can be paraphrased by

> Human language is not isomorphic, lacking any necessary exact conjunction between the linguistic signals given and the meaning of those signals. This allows a plurality of paraphrases for any one meaning intended.

or

> The communication system of humans is not isomorphic resulting in meanings not equalling the sum of the parts of the linguistic items actually spoken as well as paraphrasability for any particular meaning.

In the first paraphrase, *lacking any necessary*... means "human language lacks..." Here, we see that the message delivered is less than meaning expressed in actual words and syntax. In the second paraphrase, note that *resulting* actually means "the lack of isomorphism results in" and *the linguistic items actually spoken* means "the linguistic items that somebody actually speaks."

It is because language is not an isomorphic system that linguists find behaviorism an insufficient model for language. One cannot explain such a system in terms of responses to stimuli. There is no way to ensure that any given utterance will result from any particular stimulus. There is no way to ensure that one paraphrase will be chosen over another, or, for that matter, is there any way to predict what new combination of words and syntax that someone can come up with to express a meaning.

[2] Language is Spoken.

This title seems like a bad pun. Of course, language is spoken, as in "French is spoken here." The problem is that literate people assume that language is what resides on the printed page. Language does not reside on the printed page. What is on the page is only an evocation of language. Language itself is in the brain, or, if you will, in the mind.

Throughout all but the past 4000 or so years, humans have not had written language. What they needed to remember, they remembered by linguistic mnemonic devices. These, in short, comprise what we think of as poetry: rhyme, assonance, alliteration, melody, strong beat, unusual imagery. All of these can be seen to have an origin in the need for remembering, a need especially necessary for the essentially weak, defenseless creature *homo sapiens* is and was.

All of these devices aid memory by promoting an overabundance of connections in the brain. If one forgets a line, one can access it by recalling something that rhymed with a word in it. If one forgets one word in an alliterative string, then recalling the others helps one fill in the blank, so to speak. Beating out a rhythm or beginning to hum a tune allows one to access the words that were learned to it. This is a common occurrence when one tries to remember the words to a song which one thinks one has forgotten. As one hums it, however, the words unfold in snatches.

There are two reasons for mentioning this matter. The first is to underscore the primacy of speech. In this text, we are talking about speech, not writing. This is not to say that schizophrenic writing is not germane. It is, and much that we say of speech is true *mutatis mutandi* of writing, and, where appropriate, may be taken as applying to the latter.

The second reason is that we do find schizophrenic deviations in the use of poetic devices such as inappropriate rhyming or what seems to be a creation of a metaphor. These can be seen as a true dysfunction in linguistic abilities. Poetry and other figurative speech are part and parcel of what it means to possess a language.

[3] Sounds and Letters.

The sounds of language are not letters. Literacy causes people to think that real language is on the printed page, not in the head and certainly not in the ephemeral evanescence of sound. The reverse is actually true. Letters on a page are merely reminders of the sounds in a language. For most of human existence, there was no writing. As with technologically primitive peoples today, language resided in the head and in the waves of sound produced by speakers.

Throughout this work, when we speak of *sound,* we refer only to oral production. Even this disclaimer is not sufficient, because the orthography for English is a mess. The same sound in English can be represented by different letters. The same letters can represent different sounds. Sometimes two sounds are represented by one letter, such as the usual use of <x> to stand for the sounds [ks] or [gz] as in *exercise* and *example,* respectively. The opposite situation holds as well. One sound can be represented by two letters, such as the digraph <sh>.

Worse yet, letter-to-sound correspondences are as close to chaos as they can be and still function. For instance, the same sound occurs in each of the following words represented by the boldfaced letters: should, sugar, Cheryl, fashion, tissue, and nation. In contrast, the same letters stand for very different sounds in head, meat, great, ear, teat, and heart.

[4] The Perils of the Literacy Fallacy.

It is not merely scholarly intransigence, a pedantic insistence on details that leads me to expound on the problem of confusing language with writing. The ramifications for research can be very great. For instance, Brendan Maher's (1983) analysis of schizophrenic utterances suffers because he confounds the conventions of writing with the production of speech. It is important to note that, in general, Maher's work stands out both in breadth and depth as careful, objective, well-reasoned, insightful, and inclusive of all relevant data. In my opinion, any explanation for the etiology of schizophrenic speech has to consider the evidence Maher has presented over the past quarter century. The experimental protocol in Maher (1983) is a very promising one. Still his basic misconceptions severely compromise his conclusions regarding schizophrenic speech. There could be no more compelling evidence of the necessity of understanding language as an entity in itself before discussing schizophrenic speech than to look at this article. It shows that nobody is immune to erroneous preconceived notions about language.

Basically, what Maher has done is what most naive literate people do. They treat the written language as if it were the only real language. In this instance, he seemed unaware that commas and other punctuation marks are an artifact of writing. Such things don't occur in speech. They are not pronounced. Yes, we've all had English teachers who have said things like, "Put the commas in where you pronounce them" in sentences like

1A. My oldest brother, who is a doctor, just won the lottery.
1B. After the ball was over, Lizzie took out her false teeth.

It is true that if we are actually reading these aloud before an audience, we may drop our voices at the commas, but in normal speech no such drop necessarily occurs. Actually, even in reading, the commas are a cue for the reader to adopt a downward intonation contour, so that such contours are an artifact of the writing system, not of speech practices. There are not any comparable commas marking all of the syntactic junctures in the sentences, even the most important.

Maher (1983) even reports a famous study by Fodor and Bever (1965) as having committed the same fallacy, although it did not. Maher undertook a modification of this study in order to investigate his long-held theory of an attentional deficit in schizophrenia (Maher 1972; Maher 1983, pp. 24–26).

Fodor and Bever developed an ingenious test in which subjects listened to sentences. At various junctures within the sentences, these researchers inserted a click. They found that subjects displaced the clicks, reporting them as having occurred at syntactic boundaries when, in fact, they had not. For instance, if a click was within in the middle of a clause, subjects reported that it as having occurred instead at the boundaries of two constituents, such as that between the subject and predicate. For instance, in a sentence like

> 2. That he was happy was evident from the way he smiled.

subjects reported the click to have occurred after *happy* even if, in fact, it actually occurred on *evident*. This showed that people process language by syntactic structures, not word by word. That is, in 2, listeners grouped "That he was happy" together and then "was evident from the way he smiled." They reported the click to have occurred at the boundary of the subject and the predicate, the major constituents of the sentence.

Maher reports the Fodor and Bever experiment erroneously, saying that a click moved to "a nearby comma or period." Commas and periods are not in speech. They cannot be heard. Furthermore, they do not invariantly mark out syntactic structures. No comma or period can occur anywhere in 2 above, except at the end of the entire sentence. Certainly, there is no comma or other punctuation allowed at the juncture at which the click was perceived.

In fact, **commas cannot be used to separate any of the major constituents of the core sentence:** subjects may not be separated from their predicates, and verbs may not be separated from their complements, whether these be direct and indirect objects or predicate nominatives or adjectives. In the following, a forward (/) slash indicates the major constituent break between the subject and predicate, a backwards slash (\) indicates the break between a transitive verb and object, and an asterisk (*) separates an intransitive verb and its complement. Notice that no commas or other punctuation can be used where constituent breaks occur:

> 3A. The little old man over there/has become*senile.
> 3B. The little old man over there/broke\his leg

No matter how long we make the subject or the predicate, still no internal punctuation can occur. For instance

> 3C. The little old man over there whom I was telling you about the other day while we were at lunch/finally became*senile which was evidenced by his forgetting to let the cat out or the dog in all week.
> 3D. The little old man over there whom you met last Tuesday and thought was so wonderful/unfortunately broke\the leg which had already been injured in the Battle of the Bulge during World War II.

Another consequence of the confusion between speech and writing causes Maher (1983, p. 25) to make a corollary error, saying that "Ordinary speech does not, of course, include explicit utterance of syntax markers." Actually, it does. All human language relies on syntax. It is syntax that allows us to signal and comprehend the relationships between the words in a sentence and between sentences themselves. For instance, in "John loves Mary" we know that John has the emotion and Mary is its object because of the word order. This relationship can be signalled in other ways as well, as by the paraphrase, "Mary is loved by John." In this instance, the markers of the passive (a form of the verb *be* followed by a verb plus the participial ending *-ed*) tells us that Mary is the recipient. In some languages special prefixes or suffixes on nouns indicate such relations. In Latin, for instance, if Mary is the one loved, then she would be referred to as *Mariam,* but if she did the loving, her name would be stated as *Maria.*

Any analysis of spoken or written language must rest upon syntax, and for that, punctuation is not a reliable guide. Nor is the written language. The unsuitability of orthographic conventions for analyzing syntax is well illustrated by the fragment above. During my high school years in the 1950s, the proscription against punctuating a phrase like this was so strong that we received an automatic F for writing fragments of this sort. Nowadays, this is considered a justifiable fragment. In terms of modern syntactic theory, we can say that this is justifiable because any native speaker would recognize that it represents "The written language is not a reliable guide to syntax." By omitting the repeated material, and signalling that fact with *nor,* we have actually effected superior cohesion, as demonstrated in a subsequent chapter. The corollary to this proposition is that any analysis which does not recognize the syntactic origins of language production is suspect.

For instance, in the same work, Maher presents a model of speech based upon word associations. This is a shaky base for an analysis, because word associations have little to do with ordinary speech production (Chaika 1974, 1981, 1982a,c; Chapter 5,6,7). Word associations have a great deal to do with slips of the tongue, as when one substitutes *refrigerator* for *stove* or *up* for *down,* and we can show a correlations between these and some schizophrenic errors in word selection. What is deviant about much schizophrenic speech is the fact of associating. Normal speech is not produced according to word associations.

One can find passages in normal speech in which a word association seems to have produced a subsequent word. Maher provides several examples of normals involuntarily punning in this way. For instance (1983, p. 32) he gives

> 4. A **stable** economy requires continual reinvestment in industrial plant. Tax reductions now are a case of locking the **stable** door after the horse has gone.

In contrast to schizophrenic associational chaining, the repetition of *stable* is not simply the case of uttering the word once and then having that instigate the next use of it. The second occurrence lies several words away from the first in its own separate grammatical sentence. Moreover, the second occurrence is embedded in an aphorism, and is subordinated to and increases the sense of the former.

Speech is not produced one word at a time. We have known that since Lashley (1951). Fromkin (1973) showed conclusively that we plan our utterances before producing them. Although we are not conscious of it, we select our syntactic vehicle and the words which we are going to use in advance of our saying them. In Chapter 5 we shall see that there is no sharp dividing line between syntax and semantics, but at the same time, relations between them are arbitrary. For instance, we can and do have two words which share meaning, words which might elicit each other in word association testing, but which cannot appear in the same kinds of syntactic structures. An example is the syntactic difference allowed by the verbs *diminish* and *deplete*

> Our water supplies are **diminishing**.
> We are **depleting** our water supplies.
> Our water supplies are being **depleted**.
> *Our water supplies are **depleting**.

An asterisk indicates that the sentence is not grammatical in the sense that speakers feel that it is wrong in some way involving sentence structure. The verb *deplete* is transitive. It must have a direct object either after it or as the subject of the passive *are being depleted.* Testing for associations between individual words does not truly reflect the entire language process. Except for slips of the tongue, it does not give us adequate information upon which to explain errors in speech impaired populations.

[5] What is a Rule?

Language is not a unitary phenomenon. It is actually a set of interrelated systems, each with its own logic and each with its own rules. Salzinger et al. (1978) suggest alternative words like *principles* or *concepts,* but these do not sufficiently capture the regularity of innumerable processes in language on any of its levels. Then, too, they lend unwanted connotations, connotations which I feel would obscure the conclusions of this study.

In some quarters there is a real stigma attached to the word *rule*. It touches a raw nerve, especially in behavioral psychologists (Mowrer 1980). Mowrer (1980, pp. x–xi) speaks of a "strange revolution **instigated** by Chomsky" (boldface mine). The very word *instigate* shows Mowrer's *ad hominem* approach to Chomsky's argumentation, as does his speaking of Chomsky's theorizing "as a strange revolution." When a word becomes so loaded with far-reaching connotations that it bars reasoned argument, avoiding it is preferable. Nevertheless, it will be used in the subsequent discussion, but only because we are lacking a better term. Certainly, Chomsky's own bitter sarcasm towards behaviorists has elicited such responses, but Chomsky's arguments are intellectually serious. One need not concur with Chomsky to acknowledge the multitude of empirical studies which have effectively demonstrated that behaviorism is not a viable explanation of even the most ordinary language behavior.

The important thing to remember here is that this work is not an apologia for Chomsky or for his followers. It is strictly empirical, and one to which Occam's razor has been applied. On the one hand, it is not oriented towards behaviorism in the Skinnerian sense, because that doesn't explain the linguistic data that I have gathered or that is in the literature. On the other hand, Chomsky's works have never explained naturalistic linguistic data, normal or not.

In this discussion, *rule* is used in a weak sense, referring to whatever processes we use to encode and decode words, sentences, and discourses. It also may refer to whatever it is that makes us feel that a certain utterance is wrong in the sense of "abnormal" or "deviant." This intersects with what Chomsky called the *internalized linguistic competency* of native speakers of a language. In short, we are faced with the paradox that we can't necessarily define what a rule is and what its form is, but, empirically, we know that there have to be rules. I make no claim as to the form or forms of such knowledge, either that used to create, to understand, or to "feel" that something is deviant. I am not talking about quasimathematical rules which account for all of the grammatical sentences of the language nor am I talking about Chomsky's distinction between COMPETENCE and PERFORMANCE, which, as we have seen, is fraught with complications.

I am mindful that the very mention of the word *rule* or of competence versus performance in language causes scholars to derail, to get into squabbles over what is or isn't a rule, if there are rules, what is or isn't competence and whether it relates to performance. It would be too disruptive of our central concern to get caught up into such arguments, so the terms *rule, competence* and *performance* are used here only in the vaguest sense that a layperson would have of them: THE SOMETHING THAT ACCOUNTS FOR OUR LANGUAGE BEHAVIOR AND THAT CAUSES US TO EVALUATE LINGUISTIC PRODUCTIONS AS BEING PATHOLOGICALLY DEVIANT OR AS BEING NORMAL ERROR. On this even the most diehard behaviorists have to agree: that they have been attracted to the study of psychotic speech because of its weirdness which even they feel requires special interpretation. Something is distinctly wrong with that speech. If it weren't, they wouldn't be trying to explain it. The dissection of the kinds of deviance that occur in psychotic speech implicitly rests upon inner rules.

We certainly know when we hear or read sentences incorrect for our language. By this, I am not referring only to correctness in terms of politeness, such as not using double negatives in English but to sentences like

> 5A. I am here since six years.
> 5B. That dog all the time here comes.

In the absence of their being language-specific rules, there is no way to account for our judgment that such sentences are incorrect. If language is not governed by rules, how can we say that a language does or does not allow certain phrasings? How can we say that these sentences are not correct in English?

A clear example of a syntactic rule is what is often called the "dummy do" or "dosupport" rule in English. In order to make a question or negative in these tenses, one must use an empty auxiliary *do.* For instance,

> 6A. John goes every day. (present *goes*)
> 6B. **Does** John **go** every day?
> 6C. John **does** not **go** every day.
> 6D. John went every day. (preterit *went*)

6E. **Did** John **go** every day?
6F. John **did** not **go** every day.

The *do*'s and *did*'s here add no meaning. Their sole function is to fill the slot that an auxiliary verb would occupy if there was one in the sentence, as in

7A. **Has** John **gone** every day?
7B. John **has** not **gone** every day.

Examples such as these show clearly that language is governed by rules, many of which laypersons are not even aware of using. Language rules can be flexible, but can still be rules. J.R. Martin (1987, pp. 65–76) argues against this idea. His argument centers on the definition of the word *rule* itself. Since he has to admit that language contains regularities which must be obeyed if one is to be understood, he says that language is governed by CONVENTIONS (pp. 77–82) which people abide by in order to get their messages across. These work because "the speaker wants to signal the audience and the audience wants to be signaled" (p. 82).

Surely, this is not necessarily the case. People do talk to themselves for a variety of reasons, and when they do, they don't usually utter gibberish or deformed sentences. Those who do are considered to have a pathological condition. Then, too, in social situations, how often does one find oneself listening without really wanting to? Or even speaking when one wishes not to? In lexicon, sound system, sentence patterns, and discourses, certain words and structures must be used, others may be, and yet others cannot be used at all. For instance, Kreckel (1981, p. 204) found that, in assigning stress in a sentence, there is enough agreement between speakers to show that "... there exist phonological regularities which are part of the linguistic knowledge of naive, native speakers," but, within those rules, "... the speaker has more than one option ..." in stress placement, according to the pragmatic function or for "... distributing semantic weight."

Native speakers of a language know ill-formed sentences when they meet them. They can tell if a speaker has made a mistake in the structure of a sentence or, even, a discourse. *Mistake,* here, does not mean "solecism," but the sort of error which is made in speech pathologies like aphasia or schizophrenia. The following errors in applying *do-support* were made by an aphasic and a schizophrenic, respectively:

8A. [aphasic patient] I know you're talking, but I not talking you like I can talk you 'bout. (Buckingham, Whitaker, and Whitaker, 1979, p. 344)

8B. I still not have the thought pattern. . . . (courtesy of Dr. Bonnie Spring)

Notice that both of these violate the *do-support* rule seen in section 6 above. Laypersons, even illiterate ones, readily apprehend slips of the tongue, errors made by foreign speakers and children. All such recognition rest upon a rule-governed basis in language production. People also readily discriminate between well-formed and deviant discourse. Everyday terms for evaluating discourse, such as saying it is *rambling, incoherent,* or *irrational* presume violation of rules for making sentences cohere into a discourse (Chapter 6).

As early as the 1920s, The Prague School linguists presented by Vachek (1964) examined the mutual dependence of semantics and syntax as well as correlations between phonology and the other levels of language, and, as a result, realized that discourse requirements determined the grammar of the individual sentence. In effect, they showed that the discourse itself has a grammar (Chapters 7 and 11).

[6] Rules and Strategies.

It is never the case that only one rule can be chosen to deliver a given message. The meaning of any given utterance usually cannot be shown to inhere only in the actual syntactic rules of its sentences, even when we try to combine those with the meanings of the words used. Rules exist at all the levels of language, including the discourse level, but comprehension also depends heavily on the interaction between syntactic and lexical choice, the discourse itself and nonlinguistic strategies. These can be isolated and can be shown to be orderly. In essence, cospeakers both rely upon and control strategies along with linguistic rules in order to convey or yield meaning.

Speaking only of nondeviant, normal speech, Sanders (1987, p. 26) explains that speech production is INTELLIGENT ACTIVITY. By this he means that there are elements which one can fashion in different ways to achieve one's goal. There are always alternatives. Also, there is no guarantee that one will get the results one wants by any given organization of such elements although there are connections between what one wants, what one has chosen, and the result one gets. Therefore, despite the lack of a sure result, one can calculate the possibilities of what can happen. Sanders includes one other characteristic of intelligent action: there are elements which must be arranged according to constraints.

He avoids calling these constraints "rules," possibly to avoid a possible linkage with Chomsky's insistence on the rule-governed nature of language, an insistence which limited the linguist's domain to a very narrow domain of inquiry, one dominated by mathematical formulations of rules divined by syntacticians dipping into their own intuitions about language. This method necessarily entailed context-free interpretations of sentences. Chomsky originally insisted that the task of the linguist was to find context-free rules that would generate all and only the sentences possible in a given language. In practice, this has proven impossible. Chomsky's conception of transformational grammars is still not dead, having been revised to provide for the context-sensitivity of language (p. 123) while still affirming its context-free nature (Berwick and Weinberg 1986). In my opinion, this is an untenable position. All language is context-dependent. There is no way to achieve meaning in speech or writing without reference to context. That is the nature of the beast.

[7] Syntax and Context.

Quirk and Svartvik (1966) investigated the degree to which native speakers of English agreed upon their judgments of what is grammatical in the Chomskyan sense. They found that there was more disagreement than one would expect given the claims of transformational grammars. However, they pointed out (p. 101) that such lack of agreement on sentences was partially an artifact of the test itself. Had they provided a context for the sentences, their results might have been different. They quote Dwight Bolinger's dictum that "stripping a sentence to its minimum ... is a risky test of grammaticality; it often falsifies the potentialities of the construction."

More recently, Fauconnier (1985) lays the blame for ambiguity on uncertainties in the discourse situation itself, not in the syntax or lexicon. Wisely, studies of the accuracy of judgments of schizophrenic speech have been based upon transcripts of connected speech. This explains the high interjudge reliability. Context-free grammars based upon individual decisions of grammaticality rest on shaky foundations. Context is the key word. That is what was missing in T–G theory. More recently some attempts have been made to make rules context-sensitive, but even so, we are still faced with the abstract set of transformations—only now they include the context-sensitive rules, which are also both abstract and unproven.

[8] The Grammar of the Discourse.

Discourse itself has its own grammar, one that is partially autonomous, separate from sentence grammars, with its own phonological, lexical, and syntactic rules (Carlson 1983, p. 150; Sanders and Wirth 1985; Seuren 1985; Fillmore 1985; Halliday 1985; Ferrara 1985). Different kinds of discourses have their own rules of well-formedness. Gerald Prince (1982), for instance, has written a grammar of narrative structure and Livia Polanyi (1985) shows that conversational storytelling is constrained by culture-specific rules which are comparable to dialect differences in syntax. Phonologically, intonation contours mark out syntactic structures, prominent focus, and such paralinguistic messages as surprise, anger, and disgust (Carlson 1983, pp. 151), a point elaborated on as well by Kreckel (1981), Sanders (1987), and Lyons (1977). Sanders (1987, p. 11) likens the speaker's choice of what to say next in a discourse to " . . . the selection of lexical entries" in the sentence. Just as one chooses a word in a sentence according to sentential constraints, so one chooses the syntax of the sentence in the discourse.

Therefore, even if individual sentences taken out of context are well-formed, the discourse within which they are embedded may not be. VanDijk (1977) calls the level of phrases and sentences the MICRO-STRUCTURE, as opposed to the discourse or text, which is the MACRO-STRUCTURE. In the circumstance that microstructures by themselves show no deviance, but the discourse does, one would have to conclude that such sentences are deviantly produced because they do not properly form a macrostructure. Just as the meaning of a sentence is ultimately a function of the discourse within which it is embedded, so is the appropriateness of a sentence.

In actual usage, there is no way to separate sentences from their context and no way to judge well-formedness without considering both. Deviance at the macrostructural level comprises disruption of linguistic abilities. For instance, each of the sentences in example 9 below is well-formed, yet the entire is bizarre. In the original presentation of these data (Chaika 1974; Chapter 1), there were three utterances composed of gibberish interspersed throughout this monologue. Here, they have been omitted in order to prevent a contamination effect. Thus, the following monologue has actually been normalized to mitigate the effect of deviance, but the entire remains as deviant as before.

> 9. Good mornin' everybody.
> I don't know what that is
> Oh! It's that thorazine. I forgot I had it.
> That's Lulubelle.
> This one's Jean. J–E–A–N
> I'll write that down.
> Speeds up the metabolism.
> Makes your heart bong.
> Tranquilizes you if you've got the metabolism I have.
> I have distemper just like cats do 'cause that's what we all are, felines.
> Siamese cat balls.
> They stand out.
> I had a cat, a Manx, still around somewhere.
> You'll know him when you see him.
> His name is GI Joe, he's black and white.
> I had a little goldfish too like a clown.

On the microlinguistic level, the above phrases and sentences are well-formed, but they fail on the macrolinguistic level, and that alone establishes their deviance. Judgments of deviance depend as much on the fit of the sentence to the discourse as they do on the fit of phrases and words to sentences.

Each genre of discourse has its own set of rules. Constraints on narratives in our culture, for instance, may not operate on sermons, lectures, making small-talk, or communication of factual information (e.g., Goffman 1981; Chafe 1980; Chaika 1989, pp. 98–192). Narratives are governed by temporal ordering whereas sermons are not. Sermons require an overt moral whereas narratives do not. Such constraints on the macrostructure operate analogously to the rules for micro-structures like phrases and sentences. Additionally, there is cross-cultural variation in what is allowable in a genre and even in what is necessary, what must be included and what may not be (Labov 1969, 1972; Scollon and Scollon 1981; Tannen 1984; Jarrett 1984; Chaika 1989, pp. 98–192.) Violation of such cross-cultural constraints are more likely to be perceived as rude or pointless than as bizarre.

[9] Rules to Create.

Rules on each level of language aid in our ability to be creative. Every language has within it permissible sound combinations, some that have not yet been used, hence can be used to create new words. For instance, I could invent a game called "Bilotec" or a product called "Marfem." There could even be a new theory of psychiatry, called "Logology" (the science of words). Sentence and discourse-forming rules allow even greater creativity, albeit creativity constrained by rules. Frequently, if not most always, speakers either use old words in new contexts to force new meanings rather than make up brand-new words, although that, too, does happen. Alternatively, compounding is used, as occurred when the first person referred to stealing as *ripping off.* A third avenue of creativity is to borrow words from another language. This is typically done because of admiration for another culture, as when Latin and Greek words were adopted for the budding sciences of the 17th and 18th centuries. Native words could have been created, but the Classical languages were associated with scholarship. Neologisms and gibberish don't fail because they're creative. Language is structured to foster creativity. They fail because they are not used so that cospeakers can apply rules or strategies for decoding. This is a direct result of language's not being an isomorphic system.

[10] Notational Variations.

Why insist on the word *rule?* Why not use Martin's term and simply call them *conventions,* or, as Sanders does, call them *constraints?* Why not refer to *expectations* in discourse? These are NOTATIONAL VARIATIONS, different words for the same phenomena. The problem is that these three terms, although referring to the same phenomena, imply that adherence is not necessary, when it clearly is. Is it mere constraint, expectation, or convention that prevents

9. A: Where did you go last night?
B: No
9C. A: Are you coming?
D: I wore a yellow tulip.

Such matters as adverb placement not using the progressive form with stative verbs or the use of *do* when negating verbs are obligatory. In verbs are obligatory. In the same way, one can't answer a question asking *where* by either a *yes* or *no*. The *where* demands a location or an "I don't know." These are grammatical error on the level of the discourse itself.

These aren't just conventions, expectations, or constraints. Native speakers know that 9 A–D are wrong, and can be righted by following the rules for adverb placement or verb conjugation. The errors in 9 A–D are discourse errors, and anyone, even a quite young child would be likely to say of 9B, something like "You can't answer that question with 'no' " or of 9D "You can't answer that with 'I wore a yellow tulip.' " One might, instead, say something like, "What kind of an answer is that?" to either 9B or 9D. This is another way of saying, "You can't answer that question with . . . " The very normal and usual choice of *can't* indicates the existence of tacit rules. It takes no particular training or expertise for people to recognize and be able to correct a wide variety of linguistic errors.

[11] The Levels of Language.

As part of its lack of isomorphism, language consists of layers of interrelated rules. Each layer has its own rules, and rules which connect it to the others. PHONETIC rules, those indicating pronunciation of individual sounds, form PHONOLOGICAL rules. These in turn form MORPHEMES which form LEXICAL ITEMS which form SENTENCES which in turn form DISCOURSES.

[12] Phonetics, Phonemes, and Morphemes.

A brief consideration of the intricacies of the sounds of language illuminates both the rule governed nature of language and the FUZZY BORDERS that are also its nature. Beyond such enlightenment, phonology illuminates for us what must be accounted for in any theory of psycholinguistics. The level of phonetics is the most describable, most limited part of language, but its complexity is nevertheless boggling. In fact, even such apparently simple matters as articulating specific sounds is loaded with intricacies unsuspected by the novice in linguistics.

One would expect that schizophrenics suffering from severe speech disruption would show difficulties even at this level. Unfortunately, our phonetic record of schizophrenic articulations is almost nil. Over the years, the few researchers who have discussed gibberish have not been equipped to make phonetic transcriptions so that their discussions have been little more than vague impressionistic descriptions. Laffal (1965, p. 85), for instance, speaks of a patient who "launched into gibberish that sounded like a mixture of Chinese and Polish, with a distinct conversational prosody." Why Laffal attributed the gibberish to these quite different languages is not clear, nor does he tell us if the patient was a bilingual in these or any other languages. Robertson and Shamsie (1958) also attributed the gibberish their patient produced as belonging to different languages. If gibberish has sounds that occur in a language not native to the speaker, or one not known by the speaker, then that would indicate a deficit in the phonetic and phonemic systems. These are the lowest levels of linguistic structure, those most automatic; still they are highly sophisticated and intricately rule-governed phenomena. It is not inconceivable that severely SD patients would make errors at this level. No two languages share the same phonetic and phonemic systems; errors can be made in these systems.

Unfortunately, except for my own transcriptions of gibberish (Chaika 1974; Chaika and Alexander 1986), there are no transcriptions of reported gibberish. My own transcriptions do not reveal disruption at these levels. Holzman et al. (1986, p. 361) claim that "It is noteworthy that as the exemplar group of psychotic patients, schizophrenic patients do not violate these phonotactic rules." They do not cite corroborating studies. Looking at the pattern of linguistic disintegration, one would expect very little disruption at this level, but it is possible that some patients could regress to the point of phonetic and phonemic error. Laffal's and Robertson and Shamsie's impressions that they were hearing foreign language gibberish might arise from such regression unless the patients in question were multilingual and their gibberish could be traced to their other languages. There has not been sufficient transcription of gibberish and neologisms by trained phoneticians to verify whether or not disruption occurs at this level. If and when such studies are undertaken and even if it is found that schizophrenics do not ever make phonotactic errors, there is still plenty of evidence at the other levels of language that structural disruption does occur in schizophrenia. The rest of this chapter is devoted to showing these disruptions. In addition, it will be argued that analysis in terms of linguistic disruption does not posit factors that we cannot observe and does not demand adherence to any particular psychodynamic theory.

The above discussion shows the importance of having a basic understanding of how phonetic and phonemic systems work. Even when languages share a sound, it won't necessarily be pronounced the same way in each language. This occurs for two reasons. The first is that any sound can be articulated somewhat differently. For instance, in English, we pronounce a [t] by placing our tongue tip on the alveolar ridge behind the top teeth, but many European languages do so by placing the tongue tip behind the spot where the upper and lower teeth meet which is where English places the tongue to make a [θ], *th* in *thing*. Different languages also hold each sound for a different length of time. American English does not hold consonants as long as some other languages.

Another reason for the impression that gibberish might be in a foreign language has to do with another complexity in sound systems: the PHONEME. Each sound we think we hear is actually a group of sounds. In American English, for instance, the PHONEMES /p/, /t/, and /k/ are actually ASPIRATED before stressed vowels as in *pill, till* and *kill.* This can be felt by pronouncing these words holding a finger in front of the lips. A puff of air will be felt. No puff, or a much weaker one, will be felt when pronouncing *spill, still* and *skill,* as they are not aspirated if they follow an /s/ or occur at the end of a word, as in *spill, still, skill, rap, rat,* and *rack.* Additionally, in American English (but not British), intervocalic /t/ and /d/ are both pronounced alike, as a [D], the medial consonants heard in both *betting* and *bedding* which are pronounced alike. Disparity in phonetic rules across languages accounts for misperception of sounds in the foreign language. This, of course, is what causes us all to have foreign accents in our nonnative languages.

What this all means is that if a patient who is a monolingual native speaker produces neologisms and gibberish that sound like a foreign language, their speech may be so disrupted that they are misapplying phonetic and phonemic rules of their language. So far, there is no hard evidence of this occurring, but, so far, to my knowledge, no phonetician or linguist has transcribed large amounts of gibberish. Harry Whitaker, a neurolinguist, says that there are aphasics with what he calls the foreign accent syndrome as they misapply phonemic rules so that they sound foreign. It may also be that modern practices of medication for psychotics forestall such a complete disruption of speech that even the phonetic and phonemic systems disintegrate. If a patient is found whose gibberish shows such disintegration, not only is it caused by the most profound disruption of speech possible, it is not the sort of thing one can control. People are unaware of the intricacies of phonetic and phonemic rules until they are introduced to them by courses in linguistics, and the rules are so below the level of awareness, that such matters are very difficult to learn and next to impossible to manipulate.

To complicate matters, what we hear as separate sounds on the phonemic level may become one sound during certain word-forming processes known as MORPHOPHONEMICS. For instance, /s/ and /t/ are different sounds as in *sat* and *tat*. They are phonemically distinct. However, in sets of words like *idiot -idiocy*, the [t] alternates with [s] The <c> in *idiocy* is pronounced as an [s], but we still perceive *idiocy* as being formed from *idiot* with a suffix that indicates "state of being an idiot" (Chomsky and Halle 1968). Examples of morphophonemic regularity can be multiplied logarithmically. Think of alternations of the actual sounds in *critic-criticize, music-musician, persuade-persuasive,* and *acquire-acquisition.* Sometimes, as in the latter two examples, the sound change is indicated in the spelling. At others, as in the previous examples, it is not indicated. Still, we have no particular trouble alternating the final [k] in *critic* with the [s] in *criticize*. All languages are subject to such alternations in their word creation systems. The miracle is not that some patients with disrupted speech do produce gibberish but that there is not more disruption at these levels as they are fraught with complexities.

These examples alone show that language is neither perceived nor created by any simple equation of stimulus and response. They also show that we do not have a list of forms in our heads from which we draw when we speak. There is probably a good evolutionary reason for this. Communication would be hindered greatly if speakers had to scan through the enormous lists of words in their lexicons every time they wanted to say something, conversation would be considerably slowed. It would be slowed even more when, in the heat of talk, they first selected one word, say an adjective, and then decided to recast their sentence so that the same meaning has to be achieved by the related form of a verb, as in

- He **gets red** — uhh — **reddens** when Lola says, "hi!"
- Try to make it **prettier** — uhh — **beautify** it
- I hate to be **critic** . . . uhh — **criticize**.

If language were not rule-governed, such switching of morphologically-related words would entail scanning the lexicon until one came upon the related word. Furthermore, it would be highly inefficient to store each form with a common root word separately. That would take a great deal more "brain space" than does applying rules to sets of words. Also, if we store *critic–criticize* holistically as two separate forms, why do we have entire sets of words which follow the same rule? If there were no rules, that would be the most inefficient system of all.

Certain schizophrenic errors can be explained as failure to apply morphophonemic rules. In fact, the schizophrenic data show that such rules exist. The following response came from one patient:

10A. I am being help with the food and the **medicate**...

10B. You have to be able to **memory** the process...

10C. ... to open up the old testament and start to **memory** it.

Each of these errors was repeated in the monologue. Each boldfaced word fails morphologically by failing to add the appropriate DERIVATIONAL MORPHEMES, those which change words from one part of speech to the other. The patient has not added the *-ion* morpheme to turn the verb to its corresponding noun. He has failed to convert *medicate* into *medication*. Note that the final [t] sound in *medicate* turns to the sound represented by <*sh*> in our orthography in *medication*, so that this failure represents a morphophonemic one as well as a morphological one, and in 10B and C, he failed to change *memory* to *memorize*. It is not the case that the patient has had a general failure in syntactic rules because his word order and marking of syntax like the noun determiner *the* correctly. We can explain the deviation in 10 A–C only by referring to the morphonemic rules of noun formation from Latinate verbs. This argument is bolstered by the fact that his syntactic failures devolve upon INFLECTIONAL MORPHEMES: failure to put the preterit ending of *help* in 10A and the possessive in

10D ... to speak and think in the lord tongue

These inflectional morphemes are also governed by morphophonemic rules. The preterit ending is variably pronounced as [t], [d], or [Id] depending on the last sound of the verb. Consider the pronunciation of this morpheme in "picked, played, and lifted." They are all spelled the same, but pronounced differently. The possessive is variably pronounced as [z], [s], and [Iz], as in "lord's, patient's, and Tess's." Again, the spelling gives no clue. The patient fluctuated between omitting verb and noun morphemes and not. Given the fact that these rules are among the most every-day ordinary ones in the language, this argues for a generally impaired ability to apply morphemic rules.

In other instances, as we have seen, a patient forms recognizable morphemes into neologisms like *puterience* and *plausity*.

[13] Words.

Many researchers have attempted to find a schizophrenic deficit on the level of the word, basing their research completely upon their conception of what a word is. This is natural, but it can also lead to invalid experiments and fallacious conclusions. In order to illustrate this, we must consider the question, "What is a word?"

We all know that we form speech from words, that we give our word, and that we have words for things. In practice, however, it has proven remarkably difficult to come up with an all-encompassing definition of *word*. Phonetically, the distinction between the level of the word and the sentence is frequently obscured because inter-word phonological rules do get applied to phrases, as when we speak of "coffee to go." Typically, we pronounce the /t/ in to as a [D] in this expression. The opposite also occurs: sentence intonation may be applied to a word, as in "Coffee?" The rising intonation gives this the force of a full sentence, such as "Does anybody want some coffee?" Actually, if the full syntactic form of the question is given, the intonation is usually like that of a statement with the voice dropping at the end of the sentence.

Orthographically, for the European languages at least, we frequently think of a word as a group of letters surrounded by a space. This was not ever thus. Medieval manuscripts, for instance, crowded as many letters as possible onto a page. Consequently, such niceties as spaces between words were not provided. So ingrained is this concept that one some researchers have simply assumed that this is how a word is defined. For instance, Hart and Payne (1973) taped interviews with schizophrenics, aiming for 500 word discourse. These researchers counted as a word "a group of letters not containing a space which is preceded by and followed by a space which corresponds to a word listed in a dictionary." Dictionaries vary greatly in their listings of words, so they are hardly a foolproof source (p. 645). They say that they excluded "letter groups" such as "uh." These are not letter groups. They don't even appear in writing, unless the writing purports to be a representation of speech.

Hart and Payne report that they had to prompt most patients to get the quota of 500 words, leading one to question how natural the resulting data were. In any event, eliciting a 500-word corpus from each subject is an impossible task, even if one has a foolproof definition for *word* which as the next section shows, we do not. In any event, the researchers had a typist transcribe the tapes so that the Type-Token Ratio (TTR) could be ascertained. This is the ratio of the number of different words used to the total number of words in the sample. TTR has been used as a measure of cohesion, but it fails because one need not repeat the same word to effect cohesion. One can use its synonym or a phrase which means the same thing. In fact, in Chapter 6 we shall see that repetitions of a word or even its synonyms can impair cohesion drastically.

In order to get the TTR, there has to be an accurate word count, of course. As is true of every other study that I have ever seen utilizing a TTR, Hart and Payne do not seem aware of any of the difficulties in their procedure. For instance, does one count the sequences like *have to* or *want to* as two words or one? These are certainly pronounced as one, e.g., "hafta" and "wanna." They certainly function as one as well, being verb auxiliaries, part of a large system known as CATENATIVE auxiliaries. Should we count contractions like *can't, won't, they've,* or *they'll* as one word or two? Is *won'tcha* two words or three? Given misspellings like <should of> for *should have,* we certainly know that some even highly educated native speakers aren't sure of what the elements in a contraction actually consist of. This, too, is part of the fuzzy border phenomena.

Worse yet for TTR data, consider pronouns which refer to long noun phrases, such as the *it* in

11. Max bought the big old Victorian house on the corner. **It** needed a lot of work.

Does this *it* count as one word? Or does it count for the entire phrase which it replaces, "the big old Victorian house on the corner." There's another problem in 11: is *a lot of* three words or one? Phonologically, it is usually counted as one: "alotta."

Even as a definition for the written word the "space surrounding the word" test doesn't work. For example, consider words like *hardhearted, hard-hitting, hard hit,* and *hardihood.* The English orthographic system is notoriously inconsistent in applying hyphens to some compounds, writing others as one word, and still others as two. How, then, does one reliably count what a word is simply by counting those surrounded by a space the typist has inserted?

Regardless of the written conventions, we can tell that words are compounded by the fact that there is a special stress pattern in compound words. This is realized by the rise and fall of the voice, as well as the length of the vowel. Try saying the pairs *greenhouse* vs *green house*, *blackboard* vs *black board*. Notice that if you say *safe house* in the sense of a hideaway operated by the police for the protection of witnesses, you get the same rise and fall that you do for *greenhouse* and *blackbird*. If, instead you are speaking of a house which has been well-constructed, it is pronounced with the same patterns as *green house* and *black bird*, but the same spelling is used whether *safe* and *house* are being used as a compound or as two separate words. The writing is not as good a guide to compounding as the spoken sound patterns.

In English (and many but not all languages), part of our feeling of what constitutes a word derives from our grammatical morphemes such as plurals and tense markers. The thing that we put these morphemes on is what we consider a word, so that in *roses* and *played*, we feel that the words involved are *rose* and *play*, both of which can stand alone with no endings. In contrast, the vagaries of the English possessive play havoc with this concept of a word. Notice the way English allows a possessive to be put upon an entire phrase, such as

The woman next door's sister . . .
The guy who I dated last year's car. . . .

As awkward as these are in writing, they are commonly used in speech. Some are used even in formal writing, such as

The Queen of England's jewels.

Therefore, the definition of a word as the formation which can take inflectional endings fails.

Cross-linguistically, the problem of what a word is is even more vexatious. In some languages, however, there are few "stand-alones." For instance, note the Swahili-English equivalences:

- atanipenda "he will like me"
- atatupenda "he will like us"
- tutampenda "we will like him"
- unamsumbua "you are annoying him" (data from Gleason 1955)

Most English speakers would agree that each of the above glosses is composed of four words, the pronoun subject, auxiliary, verb, and pronoun object. The pronouns and the auxiliary are GRAMMATICAL WORDS, also known as FUNCTION WORDS, and the verbs are full LEXICAL ITEMS have to be placed on lexical items according to the rules of that particular language.

The corresponding forms to our four-word sentences look strangely like one word in Swahili. Whoever collected these data wrote the Swahili forms so that they appear as one word. In fact, anthropologists who collected languages which to us are exotic have reported that there are languages in which there are no words as we know them. Rather, what we would think of as a phrase or sentence, those languages treated as a word.

In languages which are declined like Russian, there are far fewer words that stand alone than in a language like English. Russian, being a highly inflected language, requires words to have endings on them which tell how they are being used in a sentence. English conveys such messages largely by word order. Therefore, English speakers think of Russian words, nouns, for instance, as roots to which inflectional morphemes are bound.

An even more fallacious concept of words is that they are some kind of fixed entity. Bleuler's belief that the glossomanic chaining of schizophrenics results from associative loosening rests upon such an assumption, as does Bannister's (1960, 1962) theory that schizophrenics fail to use constructs as fixed points. By "constructs" Bannister (1960, p. 135) apparently means "words." Bleuler's, Bannister's and Chapman, Chapman, and Daut's (1976) explanations based upon word association testing depend upon static constructs, but words have no fixed meanings. By their very essence, they are fluid. Lieberman criticizes those who equate words with tokens, pointing out that

> . . . one of the most salient characteristics of . . . words . . . [is that] . . . they are not tokens for things; they instead convey concepts. The meaning of a word never is precisely equivalent to a thing, a set of things, or even a property of a set of things. (Lieberman 1984, p. 80)

An even more salient characteristic of words is their inherent flexibility. By their very nature, they change according to the ingenuity of speakers in employing them in different contexts. Such change is the heart of metaphor, the ability to take a word or words from one domain and apply it to another. Without such flexibility in word usage, language wouldn't be so immediately accessible for swift encoding of messages in response to new contexts. Given the context of an utterance hearers usually can ascertain the intended meaning. In the course of a day, we all may use, hear or read new usages of old words. Zippy writing in car magazines, news weeklies, and ads attest to our abilities both to produce and comprehend. It must be emphasized, however, that I am not here referring only to artistic or professional word usage, but to an everyday capability of everyday people in everyday circumstances.

Looking at words historically shows us how pervasive the plasticity of words are, resulting over time in drastic changes in intension, all the meanings of a word. Take the word *bulb*. It originally referred to an onion, then to any plant with a bulb-like root with fleshy long, narrow leaves, then to any round bulb-like swelling as in the bottom of a thermometer, then to the round glass vehicle for the incandescent light. Now it can also mean tube-shaped lights such as fluorescent bulbs. There is even a nautical meaning referring to a cylindrical shape at the forefoot of certain ships. *Bulb* seems to have extended its original referents. Sometimes words lose their original meanings entirely. *Hackney* was originally a fine riding horse, then a horse for hire, then a worn-out horse, then, in the 17th century, a prostitute, and now a trite expression. It is easy to see how these meanings became extended with ordinary use. Perusing any historical dictionary reveals the omnipresence of changes in word meaning.

There is nothing remarkable in schizophrenic failure to maintain "fixed constructs." What is remarkable, in its original sense of "worthy of remark," is that in some way, the normal flexibility in word usage goes awry so that schizophrenic creations are perceived as being abnormal and difficult to follow.

Chapter Five

SYNTAX, SEMANTICS, AND METAPHOR: BEYOND CHOMSKY

Although many laypersons assume that the Chomskyan paradigm for language reigns supreme, here it is shown that other models of syntax, specifically context-bound ones, have far greater explanatory power. Syntax and semantics are intertwined and must be understood as such in order to analyze language data including that from psychotics. This examines the ways that semantics determines syntax and the ways that syntax can be manipulated for implications and direct meaning. The nature of metaphor, how it works, and what constitutes reasonable exegeses of it are also elaborated upon. It is shown that metaphor is not random nor can metaphorical meaning be claimed without basing it on the processes by which all metaphor is created and understood.

[1] The Importance of Syntactic Theory.

Any theory of human behavior implicitly or explicitly rests upon language. Faulty notions of the ways language works have consistently resulted in fallacious interpretations of psychotic speech. So complex is language that even when clinicans have paid some heed to linguistic theory, they have embraced too readily or rejected too summarily. A prime example is Edelson's (1978) desire to develop a psychoanalytic model based upon Chomskyan grammar. Unfortunately, formulating a theory of syntax which will explain the ways that humans speak has not proven easy. So rich are language data that a variety of explanations serve to explain at least parts of the ways grammars work. Over the years, indeed the centuries, scholars have been content to stop at the data their theories account for, seeking no further.

98

[2] The Chomskyan Paradigm.

Many scholars continue to equate linguistics with Chomsky. Julia's (1983[1]) *Explanatory Models in Linguistics* argues solely against the earlier Chomskyan grammars. One facet of the Chomskyan paradigm that has been seductive to linguists as well as to psychoanalysts was the quasi-mathematical derivation of each sentence discussed, starting from an abstract deep structure which, by a succession of stages upon which certain transformations were applied, yielded a perfect surface structure, complete with undeniable meaning. Such analysis held out the promise of our being able to prove exactly what each sentence means. This would have been an ultimate triumph of mathematics over language since the latter clearly has much fuzzier rules and boundaries between levels. Of course, T–G grammarians did not recognize that borders are fuzzy and all cannot be explained by rules.

Edelson (1978, p. 162) unabashedly looked toward the day that psycho-analysis would achieve the degree of theoretical sophistication that Chomsky had provided for linguistics. Edelson spoke of psychoanalysis as being in the state that linguistics was in before Chomsky, implying a primitive state. It is not hard to see why Edelson was so ready to embrace Chomskyan analysis with its apparent precision and abstraction utilizing the symbols and equations of mathematical logic. He (p. 159), for example, showed that the generalization "All dreams are hallucinatory wish-fulfillments" could be formulated by the Chomskyan-inspired:

> No matter what value of x is chosen, if x is a dream, then x is a hallucination of the fulfillment of a wish.

Edelson then points out that even this requires more explication, as:

> Whatever x is chosen, there is at least one y, and there is at least one z, such that: if x is a dream, and if y is a wish, and if z is a condition, and if F is a relation "fulfills" which holds between a condition z and a wish y, then x is a hallucination of $F(z,y)$-or $G(x,Fzy)$. (Edelson, p. 160)

Aside from the fact that one gains no new insights by subjecting this sentence to such an elaborate rephrasing, there is the other fact that the statement is no more valid than when it was stated in ordinary language. As one who was originally caught up in the T–G fervor of the late sixties, however, I can attest to the seductiveness of trying to bend language into such precision. To use the very term Chomsky coined, COUNTEREXAMPLE upon counterexample has already shown that T–G sentence-based grammars could not explain how people produced or understood even quite simple sentences. The pragmatists among us, sociolinguists, psycholinguists, neurolinguists, any of us mucking about with real data have found other models more felicitous.

It has turned out to be exceedingly difficult to find deep structures and transformational rules which unerringly explain very many surface sentences at all, much less to explain all possible ones. As counterexamples to Chomsky's original formulations cropped up with disturbing regularity, T–G grammars have had to be revised again and again. This has been done both in and out of the Chomsky circles (e.g., Montague 1973; Berwick and Weinberg 1984; Jacobson and Pullum 1982.). New forms of grammars multiplied, each resembling classical Chomsky to a greater or lesser degree, and each supposed to take care of data the others couldn't: generative semanticist grammars, Montague grammars, relational and arc pair grammars, grammars of the extended standard theory, and of government-binding.

Even a cursory glance at the literature debating these different schools of syntax shows how unlikely it is that any of them are to shed much light on the speech of psychosis or even of normal conversation. Their pages are filled with discussions of *it*-raising, node pruning, constraints on deep structure movement out of NP, "shunting" c-command domains (Radford 1981; Berwick and Weinberg 1984, p. 181), all of which are operations during different stages of the derivation of a sentence, stages which are nonobservable, devoid of words, and below the level of the speaker's awareness. That any of these post-hoc deep operations actually figure in speech production,[2] normal or not, has never been proven. Of course, I speak here as a pragmatist, but, as we shall see, hardly a lone one.

There are far more useful constructs in linguistics today, powerful models of conversation and comprehension. The meaning-free sentence grammars of traditional, structural, and transformational grammars have been replaced by semantico-syntactic grammatical models sensitive to the requirements of the discourse. We now know that the particular grammatical form of any sentence is dependent upon the requirements of the entire discourse, and that there is no meaning without context. Moreover, we know that the very verb one chooses will constrain the forms of the sentence in which it appears. There is, in fact, no syntax separate from the discourse, no phonology separate from the word, and no discourse the unconstrained by the social situation or the text. There are levels in language, but they are all interrelated and work in concert.

All meaning derives from context. We compare an utterance or other snatch of language to its context. That is how old words come to take on new meanings. The appropriateness of the syntax used and the words chosen depend ultimately on the context in which they appear (Lyons 1968; Seuren 1985). Lauri Carlson (1983, p. 152) maintains that we can find a context for any juxtaposition of sentences, but he does not discuss SD psychotic discourse or that from any linguistically impaired population. Truly, for some such discourse, we could provide connecting links, but these are always pure conjecture. We are justified in supplying such links only on principled grounds such as we have will see in our discussion of implication.

There is no context-free meaning. There is no context-free syntax. There is no meaningless generative cycle which produces an infinity of sentences. Actually, I should amend that last sentence. It seems to me that psychotic glossomania is the archetypal meaningless generative cycle which can be uttered as an infinite number of sentences.

[3] Case Grammars.

The Chomskyan "revolution" had barely gotten off ground before troublesome data started to pile up. There were too many data from even quite simple sentences that could not be explained by the use of Chomskyan deep structures upon which transformations operated to produce surface structures.

Fillmore, in what he originally called CASE GRAMMARS (1966; 1968) and now calls FRAME SEMANTICS pointed out that syntactico-semantic rules are intertwined rules in all languages. For instance, the verb selected in a sentence determines which sentence slots can or must be filled. In English, a word order language, there are three basic slots: subject, indirect object, direct object. Which gets filled depends upon the verb chosen. For instance, 1A allows an indirect object position to be filled with the DATIVE but 1B does not. (An * indicates an ungrammatical sentence.)

   1A. Max gave the church money.
   1B. * Max donated the church money.

However, both verbs allow the indirect object to be used with a preposition at the end of the sentence.

1C. Max gave the money to the church.

1D. Max donated the money to the church.

There are even more complex examples of this phenomena:

2A. Oscar planted peas in the garden.

2B. Oscar planted the garden with peas.

2C. The garden was planted with peas (by Oscar).

2D. Peas were planted in the garden (by Oscar).

Fillmore and others (Chafe 1970) that the very positions that can be filled in a sentence depends wholly on the verb chosen, **independently of semantic content**. Synonyms do not necessarily allow the same grammar. For example, *put* can be chosen as a paraphrase of *plant*, but with different consequences:

2E. Oscar put peas in the garden

but not

2F *Oscar put the garden with peas.

Although 2E is paraphrasable by 2A, the selection of the verb *put* in 2E prevents the locative *garden* from appearing without a preposition. It also prevents the object, *peas*, from appearing with the preposition *with*.

Bresnan (1978) in her aptly named article "A realistic transformational grammar" recognizes that verbs have markings on them in the lexicon that indicate whether or not they take objects, datives, and the like.[3] Similarly, Montague (1973) starts his derivations with words which are then mapped onto phrases as a corresponding semantics is simultaneously developed. Dowty (1982, p. 100) virtually takes it as a given that verbs govern whether or not transformations such as Dative Shift[4] can occur. Seuren (1985, p. 61) flatly avows that "There is no semantics without grammar." Halliday (1985, p. xix) insists "... there is no clear line between semantics and grammar, and a functional grammar is one that is pushed in the direction of semantics." McNeill and Levy (1982) maintain that language is generated directly from patterns of meaning, not through grammatical representation, a view now shared by many syntacticians (Halliday 1967, 1968; Chafe 1970; Lyons 1968; 1977).

Originally, Fillmore (1982, pp. 114–115) called these noun positions relative to verb cases, but later he employed the concept of VALENCY, also employed by Lyons (1977, pp. 488–489). Valency, a term originally used in chemistry, refers to the capacity of an entity to affect or interact with another in some special way. Thus, to use Lyons' (1977, pp. 488–490) examples *kill* is BIVALENT, requiring an agent and an object, and has a CAUSATIVE relationship to *die* which is MONOVALENT. *Give* is TRIVALENT, requiring that agent, object, and dative be specified.

[4] Implication, Lexical Choice, and Syntax.

Why would a mental health professional care about the differences in syntactic theories? Of what utility is a knowledge of case grammars or frame semantics, however it is called? One answer is that patients make syntactic errors explicable only in terms of such syntactico-semantic rules. The second reason is that recognition of these processes enlarges our awareness of what is grammatical and what not, surely an important issue in a scholarly field in which the thrust of much debate is whether or not the population under investigation does or does not evince deviant syntax. Another reason is that our interpretations are rendered more precise by such recognition. The last is that much implication is achieved by manipulation of syntax, and this is done according to regular syntactic rules of the language.

At times, implication is achieved by using one paraphrase or the other. There are two ways that speakers can manage such implication: by selecting one verb over another and by choosing one paraphrase of over another. We saw the latter condition with *plant* above. When *peas* were made the subject or object an implication was made that other items were planted as well; when *garden* was made subject or object, the implication was that peas were all that were planted.

A somewhat less benign example also illustrates the possibility of paraphrase. When a speaker selects one verb rather than its synonym, different implications become possible. For instance, selecting *die* rather than *kill* limits implication considerably.

   3A. Jack **died.**
   3B. Jack was **killed.**

The two can be synonymous in many instances, but 3B implies that someone or something caused Jack to die. 3A carries no such implication. Therefore, if a speaker wishes a hearer to be suspicious of Jack's death, but does not want to make a bald statement to that effect, the choice of 3B serves that purpose because English speakers know that the verb *kill* takes an AGENT or a CAUSE as well as an object. There is no way to avoid the object if *kill* is chosen, but by placing that object, here *Jack*, in the subject position as in 3B, one avoids naming the agent or cause. The use of the passive implies that there was an agent or cause. In 3A, *Jack* is merely the PATIENT, one who undergoes a process.

As noted above, there are errors in schizophrenic speech that can be analyzed in terms of syntactico-semantic relations, some involving case and some not. For instance, the error in 4A is caused by the inappropriate preposition *by* which seems to indicate that cars are the cause of the attention. Even if that is what the patient meant, and even if it is true, the prepositional phrase *because of* is required to indicate cause here. With the verb *have, by* usually is reserved for a temporal phrase, such as having it **by 10 o'clock:**

4A. They have world wide attention by the cars . . .

In 4B, below, we see a different kind of syntactico-semantic error. Here, the article *a* is used erroneously. The problem is that *people* has a plural meaning and is used with plural verbs, but its form is singular. The article *a* can only precede a singular noun. *Some* must be used with *people.* There is an inevitable mismatch between form and plurality in English, so it is not surprising that a psychotic would make an error even in the face of fact that a phrase like "some Italian people" would be quite common in the speech of a New York City resident. The error itself is not likely to have come about because of reinforced stimuli. As with the mistakes of toddlers, the speaker says what he has probably not heard.

4B. Mill Avenue is also a a I like a quiet residential n-   block like a quiet residential block with a Italian people talk.

[5] The Semantics of Syntax.

Actually, American linguists came late to a theory of grammar in which it was recognized that the components of language are not strictly separated. Chomsky actually inherited that view from the structuralist grammarians before him. Oddly, the reason that they propounded a strict separation of levels was because they were influenced by the very behaviorism that Chomsky despised. Structuralists assumed that we simply heard a message and that triggered a response. We have already seen that this doesn't even work for our processing of the sound system of language, its simplest most automatic level. Once this last vestige of Behaviorism dissolved, the way was open for powerful new meaning.

Eventually Fillmore came to think of lexical items as being in frames which evoke scenes (Fillmore 1982, pp. 116–117) that are to a great extent culturally determined. He points out that a word like *vegetarian* is important only in a meat-eating culture and that our understanding of *judge* is bound by our culture's modes of judging.[5] He also shows (p. 123) that what appears to be a grammatical category such as verb tense shapes the image of a given verb. His example is the pluperfect progressive in

5. She had been running.

The lexical item *run* gives us one image, but the pluperfect progressive shapes the image of running given here, so that it may explain at the narrative time why she is panting, sweating and tired. As a result of these insights, Fillmore now speaks of FRAME SEMANTICS.

McCawley (1986) also demonstrates the impossibility of segregating different levels and processes of language, illustrating from other grammatical constructions. He shows other syntactic~semantic configurations. For instance, it is generally conceded that making a sentence negative is a grammatical procedure according to the grammar of a given language. Even so, negation is not completely a matter of grammar. There are certain words and expressions which arbitrarily can not be used in the negative and others that can only be used as positives. That is, it is word choice itself and not grammar *per se* which forces the negative or positive polarity. McCawley gives as arbitrarily positive polarity:

6A. I would rather be in Philadelphia.
6B. *I wouldn't rather be in Philadelphia.
6C. The meatloaf is delicious.
6D. *This meatloaf isn't delicious.
6E. You could have just as well have rented a car.[6]
6F. *You couldn't have just as well as rented a car.

Examples of negative polarity [examples mine]:

7A. It couldn't be all that bad.
7B. *It could be all that bad.
7C. Max isn't all that bright.
7D. *Max is all that bright.
7E. He didn't do much for his family.
7F. *He did do much for his family.

Patricia Strauss (personal communication) commented that many of the starred (*) sentences can be used for emphasis, what linguists call CONTRASTIVE SITUATION. For instance, if someone demurs "Oh, things couldn't be that bad." The hearer, probably the complainer, retorts, "Things **could** be that bad" (with stress on the *could*). As Strauss remarked, the effect of playing with polarity works because the speaker is consciously playing with the known grammar. In turn, the hearer understands the emphasis conveyed also because he or she knows that the grammar doesn't allow this polarity on that expression.

It has occurred to me that the intertwining of lexical choice, semantics, and syntax explains the reason that paraphrases can differ so radically in their surface forms.

[6] Semantic Features.

Some meaning is derived from factoring of features as in *cub, puppy, child, calf* which share the semantic features of [young] [offspring], but differ in the features of [human], [wild], [ursine], and [canine], so that *child* is [+human, −wild], *cub* is [−human, +wild, +ursine, +canine], and *puppy* is [−human, −wild, +canine]. The very fact of being human automatically negates being ursine or canine, so those features need not be mentioned in a discussion of semantic features. However, being [−human] opens far more possibilities, so that features like [+canine] or [+ursine] have to be specified.

Certain features subsume others. *Baby*, for instance, is [+human], so that one need not specify species if that word is used for humans. If, however, it is referring to other mammalian offspring, that must be specified, as in "animal babies" or "baby Chow [a breed of dog]." Often, when attempting to be colorful or witty, people indulge in these kinds of violations of feature attachment onto words. Sometimes these can be heard as insulting to humans, as when referring to someone as a "baby whale." The conditions fostering such a meaning as opposed to one of "offspring of a whale" are rooted in the communicative situation (Chapter 7).

Weinreich (1966) tabbed another way that semantic features can be used. He noted that in expressions like *pretty boy*, the feature of [+female] that inheres in *pretty* becomes **transferred** to *boy*, thus giving an implication to that word, implying that whoever he is, he is effeminate. Dylan Thomas' line, *a grief ago* similarly transfers the feature of [+time] onto *grief*, thus implying that, at least to Thomas, life is such woe that its times can be measured in grief. Expressions like *salty humor* or *the bouquet of the wine* are other instances of transfer features. Using words together that have semantic features that don't quite jibe is a regular way of achieving implication.

A good deal of meaning does reside in inherent semantic features of lexical items, although any item can be used in novel ways. Still, there are errors in lexical choice attributable to semantic features, such as

8. Doctor, I have pains in my chest and hope and wonder if my **box** is broken and heart is **beaten**.[7] (Maher, 1968 cited in Forrest 1986).

In the absence of strong contextualizing, *box* does not usually subsume the features of a human's chest. Moreover, hearts may be *beating*, but they are not usually *beaten*. The connection between *chest* and *box* is easily seen if one considers semantic features. Boxes fall into the category of chests in some usages. Both are concrete nouns which share the meaning of [+container, +rectangle, −animate]. However, the other meaning of *chest*, that of human anatomy, is neither rectangular nor inanimate. This error is like those of glossomania discussed in Chapter 1 and 2. First one meaning is taken, one appropriate to the context. Then a synonym of that word is evoked, the one inappropriate to the context, the [−animate] meaning. One result of linkages of words based upon shared lexical features is glossomanic chaining (Chapter 1, 9).

[7] The Mental Lexicon.

Over the years, in many models of grammar including the earliest Chomsky formulations, it has been assumed that our internal vocabularies, what is now usually called our MENTAL LEXICON consisted of a listing of words out of which our syntactic operations plucked, so to speak, the correct word for our intended meaning, and put it in its correct slot in the phrase or sentence we were formulating. Early on, Chomsky noted that there were syntactic constraints on some words which he termed SELECTIONAL RESTRICTIONS. For instance, *assassinate* is restricted to a human subject and a politically important human object, unless, of course, we are talking of a cartoon world in which, perhaps, a penguin could assassinate a polar bear. Even so, T–G grammars, like their structuralist predecessor, considered lexical selection somewhat apart from the purely syntactic generation of a sentence.

George Miller (1978, p. 61) emphasizes that items in our mental lexicons have so many kinds of information attached to them that they cannot be autonomous, that even the concept of selectional restrictions is too modest to portray their role in speech and thought. Each item carries with it syntactic information such as its part of speech, inflections it may or must carry, morphological information such as possible suffixes or prefixes, variety of pronunciations possible (e.g., the variation in the ending "-ing" as opposed to "-in'" as in *singing, singin'*), ways it can be written or printed, what its synonyms are, common phrases it may be embedded in, conceptual relations to other words or spheres of thought, specific cultural information, general information about what it refers to, mental pictures evoked by the word, and even etymologies. He likens our verbal storehouses to encyclopedias and affirms that the lexicon is also tied up to "...thoughts, memories, percepts, desires, feelings, intentions." Kearns (1984, pp. 85–108) also speaks of experience as being part of the language system.

Miller reminds us that "cognitive economy depends on the intelligible organization of what is learned," so that it is not likely that our mental lexicons are mere lists of words. In essence, we saw the complexity of the relations of words when we considered glossomania, showing that it can be explained by involuntary out-of-control triggering of lexical items, and all the forms that triggering can take are explicable by the complicated networks of words and phrases in our mental lexicons. Glossomanic chaining seems to be a trip through the mental lexicon, leaping from synonyms to rhymes to phrases to subject matter related to a word to emotional reactions. What it also indicates is that there is no sharp, dividing line between syntax and semantics, or, for that matter, the other components of a language. Yes, we can define separate levels of phonology, morphology, sentential syntax, and discourse, but, no, there is no sharp demarcation among categories. Language by its very nature has fuzzy borders.

[8] Meaning and Metaphor.

Interpretations of psychotic speech rest heavily on metaphor, at least on the assumption, and it is a reasonable one, that such speech is metaphorical. In this discussion, the word *metaphor* is used in its broadest sense to indicate all figurative uses of language, the tropes, including metonymy, synonymy, irony, simile, and synecdoche.

Over the past several years more and more linguists have been acknowledging the metaphorical nature of meaning, claiming that much of what we say even in ordinary speech, is metaphorical and all our abstractions are rooted in and extended from words with originally concrete meanings, with *rooted* here being a prime example of the process itself. The great analysts have said all along that all language is metaphorical, but this does not mean that analysts and linguists perceive metaphor the same way.

Psychoanalytical exegeses of metaphor do not necessarily concur with the kinds of interpretations offered by linguists and others currently involved in unraveling the mysteries of metaphor. Of course, scholarship being what it is, variation runs rampant even in a given field. The exact nature of metaphor, its relationship to concrete language, its basis in perceptual and cognitive structures, and the ways in which it is construed have been hot topics in linguistics, cognitive science, and philosophy for the past several years (e.g., Levin 1977; Rosch 1973, 1975, 1981; Ortony 1979; Mac Cormac 1985; Lakoff 1987).

As indicated above, there are many theoretical questions about metaphor and its nature, most of which are beyond the bounds of this book. Although we cannot claim a consensus in all matters, there are already significant insights into the relations between metaphors, the world, and meaning. By examining fields of everyday metaphor, we get good insights into the ways that metaphors are built and what should be the possible bounds on our interpretations of them. Except for pathological language, even highly metaphorical language is interpretable in terms of the words and grammar their creator used. Metaphors and other figures of speech operate according to certain principles.

Although figurative language has traditionally been considered to be apart from literal meaning, and still is by many scholars (Levin 1977, p. 31), it can be seen as well as part of ordinary, everyday meaning. Ortony (1979) points out that metaphor, if taken literally, is false, but that there are regular processes by which metaphors are given and received.

The specialized metaphors in the verbal arts are, by definition, more difficult to understand. It is acknowledged that they are created to cause readers and listeners to stop and ponder, to see new and unusual connections, but they are but one end of a cline of figurative meanings. Furthermore, no matter how difficult such metaphors may be to decipher, still the author had in mind some meaning and he gives clues as to what these are. It is not the case that any author creates a work of art such that the language in it can mean anything a reader thinks it does. For instance, consider Emily Dickinson's metaphor about "Cambridge ladies." She said they had *furnished souls*. The almost oxymoronic juxtaposition between *furnished* and *souls* shows us what smug, closed-minded, insensitive women these were. They were as immutable as furnished rooms.[8] Whether or not the reader instantly gets the same meaning as I did, he or she is capable of concurring or dissenting on the basis of the words in question. This is in direct contradiction to Forrest's interpretation of the passage in example 9 below. He has followed a long-standing practice in psychiatry of giving a global and highly individual interpretation of the entire passage rather than one based upon individual words within it.

Adrienne Lehrer (1983) shows that metaphor is achieved in expressions like *velvety wine* by ignoring the inherent features of *velvet* as a fabric, transferring its meaning of "soft." Literally, wine like velvet would be disgusting.

A major problem in schizophrenic speech has been whether or not its characteristic bizarre or opaque utterances are instances of wildly metaphoric language, and, if so, how may they be interpreted. This entire question impinges on discourse analysis (Chapters 7 to 11) and will be explored further then. The question we ask today is, "How do metaphors relate to what it is that they mean?" For instance, looking at the passage also discussed in sec. 6, Brendan Maher and David Forrest have come up with dramatically different interpretations of 8 above, here repeated:

> 9. Doctor, I have pains in my chest and hope and wonder if my box is broken and heart is beaten for my soul and salvation and heaven, Amen. (Maher, 1968 cited in Forrest 1986).

Maher, I believe correctly, interprets this as the patient's complaint about physical chest pains. Forrest, on the other hand, says that this is metaphorical. "The listener is told if he has ears for it what it is like to be schizophrenic . . . , but as no one who is not schizophrenic can fully empathize with this experience, the message is redirected to God's ear." Is this passage metaphorical or is it intended as a literal message, one that has gone wrong because of a speech dysfunction?

We can compare this with passages presented by Hallowell and Smith (1983) in which a patient describes himself as imprisoned, then speaks of ebbing sand below him, and of plummeting downward towards corrosive and sharp knife-like objects, such as acid, spikes, cobra spears, "tiger-hunting forks," and numerous blades. The vivid imagery of ground that is not firm and items which give horrendous pain seem to me to be a description of what it is like to be schizophrenic. Those of us who have never had the experience of being schizophrenic certainly can feel the horror that this patient is going through.

Forrest argues within a long established tradition. Levin (1977), for instance, believes metaphor is rooted in deviance[9] and is caused by a desire to be vivid, striking, or colorful (p. 31). He also says that metaphors are used to fill lexical gaps, giving as examples *foot* (of a mountain) and *neck* (of a bottle). One cannot deny the former assertion. Clearly, one reason for metaphorizing is to say something in a new way so that it will command attention or become more memorable, and just as clearly, sometimes, metaphors are used to fill lexical gaps. However, it is never the case that a metaphor **must** be employed to fill lexical gaps. For instance, a foot of a mountain can also be called its *base* or its *bottom,* or some totally new word, like "ponge"[10] could have been made up to indicate the lowest points on a mountain. It is never the case that a lexical gap has to be filled by a metaphorical meaning of an existing word. It is the case, nevertheless, even across languages, that metaphors are often used, that certain types of metaphors are made and that metaphors show certain directions of semantic flow. To use Levin's example again, French *piedmont* is a metaphorical extension of foot. Metaphors based upon the human body are legion: the leg of the table, the arm of the law, the head on the beer.[11]

Levin (p. 31) gives as an example of deviant usage, one which calls for special construal the term "devouring books," in which a term for eating transfers to reading. Actually, there is an entire set of metaphors correlating cognitive and gustatory ingestion and excretion: *juicy story, food for thought, consuming knowledge, gulping down facts, digesting information, indigestible news, regurgitating facts, spilled the beans* and *spewing words.* Like food, knowledge is assumed to enter the body, adding to whatever is already there, and, eventually, to exit the body as well, in English by metaphors evocative of vomiting. The very fact that we can find so many metaphors analogous to Levin's indicates that we are dealing with normal aspects of language, not deviant usages.

This is confirmed by several studies. Lakoff and Johnson (1980) and Lakoff (1987) have dissected everyday metaphors, showing that metaphor making is not simply a matter of creativity. They show that metaphors refer to cognition, that there is "a coherent conceptual organization underlying" metaphorical expression (Lakoff 1987, p. 381–405). Metaphors for anger, for instance, relate to the actual physiological changes wrought by anger: increased body temperature including a rise in the heat of blood, increased blood pressure, redness in the face, interference with accurate perception, the body as a container for emotions, and agitation. To give a very few examples of these, consider

- get hot under the collar
- a heated argument
- letting off steam
- blind with rage
- burst a blood vessel
- face red with anger
- blood was boiling
- shaking with anger
- reach the boiling point
- let him stew

There are even metaphors for extreme anger which refer to exploding, a combination of heat, agitation, and pressure rising to the point of explosion, as in

- she flipped her lid
- blew his stack
- hit the ceiling
- went through the roof

Lakoff (p. 386) observes that certain otherwise inexplicable idioms for anger actually are caused by these physiologically-based metaphors. For instance, expressions like "she had kittens when I told her" are based upon the model of "something that was inside causing pressure bursts out." This is related to metaphors like "he vented his anger."

Miller (1982, p. 68) shows how deixis, actually pointing to something, which is usually considered to be straightforward and literal, can also be metaphorical. For instance, in a restaurant, a waiter can point to a ham sandwich and say "the man in red" to mean "he ordered it" or "bring it to him." Similar usages occur with "the hot fudge sundae practically licked the plate clean" meaning "the person who ordered the hot fudge sundae . . ." There is an added metaphor here, that of a dog or other animal who likes its food. Metaphor suffuses every aspect of language and any utterance can contain several. Outside of *Dick and Jane*, it is hard to find speech which is not suffused with metaphor.

Sternberg, Torangeau, and Nigro (1979) themselves using a metaphor of a rubber band, point out that one can stretch a meaning of a word only up to a point, and then it snaps (pp. 334–335). The very metaphor they use to delineate the limits of metaphor seems to be one of those physiologically based metaphors which Lakoff and Johnson so aptly showed to be at the foundation of human metaphorizing. Meaning is *elastic,* we *stretch the truth,* we *bend the meaning* to our purpose, meaning is *flexible.* All of these are based upon the tactile and visual experience of bending and stretching materials to fit a purpose. It also occurs to me that we bend and stretch our bodies for purposes, such as stretching to reach something or bending to fit under something. Their metaphor aside, Sternberg et al. make an important point, which is that there are limits on metaphorical meaning. One cannot take a word and use it to mean anything else. The hearer has to be able to expand the meaning of the word(s) used and it is part of our normal linguistic baggage both as speakers and understanders that we recognize when the extension has snapped. One has to question seriously interpretations so strained (another metaphor of the *stretch* set) that normal decodings, even normal informed decodings cannot be traced to the words used according to any of the known strategies for producing or comprehending metaphors. By insisting upon such a restriction on interpretation, I am not saying that unusual metaphors are not interpretable. The essence of wit, of comedy, of drama, of the verbal arts in all their forms all depend upon novel metaphorizing, and, as we all know, sometimes we have to have metaphors explained to us. That is one function of the Talmudic scholar, the preacher of the Gospels, and the English professor. What I am saying is that those explanations must be based upon the kinds of extensions of meaning discussed here. They are word based. They are context based. One cannot claim a meaning for an entire discourse without referring it to its parts, and relating them to regular processes of meaning.

Rumelhart (1979) claims that the same comprehension strategies are used in interpreting figurative language as literal. He (p. 83) cites a study in which a student of his found that it took no longer to assign a figurative meaning to a sentence in context than it did to assign a nonfigurative one. What did take longer was assigning a meaning to a sentence out of context. This is not surprising since we get meaning in context.

Clark and Lucy (1975) had somewhat different results in an ingenious study. They provided subjects with pictures and asked them to determine if the picture matched an indirect request that they were given. In this study, indirect requests took longer to process if their underlying meaning was negative, so that "Must you open the door?" took slightly longer to match to an appropriate picture than did "Can you open the door?" Notice that "must you" is affirmative in syntactic form, but negative in actual meaning. Since other testing has shown that negative sentences can take longer to process than equivalent affirmative ones, Clark and Lucy interpreted their results to mean that people first compute a literal meaning and then match it to the context to derive the metaphorical one, a stage which Rumelhart denies. These are empirical issues, resolvable in the laboratory. Many philosophers such as Grice also assume that a literal reading is made first and then the figurative sense is construed. It must be emphasized, however, that even in the Clark and Lucy study, we are not talking about large time differences. They speak of time differentials like 0.3 seconds and many of their examples are confounded by another problem: in some of their examples they have mixed registers of formality. For instance, they paired "Can you open the door?" with "Must you open the door?" but the latter is more formal than the former. The equivalent would be "Do you have to open the door?" The specific outcome of questions like this is not an issue. What is the issue is that metaphorical language is processed the same way as literal language, using the same context-matching strategies, and, in ordinary circumstances, if there is a time differential between decoding literal and figurative speech, it is very tiny.

Since we can find pan-human metaphorizing, we can find it in the simplest of speech amongst all peoples, we cannot in justice assume that metaphorizing *per se* is deviance. Creating metaphors is normal. So is understanding them. We have to expect that schizophrenics can suffer disruption in this language activity as they do in others.

Fraser (1979, pp. 181–184) confirms again that context is as powerful a shaper of what metaphorical meaning as it is in literal meaning. I would go one step further and point out that metaphor is possible because of the context-dependency of language. That is, all linguistic constructions ultimately mean what the context allows them to mean. For this reason, we can use phrases that are patently untrue, but still manage to convey a real meaning. Fraser gave subjects 30 zero-context short metaphorical sentences. He avoided culturally common ones like "he's a dog" except as an example. The metaphors he crafted consisted of such things as "He/she is a *peanut butter and jelly sandwich/octopus/compass,* and *ripe banana.*" Although there wasn't necessarily one "most probable" interpretation, what he did find was that certain words definitely gave negative or positive connotations and that the same words used with *she* were interpreted quite differently from their use with *he*. This conforms to more literal uses of language as well, as in "He/she is a *tramp*, or *professional* or "He/she is *loose.*[12]"

A distinction is commonly made between dead and "live" metaphors, with expressions like *the heart of the matter* being recognized as having their origin in metaphor, but which are now so common that they are virtually literal. I think that this is a false dichotomy. Virtually any nonconcrete word can be seen to have as its origin a concrete one. It must be that human language started out with words only for the palpable, the visible, the smellable, and, by extension, these became more and more abstract. It is impossible to conceive of a word so concrete that it couldn't be used metaphorically. Somebody might even find a new way to use *heart* in yet another metaphorical sense. Perhaps we should view metaphors as ranging from those which everybody would accept in a given meaning to those which only a few would agree upon. Fraser's examples are proof of this. In American culture, what could be more concrete and specific than a peanut butter and jelly sandwich? Yet, before Fraser, I never heard of its being used to refer to a person. I daresay most of Fraser's subjects hadn't either, but they did give metaphorical interpretations of it, all different, to be sure, yet understandable to a member of this culture.

The issue of metaphor can even be construed politically. Szasz' (1976) vehement insistence that schizophrenics are political prisoners is based upon his faulty conception of metaphor. Like the psychiatrists he so roundly condemns, he sees metaphor holistically, as chunks of language to be analyzed as a whole, not in terms of the parts that comprise it, nor does he bow to any psycholinguistic understanding of how people actually use language. His interpretation of schizophrenia is that sufferers are imprisoned in hospitals because they persist in talking in "metaphors unacceptable to [their] audience, in particular to [their] psychiatrist" (p. 14). That is, if you say things psychiatrists don't like, don't believe, or don't understand, you better watch out or they'll imprison you in a mental hospital.

Everyday metaphorizing requires no special talent, and examination of the epics of primitive peoples reveal that it is not a product of special cultural achievement. Artists, of course, may have special talents in creating novel metaphors, but the ability itself is a general human one. Technologically-primitive peoples have again and again been shown to have the very same language capabilities that technologically advanced ones do. So-called primitives create poetry as brilliant and using the same devices as those of us who are supposedly of an advanced culture. Meaning is derived by regular strategies. It has to be or else language would be ultimately meaningless. Anything that anyone said could mean what anyone else says it does and that is patently untrue. One can't even imagine such a system evolving, and human language certainly has taken a special evolution. Even in the most figurative of language, there is meaning which can be rationally derived. When language is so deviant that none of our normal strategies for comprehending what is said, we have to say that the fault lies in the speech itself. The speaker has a dysfunction in verbal expression at that time.

[9] Implications for Theory.

The multileveled structure of language correlates with the almost bewildering variety of deviations in schizophrenic speech seen in the previous chapter. This will be confirmed when we consider psychotic deviations on the level of discourse. If these levels of language have any psychological reality, we should expect that deviance occurs in each, deviance which can be explained only by reference to each level.

Disruption proceeds from the top (discourse level) down, with the lower levels of language becoming disrupted as the patient deteriorates. This is probably the reason that there is no evidence at this time that phonological processes *per se* are disrupted as their realization is the most automated, whereas the higher the level of language, the more choices there are, the more judgments must be made. Hence, gibberish and neologizing which apparently arise from difficulties in word retrieval seem to represent the most severe level of SD schizophrenia and the fewest, albeit them most ill, patients have this difficulty.

Specifically, using the terminology of behavioral psychology—but not to its purposes—in language, two or more stimuli can—and certainly do—evoke the same response, and the same stimulus can—and certainly does—give two or more responses. Both processes seem universal, that is, appear in all languages. These are not rare phenonema, but pervasive in all languages. For instance, by their very nature, different allophones are heard as one phoneme, so that all phonemes in a language are instances of two or more stimuli evoking the same responses, and all cases of neutralization involve the same stimulus being responded to as if they were different. Moreover, the same disjunction between stimulus and response is observable on the levels of morphemes, words, and higher structures like phrases and sentences. All cases of ambiguity, for instance, are cases of the same stimuli being responded to as if they are different. In fact, since all words typically have several meanings, understanding them is clearly never a case of simple response to a stimulus. There is no isomorphism between the given signals and the received messages in any language.

At all levels of language, the processes used both to encode and decode are not amenable to casual introspection, nor are they amenable to deliberate manipulation. Consequently, it is highly unlikely that psychotic gibberish, neologizing, word salads, and incoherent discourses are deliberate.

Notes

[1]Julia does not even mention the newer Chomskyan constructs such as Government-Binding theory. Nor does he mention Montague grammars, or case and discourse grammars. He dismisses generative semantics and functional grammars in footnotes only, and he completely ignores pragmatics, systemic grammars, and the entire body of work in text linguistics.

[2]Testing to see how long it takes subjects to process sentences with various kinds of syntactic structures has been used to "prove" that one or another derivation is real. The supposition is that if subjects take longer to process a sentence with one kind of syntactic structure than another, the former has more complex derivation than the latter.

[3]In my now hopelessly outmoded dissertation (Chaika 1972), I showed that a grammar based upon such interrelationships can be used to explain deviant sentence production, whereas transformational grammar could not.

[4]This refers to putting the indirect object at the end of a sentence with the preposition *to,* as in "Mary gave Kevin candy" and "Mary gave candy to Kevin."

[5]Fillmore also shows that miscommunication can occur because of frame conflict, as when laypersons understand one meaning of *innocent* but lawyers understand it differently.

[6]These examples are not McCawley's. Neither he nor I have even attempted a complete listing. Readers should be able to supply more examples on their own.

[7]It has struck me that the patient might really have said *beating* using the pronunciation "beatin'."

[8]In Emily Dickinson's day, people didn't usually change their furniture every few years as they do today. What was bought was bought for life. There is the added meaning here of furnished rooms for rent, which certainly indicated that the furniture was about as forever as the landlord could get away with.

[9]By deviance, he does not mean "pathological," but deviant in that the word is not being used in its original sense which here he assumes is physical eating of actual food.

[10]As one examines language change over centuries, be it in lexicon, syntax, even some aspects of phonology, one cannot help but be struck by the degree to which items already in the language are extended and eventually even changed to effect new meanings brought about by technological or other changes in a culture. Although it is possible to make up entirely new words, it is more usual to extend the meanings of old ones.

[11]It has always struck me that heads on beer are based upon human heads rather than those of other mammals because human heads are on top, but most other mammals have heads in front of their bodies, but legs of a table or chair are more easily construed on the picture of a four-legged animal.

[12]This is changing for younger speakers who are used to finding women in the professions of law, medicine, and college professorships. When I was an adolescent, however, "she's a professional" was a metaphor for "she's a prostitute." This usage still survives in the expression, "The world's oldest profession."

Chapter Six

COHESION AND COHERENCE

Cohesion and coherence are Siamese twins and one cannot be discussed without the other. Overt cohesive ties do not necessarily create coherence, however. Some kinds of cohesive ties can lead to incoherence. A study of schizophrenic, manic and normal narrations showed differences between these populations but these were not caused by incidence of cohesive ties. Rather the number of ties were related to other factors.

[1] The Difference Between Coherence and Cohesion.

All studies of discourse are really studies of cohesion and coherence, of the ways that discourses are formed. The meanings of the words *coherence* and *cohesion* overlap. There are times when one is substitutable for the other, but a distinction can be made between the two. Typically, *coherence* refers to the logical macrostructure of discourses and texts to which all must relate, whereas *cohesion* refers more specifically to devices in the linguistic code which overtly mark what goes together. This last includes ellipsis, the omission of repeated material as well as cohesive ties like *and, but, or, however, if, after,* and *unless,* any of the words used to join two sentences together or to indicate how the parts of a discourse are related. It is not necessary to use actual overt ties in the linguistic code in order to produce coherent discourse. That is, discourse can be coherent with or without overt linguistic devices. For instance,

1. S: Do you think dolphins can really talk the way people do?
   H: We don't know yet.
   S: Better not eat tuna!

This is coherent provided both parties know that tuna fishermen are killing over 100,000 dolphins each year. There is no other overt, thus countable, cohesive tie linking H's comment with S's admonishment. VanDijk (1977, p. 46) demonstrated that "...connection [of parts of a

119

discourse] is not dependent on the presence of connectives" a proposition echoed by researchers like Fauconnier (1985) and Sanders (1987).

If one is trying to determine coherence on the basis of cohesion, the problem arises that much cohesion is effected by knowledge shared because of mutual histories as well as by the cultural and perceptual bonds usually referred to as *common knowledge.* A shared history is highly idiosyncratic so that communications sometimes fail because S has presumed that H knew about an event when, in fact, the H does not remember it. Still people usually know how much to give in an interaction, and, most of the time, if they err they can repair their contribution upon receiving clues from cospeakers such as "Huh?" "What are you talking about?" "Cycle me into a subject!¹" or even a facial expression.

[2] Sentence, Discourse, and Text.

It is possible to create a set of sentences which remain just that: a set of individual sentences. Although spoken and written discourses also contain sets of sentences, they are distinguished from collections of sentences in that they are perceived as belonging together: they cohere and they are coherent. A major issue in determining whether or not schizophrenics manifest linguistic deviance has centered on the issue of coherence. It is possible to produce a series of sentences, each of which is structurally nondeviant, without producing a coherent or cohesive discourse. The whole simply may not hang together.

Meaning typically is achieved beyond the unit of the sentence. Each sentence relates to others in the text or interaction so that the entire forms a macro meaning such that each sentence is interpretable in terms of the whole. Even on the relatively rare occasions when an individual sentence comprises the entire vehicle of linguistic expression, the meaning is achieved by comparing it to the nonlinguistic context.² Failure to achieve a coherent discourse is a problem of linguistic deviance as much so as is failure to produce a syntactically correct sentence. Just as people have slips of the tongue in which they catch themselves and self-correct a word, they have them in which they start a discourse, abandon it and start over to self-correct their presentation of a discourse. These can be signalled by messages like, "Wait a minute. Uhmmm . . . " "Oops!" "Scratch that . . . " "Oh- hold up. I forgot to tell you that first. . . . " and even "Let me start over. . . . " This is evidence of actual discourse structure analogous to sentence structure.

[3] Counting Cohesive Ties.

Rochester and Martin (1979) carefully and thoroughly analyzed the cohesive ties produced in three tasks: a half-hour unstructured interview, a summarizing of a short narrative, and a description of ten cartoons accompanied by an explanation of why they were funny. Their study had the merit of eliciting connected discourse in reasonably natural situations and of providing a context against which to check verbal output. This last provided an indication of what the speaker was trying to say. Thus deviance between psychotic speech and its target could be measured.

The Rochester and Martin study rested upon the categories and definitions of cohesive ties presented by Halliday and Hasan (1976). The latter have presented the same constructs in several of their subsequent works (Halliday 1985a; 1985b; Hasan 1985), with their analyses ever more finely tuned, but not changing in orientation. Overall, the entire *oeuvre* of Halliday and Hasan present an awesome taxonomy of cohesive devices. What is seductive to the scientist about their dissection of language is its precise terminology. It allows a countable objectivity. This, of course, is its beauty for psychological research. It presents categories of cohesive markers that are easily extracted from the text and which can be subjected to statistical analysis. Its only disadvantage is that it cannot be used for the kinds of coherence not dependent on overt cohesive ties.

Halliday and Hasan (1976, p. 31) first divide the lexicon into two categories: those which are interpreted semantically in their own right, and **reference** items which indicate that information is " . . . to be retrieved elsewhere (p. 31)." These include pronouns and demonstratives like *he, they, that, those;* and comparatives like *better than last night's* (p. 82) in sentences like "That performance was better than last night's." **Reference** can be specific or not, a message typically given by the choice of article in English, *the* being definite, and *a* indefinite. There is also **deixis**[3]: determiners or pronouns which point to something in or out of the text, hence are **deictic**. These include the demonstratives like *this, that* and *those.*

Conjunctions, both coordinating and subordinating, exist primarily to create cohesion (Halliday and Hasan 1976, pp. 226–273; Halliday 1985, pp. 302–309; p. 317). Halliday and Hasan (pp. 242–243) divide these into four categories: **additive** (*and, nor, or else*), **adversative** (*but, yet, though*), **causal** (see below) and **temporal** (see below). Each of these are subcategorized. There are four[4] subcategories of causal conjunctions, for instance:

Simple causal: *so, then, hence therefore.*
Emphatic: *consequently, because of this*
Reason *for this reason*
Result *in consequence*

and subcategories of temporal conjunctions:

Sequential *then, next*
Simultaneous *just then, at the same time*
Preceding *previously, before that*
Conclusive *finally, at last*

Note the overlap of form and function on even this brief sample of their listing. That the same words do double and triple duty—or more—is no surprise, but what it means is that we are not dealing with simple unambiguous connectors. They have to be interpreted within the context that they are used, a circumstance that renders counting with attendant statistical verification dependent upon the researchers' judgment.

Ellipsis, leaving out repeated words and structures, is a powerful cohesive device (Halliday and Hasan 1976, pp. 144, 204–5; Halliday 1985, pp. 317), as it forces hearers or readers to fill in the blanks, so to speak, by reference to a prior or, more rarely, following utterance, as in (examples mine)

2A. Maxwell totaled his new car, his father's, and his sister's.
2B. Having totaled his new car, Maxwell left home.

In 2A, cohesion is effected by the hearer's having to provide the elements *Maxwell totaled . . . car* which have been left out after their first appearance. The recipient of the message is forced to go backwards to fill in the obviously missing constituents. In 2B, the hearer anticipates that the subject of *having totaled* will be provided shortly.

Chomskyan grammar called such processes DELETION of repeated material, implying that one has created the entire structure and then, before uttering it, deleted repeated material. A more pragmatic view of grammar assumes that one knows what one has just said, so one just doesn't repeat it. Rather, one utters only what is not repeated. Either way, leaving out repeated elements is a prime way of indicating cohesion between clauses and sentences. One must remember, however, that one cannot just leave out repeated material. Cohesion is forced because the hearer must bear in mind the entire discourse in order to supply the missing words. One is forced to consider the individual sentences as part of a macrostructure and to interpret in the light of that macrostructure.

Sometimes the language allows omissions, but at others, one must instead use pronouns and other such markers.[5] These also force one to go backwards to what has been mentioned. Other pronouns and markers point outward to the physical context. Halliday and Hasan subdivide reference into ANAPHORA and CATAPHORA, the first referring to reference to an already uttered word and the second to reference to what is coming. They subsume all categories of reference to other linguistic forms under ENDOPHORA, as a contrast to exophora which points outward to something in the nonverbal context. Such delicacy of categorization is unnecessary and serves no readily apparent useful purpose when applied to real language data such as schizophrenic speech. The processes of anaphora and cataphora are really two instances of the same thing: reference to another point in the verbal interaction. Giving these yet a further term, endophora, which subsumes both cataphora and anaphora in their analysis, adds no useful analytic tool. These are distinctions without differences.

Hasan and Halliday's intricacy of labelling, far from enhancing our understanding of cohesion, obfuscates it by a network of terminology which fails to capture the essential principles of cohesion: whatever is known to interactors is either omitted or replaced by a pro-word, whichever the rules of the given language allows. What is known includes the immediate physical context as well as cultural and personal matters. Furthermore, cohesion is also actuated by including the mutually shared history of interactors. Endophora is, in effect, exophora when it points to mutual knowledge given by shared interactions, pointing out of current linguistic production to a past one.[6]

In addition, within one interaction with two parties able to see and hear the same physical setting, exophora is merely a way of not repeating what is evident in the context, a fundamental principle of all successful language production. That is, it really does not function any differently from endophora. In endophora, one says, "look elsewhere in this conversation for my reference," whereas in exophora, one says, "look at the physical setting of this conversation for the elsewhere of this reference" or "look at knowledge we share by virtue of our personal histories or culture."

Admittedly, my view is a radical departure from the usual assumption that exophora is a less worthy category of reference than endophora (Bernstein 1971; Schatzman and Strauss 1972). The reason for this appears to be the assumption that the illiterate are more likely to use exophora than the literate.[7] Even Halliday and Hasan admit that exophora is a cohesive device because it ties the utterance to the immediate context even though it points out of the narrative itself. It seems to me that an effective cohesive device is effective whether or not it points out of the narrative. In fact, an argument could be made that use of anaphora when exophora would be more direct and equally cohesive comprises faulty utilization of cohesive resources. However, it is not the business of this study or any other to decide *a priori* that some modes of cohesion are more equal than others, much less superior.

More traditionally, in the sense of what scholars take as conventional wisdom, Halliday and Hasan (1976, p. 18) feel that "Exophoric reference is not cohesive, since it does not bind the two elements together in a text." This conclusion is a natural one given their emphasis on cohesion as opposed to coherence. Moreover, their position is clearly tied to written language, in which exophoric reference is highly limited. In oral communication, exophoric reference to the physical setting can be just as cohesive as endophoric reference to prior verbiage.

Ehlich (1982, p. 327–329) suggests that anaphora and deixis actually do different things. Anaphora binds, but deixis focuses. It includes terms like *over here* or *that one.* If too much deixis occurs, he says that it is tantamount to a constant request for focusing, which is confusing if you are already focused. In other words, he sees frequent instructions like, "the one over here" or "that one over there" as being confusing by asking hearers to focus. Unfortunately, neither the Rochester and Martin study nor my own elicited examples of such refocusing, so this contention could not be re-examined. However, just as skill is required in using anaphora so as not to confuse, there is skill in deixis. One is not necessarily inferior to the other in interaction. As we shall see, such apparently trivial differences in how one views one type of cohesive tie as opposed to another, can lead to quite different interpretations of results. Again, as so often, linguistic analysis is tricky, fraught with innocent perils.

Halliday and Hasan (1976, p. 10–11) and Halliday (1985) do recognize that discourse is held together by covert as well as overt cohesive ties, noting "Cohesion refers to the range of possibilities that exist for linking something with what has gone before." Cohesion includes relations in meaning, a set of semantic resources. Since one can easily find some kind of semantic relationship between disparate sentences not occurring in a discourse, Halliday and Hasan offer as a guide a useful heuristic, saying a meaning relationship that is coherent is "... one in which ONE ELEMENT IS INTERPRETED BY REFERENCE TO ANOTHER" (Halliday 1985, p. 195) (caps Halliday's). The taxonomy of overt cohesive ties presented by Halliday and Hasan produce overt messages telling how one segment relates to others. In contrast, semantic ties are covert features signalling relationships among parts of the whole discourse. My criticism is that their taxonomy creates a confusing welter of terminology without providing superior explanatory power.

Brown and Yule (1983, p. 24) explain that Halliday and Hasan's categories derive from a **text-as-product** view, which does not take into account how a text is produced. Brown and Yule's view is "best character-ized as a **discourse-as-process** view," a view implicit in Kreckel (1981), Levinson (1983), and Sanders (1987), as, of course, in my own work. Halliday (1985) claims that cohesion itself is a property of text, but how it is used makes the difference between something which is a text and something which is not, as well as the difference between one kind of text and another.

Halliday and Hasan (1976, p. 7; Halliday 1985, p. 54) actually warn that it is a mistake to use their categories of cohesion as a method of text analysis. Why have they developed them, then? Their position is that text itself is a semantic creation, so that, ultimately, all textual analysis depends upon interpretation.

Strangely, Halliday (1985, p. 54) also perceives grammar as arising from an "automatic realization of the semantic choices (p. 54)." It is true that one is not aware of the grammatical choices one makes, but there is never just one choice available to convey a meaning; therefore, choices cannot be automatic. All meanings are paraphrasable. It is precisely the automatic character of much SD speech which causes its deviance. This poses an interesting paradox. By looking at other elements in the utterance, we can **explain** glossomania because we can see how the words used are related in terms of formal description of the lexicon. However, we cannot **interpret** that same glossomania. There is never just one way to actuate cohesion. Therefore, to gain insight into our sense that speech does or does not cohere, it is fruitful to discuss the ways that language is made to cohere in discourse. The researcher is essentially working as a hearer, first figuring out what someone is trying to say and then diagnosing the locus of error.

[4] Ellipsis and Cohesion.

Ellipsis is a vital cohesive device, and must be included in any analysis of cohesion in any linguistic production. Ellipsis works because missing elements of sentence structure can be supplied. That is, the parts of the sentence which have not been overtly produced are retrievable by reference to prior utterances in the given situation. Occasionally, they are retrievable by looking forward, warning the hearer that something is on its way to elucidate. Participles commonly are placed at the start of a sentence in writing so that one knows that the missing subject is coming as in "Having totalled the car, Max left home."

Ellipsis can be seen to work across interactions so that one need not state what is known from previous interactions. Kreckel (1981) found that people who interact a great deal understand each other the most as they have a shared history. In other words, the more people know each other, the less they have to say to convey information.

With nouns, ellipsis omits the entire noun phrase, as

2A. The cat in the hat ate the mat and said his prayers.

2B. Mary, Kay, and Elizabeth went downtown, bought purple high heels, and wore them to the prom, dancing all night and getting terrible blisters on their toes.

Here *the cat in the hat* is not repeated, nor is *Mary, Kay, and Elizabeth.*

With verbs, ellipsis involves leaving out the entire repeated construction as in 3A and 3:

3. Max has been buying junk bonds, Bartholomew has been buying preferred stocks, and Andy, penny stocks.

In 3A, the entire verb phrase *has been buying* was omitted in "Andy, penny stocks," but we have no difficulty in supplying it. If a question "Who was buying junk bonds?" is asked, however, then the answer would include only the auxiliary, as in "Max has." This option is also open in instances of exact repetition of the entire verb phrase including the object, as in "Max has been buying junk bonds and Bartholomew has, too."

Ellipsis is not to be confused with unjustified omissions, items left out that are not retrievable by the hearer. In my study of schizophrenic narration (Chaika 1982e, 1983b; Chaika and Alexander 1986; Chapter 8) schizophrenic narratives were found to contain aberrant omissions. These were not ellipses because the omitted words did not refer to anything prior or subsequent in the narrative. These omissions were especially notable because they cannot be made grammatically under any circumstance, as seen in:

3A. ... he was blamed **for** and I didn't think that was fair ...

3B ... what are **the** and uh there was a scene

3C ... and asks if she can **have** then goes to the ice cream place.

In 3A and B, we know that nouns were omitted because they were preceded by a preposition and a noun determiner. In 3C, the *have* requires a direct object which isn't there. In 3C we know there has to be a noun as direct object, but it, too, is missing. These omissions are the equivalent of uttering an inflectional ending without uttering the root word in a declined language like Russian. There is no circumstance in English which allows such omissions.

These examples illustrate the dangers of mere counting in determining cohesion. If we were simply counting items left out that could fill a certain slot, we might easily accidentally confound these with ellipsis. We know that he was blamed for *it* and that she wanted *ice cream*, but these are as much in error as 3B in which the omission is not so readily retrievable. The problem inheres in the English rules for ellipses themselves which do not allow ellipses to operate by omitting the noun after a preposition, an article or a transitive verb. Pronouns are required in these positions.

Although, in most instances, the intended word could be retrieved by the listener since she had viewed the videotape with the patient, still such omissions are not allowable ellipses in normal speech. This kind of ellipsis is not cohesive. There is no reason to assume that the person who makes such an erroneous ellipsis[8] does so voluntarily. It seems truly dysfunctional, a conclusion bolstered by the fact that only schizophrenics did it. Rochester and Martin do not mention this kind of ellipsis, but it certainly occurred in my own study and only in schizophrenics.

Given the generally strong evidence that the patients were trying to cooperate in the task, and given their other genuine disruptions in speaking ability, disruptions which occur in many patients diagnosed as schizophrenic, and disruptions in speech competence not readily controlled by speakers, such as producing word salads, glossomanic strings, and leaving out a vital element in a syntactic construction, it seems most likely that these omissions are a product of deficit in speech production. 3A, B, and C illustrate. All occurred in patients with discharge diagnoses of schizophrenia. All were contained in narratives elicited by watching the same videotape.

[5] Anaphora and Pro-words.

Anaphora is also achieved by systems of pronouns and equivalent replacement forms for other parts of speech. For instance,

> 3A. Max had been looking at *the sprawling bright green ramshackle Victorian house on the corner that looks like a haunted house.* He bought **it** the other day.
>
> 3B. I'd like a **blue one** myself.

The *it*, like all of the pronouns commonly referred to as the "personal" ones, replaces the entire noun phrase starting with the determiner *the* and ending with the complete prepositional phrase ending in *haunted house*. In 3B, we see the phenomenon of the pronoun *one* which replaces every word in the noun phrase except for the one word which is different. In this instance, the adjective *green* is replaced by *blue*. Although not always recognized as such, *one* functions as an anaphoric pronoun which allows modifiers to be used with it, giving the meaning of "one just like the noun phrase just mentioned except for this one distinction."

In the following, we see both personal pronouns and the verb replacers *do* and *so do*. For the sake of convenience, I call these pro-verbs.

> 4A. Max and Alex steal cars for a living and so **do** Rob and Bob. **They** will all go to prison someday.
>
> 4B. Max steals cars for a living and so **does** Alexis. **She** was influenced by **him**.
>
> 4C. Max stole cars for a living and so **did** Alex.

There are other such replacement words like *that way* and *like this* which replace adverbs of manner and *such* which replaces adjectives.

> 5. Marilyn bakes wonderful bread by kneading the dough with her feet, so I always **do it like that**.
>
> 6. Heloise wears sexy, clingy, vinyl outfits I wish I could wear **such** outfits.

If such cohesive devices are not used, the result can be near chaos, as in

> Well I want to work for god in the mission and to work for god in the mission you have to be able to speak and think in a lord tongue in

my opinion now to speak and think in a lord tongue you have to have to be able to memory the process memory the parle—the process in the bible[9] the thought pattern the brain wave and your thought process must be healthy enough and your legs must be healthy enough to when you want to study and and from when you want to study and progress in the way of the lord you should read the bible and as you read the bible you should if you are in good shape physical and mental and mental good shape and physical good shape you should be able to acquire the memory knowledge necessary as to study the bible to speak and think in a lord tongue you should be able to memory all the knowledge down on down on the page in the bible book to work for god in the mission now in the position I am in now with the medicate and with the hospital program I am being helped but at the same time that I am being help with the food and medicate the food and medicate and the the food and medicate and the and the ah rest I feel that I still do not have this I still not have the thought pattern and the mental process and the brain wave necessary to open up a page open up the old testament and start to memory. . . . (courtesy of Bonnie Spring).

Had the speaker used *do that* for all his expressions of wanting to be able to study the bible and think in the lord's tongue, this would be far easier to follow, as it would be if he had employed pronouns and used ellipsis for the repetitions of *food and medicate.* In language, less is definitely more.

[6] Lexical Cohesion.

Another Hallidayan category, LEXICAL COHESION, presents even greater problems. Here, an apparent cohesive device turns out to be the antithesis of cohesion and coherence. Lexical cohesion consists of words which are semantically related (Halliday and Hasan 1976, pp. 318–320; Halliday 1985, pp. 310–313; p. 317). For instance, if I am speaking of my house, and then say "the door . . . ," lexical cohesion is effected, provided that I am speaking of the door to my house. Even if words in adjacent sentences or within a sentence can be shown to have a semantic connection, they may not cohere. Consider this segment produced by patient X, a segment abounding with lexical cohesion. She is discussing her medication:

... Speeds up the metabolism. Makes your life shorter. Makes your heart bong. Tranquilizes you if you've got the metabolism I have. I have distemper just like cats do, 'cause that's what we all are. Felines. [pause]. Siamese cat balls. They stand out. I had a cat, a manx, still around somewhere. You'll know him when you see him. His name is GI Joe he's black and white. I had a little goldfish too like a clown. [pause] Happy Halloween Down...." (Chaika 1974, p. 261).

It is precisely the fact of lexical cohesion that makes this narrative deviant, giving it its schizophrenic flavor (Lecours and Vanier-Clement 1976; Werner, Lewis-Matichek, Evans and Litowitz 1975; Maher, 1972; Chaika 1982a). Glossomania is lexical cohesion, although lexical cohesion is not always glossomania.

Ragin and Oltmanns (1986) found that in an acute phase of illness, schizophrenics, manics, and schizoaffectives manifested the same amount of within clause lexical cohesion, but, during remission, manics and schizoaffectives showed a significant decrease which coincided in improvement in clinical ratings of their speech. Schizophrenics, however, showed no such decrease in within clause lexical cohesion. Unfortunately, these authors, like so many psychologists, failed to give speech samples, so I am assuming, and I may be wrong, that the lexical cohesion they speak of is the same as that described here.

Lexical cohesion in itself does not advance the topic of a discourse, so that a string of lexically tied sentences can form an incoherent passage (Fahnestock 1983). Discussing the general proposition that cohesive ties as a whole do not guarantee what Halliday and Hasan call *texture*, e.g., 'textness', Enkvist gives an apparently made-up example of lexical cohesion which does not cohere. Comparing this with schizophrenic glossomania, we see the similarities:

> 7. I bought a Ford. A car in which President Wilson rode down the Champs-Elysees was black. Black English has been widely discussed. The discussions between the Presidents ended last week.... (quoted in Brown and Yule 1983, p. 197)
>
> 8. My mother's name was Bill ... and coo? St. Valentine's Day was the start of the breedin' season of the birds. I like birds ...

To my knowledge, Enkvist has done no work on the problem of psychotic speech; however, his *reductio ad absurdem* to illustrate the noncohesiveness of lexical items hits the mark. What he predicted would happen does happen with one population, SD psychotics.

The deviation in 8 is not caused by the untrue or bizarre semantic message. Enkvist's example contains only true (or potentially true) information, but it is as deviant as the schizoid passage about the mother's name and birds. It is possible to have fantastic and even absurd imagery in coherent language. *Alice in Wonderland* is a case in point. Coherence (and competence) in discourse is not a question of beliefs or cognition or of potentially true or untrue images and events. It is a matter of handling language competently. The essence of language is that it is tied neither to truth nor reality. Bizarreness in psychotic speech occurs because of incompetent handling.

Fauconnier (1985, pp. 14–15) shows that pragmatic connectors map what we have in our minds onto language so that a hearer can construct a mental representation of that. Such mapping can be achieved by expressions like *in reality, in Len's painting,* or *the little red fox was dressed in a red cape.* Fauconnier demonstrates that truth or possibility of what is said is not an issue. Fantasy is a mapping of imaginary worlds on to ordinary language. Error is a mapping of a wrong mental representation. The issue for cohesion is the link between mental representations and how they are mapped onto language. In such a view, psychotic speech would not be deviant because of what is represented, but because of how it is represented. In SD speech incoherence is perceived when we cannot find the representation of what the speaker believes because the output lacks consistency or the language used is so remote that the hearer can't build up a mental representation. Fauconnier elaborates on a system by which what is in one's mind, **mental spaces**, are introduced by what he calls **space builders**, pragmatic connectors to the mental space.

Until the ICS discussed here, the most systematic and thorough study of cohesion in a schizophrenic population, indeed, the one which inspired my own, was Rochester and Martin's (1979) *Crazy Talk.* My own study was inspired by theirs, but it differed in several respects from it, accounting for differences in our results. However, the differences were also caused by differences in orientation in our views on Hasan and Halliday and on cohesion in general. The number of cohesive ties in a discourse do not themselves account for coherence or cohesion. Apparently, psychotic deficits proceed from larger cognitive deficits at least at the time of psychotic bouts.

[7] The Rochester and Martin Study.

Rochester and Martin (1979), relying on Halliday and Hasan (1976), characterized schizophrenic narratives in terms of failures to employ cohesive ties. They considered five categories: REFERENCE, SUBSTITUTION, ELLIPSIS, CONJUNCTION, AND LEXICAL COHESION (pp. 76–77). They further analyzed these cohesive ties in terms of whether or not they were endophoric or exophoric (p. 146).

They gave subjects three tasks: a half-hour unstructured interview, a summarizing of a short narrative, and a description of ten cartoons accompanied by an explanation of why they were funny. Their study had the merit of eliciting connected discourse in reasonably natural situations and of providing a context against which to check verbal output. This last provided an indication of what the speaker was trying to say. Thus any deviance between the psychotic speech and what it was trying to encode could be measured.

Rochester and Martin found that the psychotic patients are capable of creating complex syntactic structures although they relied more on lexical cohesion and exophora than their normal controls did. These researchers concluded that TD[10] schizophrenic patients "choose not to [use complex structural elements] when the information to be encoded is provided by the situational context" (p. 203). This last conclusion is based upon the fact that TD psychotics used more exophora based upon the immediate surroundings than did others. However, the simple fact that patients used exophora does not mean that they chose not to do something else. It is as warranted to say that psychotics are not as able to handle complex routines as nonpsychotics are; hence, they rely more upon simpler kinds of cohesive devices if you believe that exophora is simpler than anaphora. In sum, Rochester and Martin did not determine that their results came from diminished linguistic capacity in TD patients. However, an assumption of diminished capacity is also a reasonable interpretation of their data.

[8] Narrative Sampling and its Effect on Results.

Rochester and Martin (1979) utilized a random sampling of normal narratives for their analysis, comparing these with non randomly selected passages from schizophrenic narratives. The passages selected were those rated most incoherent by their judges. Thus, Rochester and Martin are really talking about **passages,** not **speakers,** in their conclusions about the differences between normal and schizophrenic speech. However, they claim that their findings refer to TD schizophrenics.

They report that 10% of their normals did produce incoherent passages (Rochester, Martin and Thurston, 1977), **but these incoherent passages were not included in the analyses** unless they were randomly selected. Thus, Rochester and Martin by design compared the most disrupted schizophrenic passages with a random sampling of normal passages.

In contrast, this study compared entire narratives from each population, so that results are based upon comparisons between the entire performance of speakers. For this reason, the results reported here and those of Rochester and Martin (1979) are not directly comparable. Also, since I tested only for narrative ability but Rochester and Martin also tested for description of cartoons and for performance in an unstructured interview, again our results are not completely comparable.

[9] The Ice Cream Stories.

Because a characterization of psychotic failure in narrations did not seem to be captured by the Halliday and Hasan view of cohesion, I made an analogous study of psychotic narration (Chaika 1982e, 1983b; Chaika and Alexander 1986). My own procedure was somewhat different from Rochester and Martin's. First, being somewhat more tolerant of exophora, I devised the narrative task to be set up so that the stimulus materials were not in view; hence, ordinary exophora would not be elicited. In the Rochester and Martin study, the materials upon which patient discourses were based were in view. Hence, respondents could easily—and cohesively—use exophora. By not keeping the stimulus materials in view, I was successfully able to minimize normal effective exophora. To put it another way, Rochester and Martin's findings of increased exophora amongst schizophrenics may not have been improper exophora. Of course, it may have been. They do not present enough of their narrative samples to determine this. They simply considered it undesirable. My methodology decreased the chances of normal, proper, effective exophora, so when exophora did occur, it was not the most effective mode of reference. Narrators could not just point to the stimulus as it was no longer in view. Therefore, when exophora was used, it was improperly resorted to. Under these circumstances, exophora is less competent than anaphora by any standards.

The ICS (*The Ice Cream Stories*) was based loosely upon Wallace Chafe's (1980) *The Pear Stories*. In the latter, subjects were shown a movie, then asked to narrate what it was that they had seen. Although it was only about six minutes long, the movie was both too long and potentially too disturbing to be shown to a psychotic population as it dealt with theft of pears as well as a fall from a bicycle. Because Chafe wished to elicit narratives from speakers of a wide variety of languages, there was no dialogue in the movie. In terms of a psychotic population, a movie with its attendant paraphernalia was potentially far too distracting.

A very simple 124-second videostory, henceforth called the ICS, was prepared. The storyline was simple, but it related an incident familiar to most Americans. The first scene pans a shopping center, closing in on the figure of a little girl looking through the window of a Baskin Robbins store. The next scene shows a woman setting a table, and the same girl walking into the room asking, "Mommy, can I have some ice cream?" whereupon the mother leans down, puts an arm around her and says gently, "No, honey, it's too close to suppertime." Then a man is seen walking into the house. The child walks up to him, touching her body to his. He says, "Hello, Stefanie." Then she asks, "Daddy, can I have ice cream?" The father looks into the camera with a grin, and his hand moves towards his pants pocket. The next scene shows the child walking towards the Baskin Robbins store, entering, leaning against the counter as she waits fidgeting. Then a clerk comes into view, asking it he can help her. She responds inaudibly, but the man repeats clearly, "Double grape ice." The child plays with coins, still leaning on the counter. The man returns with a very large double-decker cone. The girl gives him the money which he looks at, then rings up on the register. A bell chimes on the register. The man gives her change, and says, "Thank you. Come again." The girl turns towards the camera with a triumphant smile, pushes the door and goes out. A sound of "Oh wow" comes from outside the door. The film ends there.

Dialogue was intentionally included in this video in order to test if patients comprehended normal speech. The father is not actually shown giving the child the money because I wanted to see if patients would make the logical deduction that he must have given her the money. The beauty of such a study is twofold. First, showing it on a small TV in a lounge area emulated a common occurrence, one familiar to all participants in the study. Second, it was easy to correlate what was said to what it was the narrator was ostensibly trying to encode.

[10] Procedure.

The videostory was shown to all subjects individually. Immediately upon its completion, each was asked to tell what it was he or she had just seen. Psychotic subjects viewed The ICS on a 12″ JVC monitor in a lounge at Butler Hospital in Providence, R.I. All responses were recorded on an Olympus Perlcorder which subjects themselves could hold. This was done to make the situation as nonthreatening as possible. Normal subjects viewed the tape individually in booths in the Providence College Audio-Visual Lab, and their narrations were then also immediately recorded with the Perlcorder upon completion of viewing. As with the hospitalized subjects, the normals were interviewed one at a time, not in groups.

This procedure of interviewing each participant immediately upon completing viewing ensured that the same amount of time had passed in between viewing and narrating for each subject. In Chafe's study, all participants viewed the movie together, but then were taken one by one to recount what they had seen. Thus, some of his subjects had more time for the story to "cook" than others did.

[11] Selection of Psychotic Subjects.

As in Rochester and Martin (1979, pp. 57–60), patients who had received ECT treatments or whose psychoses were drug-induced or due to brain lesions or tumors were excluded from this study, as were patients who did not receive a discharge diagnosis of schizophrenia or mania.

Also, like Rochester and Martin's study (1979, p. 58), diagnosis was arrived at by consensus of the attending psychiatrist, Paul Alexander, and other members of the treatment team. Diagnosis was according to DSM II and DSM III, and all diagnoses were blind as to whether or not patients had been selected for this study. The preselected patients were then invited to participate in the study.

Because this study is concerned with structurally strange speech, not necessarily strange content, mental health workers on the Intensive Treatment Unit were briefed to note patients who evinced some of the features associated with schizophrenic speech: glossomania, neologizing, gibberish, opposite speech, inappropriate rhyming or punning, word salads, perseverations, or faulty cohesion (Chaika 1974, 1982a,c). The actual examples used were:

- Gibberish

He had [fŬč] with [tʰeykraⁱmz]

- Glossomania, chaining of words or phrases which are not pertinent to a governing macrostructure, such as a topic of a conversation, as in:

...My mother's name was Bill...and coo? St. Valentine's day is the official startin' of the breedin' season of the birds. All buzzards can coo. I like to see it pronounced buzzards rightly. They work hard. So do parakeets....; (Chaika 1974, p. 260)

- Rhyming and alliterating inappropriate to the topic or occasion of the discourse: I had a little goldfish like a clown. Happy Hallowe'en down. (Chaika 1974, p. 261)

and, in response to "Hello, anyone here want some coffee?: "Head, heart, hands, health." (Chaika 1974, p. 269)

- Neologisms: "...you have to have a *plausity* of amendments to go through for the children's code, and it's no mental disturbance of *puterience,* it is an *amorition* law." (Vetter, 1968)
- Word salads and other disturbances in syntax: "...you should be able to acquire the memory knowledge down on down on the page in the bible book to work for god in the mission now in the position I am in now with the medicate and with the hospital program." (Chaika 1982a)
- Inappropriate repetitions: "...I am being helped but at the same time that I am being help with the food and the medicate and the food an medicate and the an the ah rest I feel that I still do not have this I still not have the thought pattern..." (Chaika 1982a)

It was not expected that any one would necessarily produce all or even most of these, and, in fact, nobody did. As with other disrupted speech most of each narrative was decodable, albeit not necessarily by the usual strategies for comprehension. Of the original 24, 2 were dropped because it was discovered that they probably had drug-induced psychoses. As a result of the selection procedure, 22 patients completed the experimental task. Of these, 14 had discharge diagnoses of schizophrenia and 8 had discharge diagnoses of mania.

Butler Hospital is a mental hospital affiliated with Brown University Medical School. Treatment and care is, and was at the time of this study, a staff matter. All mental health workers met daily with other staff, including psychiatrists and psychologists, and with patients. The workers, then, were encouraged, as a matter of policy, to pay close attention to patient behavior, and their observations were taken seriously. The team approach at this hospital lent itself well to selection of appropriate subjects by the mental health workers.

More importantly, confidence in their judgement was enhanced because of the precision of the criteria for selection. The workers and other staff were briefed by the principal researcher on the structural deviations as defined in the preceding section. These workers had no part in further judging the narratives. Rather, two outside raters determined whether or not each narrative was produced by a psychotic or a normal speaker. These judgments were made while listening to each tape while reading its transcript. Judges considered three narratives from normals to be psychotic and one from a psychotic to be normal. These misjudgments were not based upon any differences in use of cohesive ties; however, they were clearly based upon other features of the narratives (Chapter 8).

To assess the reliability of the lay judges' classification of the narratives, a phi coefficient was calculated (phi = .91, N = 47). This confirms the high reliability of the two judges in making the classification of narratives as produced by normal or psychotic narrators. Of the 25 normal narratives, 20 were judged normal by both judges, 3 were judged psychotic by both judges, and 2 were judged psychotic by one judge. Of the 22 psychotic, 21 were judged psychotic by both judges while 1 was judged normal by both judges. The reasons for these incorrect judgments were all related to features of the narratives as shown in Chapter 8.

Rochester and Martin (1979, pp. 58–60) used lay judges, asking them to judge written transcripts and to " . . . mark those segments which they had difficulty in following . . . in which the flow of talk seemed disrupted (p. 59)." On this basis, patients were subdivided into two groups: thought disordered or nonthought disordered, a dichotomy which commented on extensively elsewhere by me and my colleague, Richard Lambe (Chaika 1974, 1981, 1982d; Chaika and Lambe 1985, see Chapter 3). In the ICS, lay judges selected patients on the basis of disrupted speech.

The deviant speech behaviors constitute the operational definition of the selection process. In short, since we wished to characterize differences between speech identifiable as "schizophrenic" and normal speech, we invited as participants only those patients whose speech was first judged deviant by the attending staff and, upon the initial interview, by the principal investigator. This particular study is concerned solely with ascertaining what it is in some schizophrenic speech that causes people to call it "thought disordered" or "crazy." This has been the thrust in most of comparisons between normal and schizophrenic speech.

That the patients were preselected for deviance does not prejudice the formal analysis in any way since the details of the analysis are not evident in active listening, but required repeated reference to the written transcripts of the patients' narratives. The kinds of cohesive ties utilized in this study and the fine grained analysis of the data are independent of the selection criteria. This was true also of Rochester and Martin's study (1979; p. 56).

[12] Schizophrenic Versus Manic Speakers.

Several studies have shown that the performance of manics on some tasks is like that of schizophrenics, so that what is usually thought of as schizophrenic behavior, such as the constellation of speech disorders just mentioned also occurs in manics (Chaika 1977; Simpson and Davis 1985; Kufferle, Lenz, and Schanda 1985).

All psychotic subjects in this study, manics and schizophrenics, were receiving neuroleptic medications, as well as Lithium and antiparkinson medications (Alexander, VanKammer, and Bunney 1979). Since the effects of these medications are to reduce psychotic symptoms, including deviant speech, if anything they would mitigate deviation, not enhance it. Hence, any observed differences between the normal and psychotic populations may be taken to be very real.

The average stay at the hospital during the time of this study ranged from 11 to 14 days, and no subject had had previous long-term institutionalization. All appeared to understand what was required, and gave every indication of cooperating in the experiment. All, of course, signed consent forms and were free to withdraw at any time.

[13] Cooperation.

Since the question of cooperation is of prime importance in a study such as this, perhaps it should be enlarged upon briefly here. It is especially important to establish that the psychotic population was trying to fulfill the experimental task. It may be argued, and has often been, that such patients produce deviant discourse because they wish to, either because they want to confound the investigator, or because they are especially creative, a stance with which I do not agree (Chaika 1974, 1977, 1981, 1982a). Alternatively, one might argue that the psychotic participants in this study failed because they did not understand what was expected of them. If, indeed, they were not cooperating or if they did not understand the task, then our results would be meaningless, because these rest wholly on the correlation of the narrative to the videostory.

There was every evidence that the psychotic subjects were cooperating in the speech situation when they told their stories (Chaika 1982e, 1983b) Briefly, cooperation can be assumed for the following reasons:

- All told narratives that had as their recognizable point of departure, events from the story.
- Even when subjects digressed, the digressions had as their points of departure the video story, and most cycled back to the story after such a digression.
- Many commented on their own performances and/or remarked that they could not remember something.
- There were attempts to make events and comments in the digressions cohere to the narrative as a whole.
- They frequently ended their narratives formally with such phrases as "that's the way it was," "that's all," "it made me happy to see that girl get her ice cream."

Thus, there was no reason to assume that differences in performance between normals and psychotics resulted from lack of cooperation. Since, also, as noted above, none of the patients had had long-term institutionalization, and their average stay at the time of this study was two weeks, institutionalization *per se* could not be posited as a principal cause of differences.

[14] The Nonpsychotic Participants.

The normal subjects consisted of students at Providence College and members of the community who volunteered after the project was described to them. The mean age of normals was 33 and of psychotics 28.2.

The psychotic population was selected on the basis of speech disorder as described above, as this was what we were testing. Then, a population of normals was matched as closely as possible in age, occupation, and social class. Again, these procedures conform to those used by Rochester and Martin (1979, pp. 57–61).

It must be emphasized, however, that this is not a sociological study, and the data were not analyzed with social class as a factor. Indeed, one complicates an argument considerably if social class is used as the explanation for schizophrenic performance on a narrative task. For instance, failures in narration such as using gibberish, or altering time sequences, or relating incidents not appropriate to the task at hand have never been correlated with social class, and these were the sorts of dysfluencies which appeared in this study.

The entire question of class-related deficiencies in narration is very cloudy. Early studies by Bernstein (1971) and Schatzman and Strauss (1972) found deficiencies in working class narrations, but later work, such as the Labov *ouevre,* found differences in narrative techniques, but no deficits (Chaika 1982b). More recent work indicates that the differences lie more in the orality vs. the literacy of a culture than in social class *per se* (Tannen 1984). Moreover, even though Rochester and Martin found that schizophrenics perform like Bernstein's working class youth, they did not find that only working class schizophrenics performed this way.

[15] Analysis.

The tapes of the narratives were transcribed by the principal investigator. Two judges independently verified the transcriptions by comparing them to the taped interviews. For the reasons discussed below, the cohesive ties calculated here were not identical with the categories in the Rochester and Martin study. Those ties which were decided upon, below, were isolated and counted by three independent judges from the written transcription. Any discrepancies were resolved by consensus. Discrepancies were found in less than 5% of occurrences of cohesive ties. The majority of these consisted of one judge missing an obvious tie, such as inadvertently skipping over a conjunction.

- anaphora (Ap) e.g.; *he, she, it his, they, her, him, its, their, them.*
- temporals (T) e.g., *now, then, after, while*
- *and* conjunction (&C) e.g., *blue and yellow plaid*
- *and* temporal (&T) e.g., *she went home and asked her mother*
- other conjunctions (C) *but, for, or, nor, yet*
- exophora (Ex.) e.g., *I, you,* and instances of 3d person pronouns not referring backwards in the narrative itself

Given the multiplicity of cohesive devices in any language, neither Rochester and Martin's (1979) study nor this one attempted to count all possible ties. They, however, did count lexical ties, whereas this study, for two reasons, did not. First, as already shown, lexical cohesion in itself does not advance the topic of a discourse so that a string of lexically tied sentences may form an incoherent passage (Fahnestock, 1983). Second, deciding whether usage of certain words in a discourse are instances of lexical cohesion is highly subjective, and is even more so when we consider that lexical cohesion gone awry has long been considered a characteristic of what has for decades been called "schizophrenic speech." As has often been noted (Lecours and Vaniers-Clement 1976; Werner, Lewis-Matichek, Evans and Litowitz 1975; Maher 1972; Chaika 1974, 1982a), one of the most salient characteristics of schizophrenic speech is glossomania, which is lexical cohesion. To count lexical cohesion, then, is to consider the very symptom we wish to explain. Therefore, this study is confined to pronominalization and conjunctions.

Another difference between this study and Rochester and Martin's involves the crucial differences which may be covered by *and*. Because *and* clearly has both a temporal and an additive sense (Levinson 1983:98–99), each of its senses was considered as a separate class. Those that meant "plus" were counted as *and*-conjunction (&C), and those paraphrasable by *then* were counted as *and*-temporal (&T), as in:

9A. Max bought poison and fertilizer.
9B. Max went to the store and he bought poison.

In 9A, Max's purchases were poison **plus** fertilizer (&C), and in 9B, first he went to the store **and then** (&T) he bought the poison. Since the videotape offered opportunities for both additive and temporal conjoining, these were crucial for proper cohesion and for coherence as well.

The number of instances of each category was divided by the total number of words (narrative length) for each subject. The percentages thus formed were the data for the statistical analysis of cohesive ties.

[16] Results.

A one-way ANOVA with diagnostic type considered a fixed effect between subjects revealed no overall differences in mean narrative length (mean number of words per narrative) among schizophrenics, manics, and normals ($F = 0.23$; $df = 2,44$; $p > .50$).

**Table 1. Mean percentages of total number of words
devoted to different categories of cohesive ties.**

	Category of Cohesive Tie						
	AP	&T	EX	T	&C	C	Totals
Normals N = 25	13.4	5.0	2.3	2.1	1.4	0.9	25.2
Schiz. N = 14	11.6	3.9	4.5	2.4	2.1	1.4	26.9
Manic N = 8	14.9	2.8	3.8	2.3	2.7	0.9	27.2
Totals	13.1	4.3	3.2	2.3	1.8	1.1	

**Table 2. Summary table of the one-way, fixed-effects ANOVA
for narrative length compared among the three diagnostic types.**

Source	SUMSQ	df	MEANSQ	F(obt)	F(crit)	p
Diagnostic type	1440.82	2	720.41	0.23	—	›.50
Error	135508.44	44	3079.73	—	—	—
Total	136948.85	46	—	—	—	—

A two-way ANOVA with diagnostic type as a fixed effect between subjects and categories of cohesive ties as a fixed effect within subjects revealed no overall differences among the three diagnostic types in the mean percentage of total narrative devoted to cohesion (number of category instances per narrative) (F = 0.31; df = 2,44; p > .50).

Considering the narratives as a whole, undifferentiated as to diagnostic type, there is an overall difference in the mean percentage use of the six categories of cohesive ties (F = 135.5; df = 5,220; p < .01). *Post hoc* comparisons (Hays 1981; Myers 1979) revealed the following pattern of differences among the categories. Overall, the category with the highest percentage is Ap (13.1%). This is significantly higher than any other category. Next is &T (4.3%) which is significantly higher than all those below except Ex (3.24%). Ex, in turn, is not significantly higher than either T (2.25%) or &C (1.38%), but does exceed C (1.06%). T, &C and C do not differ.

There is a significant interaction of the diagnostic types (normal,

Table 3. Summary table of the two-way ANOVA on percentage of total narrative devoted to different categories of cohesive ties.
Diagnostic type (normal, manic, schizophrenic) is treated as a fixed effect between subjects while category of cohesive tie is treated as a sampled effect within subjects.

Source	SUMSQ	df	MEANSQ	F(obt)	F(crit)	p
Between Ss	292.19	46	—	—	—	—
Diagnostic type	4.11	2	2.06	0.31	—	>.50
Error (b)	288.07	44	6.55	—	—	—
Within Ss	6333.03	235	—	—	—	—
Category	4672.85	5	934.57	135.50	2.29	<.05
Category X Type	142.87	10	14.29	2.07	1.91	<.05
Error (w)	1517.31	220	6.90	—	—	—
Total	6625.22	281	—	—	—	—

manic, and schizophrenic) with the categories of cohesive ties ($F = 2.07$; $df = 10,220$; $p < .05$). The Newman-Keuls procedure (Myers, 1979) was used to further analyze the differences among the types within individual categories. Within the category Ap the schizophrenics use significantly less than either normals or manics who do not differ.

Within the category Ex, normals use significantly less than manics or schizophrenics, who do not differ. When total Ex usage is further divided into two categories on the basis of (a) personal reference (e.g., *I* saw . . . , then *we* . . .) as distinguished from (b) unprepared pronominal reference (e.g., "*she*[11] went home and asked her mother" with no referent for the *she*), the following pattern obtains: the three diagnostic types show no significant difference in personal reference, Ex(a), ($F = 2.71$; $df = 2,44$; $p > .05$). No normal subject used any unprepared pronominal reference, Ex(b), while 4 of the 14 schizophrenic subjects used such reference a total of 20 times. One of 8 manic subjects used one such reference.

Within the category &T, normals use a significantly higher percentage than manics, while the schizophrenics do not differ from either. In three categories (T, &C, and C), the three types show no differences.

To refine the interaction by comparing the categories within each type, the Bonferroni t-test was used (Myers, 1979). As noted above, there is an overall difference such that Ap has a higher percentage of use than any other category. This difference holds for all three types.

Overall, no difference was obtained between &T and Ex, and this result is sustained among the schizophrenic and manic subjects. But normal subjects did use a higher percentage of &T than Ex.

The overall difference between Ex and C was reflected in significant differences for both normal and manic subjects, but was not obtained for the schizophrenics. The remaining contrasts agreed with the main effects.

[17] Discussion: Cohesive Ties and Coherence.

Rochester and Martin's study concluded that schizophrenics chose not to use cohesive ties, and that they were more likely than normals to make exophoric reference, reference which does not refer to an antecedent word within the sentence or discourse itself.

This study did not confirm Rochester and Martin's conclusion that schizophrenics do not use cohesive ties as frequently as normals. It was found that normals, schizophrenics, and manics produced narratives of equal mean length in the ICS task, and used the same mean total percent of cohesive ties. That is, schizophrenics, manics, and normals used the same overall percentage of cohesive ties per narrative. Moreover, each group showed significantly more anaphora than other cohesive ties. This is not unexpected, as anaphora is commonly used within sentences as well as across them. Also, since anaphoric words can substitute for virtually any lexical items, there are more opportunities to use them than any other type of tie.

However, although each category of respondent used more anaphora than any other kind of tie, schizophrenics did use significantly less anaphora than either normals or manics. The relative paucity of anaphora in the schizophrenic stories appears to have been caused by another fact of schizophrenic narration. Schizophrenics were more likely than the others to include matters extraneous to The ICS. They mentioned people and occurrences that were not in the videotape, and entwined them with those that were. Thus they produced more novel references, giving them fewer opportunities for anaphora, as in:

> 10. I was watching a film of a little girl and um s bring back memories of things that happened to uh people around me that affected me during the time when I was living in that area and she just went to the store for a candy bar and by the time ooh of course her brother who was supposed to be watching wasn't paying much attention he was blamed for and I didn't think that was **fair** . . .

Note that in the above, it is not a matter of deficit in referring anaphorically. The schizophrenic speaker uses anaphoric pronouns correctly. If she had not mentioned intrusive matters (the memories that were brought back, the candy bar and the brother), none of which occurred in the videotape, she would have have had more opportunity to produce anaphora which referred to the events of the tape. Instead, she digresses to idiosyncratic associations which are, nonetheless, clearly associated to the topic. The digressions, however, produce new direct reference rather than anaphora, thus contributing to the reduction in anaphora.

The ICS study does not support the conclusion that schizophrenics and manics lack competence in using cohesive ties. Rather, their opportunity for using them is lessened because they did not adhere to a macro-structure in their narratives. Personal memories and other extraneous factors interfered. As noted above, this seems to be a cognitive factor associated with the conditions of the illness. There seems to be no confirmed explanation or intervention for this condition.

[18] The Problem of Exophora.

This study found, as did Rochester and Martin's, that normals use significantly less exophora than psychotics, perhaps for different reasons. As already noted, their result may have been task related in a way ours was not. Rochester and Martin (1979) had subjects describe cartoons which were in view, whereas ours described the videotape after it was over, hence gone from view. If the picture being described is in full view, then the simplest strategy for encoding is simply to refer to it. The exophora produced by their subjects was, for the most part, referential exophora. Although, as noted previously, some researchers consider this inferior reference, this kind of exophora is not dysfunctional and, in actual interaction, cannot be shown to be inherently less precise than anaphora.

If, as in The ICS task, the picture isn't in view, then the competent narrator will make the effort to establish who and what is being talked about before referring to it by a pronoun. Increased exophora in Rochester and Martin's study may have been a simplification of the narrative task, a simplification induced by the presence of the pictures. This is confirmed by Rochester and Martin's own finding that there was no difference between normal and schizophrenic use of exophora in free interviews. The difference occurred only when subjects were asked "to describe and interpret pictures that are in the immediate situation, but [it did] . . . not [occur] in other contexts" (Rochester and Martin 1979:157).

The factors in the Rochester and Martin study which elicited exophora were successfully prevented in the ICS, but exophora nevertheless did occur. When it did, it was dysfunctional as it appeared with no prior referent. This occurred in 5 out of the 22 psychotic narrations. No normal used such Exophora at all. It occurred among those with the most disrupted narratives so that their failing to establish a necessary referent was part of a larger deficit in narrative construction as shown below.

The following boldface examples illustrate this nonreferential exophora in:

> 11. um in an ice cream store **she** was looking in to see if **she** could get any **she** went home. Her[12] mother said wait until dinner. Then her father came home. She asked him. He said "I don't know. You're going to ask your mother." Then she went down to the ice cream store and bought her own.

There was no introduction to 11 at all, a distinct deficit in narrative production. Introductions are an integral part of narratives. Even the other disrupted psychotic narratives had introductions and part of the abnormality of this one was clearly its lack of one (Chaika 1982e). Among other functions, introductions also provide opportunities for later anaphora. The *she* probably referred to the girl in the video, but the exophora was unprepared and the form of the narrative was correspondingly degraded.

> 12 . . . and I didn't think **that** was fair the way the way **they** did **that** either, so that's why I'm kinda like asking could **we** just get together for one big party or something ezz it hey if it we'd all in which is in not **they've** been here, so why **you** jis now discovering it? . . .

Although 12 is a later portion of 10 above, there were no referents for the boldfaced pronouns. This narrative, on the sentence level, showed verbal disruption even to the point of "word salads."

[19] Conclusions.

This study of narration has import both for linguistic and for psychiatric theory. For the former, the findings are clear. Countable cohesive ties are not the sole determinant of coherence and a sense of cohesion itself. Apart from its usefulness in studying such phenomena as cross-cultural differences in narrative and other discourse studies, this has ramifications for rhetorical theory as well, an important factor in an increasingly mechanistic and literate world.

In terms of the problems posed by psychosis, this study found that overall use of cohesive ties does not distinguish between the populations under study. This result differs from Rochester and Martin's (1979:85) which found that, according to their analysis, normals used more cohesive ties overall than schizophrenics. Certainly, we did find that schizophrenics used less Anaphora than did the manics and normals. This seems to be caused by a general inability to suppress material irrelevant to the situation.

[20] The Problem of Nomenclature.

This inability to suppress has been noted often in the literature on schizophrenia, and seems to be what is meant by such terms as *derailment, tangentiality, pigeonholing, loss of set, intermingling* and *attentional deficits.* That is, several terms have been used over the years to describe the same phenomenon. Perhaps because of the great amount of cross-disciplinary research into psychotic speech, researchers describing the same phenomena give it different names, thereby thinking they have explained, when all they have done is describe.

Commonly, these terms have been based upon anecdotal rather than experimentally-gathered evidence. Where evidence has been gathered, frequently, as noted above, the task has not elicited connected discourse. Rochester and Martin (1979) corrected that problem in their study. They asked subjects to recount their narratives while their stimuli, the cartoons, were still visible, whereas we asked subjects to recount after the stimulus videostory was no longer visible. This may have created the differences in results between their study and ours, so that the differences in their results and ours may be traced to differences both in the tasks and the methods of analysis in the two studies.

This study shows that psychotics use cohesive devices as often as normals, but the pattern of such usage differed, so that exophora without establishing prior reference occurred only in highly disrupted narratives, those which digressed from the matter of the videostory. This co-occurred with other deviations in narration.

There was no general deficit in using cohesive ties in schizophrenics or manics, nor was there any evidence of deliberate choices not to use cohesive ties. Where differences occur between normal, schizophrenic, and manic populations, they seem caused by other factors, such as digressions which appeared to be genuinely uncontrollable by the patient.

Notes

[1]This is a favorite phrase of my husband's.

[2]Humans naturally interpret speech by reference to the physical, cultural, and linguistic context in which it occurs. I say "naturally" because even toddlers first learning to speak clearly expect their utterances to be interpreted in context. If they know only one word, they will use it in different contexts, expecting adults to interpret the meaning in that context. If they don't know the word for what they want, then they choose the one they do know that can be interpreted in context to give the message they want, like the toddler who uses *button* to mean "put on my clothes," "cover me with a blanket," and, pointing at the dog's face, "eyes." Babies and children cannot be taught to do with this language. They just know it.

[3]Interestingly, this derives from the Greek word for *proof*. When one points out, one proves.

[4]Both these and the temporal subcategories are actually subcategorized even further, so that, for instance, there is both **Causal general** and **Causal specific**. There is **Temporal simple (external only), Conclusive: Simple,** and **Correlative forms.**

[5]All languages utilize the same processes to effect cohesion. We know of no language which has no pronouns, for instance, nor do we know of any with no ellipsis. What differs from language to language is the specific circumstances that force speakers to use pronouns rather than ellipsis and vice versa.

[6]Rarely, for special emphasis, an interactant might repeat a known element, but this is done for emphasis or humor.

[7]The studies which "proved" this show a clear class bias, as subjects were given a task typical of middle-class education and then judged by middle-class standards. When faced with narrating the action showed on cards, nonmiddle-class speakers referred directly to the pictures, whereas middle-class ones were more likely to narrate as if the pictures were not in view a (Labov, Robins, Lewis, and Cohen 1968; Labov 1969; Chaika 1982; 1989). The middle class has more experience with books that tell stories independently of any pictures. To illustrate: if one of the pictures given to subjects showed a boy standing with a bat in his hand before a house with a broken window, the middle-class person would say, "The boy was playing baseball, and he broke the window" whereas the nonmiddle-class subject would say, "He was playing baseball and he broke the window" without first mentioning the noun "the boy."

[8]Given the generally strong evidence that the patients were trying to cooperate in the task, and given their other genuine disruptions in speaking ability, disruptions which occur in many patients diagnosed as schizophrenic, and disruptions in speech

competence not readily controlled by speakers, such as producing word salads, glossomanic strings, and leaving out a vital element in a syntactic construction, it seems most likely to us that these omissions are a product of deficit in speech production.

[9]The original from which this was taken does not use capitals except on *I.* I have repeated that practice here.

[10]Rochester and Martin speak of TD, thought disordered, subjects. This corresponds to the SD, speech disordered, label used throughout this book and my articles on this subject.

[11]Although this was technically improper because she was not in view, it did not impair cohesion since I viewed the video with each patient; hence, it could be assumed that I knew the referent.

[12]This and the subsequent examples of pronouns referring to the feminine singular could be taken as anaphoric to the first mention(s) of *she.*

Chapter Seven

PRAGMATICS, INTENTION, AND IMPLICATION

Many linguists have tried to sweep pragmatics under the rug as not being "true" linguistics, an attitude that is happily changing. Language production and comprehension can be analyzed only in the pragmatic usage. All analyses of language data have to proceed from a consideration of the discourses that sentences, both uttered and written, are embedded in. Realizing that all language is discourse based empowers analyses of speech and writing. Context-free explanations do not work. Pragmatic analyses include intention and implication, both of which impel actual speech forms and also guide the hearer's interpretation of meaning.

[1] Pragmatics.

Those aspects of meaning which cannot be explained by the breakdown of words in relation to syntactic forms are often relegated to PRAGMATICS. Gordon and Lakoff (1975, p. 83) succinctly characterize this by noting " . . . under certain circumstances, saying one thing may entail the communication of another." In practice, it has proven difficult to the point of impossible to draw borders which delimit the scope of semantics, semiotics, sociolinguistics, psycholinguistics, and pragmatics itself (Levinson 1983, pp. 1–15; Fillmore 1984). As Kearns (1984, p. 163) avers " . . . we do not begin with syntax and then add semantics; the semantics is prior."

Many linguistic scholars have labored long and hard to maintain a boundary between language itself and the practical rules for its use (Fromkin 1975). Nevertheless, it has been abundantly clear for a very long time that there is no way to divide the two (Chaika 1977, 1981, 1982b; 1989). Fauconnier (1985) emphasizes that language is pragmatics and is structured for pragmatic purposes. He gives as an instance that there is an assumption that there is a link between an author and his works, so that "Plato is on the top shelf" typically means "the book by

Plato ... " In Faucconier's terms, a TRIGGER, the antecedent of the statement, is linked to the TARGET, what is intended to be referred to. These linkages are pragmatic functions. In disrupted psychotic speech like word salads, it is precisely these kinds of triggers toward targets that are lacking.

[2] Meaning and Direct Statement.

Because language is essentially pragmatic, meanings are not always derivable by dissecting the words into their component features, nor by matching the syntax used with actual meaning. For instance,

    1A. S (in a friend's kitchen): Mmm. Something smells good.

pragmatically means "I'd like the food that smells so good." Note here, also, that although the speaker uses the indefinite *something* and there is a universe of good-smelling nonfood items, in fact 1A will be understood to mean "food." The reason for this is that it is socially unacceptable to ask for food in our society. Hence, typically we ask for food in language which does not directly request, but which nevertheless is unambiguously a request; therefore elicits a response as if it were a straightforward request. Note, for instance, one possible response to 1A.

    1B. H: I'm sorry, but it's for Mary's birthday party.

This would appear to be a bizarre response to the actual message of 1A in terms of a conventional semantic interpretation according to the features of meaning of the component words. There has been nothing overtly declared in 1A that the speaker of 1B could be apologizing for. However, if one knows the social restriction on directly asking for food, as well as the fact derived from experience (Kearns 1984, pp. 85–121) that good smelling food tastes good, such an exchange quite ordinarily means what it does. All that is needed for proper interpretation is reliance on the discourse rule that one does not state what is known to all parties in the context, unless one wishes to imply something else. In this instance, the hearer usually infers that the speaker commented on the odor because he or she wishes to eat (Sacks 1964–1972; Chaika 1989, p. 125).

Since we are talking about common, uneventful speech events, we cannot exclude them from linguistic analysis by throwing them into a wastebasket labelled *pragmatics* or *semiotics*. Language is pragmatic. It is semiotic.

[3] Formal Rules of Syntax and Semantics.

We have already seen that languages contain orderly syntactic rules that these rules in and of themselves describe how we produce our language. The *do-support* rule demonstrated in Chapter 4 is a prime example. The rules for forming questions seem quite evident and unyielding:

> in order to form questions in English invert the first member of the verb auxiliary before the subject, but if there is no auxiliary substitute *do* in the number and tense appropriate to the rest.

The problem is that many questions in social interaction do not appear in question form, nor are all syntactically well formed questions really questions. Syntactic rules exist, but without reference to motive, context, and social rules of obligation, one cannot explain how syntactic forms are actually interpreted in given interactions. For instance, it is common to hear questions like:

2A. Is the Pope Catholic?
2B. Does a bear live in the woods?

These apparent questions aren't questions at all. They are answers, specifically the answer "yes." Moreover, such answers also imply "the answer should be obvious to you." In order to know that, one must

- share cultural knowledge with the speaker.
- assess the context as appropriate for bantering

Although they are regarded as stringently rule-governed, overt syntactic forms such as questions and declarative statements may actually take on different roles in actual discourse, roles not accounted for in their rules. A statement can actually be a question, as in 2A and B above. There is nothing in the actual words and syntax used that would enable the correct semantic interpretation. Rather, the two social conditions explain the meaning. The first condition is fulfilled because we know who the Pope is and that he has to be a Catholic; therefore, the answer to 2A is "yes." Instead of saying this, the speaker has offered an obvious question to which "yes" is the answer. We will shortly see an analogous situation in which a syntactically declarative sentence is a question. Then, too, a question can really be an imperative.

[4] Speech Acts.

Although people usually think of speech as a way of stating propositions and conveying information, it frequently fulfills neither of these functions. Much speech serves the purpose of social bonding, just shootin' the breeze and passin' the time of day (Chaika 1989, pp. 43, 44, 61, 96, 117). These are out of the provenance of this discussion.

Austin (1962) delivered a now famous series of lectures entitled *How to Do Things with Words* which introduced the idea of speech acts. This has been refined and expanded by numerous scholars, notably Searle (1969), Gordon and Lakoff (1975), Bach and Harnish (1979), and Kearns (1984), drastically changing our minds about how meaning is given and gotten. Austin claimed that much speech actually is a way of doing things like betting, guaranteeing, in warning, describing, asserting, commanding, ordering, requesting, criticizing, apologizing, censuring, welcoming, promising, objecting, demanding, and arguing.[1] These they called the ILLOCUTIONARY FORCES of language.

Certain verbs known as PERFORMATIVES have been isolated as those that explicitly state the illocutionary force. This does not mean that such verbs have to precede or follow a statement for it to have an illocutionary force. Typically, they don't appear at all, but one way to test for illocutionary force is to preface a utterance with "I hereby" + the appropriate performative, as in "I hereby warn you ... " If the meaning and force remain the same, then the original utterance is considered to have had the illocutionary force denoted by the performative. For instance, one can say

3A. Get out of here

This admits of the paraphrase

3B. I hereby command you to get out of here.

If, indeed, 3A means 3B, then we can say that 3A has the illocutionary force of a command. This does not mean that "Get out of here" always has that force, however. For instance, if my husband is teasing me, and I laughingly say, "Get out of here," that can't be paraphrased by 3B; therefore, in that instance, the "get out of here" is not a true command. It has the force of a compliment on his bantering.

3C. Someone's a little noisy.
3D. This place stinks.

Both of these can mean 3B "get out of here," in one of their possible senses. That is, both are paraphrasable as "I hereby command you to leave."[2] 3C can also mean "I hereby warn you to keep quiet." 3D can mean "I hereby warn you to clean up." Actually, these paraphrases are almost absurdly strained, and many native speakers who can easily understand the illocutionary force and can easily paraphrase it accurately would never think of the *hereby*-test. I would say a better one is to paraphrase using the canonical syntactic form. 3C can be restated by, "get out of here." This is the canonical form of an imperative. In another circumstance, it could be "be quiet," another imperative.

Recognition of the illocutionary force, expressed explicitly or implicitly, explains the polysemy of any given utterance, and provides us with a heuristic for determining which meaning is to be taken in a given instance. For instance, if a friend, X, asks me to dinner, I might reply "I'm eating with Gwendolyn tonight." What this actually means depends on the relationship between X and Gwendolyn. If Gwendolyn irritates X, then X will take my utterance as a warning. If I say the same thing to another friend who is also friendly with Gwendolyn and likes her, then the same utterance would have the force of an invitation. To yet another who doesn't know Gwendolyn, it becomes merely an apology.

Additionally, as Silverstein (1987) demonstrates, there are illocutionary functions in language which do not have a corresponding illocutionary verb. One example is *insult.* There is no way to say "I hereby insult you that ..." although one can clearly insult another by overt words or by such matters as intonation and stress. Often insults are more indirect since insulting is an overt act of aggression. Still, one can speak of the act of insulting.

We can usually recognize an insult directed at others or ourselves. Certainly, people sometimes fail to recognize a particular insult, just as they sometimes think an insult was intended when it was not. Paranoids, for instance, constantly misinterpret utterances as constituting threats or insults, even though the speaker denies such intent and others present do not find a judgment of insult to be warranted. It is true after all that speakers pretend they didn't mean to insult or threaten when, in fact, they did. At some times in his or her life, the paranoid individual may well have been justified in assuming insult in the face of the insulter's denial. The major difference between a person who is paranoid and one who is not is that the former more readily judge remarks as being insulting or threatening. If speech acts were not essentially polysemous, then perhaps people would not be paranoid.

Silverstein (1987, pp. 26–28) insightfully declares that explicit performative constructions can be used nonperformatively as well. When this occurs, the performative " . . . constitutes the way one can DISCOURSE ABOUT [caps his] . . . events of social action . . . " An instance is *warn* in its illocutionary function as in "I hereby warn you . . . " This has quite a different force than when it is used in the preterit, as in "I warned you.

There are many details of Austin's and Searle's formulations which have been validly questioned, but the basic premises hold. Language is essentially social. It is not necessarily utilized to inform, although it can be. Lecturing, for instance, is speech primarily to inform. As such, lecturing typically occurs in settings like classrooms and auditoriums, which exist for the function of informing. The degree to which society restricts language in its informative function is illustrated by our avoidance of a person who habitually lectures, that is, informs us all of the time. Such a person is a bore. Informing is a part-time function of language.

Given the social purposes of language, one might well expect that psychotic speech shows rather too little illocution. Johnston (1985, p. 81) claims that developmentally disordered children, notably the autistic, show an inability to handle illocutions effectively, a finding consonant with the general social disability of such children. The disordered speech most typically considered schizophrenic also lacks illocutionary force. That is one of the problems with it. We can find no social purpose in much of it. In other words, a measure of schizophrenic social disability is seen in the infrequency of illocution in peculiarly schizophrenic language. This does not mean that schizophrenics suffer only from a social disability, as claimed by Rutter (1985).

Because speech act theory demonstrates that utterances can mean something quite different from what a segmentation of words and syntax would yield, some people have mistakenly assumed that one can willy-nilly supply "missing" phrases and sentences in highly deviant discourse to make it all come out normal. The reasoning seems to be, "if speech acts show us that much is not actually stated, then let us assume that deviant schizophrenic speech is deviant only because they left out a bit too much." However, speech act theory allows one to fill in unspoken items only by principled means.[3]

[5] Intention and Motive.

Meaning is dependent on perceived intent. Sanders (1987, p. 75) goes so far as to say that it is a truism that "uttering an expression of language is always volitional and therefore purposeful." Needless to say, he was not talking of an impaired population, although, independently, psychiatry has traditionally operated on this presumption as well.

Searle (1983, p. 150) gives a pragmatic view of intention, showing that rules become progressively irrelevant as one becomes proficient, so that one's rules become "progressively irrelevant" and one concentrates on one's intended goals. He was speaking directly about physical skills like skiing, but this view can be applied to language skills as well. Many linguistic processes do become internalized. Neural pathways get forged. Lieberman (1984) says this had to have happened in order for language to have evolved. Clearly much of our language expertise is automated. We don't have to think about the initial sound in a word we intend to retrieve. If we intend to talk about a *car,* we don't have to stop to think of its first sound, then the second, and the last. Years of teaching phonetics have shown me how difficult it is even to analyze the actual sounds one uses in words. Similarly, for ordinary spoken sentences, we don't have to think about the grammar rules we have to apply. All we do is intend to convey a message and our language processors take over. It is only when encoding new or difficult things that conscious choices have to be made once one knows one's native language. Because speech is prime, most people experience difficulty when having to write their thoughts down because that function is not so automated as speech.

Searle (1983 p. 29) declares:

> It is the performance of the utterance act with a certain set of intentions that converts the utterance act into an illocutionary act and thus imposes Intentionality on the utterance.

Whereas it is true that speakers may announce their intent, typically they do not. If one party does announce intent, they may use a performative, as in

4A. Look, Mabel, I'm **telling** you . . .
4B. I **promise** you that I'll go on a diet next week.
4C. I have to **apologize** to you for my behavior . . .

Besides the use of performative verbs, there are other devices to signal intent overtly such as the [Look + NAME] construction in 4A above.

Words like *please* announce a request. Expressions like *let's talk turkey* indicate an intent to *get down to brass tacks*, that is, to stop *beating around the bush* and to *get to the heart of the matter*. All of these indicate that the speaker wishes to negotiate directly without polite indirection. The reason that they sound so blunt is that in most social circumstances intention is deduced not overtly stated.

Our intention or motive shapes what we choose to say and how we are going to say it. Speech acts include intention as part of their meaning (Bach and Harnish 1979, pp. xiv–xv, 12; VanDijk 1980, p. 265; Searle 1983, pp. 26–29; 145–155). In fact, speech acts cannot be interpreted unless one comprehends the intent behind them. The rejoinder, "What did you mean by that?" challenges a speaker's intention in saying what he or she did. This is never used to mean, "What was your meaning?" It always means "what was your motive?." It is never a way of asking the meaning of the words and syntax used. If hearers cannot ascertain that kind of meaning the correct response is "Huh?," "Excuse me, but I don't quite understand," or a variety of other requests for a paraphrase or repetition of what was said.

An example of genuinely misunderstood intent was one that I observed in the faculty lounge. When a male professor said to a female one, "Lord, this place is dirty." The female then got up and started to clear the coffee cups and napkins off the tables. The male then said, "I didn't want you to clean up. Where's the janitor?"

A playful misinterpretation of intent occurs if I murmur, "It's a little noisy in here." and my son responds, "Yes it is," without doing anything to make the noise abate. He pretends that he has failed to perceive my intent in commenting on the noise. Like so much humor, this works as a play on ordinary pragmatic strategies which we share. He treats my utterance as a statement of fact not as a command to lower the volume. A good deal of humor depends on such misperceptions, as in the exchange:

[walking on street] S: Excuse me, sir. Do you know where the Palace Hotel is?

H: Yes. [walks on]

Silverstein (1987) maintains that illocutionary acts "represent . . . intents to perform effective, socially understood acts with speech" (p. 28)." Intention has to be derived as part of the meaning of the utterance. As we have just seen, the particular illocution that we understand depends on what we perceive the speaker's intention to be, so that "it's noisy here" could be an excuse for my leaving the room, or it could be a command to be quiet. The speech act itself is contained in the intention of its utterance.

Brown and Yule (1983, pp. 68–88; 77–78) contend that there is no way to analyze the topic of another's speech without knowing why something was said; that is, its intent. Without knowing the speaker's intent, there is no way to evaluate his or her contribution to a conversation either. We don't even know if the person is cooperating and attempting to talk on the same subject we are. If one assumes that a speaker is deliberately being obscure, then one ascribes a lack of cooperation to him or her.

DeBeaugrande and Dressler (1981, p. 112) assert that the only way utterances can be used to communicate is if the speaker intends them to be communicated and the hearer accepts them as intended. Such acceptance is a usual practice. Hearers almost always do accept utterances as intended. Therein lies a problem. Intent is derived from what the speaker has said and the general context of utterance, such context including the relationship and mutual history of the interactors. SD productions do not provide the normal cues necessary to determine intent, hence, to determine meaning. If we misperceive intent we will misperceive meaning. Notice my contention is not that the speech is purposeless. The patient might very well have intended something, but could not say it coherently enough to be understood.

Our familiarity with the forms of speech acts also aids in our interpretation. With an SD population, utterances may not be evocative of any particular speech acts and words may be mismatched to the context. The question then becomes not so much "What was the intent?" but "Can we interpret this at all? Can we ascertain what the intent was? If so, how?" For instance, what could possibly be the intent of

5. I had a little goldfish too like a clown. Happy Halloween down.
6. St. Valentine's Day is the official breedin' season of birds. All buzzards can coo. I like to see it pronounced buzzards rightly. They work hard. So do parakeets.

Sanders (1987, p. 76) attempts to show that it is possible to assign meaning even when one can not determine what illocutionary force of a sentence. His example is a sign:

We will be closed for inventory Sunday and Monday, June 12–13, and will reopen at noon on Tuesday, June 14.

He maintains that we do not know whether or not this is an excuse, a warning, advice, a promise, or an invitation to return. That is, we don't know the intent, but we do know the meaning. It seems to me to be more correct to say that we understand the event described, but we don't understand its meaning.

Sanders is correct that the same sentence could be used in all of those illocutionary forces. It is, therefore, ambiguous. However, it would be quite strange if the reader did not consider it first and foremost as an invitation to return after those dates. If the sign were posted before those dates, and if the store sold items that people could not readily purchase elsewhere, or items that cost a great deal more elsewhere, then, most likely, people would take it as a warning and an invitation to stock up before those dates. In fact, the "what can it possibly mean in this context" strategy (Chaika 1976), kicks in so that the reader matches the sentence with the date and time, the probable intentions of the poster of the sign, and other relevant knowledge to decide the illocutionary force. The illocutionary force may be potentially ambiguous, but like other ambiguities, it is resolvable by reference to the context. If it is not so resolvable, then the recipient of the message can resort to overt questioning like, "What did you mean by that?" or "What am I supposed to be getting out of that?" SD psychotics rarely can answer such questions relevantly.

An examination of discourse regarded as particularly schizophrenic reveals a paucity in the very sorts of paraphrasing and metalinguistic comments that show a stable intention or purpose in communication. Much of the speech is not paraphrasable at all, but all normal speech is. Nunberg (p. 204) says that we assume that "... speakers have no ulterior motive for behaving in a way that is irrational from a strictly informational point of view." Many of the interpretations of psychotic speech we see (i.e., Forrest 1976; Searles 1967) proceeds from a basic strategy of assuming that irrational speech can derive from rational goals, and that the speech is merely suffering from oblique phrasing. If impairment of speech processes is so degraded that normal decoding processes do not work, we cannot assume a purpose in it.

[6] Preconditions.

Besides motive and intent, another vital pragmatic consideration figures strongly in interpretation. Part of meaning lies in the social circumstances in which a meaning is appropriate, the very PRECONDITION for its utterance. Austin's term for these are FELICITY-conditions (Lyons

1972, pp. 604–606, 727–738). An example is the statement perceived as a question:

7. You live in Providence.

This evokes a reply appropriate to the question "Do you live in Providence?" such as "Yes . . . " or "No, I live in Foster."

Labov and Fanshel (1977, p. 78) explain that statements will be heard as questions, commands, or other requests if the preconditions for uttering them are met. In order to ask a question successfully, one must have the right to ask that question, the hearer must have the knowledge to answer it, and in some way must have an obligation to respond. If these three conditions are met, then, as in 7 the hearer will act as if she had been asked a question in canonical question form. Similarly, in order for a command to be successful, the commander must have the right to command and the hearer has the obligation to obey that command or is willing to. If those conditions are met, then the hearer will respond as if the command had been given in imperative form. For instance, if a boss asks "Any more coffee?" the secretary might answer. "Oh, I'll make some right away." Alternatively, she might say, "Oh, I'm sorry, but I didn't get a chance to buy any beans." An apology for noncompliance is a socially proper response in our society to what we hear as commands, even those not in overt imperative form. The essentially social rules of preconditions behind utterances override the actual syntactic form of messages.

Labov and Fanshel (1977) show how a mother manipulates her daughter by playing with these preconditions. Rhoda is locked into a power struggle with her mother. The mother goes to visit a sister, leaving Rhoda to handle the domestic affairs at home. Rhoda does not want to have to admit overtly that she needs the mother at home, so Rhoda asks, "Well, when do you plan t'come home?" The mother responds with "Oh, why?" in order to force Rhoda to admit that she needs help. The mother clinches it by saying "Well, why don't you tell Phyllis that [you need my help at home]" Phyllis is Rhoda's sister. Labov and Fanshel show that Rhoda has been outmaneuvered on two counts. First, the mother has forced the admission from Rhoda. Second, it is up to the mother to decide when she is coming home. It is not Phyllis' place to do that. Considering this, the mother has also managed to tell Rhoda that Phyllis is the favored daughter, and has done so simply by manipulation of the preconditions for questioning. Notice that the claim here is based upon general rules for interaction.

The difference between a truth-conditional interpretation and a pragmatic one is illustrated by:

    7. Max broke the crystal stemware.

If, indeed, Max has broken the item(s) referred to in 7, this would be considered to be in the realm of semantics. However, if this is said as a way of commenting on Max's clumsiness or, alternatively, on his vindictiveness, then we would be dealing with pragmatics. The actual meaning derived depends on the context of the utterance, including what the speaker and hearer have already said, what their topic of conversation is, what they know about Max from other encounters both with and without him, and what their motives are or are presumed to be.

If one accepts a dichotomy between semantics and pragmatics such that truth conditional statements alone belong in the former category, then semantics can virtually never account for meaning in social interaction. This applies *mutatis mutandis* to written sentences, except, of course, those which have been deliberately fabricated to show a dichotomy between semantics and pragmatics.

Meaning is actuated as much by implication as by direct statements.[4] By definition, implication refers to meanings not directly encoded onto syntactic structures or on the lexical items chosen in a given expression, but this does not mean that an utterance means whatever we wish it to. There are strategies and recognized conventions in a language that constrain interpretation in any given instance.

Although the necessary processes in derivation of meaning in the sorts of actual circumstances depicted above are more than passingly embarrassing for those committed to context-free grammars or to the establishment of algorithms to explain syntax and semantics, we cannot simply relegate them to some convenient bin labelled "pragmatics" or "semiotics." Pragmatics explains the actual sentences and words that are used in interactions. It is not peripheral to linguistics. In fact, any syntax that doesn't include pragmatics is trivial because it doesn't explain how people actually use grammar, nor does it explain how listeners derive meaning. Thus, it can be seen that the semantic strategies frequently relegated to pragmatics are part and parcel of how we produce and interpret language.

Fillmore (1981, p. 147) sums up the pragmatic approach to meaning

> ... an analysis [should be] carried out in sociolinguistic terms in which
> the identity, location, and relative social statuses of the participants in
> the communication act are taken into account, together with a descrip-
> tion of the social or institutional occasion within which the discourse
> was observed or within which it could be produced. Of particular
> interest, of course, is the correlation of these items with formal linguis-
> tic phenomena.

Fillmore (1984, p. 88) goes so far as to say that "there is probably no
need for a level of semantic representation ..." He argues (p. 89) that
one learns and understands words in contexts, and that words are used in
association with those contexts. He gives as an example the term *being on
land,* saying that this evokes a context of comparison with *being at sea,*
whereas *being on the ground* evokes a contrast with *being in the air.* The
truth conditional meaning, including the meaning derivable from
dissecting each word into its component features cannot account for the
actual meaning of any of these phrases. For instance, all one gains from
such a dissection of *being on land* is that it refers to the physical state of
being on dry land. In practice, however, that is not its meaning. If asked
where S is phoning from, for instance, given the response "I'm on land,"
H would be correct in assuming that the speaker had recently disembarked
even if H did not even know S[5] much less S's travel plans.

Fillmore (p. 91) offers yet another such example, this time the sentence:

8. The menfolk returned at sundown.

He points out, rightly I think, this sentence wouldn't occur in an all
male community of workers, as, in actual usage, the word *menfolk* implies
a contrast with females and children. Despite the fact that the word
literally means "men," it cannot be used to refer to men unless they are
in a heterogeneous community.

It is very important to take note of the kinds of arguments marshalled
above to justify interpretation. While it is true that the actual meaning of
an utterance may be different from what has ostensibly been said, there
are clear bounds on possible interpretations. Appeal is made to statable
rules of discourse interpretation, rules which include but are not limited
to cultural and social facts, rules which are empirically verifiable by
investigating what meanings native speakers derive from interactions
presented to them. Such interpretations do not depend on theoretical
constructs formulated in the absence of inquiry into actual speech
behavior.

[7] Implicature and Conversational Maxims.

Grice (1975; 1981) spoke of implicatures arising from the violation of the four CONVERSATIONAL MAXIMS: quality, quantity, relation, and manner (p. 45). These maxims entail such principles of discourse as

- Say what you believe to be true.
- Do not say anything for which you lack adequate evidence.
- Be as informative as required for the purpose of current exchange.
- Don't say more than required.
- Say what is relevant to the matter at hand.
- Be orderly, unambiguous, and not obscure.

It is certainly obvious that these maxims are regularly violated. People do lie, do give opinions with no evidence for them, do hold back information, are prolix, mislead intentionally or unintentionally by ambiguity, poor phrasing, and poorly sequenced narration. Then, too, what does Grice mean by *required?* How is one to know exactly how much is required? What is too little, and what too much? What will a hearer find relevant, and what is likely to strike a hearer as being not relevant or ambiguous? The partial answer to such questions is that whatever satisfies a cospeaker is enough. It is unlikely that we will ever have a firm measure which will tell us when "enough" has been achieved. There are sufficient linguistic and paralinguistic resources for cospeakers to indicate whether or not "enough" has been provided.

Grice did not say that conversants actually are cooperative, just that they are presumed to be, and from this, important facets of meaning derive. Grice (1975, p. 45) says that "Our talk exchanges do not normally consist of a succession of disconnected remarks and would not be rational if they did." Of course, it is just such disconnected utterances which gives us the feeling that certain speech is "schizophrenic." The question then is whether psychotic speech flouts (Grice's term) the maxims. Certainly normal speakers do, but there is a qualitative difference between normal flouting and psychotic SD productions. The term *flout* itself implies volition and when we examine Grice's examples of flouting we easily understand the volition behind them. That is the flouting is a deliberate way to give an implication.

[8] Violating the Maxim of Quality.

One violation of the maxim of quality is lying. Lies do not necessarily violate language rules. They violate the larger conversational rules such as Grice's maxim of quality, Searle's cooperation principle, and Gordon and Lakoff's sincerity principle (1975). Actually, the lie consists of falsifying intent, not necessarily of falsifying information. Of course, it can consist of both.

The stigma of lying inheres in its status as a violation of trust. With the exception of "white lies," lying is considered particularly despicable.[6] The white lie is represented as being intended to ameliorate the anguish that would proceed from full disclosure. Notice that this type of lie is representable as an innocent, hence not real, violation of the maxim of quality because the intent of S is beneficent.

But what of the violation that has neither an intent to deceive nor to ameliorate? If the S believes that the given utterance is true, then it is error or delusion. If S knows that it is not true and is not offering it as truth, then it is fantasy. A genuine lie occurs only if S knows that it is not true and intends to offer it as truth.

Carlson (1983, pp. 103–104) denies that implicature is derivable from violations, asserting that if true violations of conversation occur, then incorrect implications result. It is true that people deliberately deceive, but in that case, the speaker is banking on the hearer's interpreting according to usual premises. The lie works only if the hearer assumes that the truth has been told.

[9] The Maxim of Quantity: Inference.

There are always meanings left unsaid, indeed, which must be left unsaid. To specify each and every meaning and connotation intended would slow down interaction drastically. Because this would also lead to tedious belaboring of point upon point, cospeakers would get so mired in detail that they would lose the thread of organization in the communication. A plethora of information makes it difficult to get the point of what is being said. Moreover, as we have seen (Chapter 6), cohesion is enhanced by having hearers match the utterance to the context and fill in what has not been said.

Levinson (1983, p. 106) shows how the maxim of quantity adds " . . . to most utterances a pragmatic inference . . . to the effect that the statement presented is the strongest, or most informative that can be made in the situation." as in

9A. Nigel has fourteen children.

The implicature here is that Nigel has no more and no less than fourteen children. This is readily seen if one adds *only* to 9A, as in

9B. Nigel has only fourteen children.

9A and B are usually assumed to be synonymous. It would be more than passingly odd, indeed irritating, if, the speaker of 9A at a later time said, "Now, Nigel's fifteenth child. . . . " An appropriate response to that would be "I thought you said that Nigel has only fourteen children!" This response proves the implication that has been given when using the nonmodified term of quantification, as in 9A above.

The bizarreness of some psychotic speech is explicable in terms of a violation of quantity. The following response is to a request to identify the color on a chip from the Farnsworth-Munsell disc #39 (Cohen 1978, 1–34). The comment within the parens is Cohen's).

10A. Green (SHOUTS!). Hold on, the other is too! In the garden such a green is unlikely. The other is more gardenreal, piecemeal, oatmeal green, greenreal, filmreal, greenreal.

The patient correctly identifies the disc, but then goes on to add clearly extraneous material which goes way beyond what is needed to identify the disc. Moreover, as the response continues it adds on increasingly extraneous verbiage.

[10] The Maxim of Relation: Relevance.

The maxim of relation could well be termed the maxim of **assumed** relation. As part of our making sense of utterances, we assume a relevance (Chapters 9 and 10). Our doing this leads to some interesting implications. For instance, one of the ways that people **waffle,** is to imply relevance where none exists.

For instance, Z wishes to take a day out of work for personal reasons, but has no "personal days" left, so he informs the boss that he is not coming in Monday. When the boss asks why, he responds, perhaps with truth, "I'm having some nasty physical problems I'd rather not talk about." The boss naturally assumes that the day off is related to the problems, even if it is not. Moreover, the boss assumes that the problems are not self-imposed, like having a hangover from a wild party Sunday. Here the maxim of relevance leads to implications based upon the hearer's strategy of assuming relevance.

Perhaps the trait many would consider most characteristic of schizophrenic speech,[7] is its frequent inappropriateness to whatever task is at hand, or, rather, the difficulty in uncovering any relevance. Again using Cohen's (1978) data elicited from Farnsworth-Munsell disc #39:

> 10B. The eentsy beentsy spider went up his mother's spot. Out came the rain the color of green snot.
>
> 10C. This isn't such a bad green. Reminds me of a picnic on the green. Yes! Picnic green.

One problem with 10B is that the situation called for a direct answer as the first part of the response. The patient nowhere indicates that this is an answer to the question posed. One supposes it must have been an answer only by the reference to green snot. Similarly, 10C starts with a value judgment rather than the direct labelling of the color. Then, in the reverse order of what the speaker of 10A did, he goes from the extraneous to the specific. Neither the value judgment nor the comparison is called for here, as the conventions of American questioning demand that first one must answer the question asked as directly and economically as possible.

[11] The Maxim of Manner: Orderliness.

The maxim requiring speakers to be orderly results in the implication that if actions are presented in a certain order, that is the order in which they occurred. For instance, to use his example

> 11A. Taking off his trousers, the King of France went to bed.
>
> 11B. The King of France took off his trousers and went to bed.
>
> 11C. The King of France went to bed and took off his trousers.

The implication is clear in the first two that the King took his trousers off first, but in the third, he went to bed before divesting himself of trousers. It is, of course, possible to present events out of their actual order, but only by using words indicating the actual order, as in

> 11D. **Before** he went to bed, the King of France took off his trousers.
>
> 11E. **After** he went to bed, the King of France took off his trousers.

Similarly, cause and effect can be implied by order of presentation, as in

12A. She went skiing and broke her leg.

The implication is that the skiing was the cause of the injury. Notice the change in meaning of

12B. She broke her leg and went skiing.

So strong is the assumption that the order in which utterances are given is significant for interpretation that some implications can simply occur by juxtaposing two comments. Sometimes this itself creates a lie. For instance, consider this exchange

13A. Max: Bobby's gas station was robbed last night.
13B. Tony: I saw Melvyn there at midnight.

The implication is that Melvyn must have committed the robbery. Why else would Tony have made that remark localizing someone's presence at a time that qualified as being the time of robbery. Note that this implication can be directly negated

13C. Max: No, dummy. Melvyn noticed the open door and went to check it out. He was the one who called the police! He couldn't have done it.

The very denial in 13C shows the implicated meaning caused by the juxtaposition. Like the giving of false information, creations of false implication do not always proceed from the desire to deceive. There can be many sources of violations. They can be a result of poor judgment of what the context requires, of cross-cultural differences in communicative practices, of misexecution of intended speech, or of impaired faculties.

Violation of orderings abound in schizophrenic speech, so much so that that even simple cause and effect relations are misordered. This occurs when there is no implication derivable from such misordering, as in

14A. She . . . leaves the ice cream and eats it.
14B. She ate the ice cream and brought it home.

Insufficient contextualizing also causes problems of interpretation. Fauconnier (1985) lays the blame for ambiguity on uncertainties in the discourse situation itself. Context also changes our perception of presuppositions (Gazdar 1978). Carlson (1983, p. 152) claims the contrary situation: that one can almost always invent a context for any sequence of sentences which seems unrelated. This is too strong a claim. First, in order to prove such a contention even for normal speech, we would have to present subjects with a potpourri of sentences, possibly taken from widely different sources, and then see if they could invent contexts for such a conglomerate of sources. Second, he was speaking of normal linguistic production. One of the problems with disorganized psychotic speech is that it defies our ability to provide a context to make it intelligible. A reprise of two utterances shows the problem:

> 15A. After John Black has recovered in special neutral form of life the honest bring back to doctor's agents must take John Black out through making up design meaning straight neutral underworld shadow tunnel (Lorenz 1961)
>
> 15B. ... you have to have a plausity of amendments to go through for the children's code and it's no mental disturbance of puterience, it is an amorition law. (Laffal 1965)

Finally, even if one can find a context in which those utterances would fit, one still cannot be sure that the speaker intended the unrelated sentences to belong to the invented context.

Along with being disorderly, schizophrenics may also appear obscure and ambiguous, Grice's term for other violations of maxim of order,[8] seen in 15A and B above. If we assume that speech has been purposely produced in accordance with the maxims, the very terms Grice has chosen, *obscure* and *ambiguous*, carry as part of their semantic load the "deliberate obfuscating." Hence, except perhaps in scholarly writing, these terms comprise negative evaluation.

[12] The Maxim of Response.

To the above maxims, Grice (1981, p. 189) later added yet another:

Facilitate in your form of expression the appropriate reply.

In other words, cospeakers assume that they are to respond according to the form and content of each others' utterances. This is both a social and a linguistic matter. Obviously, such matters as topic and lexical choice are constrained by previous utterances in an interaction, by those of previous interactions or other matters pertinent to the context of interaction. Constructions are also syntactically formed so that certain replies are both possible and invited. To illustrate, *how, who, what, when,* and *where* all are words referring to specific constituents of the sentence or of the discourse, asking the cospeaker(s) to supply, respectively, a reason, a person, a thing, a time, and a place. Here, too, one sees that much speech disordered schizophrenic speech is not formed so that it controls responses. For instance

> 16. My mother's name was Bill . . . And coo? St. Valentine's day is the start of the breedin' season of the birds. . . .

[13] Violations.

The maxims which Grice proposed will generate meaning as much by their being breached as by their being honored (1975, pp. 52–56). Understanding their role in meaning equips us to explain many implicatures[9] in a non-ad hoc manner. For instance, Grice (1982, p. 184) demonstrates the effect of a speaker's deliberately violating the maxim of quantity by damning with faint praise when asked to give a recommendation is such an example. Consider the situation in which X has applied for a teaching job in a philosophy department, and his mentor, A, writes as a recommendation:

> Dear Sir, Mr. X's handwriting is clear and he is always neatly dressed.

This strongly implies that X is not a good philosopher. Why else would A not mention his abilities? It is not that A is uncooperative. If that were the case, then he or she wouldn't have written at all. Similarly, if A is X's mentor, then A must know X's worth as a philosopher. Since A knows that the future employer is expecting to hear about a person's abilities relevant to the job being applied for, he or she can assume that if A doesn't mention those, but instead mentions clearly irrelevant facts, then the employer would get the implication that speaker doesn't want to say that the person has poor capabilities. A failure to mention relevant information is clearly perceived as **evasion,** and evasion itself is frequently perceived as an unwillingness to give bad news, in this instance that the candidate is not fit for the job.

What the violations show is that we cannot assume that speakers always or even usually follow conversational maxims, but that **cospeakers typically assume that the maxims are being followed.** In other words, maxims characterize effects on the hearer. They don't necessarily characterize speaker behavior.

Sanders cautions that the possibility of an implicature does not guarantee that one will be inferred (1987, pp. 67–68). Even when an implicature can potentially be achieved by a breach of a maxim, H may attend only to the propositional content of the utterance. This, of course, can also occur when H realizes that an implicature has been made, but chooses to ignore it. In this instance, H may decide to comment on or otherwise respond to an implicature at a later date as if it had actually been encoded in words.[10]

[14] Modality.

The very syntax of a language itself has syntactic forms designed to express the speaker's attitude towards what he or she is saying. These are MODALITY markers. The examples that spring to mind are the MODAL AUXILIARIES like *can, may, might, should, could, will, would,* and *must.* Introductory adverbs like *probably, surprisingly, doubtfully,* and phrasal adverbs like *it is certain that* and *it is supposed that* all fill this function.

[15] Mitigating.

MITIGATORS are speech forms which background their messages, lessening the possibility of overt confrontation. They may be used to deny what one feels. These are directly involved in what is called *saving face* (Goffman 1955), and are important determiners of how messages are given. We have already seen these in the guise of commands or questions that are couched in apparently ordinary statements. Language abounds with mitigators, such as

> 17A. You'll never believe this, but . . .
> 17B. I know I'm no expert, but . . .
> 17C. And I haven't got into that but — I don't know — I—I just—like, you have your set way of doing things and you're in control . . .

This last, 17C, comes from a conversation between a female schizophrenic and a medical student (Chaika 1981, 1983a). The patient is speaking, trying to indicate disagreement with the medical student. Because social and professional power clearly reside in him, she has to mitigate her expressions of doubt (Chapter 11).

Robin Lakoff (1975) documents such excessive mitigating as being typical of women, showing that they are actually inferior to men in social status even under the best of circumstances.[11] O'Barr (1982) amends this to include males in an inferior position as well, a discovery he made while investigating weak versus powerful language amongst witnesses in court trials.

Fowler (1985, p. 73) includes mitigators in the category of modality, a sound practice since they can often be used interchangeably, so that the following seem to be equivalent for many contexts

- **I might** accept his apology.
- **Perhaps** I will accept his apology.
- **It is possible that** I will accept his apology.

Fowler also shows that **tag questions** are mitigators, often used as expressions of doubt. Robin Lakoff pegged these early on as being softeners of assertions, as in

- You're not going, **are you?**
- Tastes good, **doesn't it?**

All of the mitigators in language are so pervasive that we frequently don't notice the effect they have on our judgments about the speaker. Sometimes our "intuitive" feeling that someone is especially uncertain and ill at ease arises because of the number of mitigators in his or her speech.[12]

[16] Indirect Meaning.

We have already seen that meaning can be gained directly from the semantic features on words. Factorial analysis of features explains some IMPLICATIONS as well (Chapter 5). Many words in and of themselves connote opinion: *riot* or *demonstration; invade* or *land; instigate* or *encourage,* all can be used to indicate whether or not the speaker approves of what is being spoken. Such terminology is not confined to the press. We even see it in putative objective scholarship. In his book on psycholinguistics, Mowrer speaks of Chomsky as *instigating* a theory of grammar. The verb alone tells us of Mowrer's disapproval of Chomsky.

Sometimes word choice can indicate far more reaching implications, as in:

18A. The tuna fishermen are still murdering the dolphins.
18B. The tuna fishermen are still killing the dolphins.

The word *murder* literally means that killing was done by a human to a human. This is what distinguishes it from *kill* for instance.[13] As part of the actual meaning of the expressions in 18A, simply by my choice of *murder* I have claimed that, in my eyes, what the fishermen are doing is as bad as killing humans. We assume that this is my belief because I have chosen that particular verb and it is always presumed that an utterance reflects the speaker's point of view. This, of course, has tremendous implications about my belief systems, my moral codes, and my empathy.

In contrast, although 18B can be used to express my disapproval of what the tuna fishermen are doing, it does not necessarily entail my belief that causing dolphins to suffer is as wrong as causing people to. However, in context it certainly could both mean and imply what 18A does if, for instance, prior experience with me or overt statements made before 18B established such feelings.

[17] Implicature and the Sentence.

Implication can be effected on the level of the sentence by using or not using certain paraphrases. Thus, one reason for using the passive is to be able to omit the agent or cause, but all the while implying that one was there. Even if the agent or cause is omitted, the implication of a passive is that one or the other was involved, that the proposition is not about something which just happened. This is the difference between "he died" and "he was killed."

Another implication of an agentless sentence is that the agent is not important enough to mention, or that such mention is beside the point. In this category, there is what I call the "housewifeless" passive, as in

19A. The beds got made.
19B. The dinner is cooked.
19C. The house was cleaned.

These examples of agency or its lack thereof by no means exhaust all of the resources of sentence grammars to create implications, but is sufficient to the task at hand. Kearns (1984, p. 67) maintains that sentences are fundamental in imparting inferential meaning, as we have just seen in the instance of agentless passives [not his example]. The very use of a certain grammatical form creates entailment.

My oft-quoted example (from Cohen 1978) is an interesting example of incompatibility between terms and sentences:

20. Looks like clay. Sounds like gray. Take you for a roll in the hay. Hay day. May day. Help! I need help.

Clay is both a tactile and visual stimulus, so the first simile is fine, but *gray* is a color, not a sound, so that the "Sounds like gray" is incompatible. The subsequent sentences in this uttered passage do not add any information which would modify the oxymoronic construction entailed by the reference to gray as a sound. Nor do they give any clue as to how sounding like gray is relevant to looking like clay. The individual terms in this utterance cannot be forged into a discourse because of the their fundamental incompatibility. This is not to say that someone could never forge such incompatible terms into a coherent structure by adding other terms to it. That is not the issue. The issue is that the speaker of 20 above has not done so and has given no clues in the given utterance that would allow us to make such additions or to normalize the sequence in any way. Consequently, part of the abnormality of this utterance lies in its incompatible entailments.

[18] Testing for Implicature.

Since Grice attempts to distinguish between implicated and direct meanings, he adopts verification procedures in order to provide criteria for determining whether or not a meaning is implied at all as well as for exactly what it is that has been implied. Grice naturally assumes that if there are two kinds of meaning, one inhering in lexical items and syntactic form, and another not arising from linguistic constructions *per se*, but derivable by implication, then these should be distinguishable by different modes of analysis (1981, p. 185). His first criterion is that what is conversationally implicated is not part of the meaning of the expressions used to convey the implicature. Obviously, if it is part of that meaning, then it is direct statement, not implication. Grice suggests three salient criteria to distinguish implicatures. They are:

- DENIABILITY, e.g., they can be denied by demurring "but not necessarily in that order" or "but not in the usual meaning of that word."
- NONDETACHABILITY, e.g., synonyms give same implication.
- CALCULABILITY, e.g., they constitute a reasonable inference in the context assuming the cooperative principle; The first criterion simply means that you can deny an implication. For instance, the

implicature that the order of encoding is the order of occurrence can be denied by saying " . . . but not necessarily in that order," as in

21. The King of France went to bed and divested himself of his trousers, but not necessarily in that order.

The order of narration in "She ate the ice cream and brought it home" is literally impossible. Adding "but not necessarily in that order" does fix it, but, in this case, the fix is perceived as a correction to a slip-of-the-tongue.

Grice's second test (1981, p. 186) that of synonymy, says that if synonyms of the expressions actually used provide the same implicature, then it is unlikely that the implicature inhered in the original words. Rather, it occurs because of a conversational situation that calls for the given semantic message. Nunberg (1981), objects that nondetachability fails as a necessary test for implication because semantic entailments of conventional messages also are preserved if one uses the right synonym. Thus, a test based upon synonymy does not separate out implicature from meanings derivable directly from the expressions used.

Both of these opinions presuppose that exact synonyms can usually be found for all or most expressions. It is important to note that it is actually extremely difficult to find individual words which are truly synonymous in the sense of complete substitutability. In the first place, it is quite usual for synonyms to require somewhat different syntactic frames, as shown below. Furthermore, typically, as a perusal of any thesaurus shows, each word has its own network of meanings, and synonymy is typically a case of partial matches of meanings. For instance, consider this set: *belief, tenet, thought* and *conviction*. Although one can find contexts in which any one of these can be selected without changing meaning, one need not stray far to find contexts in which their synonymy fails.

For instance, I can utilize each of the above nouns in the context of expressing my belief in God as One. The sentence frame might have to be changed in accordance with the syntactic frame the different synonyms demand, but I can still say the following are synonymous:

I abide by a *belief* in God as One.
I hold a *tenet* that God is One.
I hold the *thought* that God is One.
I have a *conviction* that God is One.

All of these entail an implicature that I am either a Jew, a Unitarian, or a Moslem, but not a Christian, because Christians believe that God is a Trinity. Although synonymy works well for the religious senses attaching to these words, it certainly doesn't work if *conviction* is used in the sense of a prosecutor getting a conviction, or if *belief* is used in the sense of my belief that the color of a tomato I am looking at is red, or if *thought* is used in a complaint that I just lost my train of thought.

Grice (1981, pp. 187–191) is very adamant that neither deniability nor synonymy comprise final tests for implicature. They are but rules of thumb. The final test rests on his third criterion, calculability, that one is able to give a derivation of the implication. For a derivation to be valid, a principled connection must be constructed between the overtly expressed proposition, the maxim it breached and the resulting implication (Sanders 1987, p. 61). The major obstacle in applying the test of calculability is the degree to which one can come up with an apparently consistent and all-embracing interpretation which impresses by its brilliance and originality but is not verifiable by anything except the analyzers intuitions. Chomskyan linguistics ultimately failed because of its reliance on intuition. The same problem occurs in fields as diverse as literary criticism and psychotherapy.

Nunberg (1981, p. 202) mitigates this danger by offering more precise guidelines for a "satisfactory pragmatic explanation" of an expression.

- specifying its conventional use
- the use to be explained
- information speaker and hearer presuppose about each others' intentions
- background knowledge
- physical setting
- ... a demonstration, usually in the form of a set of inferences, that the use in question is the best way available to the speaker to the accomplishing a particular conversational purpose ... "

I would amend this last to " ... the way that works at the moment to attain one's purpose." If it does not, the cospeaker may indicate linguistically or not that there is a communicative glitch and the speaker can take another turn, so to speak and reformulate.

In practice, formal distinctions between implied and overtly encoded meaning may not always be easily achieved, because linguistic units do not form an algorithm from which meaning is automatically derivable. Extracting meaning directly from the expressions used relies on pragmatic strategies (Chaika 1976) as well as syntactico-semantic factoring of meaning. Early on, Gordon and Lakoff (1975, p. 83) showed that implications have their usual literal meanings as well as their implied ones. One of their more amusing examples illustrates this beautifully. If a friend of mine comes up to me and out of the blue confides, "Your husband is faithful," I would take that as meaning that he is, in fact, being faithful, but I would also get the implication that he has not been faithful in the recent past. If I had earlier voiced doubts about my husband's faithfulness to this friend, then her comment would be a reassurance that my suspicions are unfounded and no negative implications would be derived. If I had not, the friend's words would be tantamount to letting me know that I had been deceived.

Sweetser (1987, p. 45) puts it well, pointing out that implication and other indirect speech is parasitic on informational speech. In other words, the indirect meaning is based on the actual utterance in oblique but derivable ways. Some speech inappropriate enough to render usual decoding strategies inoperable may still be at least partly interpretable by reference to normal expectations combined with an analysis of what seems to have gone wrong. We will take this matter up subsequently (Chapter 11) but first other treatments of the question of maxims and implicature.

[19] Decision-theoretic Strategies.

Sanders (1987) declares that there is no objective rule which will tell us that a maxim is breached. Rather, in conversations, cospeakers subjectively judge whether or not each others' contributions are irrelevant, imprecise, insufficient, or insincere. He (p. 64) offers the interesting suggestion that this is done by identifying the cospeaker's state of mind about whatever is being communicated. For instance, if an utterance does not seem relevant, then the hearer assumes that the speaker thinks that something in the present or past shared context should be bridging the gap between what has just been said and the general topic.

Sanders (1987, p. 65) offers a similar explanation for what happens if the maxim of manner is breached, the maxim which says the speaker must be clear and precise, " . . . there is a state of affairs that (the speaker considers sufficient to prevent or dissuade him/her from being clearer." Therefore, in his view, the hearer searches for the implication that results from the disparity between utterance and breached maxim.

By way of demonstration, Sanders offers scenarios, such as that in which a student asks a professor what should be done to prepare for a forthcoming exam, and the professor replies "Read the book." Because the professor clearly knows the content of the exam, this response breaches the maxim of quantity. Therefore, it may imply at least one of the following or all three:

- it is up to the student to figure that out
- offering advice would reveal too much
- reading is the best preparation.[14]

The student takes the meaning that best fits his or her view of the professor's beliefs and attitudes.

Sanders offers an interesting and, I think, important approach to meaning. This is not to say that this is all there is to it, however. Even in such a simple scenario, other implicatures can be taken. If the professor intended to convey the second implication above, the response could easily have responded, "I'm sorry, I can't help you with that without giving away too much."

Certain implications arise from a curt, "Read the book." One implication is that the professor doesn't like the inquirer, or that the professor considers him or her stupid.[15] This comes about from the very obviousness of the response. One of the working assumptions of education is that one must read the assigned book in order to prepare for an exam.[16] The professor's words can also be construed as being sarcastic, saying, in effect, "You've got to be pretty dumb to ask me that."

If prior experience warrants it, the student may simply assume that the professor is in a bad mood that day. This highlights the truism that the more experience cospeakers share the more accurate they are in interpreting the other's implicata. It is for this reason that one feels another "isn't so bad" as one gets to know, hence to understand, him or her. This proposition entails a discussion of relevance and of mutual knowledge. Before tackling these, we must examine Carlson's (1983) game-theoretic model of discourse and compare it to the decision-theoretic model presented by Sanders (1987). The model of social interaction as a game is a persistent one. Carlson, for instance, adopts it from Wittgenstein.

[20] Conversation as a Game.

Carlson (1983, p. 102) claims that specific implicatures arise as a result of DIALOGICAL ENTAILMENT. By this he means that the implication arises because it is logically binding given the position of the sentence as a move in the dialogue. That is, implication results from the dialogue as a whole and the position of each sentence within it. As true as this might be, neither context nor position within the sentence guarantees that any given implication arises as the singular logically binding one. If it did, there would be no ambiguity, no misinterpretation, and, probably, no paranoia.

Carlson's central metaphor of conversation being a game, leads him to portray specific utterances as moves in a game in order to achieve one's goals, thereby winning. If one wins, then another loses. This implies that one party to an interaction wins to the detriment of the other. In his view, a coherent text is *"... (well-formed) if it can be extended into a well-formed dialogue game"* (p. 146). This sounds like a debate or a jury trial, not a dialogue.

Both Carlson's teleology and metaphor are suspect. His redefinition of implication presupposes that participants always have in mind clear goals and that each sentence is produced deliberately in order to achieve those goals. It is well known that at least some conversation is produced PHATICALLY, that is for the purpose of social bonding or to conform to cultural norms. Conversations about the weather and inquiring after the health of acquaintances fall into this category, but so may discussions of the upcoming elections, the dissolution of social values, or how funny a recently seen movie is. Although there is conversation designed to achieve goals, much ordinary talking is not so ordered. Patricia Strauss (personal communication) points out that some games are cooperative, therefore do not have winners and losers. This kind of game might provide a better metaphor for conversations.

A major problem with viewing conversation as any kind of game is that speakers can never predict the hearer's response to any conversational "move." Even in complex games like bridge or chess, there are rules which limit, hence help predict, possible actions, and in cooperative ones the goals are clear even if they aren't about winners and losers.

This is not at all true in conversation. As Sanders (1987, p. 183) demonstrates, a game-theoretic model "assumes that the competing agents have to share the same finite pool of resources in pursuing their own interests." Each person's language stock is dependent upon his or own personal histories and there is no way to know all of a cospeakers motives. The research on language acquisition has shown beyond a doubt that children figure out language by themselves from what they hear around them. It has also been known for a long time that no two people have quite the same grammatical system in their heads even if they are native adult speakers (Quirk and Svartvik 1966; Gleitman and Gleitman 1970).[17]

Then, too, what each cospeaker offers affects what the other will then say, and each chooses from an array of multiple messages neither known to nor always guessable by the other, although the messages are usually immediately interpretable. In any conversation, one never knows for sure where the entire is going until it has gone there, no matter how goal-directed the participants were at the outset. Even such goal-directed activities as lecturing may become derailed by unexpected comments or questions. Only in the most formal of speaking activities such as sermons or lectures by invited exalted personages can we be assured of sentences produced so that the conglomerate achieves a predicted goal. If dialogue were truly a game, social interaction would become as glacially slow as an expert chess game, with each participant mulling over possible strategies before entering his or her own move. In actual fact, dialogue with the aim of winning a point or an argument is a special activity, one not necessarily engaged in by most people much of the time. Scholars and attorneys do engage in such competition, but this is part of their professional life, and, as such, acknowledged to be a special activity.[18]

Carlson claims that implications do not arise from violations of maxims. Rather, he says, " . . . they play a prominent role only when they are brought in to account for *apparent* violations . . . " (p. 103, italics his). Therefore, he defines implicature as arising from " . . . an assumption that has to be made about a player's aims or assumptions in order to construe his choice of strategy as a rational one" (p. 103). The problem with this formulation is that it describes all social interaction, not just those construable as violations of maxims. As we saw in the discussion of intention earlier on in this chapter, part of the meaning we get from any utterance depends on the assumptions we make about the person's intention in saying what he or she did. This holds for even apparently uncomplicated straightforward messages like "Joey got mud on the floor."

If I call Scrooge "miserly" but his brother "thrifty" I am certainly implying quite different things, but in no sense can I be said to be violating rules apparent or not. If I say "I always knew Max to be honorable" I am implying a doubt that is not there in "I always knew that Max was honorable." If I say "Max was murdered," I am implying that someone did the dastardly deed again without my violating any rules.

The overriding fact uncovered in all objective studies is that meanings are given and gotten in a very great number of ways. What we can do is chart those ways and interpret in their light, and not resort to nontestable and nonobservable phenomena. Nor should we be seduced by a metaphor purporting to explain all interaction. There are many different kinds of interactions, each yielding its own set of viable interpretations. Neither game theory nor, as we shall see, Freudian theory explains all. Each has its verities, but each is incomplete. Intensive work in sociolinguistics (Chaika 1982b, 1989) and related fields has shown us the multiplicity of interactions occurring in any society, each with its own purpose, its own strategies, and each with its own ego-fulfillment for the individual as well as its social purposes.

Notes

[1]John Lyons (1972, pp. 725–744) does not approve of the term *speech acts* for these phenomena as they don't actually refer to an act of speech, but to a semantic phenomenon. He also demonstrates that speech acts can be carried out without speaking, as in waving someone away. However, he uses the term because, as he says, that is pretty much what everyone else uses. I agree with him on all counts.

[2]If the situation is one in which the speaker had agreed to allow someone to stay in the room on the condition that she be quiet, then "get out of here" is an appropriate paraphrase. In other circumstances it might simply mean, "be less noisy" or "be completely quiet." Similarly *this place stinks* can mean "get out of here" or it can also mean "let [all of] us get out of here" or "clean this place up," or "I have to clean this place up."

[3]Of course, one of the reasons that paranoids can be paranoid is also that people do lie about their intent.

[4]There is also purely social speech such as greetings, untruths intended to "butter people up," and ritualized complimenting as at a wedding. Such speech has been extensively studied ever since Malinowski's insights into phatic communication. We are indebted to the extensive *oeuvre* of scholars like Harvey Sacks and Erving Goffman in delineating such speech (Chaika 1988).

[5]This is not so farfetched as one would imagine. As the wife of a trial attorney, I frequently get phone calls late at night, and, in response to questions about whereabouts, I am often given analogous answers. For instance, "I'm at the airport" tells me that they are at Greene Airport, Rhode Island's only commercial one. If they say, "I'm at North Central," I assume that they pilot and/or own a plane. If they

say, "I'm in Dallas," I assume that they are likely to be in the airport, at a hotel, or in someone else's home, so that their usual home number will not be operative.

[6]Falsehoods strike at the heart of society. Our actions are predicated upon what we perceive are the motives of cospeakers as well as upon their representation of facts.

[7]And, to be sure, general behavior.

[8]All speakers are sometimes ambiguous, but in pathological cases, it seems as if the speaker cannot disambiguate. Of course, we could claim that the one who cannot actually will not, so that it is a matter of cooperation, not pathology. But then we have to ask why this is so typical of schizophrenics and aphasics, but not of people adjudged not afflicted with either condition.

[9]Meaning is not wholly derivable by reference to these maxims, as shown in the sections in this book devoted to semantics, syntax, and cohesion in sentences as well as in discourse analysis.

[10]Although I have no hard data from experimentation on the phenomenon, I have noticed that people often store in memory an implication heard but not acted upon, later recalling it as if it had actually been said. Similarly, they will note a facial expression or kinesic cue, and store its meaning as if it had been said. This seems to account for the situation in which one is retroactively blamed for saying something which one has never said. For instance, one may be accused of having made a negative evaluative comment, when, in fact, the sole "comment" made was by implication or expression. The idiom "turn up your nose at . . . " characterizes such meanings.

[11]As I write this in 1988, I realize that this may have changed for many women in the years since Lakoff, although my students claim that this is true in mixed gender discussions. However, since the interaction in question took place before 1977, we are dealing with a double whammy: a patient who, by definition, is in inferior status, and by being a woman as well, was in actuality in an inferior position. Hence, the extreme mitigation evidenced.

[12]In speech, mitigation can also be effected by prosody, voice quality, amplitude, tempo, pausing, or false starts. In general, paralinguistic cues like these also indicate the speaker's stance towards what he or she is conveying (Kreckel 1981).

[13]*Kill* itself is distinguished from *die* in that *kill* means that someone or something caused something else to die.

[14]It seems to me that this last is a direct answer not an implicature.

[15]This is an implication that students are wont to take. They tend to interpret almost all even remotely negative speech as the professor's not liking them. Perhaps this occurs because of the fact that the professor has to judge the student's worth. Like the sufferer of paranoia, students seem all too often ready to ascribe dislike when it isn't intended.

[16]The truth of this assumption is not the issue. There are courses in which one need not read the books; however, it would be the rare professor who admits that.

[17]For instance, in an investigation of subject-verb agreement in Brown University undergraduates, I found that people didn't agree with their own judgments. Following Quirk and Svartvik, I first administered a written test in which students were given a test which of the same sentences, but with the verb form already selected.

They were asked to reject or accept the sentence. To my astonishment, people often rejected the very forms they had previously selected. This was not random behavior. In all such cases there were clear disparities between the meaning of the noun and the correct grammatical form of the verb. For instance, some chose a singular verb for *There has always been a time to speak and a time to be silent,* but when given this identical sentence later on, they rejected it, saying it should be *there have* ... More recently, I have discovered a disjunction in acceptability of *Let no man rejoice until he* **find** *life.* About half the students in one class no longer would use that subjunctive, insisting on *Let no man rejoice until he* **finds** *life.* Those who, like me, can use both get the meaning in the first that he is not likely to find life, whereas the latter indicates he has a good chance. Others who only allow the first got no such meaning differential, and simply found the second wrong.

[18]Additionally, those persons who treat each dialogue as a game from which they have to emerge as a victor is highly confrontational, and are often perceived as having an ego problem, not to mention obnoxious.

Chapter Eight

THE ICE CREAM STORIES:
A STUDY OF NARRATION

The study of psychotic and normal narratives discussed in Chapter 6 demonstrated speech disruptions peculiar to psychotics. Some occurred only in schizophrenics. Normals produced as much error, but it was different both in degree and in kind from the pscyhotic one. Both normals and psychotics had the same amount of misperceptions, but these were often mutually exclusive to each population. This study showed that psychotic deviation is neither normal nor creative.

[1] The Nature of Schizophrenic Error.

Close examination of the narratives in the Ice Cream Story task discussed in this chapter revealed that Fromkin (1975) was in error when she claimed that schizophrenics make the same kinds of errors that normals do. It will be shown here that the former population differs from the latter both in degree and in kind of error. Psychotic error is very real and displays a true disintegration of linguistic ability on every level except, perhaps, the phonemic, but word retrieval, syntactic error, narrative construction, all the facets of informing and commenting indicate a far from intact linguistic ability even in the very simple task presented to the population discussed here.

More recently Allen (1985) maintains that schizophrenic speech, both SD and NSD, can be reliably discriminated from normal speech by a clinician with acumen, but that the ways it is different cannot be specified. Actually, as we have seen, it has long been known that even laypersons can discriminate schizophrenic speech from normal. It is no surprise that a clinician can do so reliably, but to say that this is only because of acumen, not from specifiable features is a strange conclusion by a scientist. It is true that people do seem to react intuitively towards language, but it is still possible to analyze the bases of intuitions by comparison between populations. True, the average clinician has not studied much linguistics, but there are linguists of many stripes who study language objectively. As we saw in Chapter 1, the features of schizophrenic speech can be depicted.

The ICS studies described here directly compare the features of schizophrenic, manic, and normal speech elicited by the task discussed in the previous chapter.

[2] Rating and Testing of Participants.

As we have just seen, the differences between normal and psychotic narrations are not necessarily caused by differences in the number of cohesive ties used by each population. Nor were they caused by differences in the length of narrations between the two populations, nor, as we shall see here, are they caused by differences in the amount of misperception by each group. Rather, as shown below, other features of the narratives were implicated. There are real differences between the two populations, psychotics and normals, and these coincide with those features of speech long known to be pathognomic of schizophrenia. One psychotic was judged normal, but he was taped at the time of discharge. Upon his initial selection his speech did show deviation but had improved by the time of his participation.

Two normals were rated as schizophrenic by one judge. A third normal was rated that way by both judges. The normals erroneously judged as schizophrenic produced features in their narratives which correlated with the deviations in the psychotic group. Whether or not these normals were at risk for schizophrenia or whether their deviations could be attributed to excessive nervousness or the like could not be determined within the confines of this study. The procedures for testing were particularly nonthreatening. All subjects were even allowed to hold the tape recorder in their hands to lessen anxiety. All we can say is that there are definitely features of narration which lead to judgments of psychosis and some ostensible normals may evince these. One conclusion that can't be made, however, is that SD schizophrenics speak normally during their psychotic bouts.

It bears repeating that we must test for those skills necessary for daily speech activities. We must ensure that our explanations take into account the skills needed for normal speech production because speech readily labeled "schizophrenic" is evident in ordinary interaction. It is equally vital to employ a narrative task that can be matched to what the participant is trying to encode so that we can compare the utterance with its target. Narration, in itself, also requires the encoding of ongoing events, which in turn demands temporal sequencing and shifting references, thus testing for a variety of speaking skills and simulating everyday speaking situations.

The narrative task employed here also carries a lighter cognitive load than did Rochester and Martin's. Explaining the points of cartoons, retelling anecdotes, and describing unusual colors are not everyday activities and would seem to present a greater cognitive load than a mere retelling of an ordinary sequence of events. As a result, it is sometimes difficult to correlate utterances with intended meaning. As Maher et al. (1966) and Maher (1972) noted, the more unconstrained the speech activity, the more disorganized schizophrenic speech becomes.

Because of the strong constraints put on responses in the task reported on here, glossomanic chaining, for instance, in its above-shown "classic" forms did not occur, although a variant of it did. What is perhaps most surprising is that patients did utter both gibberish and agrammatisms despite the constraints on the task, and despite claims of researchers that such aphasia-like symptoms are rare in schizophrenia.

As previously explained, actively psychotic patients frequently have a short attention span so that the ICS could not be as complex as Chafe's Pear Story. Still, some extraneous material was included because one of the characteristics of the speech of schizophrenics frequently mentioned in the psychiatric literature in their veering from the topic at hand. Given hypotheses about the nature of schizophrenic malfunctioning in attention and filtering, it was expected that the extraneous material would cause derailment. Actually, when derailment occurred, it was from the essential plot and appeared to be caused by intrusions from memory, as is shown below.

Despite its simplicity, the Ice Cream Stories tested for many language skills and attentional and logical phenomena. For instance, the viewer had to leap one important gap. The father is not actually seen giving the child money, nor does he answer her in words. When one sees her walking in to buy the ice cream, one might surmise that the father must have given some money to her. Scenes such as one showing the mother setting the table were included to see if they would cause the narrator to be deflected from the major progression of action, perhaps starting off on something relative to mealtimes or mothers or family incidents (Chaika 1982a; Lecours and Vanier-Clement 1976). However, deflection caused by these side actions did not happen.

The 124-second story proved to be well within the attention span of all participants. The opening shot, panning a shopping center, focusing on a child wearing a plaid skirt and vest with a long-sleeved jersey peering into the window of a Baskin Robbins, took 20 seconds. Later, when the child enters the ice cream store, it takes 23 second for her to be waited on. In terms of effects on the narrations, these seemed to be the only significant time spans.

Originally, there was to be a memory task as well, in which I asked subjects to recall what they had seen the previous week. Unfortunately, too often patients were discharged before the week was up or received ECT in the interim which wiped out their recall entirely. Consequently, although I may allude to the memory task from time to time, no attempt was made to analyze their relation to the first narrative or to run any kind of statistical measures on them.

[3] Selecting Participants.

All patients were being treated with antipsychotic medication as well as antiparkinsonian medication designed to mitigate the side effects of the former. All also were receiving lithium (Alexander, VanKammer, and Bunney 1979). The effect of these is to lessen the effects of psychosis, so that speech is made more normal. This makes even more important the very real differences found between the normal and psychotic narratives. The average stay at the hospital during the time of this study was less than 2 weeks. No participant had been institutionalized or heavily medicated for long periods. Hence our results could not be traced to social or cognitive deficits on those grounds.

Twenty-five normal volunteers matched the psychotic population as closely as possible in age, occupation, and social class. Both groups consisted of blue-collar workers and college students. As is usual between psychotic and normal groups, the normals were somewhat higher in achievement. This effect was mitigated by including normal college students with working-class parents and psychotics with college-educated parents.

As already discussed, social class is not a factor in this study. Patients were selected solely on the bases of diagnosis and observed speech dysfunction. However, we still have to contend with Bernstein's theory of **restricted** and **elaborated codes.** He assumed, and so have his followers, that working class is limited in their ability to discuss issues intellectually because they have been socialized to speak of the here and now rather than of hypothetical and abstract issues. Because both our patient and control populations came from mixed social backgrounds, we could observe any mitigating effect of early socialization on speech performance.

Bernstein's theory of differential narrative adequacy rests upon a theory of socialization such that, if it were valid, parental status should be as important as earned achievement, especially for nonachieving children of educated parents. One could argue that those who rise from the working class do so because they somehow learn on their own what Bernstein calls the elaborated code (Bernstein 1971). However, it is difficult to claim the reverse, the scions of the middle class sink, as it were, because they, despite their socialization, only learned a restricted code, for Bernstein's claim is that the latter is different in kind from the former, not just in degree and that this is a product of different communicative styles of families who come from different social classes (Chaika 1982b, 1989 for further arguments against Bernstein's theories). In any event, the data presented here correlated with diagnosis of psychosis versus normality, not with social class. There was no effect traceable to social class, but there certainly was one related to illness or lack of it.

The three normals judged psychotic by both raters were all college educated. Their narratives showed definite correlates with the psychotic ones. Rochester and Martin (1979) likened increased use of exophora by schizophrenics to Bernstein's theory of restricted code amongst the working classes. No evidence emerged that differential social class membership affects reference.

[4] Intentionality and Cooperation.

Intentionality is always an integral part both of speech production and of meaning itself (Searle 1983. (p. 3). He defines intentionality as directedness, and shows that meaning is comprised of " ... Intentional content that goes with the form of externalization" (Searle, pp. 28–29). Thus normal comprehension demands that we derive Intentionality as well as truth value (Chaika 1982b, p. 71, 1989; Goody 1978). If speech is so deviant that we cannot do so, then we fault the speaker. If the speaker does not encode so that his or her Intentionality (or truth value) can be derived, and, if further, the speaker cannot explain when asked, we fault the speaker, not the hearer. Hence, we consider the opaque or deviant speech of psychotics as evidence of a person's being "out of his/her mind." Similarly, as Searle (1983 (p. 43) shows with visual perceptions, when people see things that are not objectively there, we say " . . . it is the visual experience and not the world which is at fault."

Searle (1983, p. 147) introduces another component to meaning, one especially valuable in this discussion: the Background. He defines this as ". . . . capacities and social practices." Hence, Background includes " . . . skills, preintentional assumptions and presuppositions, practices and habits" (Searle 1983, p. 154). Under this view, a breakdown in surface performance is a failure of " . . . preintentional capacities that underlie the intentional states in question" (Searle 1983, p. 155). To treat that which arises from faulty Background as if it were " . . . a sort of Intentionality, it immediately becomes problematic" (Searle 1983, p. 159).

What this means here is that we assume that narratives which are deviant arise from impaired skills in narration, not from a separate language or an attempt to hide taboo desires or an attempt to convey what it means to be schizophrenic or the like. This applies to deviation in what is reported or in the way that it is reported. This is the simplest explanation that fits the facts; therefore, in accordance with the application of Occam's razor, it is the one adopted in the explanations below.

We have already seen that there are five reasons for believing that the participants in this study understood the task, were cooperating in it, and intended to fulfill it. The following passages from SD narratives show this. Even those whose narratives were not accurate took as their point of departure the sequence shown. Moreover, when they digressed from this, they related stories similar to that on the screen, and kept returning the events (boldface) actually shown them, as in

> 1A. What do you want me to say? I say my brother Gene. He says he said I buy the things I wanted. **I saw a little girl who wanted ice cream.** Today you have to pay for it. Today she paid for it . . .

This starts out with an irrelevant comment about her brother, but quickly reverts to the business of the video. Actually, since this was about somebody wanting something, even the bit about her brother Gene saying that she should buy what she wanted can be seen to have been triggered by the video.

Second, where someone hallucinated or misperceived action, he or she indicated an effort to integrate it into the story. In 2A, for instance, when the patient says, "I don't know what . . . that was about," he indicates that he cannot fit what he perceives into the story. The description of the cars was also accurate, although he misperceived that the girl was moving a counter and was looking in a trash can:

2A. I saw a little girl who was moving a counter for some reason and **I don't know what the heck that was about. She was pressing against it okay.** In the beginning I saw a white car with a red vinyl top and then this little girl was lookin' in the store was **looking in the trashcan or something** and then she turned around and she went on she talked to her mother and her father and neither one of them was listening to her . . .

Here, note also the "okay" as indicating that although he didn't "know what the heck that was about" he was going forth with the narrative anyway. Interestingly, the following week, on recall, the same patient said

2B. . . . I remember seein' the little girl **I don' know if her head was in a trash, she was lookin' in the trash or she was lookin' in the window to a store** . . .

He did not mention moving a counter, but he had obviously recalled his misperception about the trashcan. In both narratives, the patient proceeded to recount the events clearly triggered by the videostory, although lexical selection was clearly deviant, a matter discussed below. the first mention of *trash* either omitted *can* or or used *a* instead of the *the*. Since *trash* belongs to the category of MASS NOUNS,[1] therefore cannot be used with *a.*

Third, several made overt comments about their ability to speak or to remember something on the tape. For instance, one apologized:

3 . . . she just cunna's cunna get anything home so she's hafta go out on her and get it. okay. **I'm sorry. I'm sorry. I'm sorry about my speech. I stutter a lot though.** That's about it.

Another indicated that he had a "memory lapse." This also shows an effort to recount what was shown:

4. . . . and I noticed a little girl looking into the window and I guess he walked back into the store and then a [kif] thing switched where the girl was at home and I dunno asked her mother for something and she had a kni- **got a little memory lapse there.** Then it switched again and her father came in . . .

Self-corrections also indicated the patient's attempts to recount the story, thus to cooperate in the task as did expressing happiness that the girl got her ice cream, both shown in:

> 5. . . . so then she went and she went to the candy store by herself **or ice cream shop** and bought a double-decker ice cream cone. **That actually brought me happiness to see that little girl with a mind of her own. Okay.**

Even the most deviant narratives signalled endings formally, marking the narrative as an entity. The "That's about it" in 3 above is one example, as is the "Okay" in 5. Normals often ended their narratives the same way.

[5] Visual and Verbal Scanning.

The parallel between visual scanning and narration made by Chafe (1980) was borne out in this study. His claim is that the narrative itself progresses in a fashion similar to the way the eye searches a scene. As we have already seen, there is a correlation between schizophrenic dysfunction in visual tracking (Holzman et al. 1978; Holzman 1978) with dysfunctions in their free speech. Chaika (1982a) showed that both the sacades and the spiky-type movement are analogous to schizophrenic utterances. The sacades show lack of focusing ability, a deficit in tracking, what Holzman terms a failure to turn on the system. The spiky type movement represents perseverations along associative pathways. The entire narrative from which 1A above comes illustrates these remarks:

> 1B. What do you want me to say? I saw my brother Gene. He says he said I buy the things that I wanted. I saw a little girl who wanted ice cream. Today you have to pay for it but today she paid for it.I want Gene to come visit me soon at 1:30 and I saw a little girl with the baby and her father's gonna be home and and oh yeah and [hehe] my mother loves me [aw hehe] I don't know what I want to say. Can I stop now?

Note that the first question is entirely appropriate as a narrative opener. However, the story line is intertwined with her memories and desires. She "sees" her brother Gene and even gives a sentence to expand on her mention of him. Except for the fact that the video had nothing whatsoever to do with Gene, the opening statements are appropriate for a narrative. It can be seen that the sentences about the brother were triggered by the video and were a **parallel encoding** to the tale about the girl wanting to buy ice cream. This is analogous to what Holzman found in visual sacades. The story is not tracked from start to finish.

In the next sentence, the narrator jumps back to the videostory proper. Since this does deal with buying which entails paying, she veers off the narrative track to the cliché, *today you have to pay for it,* then changes the pronoun to one appropriate to the story, *but today she paid for it.* Note the slight mismatch of meaning and the story. *Today you have to pay for it* implies that yesterday you didn't which is patently untrue. In its sense as a cliché, this refers to moral issues, not money.

This patient gives other verbal sacades. She first follows her inner story about Gene, then jumps to the videostory, then jerks back to Gene, then jumps to a girl with a baby, then the father who is going to be home then her mother who loves her.

Another patient encoded a visual pun. He noticed a similarity in stance between two actions and attributed it to the wrong one despite the fact that the context itself did not lend itself to this alternate interpretation. This occurred in the statement "I saw a little girl who was moving a counter for some reason and I don't know what the heck that was about." The girl's stance, leaning forward against the ice cream case as she is waiting to be served, is similar to that when one is moving a heavy object. Such similarities in body positions are not usually noticed when the circumstances eliciting them are so very different. Nothing else in the video lent itself to a theory of "moving a counter," and one doesn't usually even think of moving counters, and one especially would not think that a child would be moving the counter. Still, the narrator gave the wrong interpretation to this stance. We can only be reminded of the wild puns that schizophrenics fall victim to, such as the punning of *wise, whys, noble, and no-bill,* connections that most others would not notice.

The opening scene, 20 seconds long, started with almost random shots of a parking lot: people walking by, cars pulling in. Because of this, there was a verbal parallel to the visual process upon first seeing a scene and not having a frame to put it in. Not knowing what is going to be relevant, the person tries to note everything that is going on until he or she figures out a frame for the unfolding scenario. Once this frame is constructed for normals, only matters relevant to the story line get mentioned. Because all participants, normal and psychotic, were recounting the story immediately after seeing it, they didn't all get the correct frame at first. Those who displayed this searching behavior spoke as if their initial narration was wholly unedited, so that they verbally recounted the visual scanning upon first seeing a scene. Many of both populations started by describing the cars and the people in the opening scene. Note the similarity of the normal opener in 6A to the psychotic one in 6B.

> 6A. First I saw a parking lot with a lot of cars and I noticed an ice cream shop I think it was a Baskin Robbins store. A woman walked by and another gentleman came from the opposite direction and he walked past the screen and then I noticed a little girl standing outside looking into the ice cream shop . . .
>
> 6B. Okay. There's a lady who was walking toward the car and I forget it she was wa—she walked by the car is what it was and they went past the car and a man walked by a store a Baskin and Robbins sign it was the scene before so wa let's see then one once they went past the man zooming in they they zoomed in on a girl . . .

There is no substantive difference between these narrations up to this point. The psychotic rendering is more detailed than any normal one was, but still, up to this point, 6B above is well within the bounds of normal.

The differences between populations occurred right after these initial scannings. Once normals zeroed in on the girl staring in the window, they related only those points of action that furthered the plot, typically that the child went home, asked her mother for ice cream, the mother refused her because it was too near suppertime, the father came home, the child asked him for ice cream, the child went back to the ice cream shop and ordered ice cream which she received.

This "zeroing-in" tactic, also a finding in Chafe (1980), is easily seen in the degree of detail in description of characters first seen, such as noting that "a man with a three-piece suit minus the jacket walked by" or that a woman with a shopping bag also walked by. However, such matters were never again mentioned once the narrator got his or her bearings. This was true of normals and psychotics. Not one person mentioned the clothing of either parent, although each was on film far longer than the casual passersby at the outset. Similarly, many carefully described the opening parking-lot scenario but the kitchen, which was important to the plot, received only one mention and that, by a psychotic, commented on color: "There were cur-blue curtains. It was kinda brown the room they're in."

This scanning was not the only initial tactic. Some immediately focused on the girl. Again, the two populations made substantially similar openings. For instance, compare the normal

> 6C. It began with a girl staring through a window at a Baskin Robbins store

to the psychotic

> 6D. I seen a little girl looking in the window and she want some ice cream. . . .

[6] Temporal Ordering.

After the openers just illustrated, differences between the two populations quickly became evident. Once normals got their bearings, so to speak, they usually followed a strict temporal ordering in narration. They gave the impression of play-by-play description. First this happened, then that, and that, and so on to the conclusion. For example, the following is an exceptionally detailed opening scene by a normal who seemed to have a bit of a problem knowing what to zero in on. His narrative was the most detailed one evoked.

> 7A. When it first came on a car drove by and then we were looking at the Baskin-Robbins store and another car . . . As we closed in towards the store the [pause] picture started and stopped, stopped and started[2] and we saw a man walk by and then came into a little girl no it was a lady walked by then we came in to a little girl standing by a window in a plaid dress and a white, it appeared to be a white, long sleeved shirt. Then we went to a home and it was the same little girl asking her mother if she could have something and then her mother said no, it was too close to supper. Later, she went up to her father who had just walked in the door and asked him if she could have some ice cream which is I guess what she asked her mother and we didn't hear her father's answer but then we return to Baskin-Robbins and she walked into the door and ordered some kind of ice it looked like raspberry and um the man she waited for the ice cream cone at this time her shirt appeared yellow. [heh] and the man gave her the ice cream cone, she paid for it and left.

In contrast, psychotics often failed to create an orderly progression. For instance, the following is a psychotic rendering with a detailed opening. Despite the fact that it is longer than 7A, it does not provide as much detail.

> 7B. All right. The first thing we see is an ice cream ayuh it could've been a shopping center with two cars parked in front or drives up in front and waits get the impression that someone goes [aᵘ] out of the car and walks in front and sees in the window of the same one of these shopping center stores a little girl waiting for some ice cream or something or other because she goes home to her house asks her father for ice cream he says well what the heck give it to her [noowee] Sh-sh- she's a little daughter so he gets her the coins and she goes up ice cream stand and stands in line[3] and gets a giant sized cone and she uh is so happy with her ice cream a simple pleasure but that's what kids are like these days always have but th- it means that [shinchuer] her parents that she's [shuh] so proud of **she goes out leaves the ice cream 'n eats it** and on the way 'n we don't know what happens [smæ] the fact. You can interpolate and say that **she ate the ice cream and brought it home** and said thank you daddy or thank you mummy but she still is her destination is not known in a few minutes and you say that's just one pen memory in the brain? How does that how does that able to reach that conclusion.

Besides the neologisms, the boldfaced segments are narrating completely impossible temporal sequences. In the second sequence, the action has been flip-flopped. She would have had to take the ice cream home and then eat it. The first sequence involves mutually exclusive occurrences. If the ice cream is eaten it can't be left, and if it is left then it can't be eaten if the girl goes out. Notice that the individual items in each phrase are linguistically correct. They just have not been organized correctly into the narrative. Additionally, for all its verbiage, this telling omits the entire scene of the child asking the mother for ice cream, but it does contain matters absolutely underivable from the video, such as the girl's being proud of her parents. With all its length it shows far less detail of what had transpired than did short normal narratives, like:

> 8A. I saw a little girl looking into an ice cream store and she went home and asked her mother if she could have some ice cream and her mother said no because it was too close to supper and then she asked her father and her father gave her the money and she went back to the ice cream store and bought some ice cream.

Comparing this with a short narrative from a psychotic, we still see a similar disparity in reporting of detail and the actual events encoded, as in

8B. A little girl wanted things and her mother said no and her father came home and she asked for some ice cream and then she went back to the store and then she ordered some ice cream and the man said thank you.

In 8B, there is no introduction at all. It says that the girl wanted "things" which is not an accurate encoding of the desired commodity. No reason is given for the mother's refusal. Although the patient did say that the girl went *back* to the store, nowhere previously did it say that she had been at a store. There is also a strange gap between the girl's ordering ice cream and the man's thank you. No little gaps like this occur in normal narratives. In those, the "thank you" might not be mentioned, but the girl's receiving the ice cream was.

Actually, 8B was very accurate and even detailed for a psychotic narrative. Consider the paucity of:

8C. Well I saw a young lady peekin' in a win- no lookin' through the window an 'uh other men passing by and then she went in there an' she bought some ice cream for herself. Um I really don't know what else to say um because that's all I saw.

Although the germ of the story is there, that the young lady bought ice cream, all the other detail is missing. The significance of the men, and what *in there* refers to are never explained. There's no plot or purpose to this.

8D. All about ice cream 'n I coulda really went for a cone. . . . I saw a parked car near an ice cream parlor 'n a little girl wantin' ice cream her mother refused her but her father gave her the money for it. And she bought the ice cream 'n she was gonna **neat** it.

Often the poverty of the narrative in terms of what is included and the order of presentation is matched by other disintegrated speech:

9A. A little girl, she's uh she's on her own. She's so [weh] she gets her [aᵘsoh uh uh oᵘ] after she ask her own father if she can go out for ice ice cream and he says eh answers her [shi] dunno and get ice cream for herself ice cream for herself and [ess] pass by [sh wu] and so it all happened [eh] that they're all happy . . . She just cunna's cunna get anything home so she's hafta go out on her and get it. Okay. I'm sorry, I'm sorry. I'm sorry about my speech. [me: your speech is fine]. I stutter a lot though.

9B. Well I saw it divided up into three segments. First segment was outdoors. It involved automobiles and a small child and it was kind of disturbing because to me because I don't like the noises of cars. The camera was quite shaky um that was sort of disturbing but that's usually happens with videotape um kinda worried me to see the girl leaning her head against the glass that's kinda disturbing um only because I identify with that um the second segment was filmed in almost an orange very warm sort of color.

9C. What I saw? Uh, a car waiting in front of an ice cream shop a car drove by a girl looking through a window into an ice cream shop uh mmm a man a lady walkin' by with groceries [uhnu] when she switched into a family's house the girl talking to her mother her mother her mother setting dishes her father came through the door there were cur- blue curtains 'n it was kinda brown the room they're in uh ask girl if she din't have ice cream 'n the girl went and bought ice cream.

These psychotic narratives supply detail not germane to the plot and omit essential ones. The color of the curtains had no relevance to the story nor did an orange tone in the second segment. The repetitions about feeling disturbed, the shakiness of the camera, none of these were made relevant. Even though one narrator said that she identified with "that," ostensibly with the girl looking in the window, we are not told why she identifies with that, what import it had.

Some psychotic narratives did manifest detailed tracking, as in

10A. Okay. There's a lady who was ah walking towards a car and uh, I forget it she walked by the car is what it was okay and then uh it zoomed in past the car 'n they went past the car a man walked by a store a Baskin-Robbins sign it was the scene before [laughs] so wa le's see. Then once they went past the man they zoomed in on a girl and the girl looking in a window so wa- from there they were on that for a while then they switched to the family scene where ah the lady . . . I guess the girl was asking the mother for ah some money for ice cream 'n I guess she didn't give her any 'n her father came in [shavaw][4] they switched to the front door[5] 'n her father came in 'n the girl ran up and asked for some money. I guess he gave in 'n [laughing] he gave her some money. So wa she ran down to the ice cream store and bought a double scoop of chocolate ice cream.

The difference between this and the normal narratives above, is that the greatest detail occurs at the outset with extraneous matters. Fully half of this is concerned with the lady, the man, and the cars. Even so, it does not encode the opening sequence so that a hearer can form a picture of what happened. It was impossible for anybody not to walk by or towards a car in the crowded parking lot portrayed. Neither walked to any particular car, nor were they shown getting out of cars. We simply see them walking separately. This is encoded as if the focus was on the pedestrians and it wasn't. For instance, notice that the patient says that "once they went past the man they zoomed in on a girl." This sounds as if these actions were related and they weren't. After all opening detail, we are not told what kind of window the girl is looking in, the phrase "switched to the family scene" is a vague encoding. The patient does mention that the girl requested ice cream from the mother, but she is said only to ask her father for money without specifying what for. This is recognizably psychotic, but there is no bizarre imagery; it does pretty much say what was on the video; it is grammatical. It is the narration itself that is perceived as abnormal.

In contrast, in all narratives judged normal regardless of length, the narrator typically tracks the events. Even if undirected visual scanning occurs at the outset, once the participant gets his or her bearing so to speak, the events are encoded as they happened with no crucial part of the story being left out, **crucial in the sense of what motivated subsequent action.** One normal narrator adjudged psychotic by both raters failed to mention that the girl asked the mother for the ice cream and failed to maintain temporal ordering[6]:

> 10B. A young girl getting ice cream at a ice cream parlor. Let's see what are the—and there was a scene with her and her parents. She asked her father if he would give her some money to get the ice cream and before that she was hanging around outside the ice cream parlor. Okay, let's see. How about she had a yellow shirt on. Whatever. A sort of jumpsuit.

10C was judged psychotic by one of the raters. In part, this may have been because of his faulty tracking.

> 10C. What I saw was [uh] a young girl looking through uh an ice

cream parlor window I saw her go home to her parents, I guess they were her parents, I saw her go home and ask what I assume to be her parents if she could have an ice cream. I saw her get rejected by one. I saw one give in and gave her money to go get an ice cream cone. She went down she bought it and left.

He starts out correctly saying that first she looked in the window, then she went home to her parents. Then he backtracked and said he guessed they were her parents, and then said he assumed they were. He was the only normal who perseverated on a point. This kind of overprecision is otherwise seen only in psychotics. Like the previous narrator erroneously judged as psychotic, this one collapses the request to "a scene with her and her parents." Notice that neither of these encodes error. "Asking parents" certainly would be an acceptable paraphrase of a child's asking first one parent and then the other, but in this task, hearers apparently expect certain kinds of orderly encoding of events. As we shall see with misperceptions, it is not truth *per se* that causes speech to be judged normal or abnormal, but structure.

All other normals said that the girl wanted ice cream, asked her mother for some, was refused, asked her father, and then went back to the store to buy her ice cream. The only point of difference in this tracking of events was whether or not the narrator mentioned that the father must have given the child money. Apart from the two exceptions mentioned above, if normals evinced a gap it was that they simply didn't mention if the father gave her the money. For instance:

10D. I saw [uh] a young girl enter the kitchen ask her mother if she could have an ice cream cone and the mother says no it's too close to your dinner and she walked out of the room and a moment later her father walked in from work an' she says to her father, "Can I have an ice cream cone?" and the next sequence showed her walkin' into an ice cream parlor an' buying the ice cream cone and walkin' out.

10E. . . . her father walked in from work and' she says to her father, "Can I have an ice cream cone?" an' the next sequence showed her walkin' into the ice cream parlor . . .

10F. . . . she asked her father who she bumped into[7] As he walked through the door same question he didn't answer [ah ne] it all it does show her go walking into the ice cream stand . . .

These gaps are exact renderings of the video in which the child asks for ice cream, but the father's response is not given. Six normals encoded the gap, but since it was a factual tracking of the video, none were judged psychotic.

Another apparent exception to temporal ordering in a normal seems to have been a slip of the tongue. One subject said, "He [her father] stuck his hand in his pocket and then the film ended," but then proceeded to describe the girl going back to the store and buying the ice cream. Apparently, what this subject was encoding was that the scene in which the father is seen putting his hand towards his pants pocket is abruptly cut off. She did not mean that the narrative was through. She was rated normal by both judges and her narrative conformed to the normal ones in every other way.

[7] Narrative Glitches.

Both normals and psychotics produced glitches which interrupted the flow in the narratives. Fromkin's (1975) assertion that schizophrenic error is not different from normal error was not borne out as there were three categories of glitching produced only by psychotics, and one produced only by normals. Both populations started a word, broke off, and then restarted as in

START-RESTART

11A. f-f-for
11B. she we-went
11C. the way the way they did that either.

but only normals started a phrase, broke it off to insert a prior event or a comment on their word choice and then resumed the phrase as in (underlining shows interrupted phrase and its pickup. Boldface is interruption):

COMMENT-CORRECTION

12A. and then she—her father came home from work, whatever —she asked her father for money.
12B. and a white—it appeared to be white —long-sleeved shirt
12C. so when her father came home—or the man who came in the door I thought it was her father —came in the door.

In contrast, if psychotics broke off in the middle of a phrase, they never picked it up, creating strange syntactic gapping.

Both populations evinced false starts but only the psychotic ones were unrelated to the ultimate selection of words as in

12D. he ch- told where to go

Some of the neologizing and gibberish below could also be counted as evidence of such unrelated false starting. In contrast, normal false starts could be seen to be self-correction, as in

12E. **she-we** saw
12F. it looked like a chocolate **su**- a chocolate ice cream **cone**

The first involved a correct pronoun change, and in the second, the speaker apparently started to say *sundae,* but corrected it to the proper word *cone.* The perceptual error of calling the ice cream chocolate was one made by many normals, none of whom corrected it.

Only psychotics produced words which rhymed with the apparent target, as in

13A. he **twitched** through the door.
13B. that's all I can **stew**

The *twitch* was probably intended to be *switched* as it was a reference to the camera action and the *stew* was apparently a misretrieval for *do* as it ended the narrative.

[8] Neologizing and Gibberish.

Neologizing and gibberish occurred in psychotic narratives, although one normal also produced a short stretch of gibberish. Given the constraints on the task this was not wholly expected. Actually, there were no neologisms comprised of recognizable morphemes, such as *puterience* or *plausity.* All of the examples here could as easily be called neologisms or gibberish. What occurred is a stretch that sounded like a short word in an otherwise comprehensible passage or two or three syllable stretches. We have already seen some of these like *kif* in 4 above. This is unusual in that there were few other such errors in that narrative. Typically, nonwords like [aᵘsoh uh uh oᵘ], [shi], [ess], [sh wu] [cunna's cunna] were produced by patients who displayed other lexical problems as in

14A. a little girl taking a **dit** asking for ice cream from her mother her says says that it's too close to dinnertime so she goes to her father an' asked if she can have then goes to the ice cream **place** and orders a double scoop of **something which I didn't understand** just taking

efu taking control away from her mother asking mm asking her father **fsh** if her father said no she should've gone to her mother.

Besides the obvious neologizing, *dit, efu,* and *fsh,* we see nonaccurate lexical choice or circumlocution as in speaking of *the ice cream place,* rather than *parlor* or *shop,* and *something which I didn't understand* instead of a cover term like "ice cream." (See sec 10 for syntax error.) The patient above who said [shinchuer] and [smæ] showed other not quite normal lexical choices such as "she's a little daughter."

There was even one normal lapse into gibberish

14B. So therefore she **etuh** she **ed** she listened.

Even though this normal produced these apparent neologisms in her two false starts, she recouped almost immediately finishing the construction she had stumbled on. In all other respects her narrative was normal. It encoded the events correctly. Given her recouping here, this is more like the COMMENT-CORRECTION of normals seen above. She starts out with an error but is able to go back to the target utterance despite the interruption. There is still control.

[9] Lexical Choices.

There were three other problems with lexical choice. The first involved selection of words that rhymed with the apparent target word, but bore no semantic similarity with it, as in 13A—B above. The second was inexact wording, using a HYPONYM, the general classification under which the word falls, rather than the exact word for the meaning. The third consisted of selecting several words to add up to a target word. These typically overinflated what was intended.

The use of hyponyms is illustrated by subjects who said that the girl wanted *things* or *something* rather than saying she wanted ice cream fell into this category. The one normal who did this, in A above, recouped later on in the narrative, indicating that he realized his error, by saying she asked her father for ice cream "which is I guess what she asked her mother." In contrast, vague wording by psychotics did not get corrected. Notice the misencodings of

15A. What I saw. Uh a car waiting in front of an ice cream shop a car drove by a girl looking through a window into an ice cream shop uh mmm a man . . . a lady walking by with groceries [uh'n nu] when she switched **into a family's house** the girl **talking to her mother** her mother setting dishes her father came through the door there were cur- blue curtains 'n it was kinda brown the room they're in uh ask girl **if she din't have ice cream** 'n the girl went and bought ice cream.

Notice the inexact wording. The scene changed to "a family's house." It is usually assumed that families reside in houses so that one doesn't qualify by specifying that. The opposite occurrence, a house occupied by persons other than a family, is the one that has to be specified, even with today's current changes in family life. This improper specification is matched by the fact that the narrator uses the indefinite article *a* rather than the specific *her* in introducing the house. This is as much a syntactic error as a lexical one as the grammar of English requires that a marker of old information, such as a personal pronoun or *the,* introduce an item or location belonging to some one who has been introduced. Then, the narrator encodes the girl's request to her mother as "talking to her mother." Nowhere is it mentioned what she is talking about. Another patient made an analogous error:

15B. He says well what the heck give it to her [nooee] **sh-she's a little daughter.**

Strictly speaking, all girls are little daughters, but usually, when someone mentions a little daughter they precede it by a possessive, such as saying that Betty is "Max's little daughter" or that the girl over there is "my little daughter." Other than that, one might say of someone else's child, "she's like a little daughter to me," but the plain unvarnished "she's a little daughter" is not usual.[8]

Some psychotic lexical choices are reminiscent of mild anomic aphasia.[9] For instance, when the child pays for her ice cream, one patient encoded this as

15C. The cash register man handled the financial matters.

Calling a clerk a "cash register man," although readily understandable, spreads the semantic features adhering to *clerk* over too many words. Using such a roundabout phrasing implies that the "cash register man" is not a normal clerk. In this instance, such special implications were not appropriate. The clerk behind the counter who dipped the ice cream was in every respect an ordinary young male clerk. Similarly, handling financial matters refers to transactions far more glorious and important than ringing up the sale of an ice cream cone.

Another patient, C.T., couched the act of the father's giving the child money thusly:

15D. He says "well, what the heck give it to her [nooee] she's a little daughter so he **gets her the coins** . . . "

To speak of getting the coins implies that one is fetching some coins of great value or those in a coin collection. The father *gives* her *change* or *money.*

C.T., the patient who uttered both 15B and 15D above also created several neologisms indicating that he had a general problem in lexical retrieval. He frequently used literary words, such as saying

15E. You can **interpolate** and say that she ate the ice cream and brought it home and said thank you daddy thank you daddy or thank you mummy but she still is **her destination is not known in a few minutes.**

In such a narrative, one would expect "I'm not sure she went home." both the word *destination* and the passive voice *is not known* are the wrong register for the situation. Although this patient spoke copiously, his speech was larded with such inappropriate phrasings. A straightforward misencoding occurred as he was setting the scene

15F. All right. The first thing we see is an ice cream [ayuh] it could've been a shopping center with two cars parked in front car drives up in front and waits get the impression that someone goes out of the car and walks in front and **sees in the window of the same one of these shopping center stores a little girl waiting for some ice cream or something or other** . . .

The girl is looking in the window, but she is not in the window. Notice also the inappropriate reference to the "same one of these shopping center stores." He has not singled out which store that is. *The same one* can only refer back to a previously mentioned item. This is clearly a circumlocution, again evidence of his difficulties in lexical selection.

An analysis of these wordings as being evidence of a linguistic deficit is reinforced by his frequent neologizing and his grossly misordered sequences. It was also C.T. who said

15G. . . . that's what kids are like these days always have but th- it means that [shinchuer] her parents that she's so proud of she goes out leaves the ice cream 'n eats it on the way 'n we don't know what happens [smə] the fact . . .

[10] Syntactic Errors.

However we wish to term it, the undeniable fact that emerged from this study was that psychotic speakers do show genuine disruption in syntax. Because, as we have seen, the borders of language tend to be fuzzy, certain errors can be assigned either to the lexicon or to the syntactic system. Those mentioned above dealing with choice of indefinite or definite noun determiner are cases in point. If a patient uses an *a* in lieu of a correct *the* or *my*, it is true that he or she selected the wrong word, but it is equally true that he or she failed to use the proper syntactic marking for indicating definite versus indefinite mention.

Apart from these fuzzier matters, however, psychotic narratives showed agrammatisms, hard instances of agrammatisms. For instance, let us reprise from C.T.'s narrative:

- ... that's what kids are like these days **always have but** th- it
- ... she still **is** her destination is not known in a few minutes.

In the first of these, C.T. has not completed the construction started with *have*. There is no prior phrase to which this is anaphoric reference. Similarly, in the second the *is* requires an adjective, noun or verb to complete it. Again this is not anaphoric reference. There is no hesitation or backtracking in either of these to indicate that the speaker has started to say something and then has changed his mind. The patient simply starts the construction and changes to a different one with no warning or later correction.

This kind of error, what I call *syntactic gapping* occurred only in psychotic patients. This is another category of error not produced by normals, again proving that Fromkin is in error in her claim that schizophrenics evince the same errors as normals. Not surprisingly, the gapping occurred in patients who evinced other linguistic disabilities like neologizing, imprecise lexical retrieval, and misordering of temporal events. Other examples are

- he was blamed **for** and I don't think that was fair the way they did that either
- what are **the** and uh there was a scene
- and asks if she can **have** then goes to the ice cream place.
- Another car **pulls** and then a little girl is peeking. . . .

It must be emphasized that errors like these were not only exclusive to psychotics, but the sentences in which they occurred were said as if nothing had been omitted. There was no break in intonation or stress, but a vital word to a syntactic construction was never uttered. In contrast to this kind of gapping there exist devices for starting a syntactic construction, then before completion abandoning it and starting anew. We see the difference in the reprise of:

> I saw a movie with a girl and she wanted ice cream and it wasn't really ice cream she wanted, **it was uh she ordered frozen grape ice,** a double order, and her mother said no and her father said no and it seemed like she defied them and went for it anyhow.

The speaker started to say "it was.." This could have been the comment on the previous sentence, as in "it wasn't really ice cream she wanted, it was grape ice." He indicates that he is breaking off to rephrase the sentence by the *uh* followed by a pause. Then he restarted with another whole sentence which fit the context including the observation that she didn't want ice cream. In contrast, in the gapping above, there were no pauses to indicate a rephrasing and what follows is not a new phrasing. It just continues as if the prior constructions were complete.

Both normals and psychotics evinced a less disruptive kind of syntactic error.

16 . . . he charged **it for her**
17. . . . it's too close **for dinnertime**

18. . . . two three minutes **for get waited on** (see 20 below)
19. **There was** and when she got home **there was** too near suppertime.

The first of these, from a normal, was simple reversal of words. It should have been "he charged her for it." The next two both substitute *for* for *to*. This is not so surprising as it might appear at first blush. *For—to* together constitute the infinitive after some verbs,[10] as in "I would love for you to come." In 16 and 17 the *for* is not grammatically correct, but it is easy to see that this is a typical slip-of-the-tongue error of substituting one word in a set for another. 16 was said by a normal and 17 by a psychotic. The last, 19, was said by a psychotic. Both *it* and *there* can function as dummy subjects as in "it's raining out" and "there are napkins on the table." Unlike *for* and *to*, however, they never occur in the same construction. Complex syntactic rules determine which can be used in a given instance.

Some patients displayed common errors in pronoun selection of the kind prevalent in slips of the tongue.[11] However, when this occurred in psychotic narrative, it typically persevered over a stretch of several references. The underlining shows the wavering between pronoun choices.

> 20. I seen a little girl looking in the window 'n ah say wan' some ice cream but didn't have money to get it so <u>she</u> asked <u>her</u> mother 'n <u>her</u> mother said not now because it's too near suppertime uh the kid was put down so <u>he</u> goes to the father 'n the father **ch-told where to go** 'n gave <u>him</u> the money so <u>she</u> could buy ice cream. While <u>she</u> was in the ice cream parlor <u>she</u> was **sittin' there** waitin' for somebody to get—musta waited two three minutes **for get waited on** a place like that should have <u>it</u> all the time soon as <u>she</u> comes in the door. Then finally <u>she</u> got the ice cream. <u>She</u> was happy 'n that's the way <u>it</u> is.

Again this passage shows how difficult it is to discuss a level of syntax separately from one of semantics and lexical choice. The incorrect pronoun usage can be viewed as opposite speech which we think of as a problem of lexical choice. Another example of undeniably opposite speech in 20 occurs when the speaker said the girl was sitting there. She was actually **standing** there. The boldfaced segments highlight other deviations here: a syntactic error, and another improper lexical choice. Unless one is specifically giving directions, usually in response to a question, telling another *where to go* usually means you have been refused roundly.

One patient with speech disintegrated to the point of gibberish also produced word salads. Underlined words indicate faulty pronoun reference, another semantic-syntactic category:

> 21. Okay. I was watchin a film of a little girl and um s bring back memories of things that happened to uh people around me that affected me durin' the time when I was livin' in that area and uh she jus' went to the store for candy bar and by the time ooh of course her brother who was supposed to be watchin' wasn't payin' much attention he was blamed for and I didn' think that was fair the way the way they did that either so that's why I'm kinda like askin' yah could we just get together and try to you know work it out all together for one big party or something **ezz it hey if it we'd all in which is in not** they've been here so why you jis now discoverin' it. You know they they've been <u>men</u> will try to use you every time for everything <u>he</u> wants so ain't no need and you tryin' to get upset for't that's all that's all.

This, of course, fails on every level. The narrative tracking is off. Personal memories intrude on the narrative. Very little of what was seen in the film ever gets encoded. There is syntactic gapping (he was blamed for and I didn't think . . .), gibberish, word salad. Generally, narratives deviant enough to manifest severe syntactic and lexical retrieval problems are those which manifest about every other evidence of disintegrated discourse abilities.

[11] Misperceptions.

One unexpected finding was that normals do about the same amount of misperceiving as do psychotics. The differences lie both in the order of scanning the memory which seems to underlie narrative production, and the kinds of misperceptions which each group had. This last was partially a result of the first.

The misperceptions of the two populations were almost mutually exclusive. Misperceptions by normals arose out of their summing up the action in order to get a smooth, logical progression of activity, all subordinated to what was apparently seen as the central theme: the girl's desiring and then getting ice cream. Hence, many normals, but not psychotics, reported that the father as well as the mother refused the child. The story could be told either way. Normals ignored the mother's affectionate and kind refusal. Rather, it became converted to a flat, even unpleasant, denial of the girl's request. It was this scene that caused one normal to say that the child was "rejected by one [parent]." Another reported the mother as giving an abrupt "nope." What is essential for the overall story line is that the mother refused the request, or else there was no reason for the girl to ask her father. Therefore, normals not only said that the mother refused, but they grossly misrepresented the character of the refusal. One normal even misinterpreted the father's putting his hand in his pocket as a specific gesture:

> 22 . . . she asked her mother if she could have some ice cream and the mother said not it's too near supper so then the girl's father, I assume it was came home and she asked the father the same question and he sa— . . . He didn't actually say but he **gave the gestures for no** and the next scene was the little girl went to an ice cream store and she ordered a double grape ice and the man gave it to her

and she paid the man and he said "Thank you come again," and she left the store.

Similarly, it made no difference to the story exactly what flavor ice cream the girl gets, so normals did not seem to process the clearly enunciated "double grape ice" in the videostory. So far as the central storyline goes, it makes no difference if the mother is preparing dinner rather than setting the table. Consequently, a normal misperceived this sequence as well.

Two normals misperceived the white cases barely visible through the window which the child was looking into in the opening scene. One termed the store a deli, and the other thought it was a laundromat. Although the cases do look like those in delicatessen's or laundry equipment, it was surprising given the entire videostory that they did not perceive that she was looking at ice cream cases, especially given the normals' penchant for fitting the facts to the perceived story. However, even these errors did not mar the storyline. Neither of these misperceptions caused a rating of psychotic. In sum, normals do misperceive even in such a short and simple task as this was, but their misperceptions fit into the gist of what they assume the story to be about. It is as if normals first figure what the point of the story is, and then fit facts in to suit.

Psychotic misperceptions, although no more frequent than normals, are far more disparate. Sometimes in what appear to be psychotic misperceptions, we are not sure if the patient is hallucinating, accidentally accessing chance associations to the target utterances, or simply is suffering from difficulties in lexical retrieving. For instance, in 2A, the manic narrator says that the girl is looking in a trashcan, a statement repeated the next week on recall. There is no way to know if he was actually hallucinating this, but it seems unlikely because he says, "This little girl was looking in the store was looking in a trashcan or something." The "or something" indicates that he was not discussing a hallucinatory trashcan, but that he could not recall what she was actually looking into or that he had not registered that information or couldn't think of the correct word. This usage of "or something" is frequently used to indicate that a word just selected is not quite on target. Alternatively, the word *trashcan* might have been a syntagmatic association. The phrasal verb *looking in* can be completed by *trashcan*, although it does seem quite farfetched. Although one can look into a trashcan, looking into windows and stores is far more likely.

The patient who reported the father's question as asking the girl if she had ice cream, was a clear misperception. The girl did the asking and she didn't ask if anyone had any. She asked for ice cream directly.

Another misperception of dialogue seems responsible for

> 23. Ummm. First one car pulls up near an ice cream parlor. Another car pulls 'n then a little girl is peeking in a ice cream parlor 'n' then later after that the little girl is at home and she asked her mother **she wants to eat supper and her mother says it's too early.** Then her father walks in and she says, "Hello Daddy"[12] an' the next thing she goes back to the ice cream parlor an gets the ice cream and walks out and meet her friends waitin' for her.

The misperception of what the girl asked is especially blatant since it does not cohere with any of the action at the ice cream parlor. In contrast to the normal misperceptions, this did not fit in with any overall action. Indeed, the misperception disrupts the story.

When a psychotic encodes the child's request to her parents as "She talked to her mother and father," we do not know if he actually saw the child conversing with, but not requesting anything from, her parents. Whereas requesting is a form of talking, still *talking* is not a usual synonym for it. It is as if the patient hit upon a hyponym under which requesting or asking is categorized, but did not quite get to his goal. Similarly, some psychotics spoke of the "candy store" rather than the ice cream store. Interestingly, in Rhode Island, one does not buy ice cream at a candy store. One purchases it from a dairy, creamery, ice cream parlor, supermarket, variety store, or spa. Only gourmet candy is bought at a candy store. Every one of the subjects who substituted *candy store* for *ice cream parlor* came from Rhode Island, as did all but one who said the girl was going for a candy bar instead of an ice cream cone, and she seems to have been speaking of a hallucinatory girl with a baby. Whether those who spoke of a candy store and candy bars misperceived or simply made lexical errors could not be determined.

[12] Constraints, Organization and Psychosis.

In sum, although both normals and psychotics were astonishingly prone to errors even in such a simple task, this study verified that there are distinct differences in the kinds of errors each produces. Only psychotics manifested syntactic gapping.[13] They alone generated word salads and made slips of the tongue based upon words rhyming with their targets. With only one exception, it was they who produced neologizing and only they uttered false starts with elements unlike those that followed. They alone produced narratives with events misordered, cause and effect reversed, and interpolations of personal memories and conjectures not germane to the film.

Only psychotics created unusual, almost literary circumlocutions as in "he gets her the coins" and "the cash register man handled the financial matters." Unfortunately, these were their only felicities. The other features peculiar to psychotic narratives were disruptive, not creative. Psychotic speech was not indicative of exceptional creativity as posited by Forrest (1976) and Lecours and Vanier-Clement (1976). So infelicitous were all the other features of psychotic narrating that the few unusual circumlocutions seem to have been accidental, a result of a general difficulty in getting the correct word for the situation. These fortuitous circumlocutions were overshadowed by opaque unbeautiful meaninglessness of the rest.

In sum, it was found that psychotics produced error at almost every level of speech: word formation, sentence production, and narrative production. With the exception of cohesive ties, their errors and those of normals were almost entirely mutually exclusive. Their speech was characterized by a general deficit in ability to order and to organize. There were individual differences among the patients in the levels of speech that were affected as well as in the severity of disruption, but the general pattern was the same for all. Those normal narratives judged psychotic shared one or more of these features, although no normal failed to complete the telling of the events of the narratives. Normals always were able to recoup.

Normals organize their narratives far more tightly than do psychotics, utilizing temporal order and attempting to reproduce the details of what they have seen. Although they do display linguistic errors, their target is easily retrieved by hearers. Not surprisingly, normals are both capable of self-correction and likely to indulge in it. Where they err in reporting events, they do so because they produce a coherent whole, so that they fit the facts to what they perceive to be the central issues in the story. They also suppress personal associations to events depicted. They did not comment on the outcome of the story nor did they "remember" personal events. Interestingly, several normals at the end of the taping commented that they used to play one parent off against the other as did the girl in the film, but none told me this as part of their narrative.

In contrast, psychotics were often unable to repress internal stimuli, such as the patient who introduced the narrative with "All about ice cream 'n I coulda really went for a cone." Shortly thereafter the patient said "neat" for *eat.* Another correctly said the girl got a cone of double grape ice and then interpolated, "my favorite flavor." Only psychotics commented that they were happy that she got her ice cream or even that she was happy. Only psychotics mentioned that certain things disturbed them or got them angry. C.T., to use his own word, interpolated all kinds of comments about what kids are like these days, the girl's pride in her parents, and her probable "thank you's" to "mummy and daddy."

Typically, the more such extraneous matters intruded, the more disrupted the entire narrative was. C.T.'s was the one with the bizarre temporal misorderings as well as neologisms and other disruptions in lexical retrieval. In the most disrupted narratives, personal memories blended with the events on the screen, as in the narrative that spoke of "memories of things that happened to uh people around me that affected me durin' the time when I was livin' in that area and uh she jus' went . . ." Where the area was; who "she" was, indeed, the entire leaping from one event to another with lapses into word salad and neologizing show a total lack of organization and of repression of matters extraneous to the matter at hand. Because of their inability to filter out stimuli not relevant to the task at hand and to organize, psychotic misperception, unlike that of normals, does not form a coherent narrative.

Their deviations were not what Lecours and Vanier-Clement call "plus deviations." They were almost all "minus deviations" hindering comprehension and/or failing to encode the story. Because in a variety of ways they showed that they were trying to narrate it, one can conclude that they were not always able to say what they meant. This argues for disrupted speaking skills. This disruption includes hard instances of agrammatism. Moreover, such instances were not at all difficult to find even in a short task given to short-term patients.

We can characterize a general dysfunction caused by a generalized lowering of constraints in speech activities. It is possible, indeed it does happen, that in some psychotics, at least some of the time, the lowering of constraints can be controlled enough to produce artistic endeavors like the wildly creative poetry of a patient reported on in Hallowell and

Smith (1983), for instance. In one of those, the patient describes his terror as being like a plummeting toward acid and spikes, cobra spears, and tiger-hunting forks, and he says that he is impaled upon a dozen blades. As vivid and really wild as some of his imagery is, it is all in control, all subordinated to his description of his feelings. Furthermore, this poem is appropriately rhymed and was written down by the patient, correctly spelled and lined up as poetry on the page. However, this certainly is not the usual psychotic speech. As we have seen in the Ice Cream Stories, the problem is that the productions are not subordinated to form or to a coherent meaning. They are not controlled, and control is the essence of art and of ordinary communication.

Many theories advanced for the oddities of schizophrenic speech have discussed its strange associational character, including this mix of memories with other verbal output. Terms like "filtering defects," "faulty pigeonholing," "attentional deficits," and "weakening of constructs" have all been used both as explanation of the cause of such language and as a description of it. All of these terms seem to be referring to the same phenomena. This study indicates that schizophrenic and manic narration is marred by intrusions from personal memory, such that it seems to be suffering from "faulty filtering" mechanisms. It should be stressed, however, that other terms might be—and have been—used to label the same phenomena. In short, the Ice Cream Stories support the model of disrupted speech with the analogous disruption in visual tracking as discovered by Holzman.

Notes

[1]Mass nouns are those which cannot be counted. That is, one cannot say "one trash," "two trashes." Also, if one puts *some* in front of a mass noun, the noun remains singular, as in "some trash." With count nouns, if one puts *some* in front of them, they become plural, as in "some apples."

[2]He was referring to the rather jerky camera action at the outset of the video. It literally did stop and start.

[3]There is no line

[4]This was a neologism

[5]There was no switch to the front door. The father clearly entered by the kitchen door clearly visible in the room.

[6]This subject was exceptionally nervous when recounting the narrative. He gripped the tape recorder tightly, was flushed, and appeared unsure of himself. Since he had volunteered for the project, his behavior was inexplicable. Normal

participants were not asked if they had schizophrenic or otherwise mentally ill family members, but studies have shown that people genetically at risk for schizophrenia do show abnormalities in speech similar to schizophrenics. Whether or not this person is at risk I do not know. As we saw in the last chapter, Rochester and Martin also found that they got some highly deviant passages from normals.

[7]She actually walked up to the father and made body contact with him as she makes the request.

[8]A similar phrase is fine, however, as when one says "she's a little sister" or "she's a little lady" when explaining someone's role behavior.

[9]Notice that I am not claiming that the patient does have anomic aphasia; only that his or her wording is like that.

[10]This is a matter of dialect as well. Some dialects use both the *for* and the *to* where others would be more likely just to use the *to.* I would be more likely to say, "I'd love you to go." Either encoding seems to be equally socially correct and all English speakers at some times at least would use both *for* and *to.*

[11]We have to exclude here the confusion between the gender marking on English pronouns by native speakers of languages like Chinese and Filipino. Because these languages use one pronoun for all genders in the singular, speakers often confuse *he, his, she,* and *her.* Lest the English speaking reader feel superior, I must point out that English shows no gender marking in the plural.

[12]The patient's voice dropped and she adopted a very seductive tone and elongated the words "hello Daddy."

[13]This is not a claim that psychotics are the only population who ever produce these. In more open-ended situations, more exciting or fatiguing ones, or amongst other impaired populations, we might find these as well. In this situation, one which required narration of a relatively simple and short (124 second) videostory, only psychotics omitted head words of constructions.

Chapter Nine

RELEVANCE

Schizophrenic speech is notoriously irrelevant, although this has been called by many other names such as being *tangential* or *derailed*. What is it that causes such evaluation? What exactly is relevance? How can we determine whether or not speech is relevant? How is relevance achieved? This chapter will show that relevance and truth are not the same thing, that utterances may be untrue, impossible, even fantastic, but still be relevant. Allied to relevance is the problem of establishing mutual ground, including the ways that this is done. The factors leading to judgments of irrelevance can be isolated so that schizophrenic and other psychotic speech can be analyzed as relevant or not by objective standards.

[1] Relevance.

For those involved with psychotic speech, the problem of relevance is especially pressing because the most remarked upon feature of schizophrenic speech is its lack of relevance. Labels like **incoherent, tangential, and distracted** are all commonly applied to describe schizophrenic speech. Before discussing these, we need to consider what it is that makes sentences relevant to the context so that a topic can be inferred in oral and written communications. What is it that leads to the judgment that what has been said is coherent, relevant, and sensible.

Relevance has two faces: first, how speech is connected to the interaction under examination; and second how it relates to a topic. It is, admittedly, difficult to separate the two as they are Siamese twins. One keeps to a topic by making relevant allusions to it. The overlap is unavoidable, but we can still see a difference between them. Relevance is an ongoing cognitive process. Topic, a MACROSTRUCTURE category, is more directly concerned with syntax.

[2] Common Ground.

In order for successful communication to take place, common ground has to be established between participants in the interaction. Obviously, the longer their mutual history, the more that each can assume the other (or others) know and this will affect what they have to overtly encode (Kreckel 1981). Beyond these social conditions there are syntactic constructions which indicate that a constituent in the sentence or the discourse is COMMON GROUND. What interests us here is the sorts of devices speakers use to establish common ground without participants' overtly reviewing their MUTUAL or SHARED KNOWLEDGE in each interaction.

We typically take anything in the physical environment as being common ground, and we encode on that basis. For instance, if we are sitting at a restaurant table, and there is a candle burning on the table, we could at first reference say, "The wax is getting all over the tablecloth." One need not mention that there is a candle, it is burning and it is melting. Indeed, to mention that would be odd since anyone sitting at the table can see (or, if blind, feel) the flame. It is just such extraneous mention which we associate with schizophrenicity.

Common ground also comes about by simple mention. If someone says, "Darn, the books are on the table," nobody would think that all books on all tables were meant. Rather a hearer would look for a likely table nearby or in view. Failing that, if the interactors had just left a place with a table upon which relevant books could have been left, the statement would cause a hearer to think back to that spot or would assume that the speaker had left the books on some table before meeting up with the hearer. Mention, then, simply because it has been made indicates that a certain scenario must have taken place, in this case, leaving books that the speaker wants or needs. Mention need not be represented as truth. Within a story or other fiction a character might say, "Drats! They've painted the roses red." So long as the narrator then mentions causes or consequences of the painted roses, listeners will consider their existence common ground in that fictional world. If no prior or further reference is made to them, then their mention is perceived as odd, not relevant. In fact, at the end of such a story, someone might say, "But what about the roses?"

Mention of items that cannot be located by such natural strategies may be taken as evidence of a wandering or otherwise incapacitated mind, especially if the mentioner cannot direct the hearer to an appropriate scene or object. For instance, if one meets up with a person who suddenly says, "Darn, the books are on the table!" with nothing in the environment or present interaction accounting for this exclamation, the hearer might well ask, "What books?" Presumably, then, the original speaker might answer, "Some books that are 30 days overdue at the library." That explains the expletive and the concern. If, however, the original speaker responded with "Tippecanoe and Tyler too," the hearer would be justified in thinking something was wrong with that speaker, unless, of course, the interaction was taking place in an American history lecture or the hearer knew that the speaker was a specialist in American elections. We don't feel an abnormality in the response unless there is no context, including mutual personal knowledge, that the present item can be fit into. Given the very wide latitude and longitude that we have in establishing common ground, the speaker who fails to do so can be seen to be suffering from a serious, indeed primary, deficit.

Mutual cultural and personal knowledge such as matters pertaining to a given job or profession are also givens in establishing common ground. Frequently, at parties when people ask what kind of job I have, and I respond that I teach, they will say things like "Oh, I better watch how I talk." In our society, teachers are the repository of socially correct speech.

Until the past few years if someone told me that they had to prepare for a Passover Seder I would assume that they were Jewish. Now that Catholics are having seders on Maundy Thursday, that assumption cannot be made. However, if the person were preparing for a seder but not on Maundy Thursday, I would then be justified in still assuming that the person was Jewish.

This last example pertains to another facet of establishing common ground. Peter Seuren (1985, p. 65) reminds us that the lexicon is dynamic. It is not a simple store of meaningful building blocks for sentences. Rather, the lexicon is "an extremely rich quarry whose creative principles are of the highest explanatory value in linguistic theory." Certainly, speakers can tap into each other's lexicons forcing new connections between elements and adding meaning to preexisting items. Frequently, this is how common ground is achieved. To give a trivial example, this sort of thing is frequently done with food. Trying to describe Vindaloo to a novice in Indian food, I said, "Try to imagine the hottest chili you ever tasted. Real Tex-Mex. It's hotter than that." another party present added, "Try to imagine food so hot your ears hurt by the second bite. That's Vindaloo." My comment then was, "Imagine the smoke coming out of your ears. That's Vindaloo." Each of these images extended the novice's idea of what hot food could be as well as defining Vindaloo. Notice that both real and imaginary experiences may be blended in order to extend meanings and relationships between items in the lexicon. People don't necessarily associate pain in the ears with spicy food, for instance, and outside of a Mel Brooks' movie, smoke doesn't come out of people's ears. No matter how outlandish such images are, they are not taken as evidence of insanity or other incapacity. What counts is that they have been presented skillfully enough so that the hearer can find their relevance to the topic.

Another technique for establishing mutual ground, one which also can cause shifts in the lexicon, is to localize something in a known shared experience and then extend it from there. For instance, "You think Jerry used to be fat! You should see him now. His stomach looks as if he swallowed a 20 pound watermelon." or "You know the gown Liz wore for her wedding? Well, this looked exactly the same except there were about double the pearls on the neck—sort of like a turtle neck all with pearls sewn on."

Clark and Marshall (1981) maintain "The world in which a thing is claimed to exist can be real or imaginary, past, present, or future." They give the example of a possible world in which the following can be said:

> 1. A deer and a unicorn were grazing beside a stream when the unicorn complimented the deer on his beautiful extra horn.

By virtue of the verb tenses and the adverbials *beside a stream* and *when,* 1 is presented as a factual occurrence. What occurs to me is that we don't have to posit a possible world; we start with this one. Except for very young children, hearers know that unicorns don't exist and that animals don't talk, although herbivorous, animals do graze by streams. Therefore, hearers know that they have to suspend some reality when they hear sentences like 1. At the same time they can imagine the event because of the inclusion of the real. The imaginary is imaginary because of what we know of this world. It seems to me that hearers don't maintain several worlds in their brains. If they did communication would require longer processing time because a great many extraneous questions would arise: how much of the "possible worlds" would need constructing; would we be forced to imagine possible weather systems? Housing forms? Vegetation? It's not so much a case of possible worlds which are constructed, but of this world with some imaginary elements.

Utterances, written or spoken, that do not establish enough common ground so that we can cycle into a subject matter, are incoherent even if the individual phrases and sentences used are normal enough. For instance, part of what is wrong with the following is that we can find no common ground on which to build up an event or explanation.

> 2. After John Black has recovered in special neutral form of life the honest bring back to doctor's agents must take John Black out through making up design meaning straight neutral underworld shadow tunnel. (Lorenz 1961)

We can assume that there is a person named John Black and that something was wrong with him from which he recovered, but what a "neutral form of life" is remains a mystery. Similarly, although we can assume that a person can be brought out of a tunnel, we aren't given a clue as to what a "design meaning straight neutral" tunnel can be. This can be seen as a failure to provide proper syntactic cues, but even if these were present, common ground as to the kind of tunnel still has not been established. That is, there may be a syntactic deficiency, but there is also one in the larger discourse task of providing common ground:

Similarly, despite the syntactic errors, the bizarre quality of 3 comes about because it fails to establish what should be answered and the relevance of Paradise to the rest of it.

> 3. Mill Avenue is a house in between avenues U and avenue T I live on Mill Avenue for a period of for now a period of maybe fifteen year for around approximate fifteen years I like it the fam—I like every family on Mill Avenue I like every family in the world I like every family in the United State of America I like every family on on Mill Avenue I like Mill Avenue is a is a block with that is busy cars always pass by all the time I always look out the window of my front porch front porch at time when I s- when I'm not sure if it's possible about the way I think I could read people mind about people's society attitude plot and spirit so I think I could read their mind as they drive by in the car sh- will I see Paradise will I not see Paradise should I answer should I not answer I not answer w- their thought of how I read think I could read their mind about when they pass by in the car in the house pass by in the car from my house I just correct for them for having me feel better about myself not answer will I should I answer should I not answer will I see paradise will I not see paradise I just correct them to have me feel better

about myself about the way I think I can hear their mind r- about the way I think I could read their mind as they pass by the house . . . (data courtesy of Dr. Bonnie Spring)[1]

Interestingly, the matter of reading people's minds as they drive by in their cars is established as this is part of a response about what it is like living in the patient's neighborhood. After localizing the street, the patient then comments on people riding by in cars, and expresses doubt that their minds could be read and that there might be plots in the minds of the passers-by. Note that this is understandable despite the syntactic errors in the passage, but the syntactically intact questions about seeing Paradise and answering are precisely what are incomprehensible. "Should I answer, should I not answer" and "will I see paradise, will I not see paradise" are well-formed, but they don't many any "sense." Thus, although they would appear to be contradictory, common ground can be established in otherwise disrupted speech and syntactically undisrupted speech can yield a feeling of incoherence. Common ground and relevance are not wholly a matter of sentence structure.

Whenever someone speaks, in the absence of other evidence, we assume that at least part of his or her utterance is true. In fiction, we assume that we are to take it as true. Grice (1981) offers:

4. The King of France is bald.

In such a sentence, the hearer takes as factual the underlying proposition that there is a king of France. It is not that someone could not deny that there is a king of France, but, in practice, one is more likely to deny that he is bald, not that there is a king of France. Grice (1981, p. 190) feels this is so because both the speaker and hearer usually assume that at least one conjunct in a sentence is undeniable thus having common ground status. Even if the hearer has never heard of an existing king of France, much less whether or not he is bald, still the hearer will assume that the speaker is correct and that such a person exists.

I find another reason for such an assumption. The article *the* specifically has the meaning of mutual knowledge. That is, by prefacing a noun with *the,* the speaker is asserting "this noun is one that we both know of." Hence, for instance, if one American says to another "The President," in the absence of more restrictive context, both will assume that the speaker meant the current President of the United States. Additionally, the topic of the sentence, the first NP, is often taken as given and the predicate is taken as the comment on that topic. This is what demagogues or even less venal politicians bank on. The hearer assumes that part of the sentence containing the topic is common knowledge and regards it as common knowledge.

Grice adds that another way to achieve undeniability is to mention uncontroversial matters, i.e., "my aunt's cousin." Noone would question that you have an aunt or that she has a cousin. To this, one could add a whole host of people whose existence you would accept as real: my husband, my high school English teacher, your nemesis, or his brother. None of these need any particular introduction as we assume that just about everyone has or has had such human relationships. Moreover, the possessive *my* like *the* is used to signal something already known to participants.

Similarly, "my home" used to be taken as a given, because in America everybody supposedly had a home. Now that has changed, so in a circumstance in which the speaker is homeless and says to the hearer, also homeless, "My home is comfortable," the hearer knowing that the speaker is homeless, could easily deny that the speaker has a home. For that matter if someone was laden with overstuffed bags and had a general ragged look, almost anyone might doubt that he or she really had a home. It is not necessarily the case that certain utterances or positions in sentences are automatically taken as true or not.

Both Sanders (1987) and Kreckel (1981) stress that a history of shared interactions leads to more accurate understandings between parties. There are more bases upon which to establish common grounds. Shared histories mean that less needs to be said to indicate what common ground is to be assumed, and the more accurately implicatures will be achieved. However, even strangers have ways of establishing common ground.

[3] Relevant Contributions.

Apart from formal cohesive devices like conjunctions, relevance can be achieved by the meaning of sentences themselves. If I am talking about rules, for instance, and suddenly mention *infractions*, relevance is achieved simply because that word is semantically relevant to our concept of rules. All that is necessary for relevance is that the talk of infractions relates to the rules that were discussed previously, or to ones that are going to be mentioned. In contrast, the semantic chaining in schizophrenia does not refer to other segments of the discourse in question and does not stand in any logical or real-life relationship to them.

Fauconnier's (1985) metaphor of mental spaces pertains to relevance as well as to pragmatics. He says that language forms refer to elements which are set up and mentally pointed to. Language makes its own constructions, building up mental spaces, the relations between them and the relations between elements within them. He portrays language forms as being plucked out of internal networks and pointing outward, perceiving speakers as creating mental spaces which are then populated with language. It seems to me that this view has special explanatory significance for the analysis of schizophrenic speech. Whereas relevance is achieved by mental pointing, schizophrenic irrelevancies seem to be caused by roaming around in internal networks without indications of connection between exterior or interior relations.

Sanders (1987, p. 186) maintains that relevant entries in a discourse affirm, deny, add, or seek information about a proposition or combination of propositions already mentioned. I would amend this to include as well entries which have been suggested laterally, so to speak, by something just said. These are shown to be relevant by further propositions which develop another aspect of the proposition or even a new proposition. Thus topics can and do advance and change within one normal discourse provided that entries are relevant. It is not change of topic *per se*, then, that gives some discourse its schizophrenic flavor, nor is it necessarily the formal ways of indicating change. It is that schizophrenics do not then produce subsequent entries which affirm, deny, add, or seek information about what they have just said. This is one of the things wrong with the following:

5A. Looks like clay. Sounds like gray. Take you for a roll in the hay. . . . (Cohen 1978)

5B. I was watching a film of a girl and um s bring back memories of things that happened to people around me that affected me during the time when I was living in the area and she just went to the store for a candy bar and by the time ooh of course her brother who was supposed to be watching wasn't paying much attention he was blamed for and I didn't think that was fair the way the way they did that either so that's why I'm just asking yah could we just get together and try to work it out all together for one big party or something ezz it hey if it we'd all in which is in not they've been here so why you just now discovering it. You know they they've been men will try to use you every time for everything he wants so ain't no need and you trying to get upset for it. That's all. That's all.

5C. You want me to talk about -um- last week experience I had?'n it was funny, 'is experience seems to sum up all of what's been goin' on because I've been walkin' around recitin' things. I've written to people and people been listening but then when you get down to it you've got to scrub your own dishes or else nobody's gonna an' I've just been so totally against the idea of people feelin' they have a ticket to carry them along because it's a ticket is not an easy trip along by no means is probably harder if you understand what I mean.

In 5A the first phrase, *looks like clay* is accurate, but the next *sounds like* tells us nothing about looking like gray, and taking someone for a roll in the hay advances neither preceding proposition. The only way to make sense out of this is not to try to understand what it means, but to understand the processes that could have produced it.

5B starts out just fine with a recollection brought about by the film. Then the brother is mentioned and the fact that he was supposed to be watching but didn't do it. Then the statements cease to advance the topic. We never find out what he was blamed for, nor who *they* are nor what they did, nor do we find out what relevance the party has to the preceding. The word salad "hey if it we'd all in which is in not they've been here . . ." cannot be interpreted in terms of relevance at all, since we don't know what it means,[2] but the irrelevancy of the entire is not caused by this lapse.

5C was produced in answer to the question, "Do you remember the video you saw with me last week?" This is acknowledged in the first statement. Actually, it is possible to give an interpretation of the entire. It seems as if the patient is commenting on the need for self-reliance, of not depending on anybody else. This assumption is based upon the passage *when you get down to it you've gotta scrub your own dishes* and the references to a *ticket.* In that context, it is reasonable to assume that the patient is talking about people getting a "free ride." As with so much of SD speech, it is interpretable if you tape it and then examine it at leisure. The irrelevancies get in the way of ordinary interpretation in face-to-face interactions. We are not told how the experience "last week" pertains to his walking around reciting things. There is no elucidation of *things,* nor are we told what he has written and what people have been listening to. The *but*, far from introducing a contrastive statement to what has gone immediately before simply introduces another statement not made relevant, nor are we told why having a ticket makes things harder. This lacks sufficient relevant entries although it is loaded with expressions of time, place, and cohesion.

Normal discourse does not always shows adherence to one topic. As we saw earlier, it often doesn't. In some instances, in normal conversation, overt topic changing markers are used, such as "ooh, that reminds me . . . " or "not to change the subject, but . . . " which are instructions not to interpret following remarks as belonging in sequence. Stubbs (1983, p. 183) points out that these are used strategically, but are not required in the sense that certain syntactic rules are.

Even if such markers are not used in normal discourse, the new topic itself becomes the source of other entries relevant to it. In glossomania, often within sentences, our feeling that a topic is not being adhered results from the lack of affirmations, denials, additions, or questions about any of the propositions singly or in combination. Our sense that there is no STRATEGY in schizophrenic passages like 5A and B, our sense that the sentences seem to be thrown together arises from the absence of such relevant additions to anything mentioned. That is what makes people characterize schizophrenic speech as having "loose associations."[3]

In order to make entries relevant, one need only formulate in any way possible structures which can be construed as adding to the macro-topic or otherwise alluding to it (Chaika 1976). Relevant entries in and of themselves effect coherence and cohesion aside from any particular overt syntactic cohesive devices which may be used. vanDijk (1977, p. 148; 1980, pp. 105, 194) himself frequently confirms that local coherence is not a matter of connecting facts linearly, but of connecting them to the topic of the sequence. Sanders says:

> For strategic purposes, the disposition to say or do something in particular is a secondary consideration to the following ones: (1) whether that utterance . . . can be relevantly entered in the discourse or dialogue at that juncture, and (2) which outcomes become possible (i.e., relevant) and which do not if contemplated utterances . . . are entered at that juncture. (Sanders 1987, p. 11)

VanDijk (1980, p. 77) further points out that macrostructures allow us to " . . . specify a set of possible inferences . . . " These are not paraphrases of the actual sentences used, but are *semantic transformations* which reduce and organize information as well as limit the conclusions. Well-formed macrostructures consisting of relevant microstructures allow such transformations, but ill-formed ones do not. We often find it impossible to infer anything from schizophrenic discourse by referring to the macrostructure itself. Similarly, and from the same cause, we have difficulty coming to conclusions about what the schizophrenic meant. Perhaps because of this, the history of psychotherapy has largely been a history of trying to devise extraordinary ways of achieving inferences and conclusions (Chaika 1981).

For instance, the preceding paragraph can be summarized by saying that well-formed macrostructures allow us to make inferences and conclusions in a non-ad hoc manner. From that paragraph, one can conclude that I believe this is one definable difference between normal and schizophrenic discourse. One can also infer that I believe that psychotherapeutic analyses are fallacious.

Note that these observations are not to be construed as saying that schizophrenic speech never allows inference and conclusions. Some of it obviously does. Some of it can be summarized. In fact, 5B above can be. With some justice, one can even infer that the speaker feels that it is useless for women to complain about being used by men, but the passage is still recognizably schizophrenic (Chaika and Alexander 1986 and Chapter 1).

In contrast, "my mother's name is Bill . . . and coo" is not amenable to summarizing beyond saying something like "The speaker talked crazy about her mother's name and birds." We are told that the speaker likes buzzards and thinks they and parakeets work hard, but what can we infer from the rest? About all we can do is repeat what she has said.

We cannot suppose, however, that relevance is foreordained by the macrostructure. We must also allow for the skill of the speaker in creating newly relevant sentences by making connections never before made. This is quite usual in scholarship, for instance. In fact, creating new relations is inherent in scholarship, but is not at all confined to it. Anyone who has a different slant on things can make sentences relevant to a topic that has not previously been conceived of as being relevant. This effectively excludes glossomanic chaining as being in any way a manifestation of intact linguistic ability (Fromkin 1975). Although the patient is connecting sentences and phrases in wholly new ways, these cannot be construed as being relevant. For precisely this reason, such chaining has always struck observers as being pathological.

[4] The Decision-theoretic Model.

Sanders (1987) calls his model of relevance a decision-theoretic model of meaning because, he says, speakers make decisions about what to present as the discourse unfolds. They decide what will best achieve their goals, whether or not a certain utterance is relevant. These decisions change as the situation unfolds. The decision-theoretic model has the distinct advantage of accounting for the ways that relevance is achieved in interaction and what happens and why when it does not. It also avoids the problem of topic-centered theories of discourse in that it shows how topics do get changed in an ongoing interaction with no overt announcement.

Despite his theory of macrostructure, Van Dijk (1980, p. 215) implicitly admits that the construction of relevance is ongoing in a conversation or other discourse mode. He asserts that a proposition is irrelevant if " . . . it is not an interpretation condition of a following proposition in the sequence." This claim should be amended to recognize the reversibility of relevant utterances. Thus we can say that a contribution is relevant if it influences a subsequent contribution or if a subsequent contribution is interpretable by reference to a prior one. That is, for any sentence in a discourse, we can determine relevance either by its influence on a subsequent sentence or by determining that it has been influenced by a prior one.

A contribution need not be specifically relevant to its immediate progenitor, nor to its immediate successor. We have already seen the samples of glossomania in which phrases are contiguous but nonsensical. Proximity is no guarantee of relevance. The requisite condition is just that some subsequent or prior contribution relate to it. To my knowledge, nobody has yet computed exactly the degree of proximity requisite for one sentence to be counted as relevant to another in the discourse. It may be that there is no such metric, at least not as a hard and fast rule. We might sensibly expect that there is individual variation in how much space or time can elapse before entries are too far apart to be perceived as relevant.

In any event, there are many linguistic devices which serve the purpose of reminding a cospeaker or reader that a nonimmediately prior statement is to be taken as relevant. Typical examples are:

- As noted above . . .
- The reader may recall that . . .
- As I was saying before we got off the track . . .
- Well, look, to finish what I was telling you about. . . .
- Oh, remember what I was telling you . . .
- To get back to what happened last night . . .
- Do you remember when we went to the Yale game last year?

These last can be used to refer to a discourse prior to the current one. Relevance can be created when the mutually influential sentences are not adjacent simply by localizing the time and place being spoken of, or, in Fauconnier's terms, by mentally pointing to them. By the use of HYPOTHETICALS, even imaginary events or events not shared mutually are made relevant.

Even within the context of one discourse mutually relevant normal utterances may not be proximate for several reasons, including, but not necessarily limited to:

- intervening material which elucidates a prior or coming utterance
- reference to a disturbance in the physical atmosphere
- deliberate digression to recount a non-relevant experience or idea which the speaker has just been reminded of and is afraid of forgetting
- apology for content or mode of presentation
- correcting a cospeaker's misinterpretation of a prior utterance

Sanders (1987, pp. 175–206) shows that any entry in a discourse has further entries as its consequence, but no single entry must be made. The possibilities of what can be made is constrained but not ordained. At each juncture, the situation changes, and with it, so do the co-speakers' options. As it unfolds, the speaking situation allows each participant to project different consequences of what must be said next. Of course, this also means that cospeakers cannot predict each other's reactions with complete certainty. Besides the obvious problem that each person relates what is said to his or her personal experiences, there is also the fact that comprehension is not effected by an algorithm any more than speech is produced by one. Rarely does an utterance mean only one thing, and one cannot predict exactly what meaning a cospeaker may derive from it.

When it does become evident that the cospeaker has misinterpreted, correction can be made. This, then, further affects subsequent relevant contributions. It strikes me that Sanders' model of relevance explains one important facet of conversation that no other model does: the ways that topics change during the course of a conversation.

It cannot be stressed too much that these conditions of interpretation in the light of the unfolding of meaning in a discourse are based upon verifiable strategies and canons of comprehension, and that any meanings not so derived are suspect.

An integral part of a decision model of discourse is projecting how one's contribution will advance the goal of the interaction. The goal need not be a definite one; it can be nothing more than a desire to promote self-interest no matter what occurs in the situation (Sanders, p. 178), or it can be purely phatic such as "shooting the breeze."

We can even rehearse our contributions as in those conversations we have with ourselves in which we project what the other person is going to say and how we will, therefore, answer. Of course, the same can go on after the fact when we ruefully think of what we should have said and how it would have affected the outcome. The latter activity is proof of the difficulty of responding adequately in the midst of conversation to the cospeaker, all the while trying to formulate how self-interest is best served in the situation. This problem is compounded by the necessity of making our contribution relevant both to our goals, and to what has been said or implied by each cospeaker in this interaction or prior ones.

For that matter, it is not inconceivable for our goals to change during the course of an interaction. Perhaps the cospeaker turns out to be far nicer and more accommodating than originally thought. Perhaps he or she turns out to have been duplicitous or guilty or suddenly revealed to be quite stupid and uncomprehending. Whichever, each contribution to the conversation can change its course all the while remaining relevant in terms of what has gone before. Sanders himself assumes a steadiness of goal or of self-interest, but there is nothing in his presentation that denies such changes.

In sum, cospeakers who are perceived as maintaining relevance make their contributions in light of what has been said. They may change the subject, but this is done in orderly ways, such as

- Not to change the subject, but . . .
- That reminds me . . .
- Before we go on a tangent. . . .

Then new entries into the conversation will refer to the new topic. Topics are continuously being negotiated in the course of an interaction or in the course of reading. Contributions heard as schizophrenic do not do that. As we have seen, these utterances are often governed by chance phonological or semantic features of a prior utterance.

This conception of the sequential nature of the consequences of what has been said illuminates the difference between SD psychotic utterances and those heard as normal. As we have seen, SD narratives and conversations frequently start out all right, but as they go along they become progressively more deviant. A sequential model of discourse predicts such derailing in a group generally acknowledged to suffer from cognitive deficits. The longer the conversation the more that must be kept in mind in formulating next entries. This is true within one turn. The longer the dialogue, the more challenging it is to remember all that one has said.

[5] Syntax and Relevance.

There are syntactic clues which interpreters can look for in determining the relevance of statements to the time of speaking or writing as well as for determining semantic relevance. The syntax of English[4] has codified relevance onto the system of verb tense and aspect. Robin Lakoff (1972) noted that it is not possible to say

- Shakespeare is a noted drunkard.

but that it is fine to say

- Shakespeare is a noted playwright.

and, if we believe it true

- Shakespeare was a noted drunkard.

The reason that we can use the present tense of his being a playwright is that his literary works are still relevant to his reputation, but that his being or not being a drunk is not. Similarly, if one says "my uncle had blue eyes," the very use of the past tense indicates that my blue-eyed uncle is dead.

In contrast, if someone says, "My dog died," one would be surprised to discover that this occurred 25 years ago. The use of the unadorned past tense here indicates that the death was in the recent past. I suspect that the reason for this interpretation is that we usually qualify a change of state with an adverbial of time, especially if the change was long ago. That is, if the event is proximate, we signal that by not mentioning time. If it is distant, then we do mention time.

There is a corollary presumption of relevance when mentioning locations. The very fact that a place is mentioned[5] without a qualifying locative term often means that it is relevant because it is close by. If Myrtle tells me, "I found the greatest place to get Liz Claiborne clothes cheap!" because I live in Rhode Island, I would not expect the store to be in California. I assume that the store will be within an hour or so's drive. Otherwise, Myrtle should append something like, "too bad it's 3000 miles away" or "I found the greatest place in L.A." or the like.

Presumed relevance is a key ingredient in how we understand. As the above sections show, we ordinarily assume that speech is relevant to the topic and, therefore, the context. Such an assumption underlies our interpretation of when the dog died or where the Liz Claiborne store is.

[6] Relevance and Comprehension.

Part of our ordinary conversational strategy is to figure out how what has been said can be relevant to the matter at hand. The relevant meaning is the one we take as having been meant. In instances of ambiguity we disambiguate, or try to, in terms of what is relevant, ignoring any irrelevant meanings which may accidentally inhere to the words and grammar used. For this reason, failure to "get" a pun is not unusual, nor does it seem easy for most people to create puns. Therefore, it is a true dysfunction in schizophrenia that patients are conscious of meanings which are irrelevant for the context, a circumstance apparently leading to the glossomanic punning so characteristic of that population. Maher (1983, p. 8) gives as an example

6. To Wise and Company,

If you think that you are being wise to send me a bill for money I have already paid I am in nowise going to do so unless I get the whys and wherefores from you to me. But where fours have been then fives will be and other numbers and calculations and accounts to your no-account no-bill, noble, nothing.

Here the name *Wise* becomes the source of puns on *wise* meaning "wiseguy," *nowise,* and *whys,* just as *noble* forms a punning relations with *no-bill* which is a pun on *no-account* (in the meaning of *account* which means "bill." The inherent abnormality of this is that the puns are not relevant to anything except their chance resemblances to each other, and relevance assumes meaning coherent with the context.

[7] Achieving Relevance.

Oddly, it is possible to have a highly deviant passage in which one can find the relevance of the parts to the whole. Consider the entire passage presented as failure of cohesive ties in Chapter 6:

> 7. Well I want to work for god in the mission and to work for god in the mission you have to be able to speak and think in a lord tongue in my opinion now to speak and think in a lord tongue you have to have to be able to memory the process memory the parle—the process in the bible the thought pattern the brain wave and your thought process must be healthy enough and your legs must be healthy enough to when you want to study and and from when you want to study and progress in the way of the lord you should read the bible and as you read the bible you should if you are in good shape physical and mental and mental good shape and physical good shape you should be able to acquire the memory knowledge necessary as to study the bible to speak and think in a lord tongue you should be able to memory all the knowledge down on down on the page in the bible book to work for god in the mission now in the position I am in now with the medicate and with the hospital program I am being helped but at the same time that I am being help with the food and medicate the food and medicate and the the food and medicate and the and the ah rest I feel that I still do not have this I still not have the thought pattern and the mental process and the brain wave necessary to open up a page open up the old testament and start to memory it the old te- the old new testament page of the bible start to have me- memory knowledge necessary to speak to think in the lo- speak and think in the lord's tongue while you study while you study the bible while you study the bible the memory the knowledge necessary to go to work for god in the mission so when your thought problem your brain wave and your mental process is quick enough you will be able to memory the

knowledge in in the old and new testament bible and from memory knowledge in the old testament and new testament bible you are able to memory the knowledge necessary necessary to think and speak in the lord's tongue and go to work for god in the mission. (courtesy of Dr. Bonnie Spring)

There are some grammatical errors here, notably the lack of derivational morphemes like *-tion* on *medicate* and *-ize* on *to memory*. Even without these we feel that this is highly deviant. We understand that the speaker wishes to work in a mission, is concerned with being able to read both testaments, and needs help for his brain problems before he can do this. He also acknowledges that the food and the medication are helping him, but they haven't yet allowed him to fulfill his goals. Additionally, he seems to be concerned with his memory which he feels is not up to the snuff required for biblical study. The problem with the passage inheres in the constant repetitions which do not advance any message; indeed, they get in the way. The entire does not progress. It has a distinct circular movement, starting and ending on the same note, with the same phrases being recycled.

Sanders (1987) concerns himself with the things that can ordinarily go wrong in a conversation. He does not deal with pathologies of any kind, although he does account for cross-cultural miscommunication. Still, his observations bear fruit. Speaking only of normal interactions, Sanders points out that disordered conversation can result from poor exercise of what he terms as STRATEGIC OPTIONS. That is, when faced with a juncture in conversation, cospeakers choose from various options. If the speaker is not successful in those choices, then disorder can result. Thus Sanders locates the source of incoherence[6] specifically in choices made in accordance with the utterances in the developing conversation. Incoherence results when relevance to the context cannot be ascertained by cospeakers. However, this is not just a problem on the part of hearers.

Incoherence ultimately rests upon the choices of speakers or, as seems probable at least some of the time with schizophrenics, the lack of choices. The most disrupted speech, glossomania, seems to be choiceless. The curiously "automatic" flavor of such speech seems to derive from this sense we have that no choices were made, except perhaps for the first part of the utterance. Such[7] speech seems to derive from distraction so great that speakers cannot focus on what needs to be said to advance a discourse coherently. As shown in Chapter 2, SD speech shows the kinds of patterns one would expect if automatic language functions took over, so to speak, precluding direction afforded by choice. The result is incoherence and irrelevance.

Sanders' insights do give us a working definition of what makes schizophrenic speech tangential and obscure even when it is not accompanied by disruptions in word formation and the structure of the individual sentence. Simply put, it does not seem to contribute to any agenda. Cospeakers cannot find a connection between the schizophrenic speech and what has transpired previously in the interaction, nor can they find an appropriate response. **This is because the schizophrenic's contribution may not itself set up the condition for possible responses.**

[8] Cognitive Strain.

If Sanders account is correct, and I feel that it is substantively so, there is a great cognitive burden on conversants. They must manage turntaking, consider the effect of their speech and of their silence on the ongoing interaction, at the same time divining others' intentions in order to understand in the manner intended.

> ...conversants must...[identify]...transition boundaries within turns and topics, distinguishing between entries intended to be contributions and spurious ones, and organizing contributions into coherent wholes (e.g., episodes). (Sanders 1987, p. 210)

It is no wonder, then, that schizophrenics so often seem to fail in conversation, even when they are evincing no apparent breakdown in structuring sentences. Sanders specifically talks about populations with presumably intact linguistic and cognitive processes, not aphasics or the mentally ill.

Considering peculiarly schizophrenic speech as emanating from the cognitive strains of conversation makes explicit the connection between SD and NSD schizophrenics. Incoherence proceeds on a cline of severity from structurally well-formed but inappropriate responses to a general disintegration of sentence structure and word formation that in the worst cases manifests itself as gibberish and word salads. Dealing with speech as a competency in itself allows us to formulate a coherent account of the illness, one that shows us the connection between SD and NSD[8] schizophrenics. It also explains why some patients manifest different degrees of pathology in their speech.

The cognitive strains spoken of here are not necessarily limited to those patients who are so often called thought disordered. They, of course, show the greatest cognitive disruption. Many patients who would be termed NTD, whose speech doesn't consist of word salads or glossomania, but is considered merely obscure or peculiar can be seen to be evincing cognitive strain. They are not up to the strains of monitoring cospeakers, figuring out what words and syntax were used by cospeakers, figuring out their intent, matching utterances to context, choosing words and syntax themselves to encode responses relevant to the cospeakers contributions and to their own goals, figuring out how the cospeakers' utterances as they unfold are relevant to what has been said previously, and figuring out to keep their own relevant. Grice (1975, p. 45) points out that "Our talk exchanges do not normally consist of a succession of disconnected remarks and would not be rational if they did." Of course, it is just such disconnected utterances which gives us the feeling that certain speech is "schizophrenic."

[9] Constrained Verbal Forms: Narratives and Responses.

Relevance is also achieved by conforming to a GENRE of discourse. A genre is a speech form such as a joke, a sermon, or a narrative. These can vary widely in different cultures. Dennis Jarrett (1984) makes an excellent case for his proposition that blacks understand the genre of the blues, but that whites and Hispanics find that the lyrics don't quite make sense, but in the black culture they do. The blues are intended to describe the singer's feelings and to satirize aspects of black life, such as preachers. For this reason, they never mention nature.

The genre typically has an opener which announces which genre it is. For instance, if someone in mainstream American culture hears, "The King of Tobolopol proclaimed an edict," he or she would then expect a fulfillment of the genre of fairy tales or an opera. The use of the definite article presupposes that one is to believe that there is a king. That the king is fictional is established in the predicate "proclaimed an edict." This is a typical opener in fantasies like fairy tales and operas. It is not used in spy stories, so far as I know, or even in historical romances. Real life knowledge plays a part in this as well. There is no country called Tobolopal. If the hearer later found out there is, he or she could revise that judgment. However, fantasy-hood still would not be ruled out because nowadays only fictional kings proclaim edicts. The hearer also knows that the fairy tale ends when he or she hears the words "and they lived happily ever after."

Narratives are a ubiquitous genre, both in the telling of real-life happenings and in fiction. Deborah Tannen notes that both in written and spoken language, narrative has distinctive structure. The ways that psychotic speech are not relevant are illuminated by a comparison of a narrative fragment to a response to an open-ended question, both produced by schizophrenics. The narrative is a portion of one of the ICS (Chaika and Alexander 1986; Chapter 8). Here a subject is describing the final scene in the videotaped story of a child who has managed to get some ice cream:

> 8A. . . . she goes out leaves the ice cream and eats it and on the way and we don't know what happens [smə] the fact you can interpolate and say that she ate the ice cream and brought it home. . . .

Here, with the exception of the [smə] all words and phrases are normal, but still the entire is not. Its failure resides in the two temporal misorderings of the encoded events, both impossible according to what we know of the real world. The first error lies in the statement that the girl leaves the ice cream, but then eats it after she has left the store. The second impossible sequence relates that she has eaten the ice cream, but brings it home. The events themselves are correctly encoded. They fail at the level of the macrostructure, the discourse itself.

The phrase "and on the way" in 8A is misplaced. This is one of a class of phrases I call NARRATIVE DEICTICS. These are employed to help hearers/readers keep their mental places. This one is proper to narratives. It just has not been placed properly.

Because of the general constraint on narration which demands that correct temporal ordering be followed, 8A is erroneous. Real life constraints apply here. We know that certain events have to follow certain temporal orderings. This may be done in two ways. First, one may simply relate the events in the narrative in the order in which they occurred or are imagined to occur. Second, one may indicate the correct ordering lexically or syntactically without necessarily presenting events in the order in which they occurred. For instance, 8A could have been correctly phrased as

> 8B. She eats the ice cream on the way [home], after she goes out [of the store]. [Actually], we don't know what happens but you can

interpolate and say that she ate the ice cream [before] bringing it
home

The words in brackets represent words not actually used by the narrator.
I am not claiming that he intended to say 8B, just showing how it could
have been said nondeviantly employing syntactic devices to indicate
ordering. **Notice that I have not added to the meaning of the information
given. All I have done is to make it cohere.**[9]

Another sort of ill-formed speech on the level of discourse is seen in
examples in 9 and 7 above.[10] Forgetting for now the obvious errors in
syntax, these are deviant because of their lack of relevant progression.
Their "schizophrenic" flavor inheres primarily in their repetitions. The
sheer number of them makes each passage very difficult to understand,
and contributes to our feeling that they are inherently abnormal. As we
have seen, in order to achieve coherence in discourse, speakers must not
repeat words, phrases, or sentences. Rather, appropriate anaphoric words
or ellipsis must be used. For instance, perfectly prosaic and reasonable
information is imparted in

9 Mill Avenue is also a place where **people gather in back yards** to
have **people gather in back yards** to have a barbecue **in the back yard**
to have relative over to have friend over to talk **in the back yard** to
be merry with each other."

What makes it wrong is the repetition to no apparent purpose of
"people gather" and "in the back yard." As we have already seen, such
repetition is a hallmark of schizophrenic speech, evincing itself on every
level. It is also what causes us to feel that such speech lacks relevance.
The repetition creates circularity as it fails to advance topics.

There is another problem with the responses in the examples in 3 and
7 as well. They do not adhere to the requirements of the macrostructure
which was elicited, that of the answer. Answers require that one encode
only that information which is relevant to the question asked, and when
that information is given, it is proper either to stop speaking or to ask the
equivalent of "Is that sufficient?" or "Did that tell you what you want to
know?" When one is asked what one's neighborhood is like, it is not
appropriate to interject over and over again one's inner doubts about
going to heaven or about one's ability to read people's minds or one's
need to speak in a lord tongue.

People who are bores or nags do repeat the same information cyclically
over and over, but the repeating in 3 and 7 above are clearly not the work

of sane bores or nags. For instance, one of the oddities in each are their respective REFRAINS. Let's consider one[11] of those in 3:

> 10 . . . will I see paradise will I not see paradise should I answer should I not answer.

This is a direct repetition of the same words and syntax such as one gets in songs or poems. In songs and poems, the refrain reinforces the topic and is clearly related to it. In contrast, the refrains here does neither. At no time in the discourse of which 10 is a part does the speaker say what it is he should or should not be answering. In normal refrains, the entire is sung or said at stated intervals. In the schizophrenic refrains, the repetition does not come at such regular intervals, after a verse, for instance. Moreover, this refrain frequently starts in the middle of a word, as in

> sh—will I see Paradise will I not see paradise should I answer should I not answer I not answer w- their mind

It seems to be randomly accessed both in terms of where it falls in the entire discourse and even at what point in the refrain the patient picked it up. In context it seems as if the "sh-will" started out to be the "should" of "should I answer" and the "w-their" started out to be the "will" of "will I see . . ."

In contrast, the repetitions of bores and nags are tied to their topics, often with a dreadful relentlessness. Moreover, the repetitions of bores and nags repeat the information, but not the actual phrasing as is done in a refrain. Nags may also preface their repeated remarks by complaints like "I told you . . . ," "How many times do I have to tell you . . . ," and "You never listen . . ." Such remarks indicate that the nag is in control and is aware of the repetitions. Similarly, bores may ask rhetorically, "Did I tell you about . . . " and "That reminds me of. . . ." The point here is not that bores and nags always preface their remarks this way, but that they may. The fact of their being bores or nags rests ultimately upon their propensity for repeating information beyond necessity to inform, the nags combining this overinformation with complaints about the hearer.

Most importantly, the criterion of **relevance** demarcates the repetition of bores and nags from the psychotic repetition above. To be relevant, an answer should contain the information requested. The response should have been confined to information about the physical properties of

Mill Street and its inhabitants. Some digression or added explanation is always allowable in an answer, but only insofar as it advances the topic requested. Bores are guilty of overinformation, of adding too much, but their "too much" is of the nature of providing excessive information which is, however, connected to the question asked. For instance, a bore might tell you that his grandparents first bought their house on such a street and that he grew up with his uncle Teddy, and he had certain neighbors who always did certain things, and changes that were wrought when so-and-so moved away.

In contrast, in *number* some of the overinformation above is not relevant to the questions asked. In our culture one's religious beliefs and deepest doubts are not appropriate responses to a question about one's neighborhood. Far from reaching a conclusion or advancing a topic, the profusion of verbiage is simply circular, a jumbling of words and phrases in an almost random ordering. What eventually does get said in *sample above*, that the neighborhood is one in which people get together to have a good time, is an appropriate enough response. It gets drowned in a sea of verbosity not subordinated to the question asked.

Notes

[1]Dr. Spring does not necessarily endorse my interpretations of these data, however.

[2]This doesn't mean that people won't try to assign an interpretation to it, but there is no way to verify what it actually means because of its syntactic deviance.

[3]Actually, the problem is more of "tight" associations, not loose ones. Each word is glued to the next by associations that nonschizophrenics usually don't notice, and if they do notice, they still refrain from saying unless they can worm it into the conversation as an apropos bit of wit or topic change.

[4]It is not possible to say whether such relevancy marking operates in all languages, but it does operate in many others. However, it may not inhere so closely to verb tense selection as it does in English. In other words, one cannot expect it to be encoded exactly as it is in English. One has to find the equivalent construction.

[5]Time and space frequently are governed by the same words and conventions of usage. For instance, both time and space may *behind* us. One event can take place *after* another, just as one person can be *after* us. Notice that an event "takes place" in time, just as one event *follows* the other. It is as if we perceive.

[6]Sanders (pp. 220–228) also speaks of conversational disorder, by which he means people's interrupting others, controlling the topic, and other such "disorderly" behavior. This is quite different from the kinds of disorder we are discussing here. Typically, there is no problem understanding what is meant, what the speaker's agenda is, etc. Furthermore, such behavior varies greatly with different social

groups, so that it is perceived as disorderly by some, but simply normal warmth and interest by others (Tannen 1984; Chaika 1989, pp. 100–106)

[7]This is possibly true for other kinds of incoherence as well, such as that proceeding from alchohol, drugs, and brain injuries. Since I have made no in-depth study of such populations, I do not make any claims for the provenance of incoherence in them, but I suspect they have a great similarity.

[8]Traditionally called TD and NTD patients. In my view, the latter terminology is oxymoronic.

[9]It is necessary to make this point as so many have attempted to "explain" schizophrenic speech by adding elements that change its meaning or by interpreting as if it had had such meaning (see Chapter 11).

[10]In the original transcript furnished to me, there was no capitalization of street addresses or of recognized terms for nationalities like *Italian*. I have added those capitals so that the written form of the data looks no more deviant than it actually is. That is, we are used to the convention of seeing capitals on proper names and to omit them is likely to be interpreted as evidence of an even greater deviance than it is.

[11]There are actually many refrains in both passages, but whatever theoretical point can be made of one can be made about the others.

Chapter Ten
TOPIC

The literature on schizophrenic speech teems with reference to the lack of discernible topic. This chapter demonstrates what a topic is and how it is signalled by the syntax of the language. There are two kinds of topic: that of the sentence and that of the discourse as a whole. These are determined in different ways as each is expressed in somewhat different ways. Fortunately, there are tests which can be applied to determine what the topic is. The difference between normal changes of topic and schizophrenic ones is elaborated. The ways that topic is used to express the speaker's empathy towards the topic being expressed are also explored here.

[1] Topic.

The word *topic* refers to two distinctly different entities: the topic of the discourse, and the topic of the sentence. The discourse topic is at the heart of relevance because all entries in a discourse are relevant by reference to their topics. The discourse topic need not be overtly expressed. It derives from the text as a whole, " ... what the upshot is ... " (VanDijk 1980) of the information provided by the discourse as a whole. It provides the linguistic context. The topic of the discourse works to constrain meaning by making individual sentences relevant to it. Thus, the topic is the prime disambiguating force in language. In other words, each sentence is interpreted as if it is relevant to the topic, which is why topic is so strong a determiner of meaning. If a global topic cannot be ascertained for any group of sentences, then the language used is perceived as obscure, strange, vague, or incoherent, and we are baffled.

The topic of the sentence, also known as the SUBJECT of the sentence, differs from the discourse topic by adding information to it. VanDijk explains that the subject of a sentence is

> ... the semantic-pragmatic function that selects which concept of the contextual information will be extended with new information. (1980. P. 97)

In the previous chapter we considered such selection in terms of relevance. In this chapter first we examine the factors leading to the choice of the subject itself, and how it pertains to the speaker's point of view. Then the topic of the discourse and its relation to our understanding of psychotic speech will be analyzed.

[2] Subject of a Sentence.

Traditionally, it has been assumed that the basic structure in language is the sentence, and that the sentence is composed of the subject and predicate. We intuitively recognize that the subject-predicate relationship gives a COMPLETE STRUCTURE; hence the common misconception that sentences are complete thoughts. Case grammars (Chapter 4) have shown us the many kinds of relations subsumed under the rubric of "subject of the sentence." As we have already seen, these deeper relations explain aspects of meaning, implication, and even permissible paraphrases of a given proposition. More recently, relationships have been found between the noun chosen for the subject and the empathy and general perspective of the speaker.

[3] Empathy and Syntax.

Kuno (1987, pp. 203–267) develops the interesting proposition that the syntax chosen for a given sentence corresponds to the perspective of the speaker. Kuno (p. 204) explains that

> ... speakers unconsciously make the same kind of decisions that film directors make about where to place themselves with respect to the events and states that their sentences are intended to describe ...

Such decisions are describable in terms of empathy. Kuno shows, for instance, that 1A is an unmarked empathy condition. It projects an objective view. In this encoding, no particular empathy is being shown either to John or to Bill. It merely states that John initiated the blow and that Bill has received it:

1A. John hit Bill.

However, if the same speaker says

1B. John's brother hit him.

he or she has identified more with John than with his brother. Kuno observes that it "seems commonsensical" that the possessive chosen, here *John's brother*, would be used to refer to Bill only " . . . when the speaker has placed himself[1] closer to John than his brother." This is because the brother is seen in this construction only through his relationship with John, not as an independent person. In other words, John's relationship is more important than the independent characterization of calling him Bill.

Yet another empathy condition occurs in passives:

1C. Bill was hit by his brother.
1D. Bill was hit by John.

Kuno says that passives always indicate empathy, because they show that the speaker has identified with the subject of the passive verb, in this instance, Bill. Kuno observes (p. 205) that the subject of the passive is "new" because the passive is formed by placing the object in what is usually the subject position. Doing this is more unusual so that hearers perceive the extra effort, so to speak, as a signal of empathy. If a speaker creates a MARKED construction, hearers will suspect that some special message is being implied. Actually, each of these has done something unusual, thereby creating empathy for Bill.

In 1C, the very fact that the brother's name is not mentioned is an overriding empathy condition on two grounds. First, use of a possessive ordinarily indicates the point of view of the possessor. The second is that failure to directly name someone whose name you presumably know, shows empathy for the one whose name you did use. Using a person's name indicates familiarity. Identifying another person simply by an anaphoric possessive like *his* again shows that one is telling this from the point of view of the named person. We shall see clear instances of this in the Ice Cream story narratives discussed below.

In 1D, the message indicating empathy for Bill works because passives with one word agents like *John* are rarely made (Svartvik 1966). Even if the passive were selected, ordinarily the agent wouldn't be mentioned. If the agent must be named, then the sentence usually would be in the active voice as in 1A above. The passive is used most habitually to enable the speaker to omit the agent or cause. There are two reasons for keeping the agent in at the end of the sentence. The first holds if the agent is heavily modified as in 1E and F. 1F is awkward. One expects that the sentence stopped too short as one would expect the object to be at least as long as the subject.

1E. Bill was hit by the short, skinny guy with curly red hair.

1F. The short, skinny guy with the curly red hair hit Bill.

There is a strong tendency in English to throw heavy constituents to the end of the sentence. A heavy constituent is one with a great deal of modification: adjective, relative clauses, and the like. These are either newly introduced items, hence the modification, or they are being especially emphasized. In 1D, since there is no heavily modified agent, choosing the object, Bill, to be subject indicates that there is some out-of-the way connotation. Hence, the reason for putting the agent at the end must be because the speaker wishes to emphasize who did it. A major reason for emphasizing the agent is that he or she is blameworthy.

Kuno uses *empathy* and *perspective* almost interchangeably as in his discussion of the choice between *comes/came up to* and *goes/went up to*. He says that this indicates the speaker's "camera angle" and empathy (p. 225)

2A. So Mary comes up to Max and says. . . .

2B. So Mary goes up to Max and says. . . .

In 2A, the action is being seen from Max's angle, whereas in 2B, it is seen from Mary's.

Kuno's approach to sentence analysis has a great deal to offer. He points out that certain verbs demand certain kinds of subjects. For instance, the agent of *assassinate* (example mine) has to be reprehensible and the object has to be a victim, which implies "not reprehensible." It is difficult to express empathy for an assassin. If we wish to we have to use other terminology, such as *freedom fighter*. Other verbs, like *hit* and *go* can be designed (Kuno's term) in terms of perspective; hence, they can be manipulated to imply empathy or its lack.

The reader must beware, however. Although Kuno formalizes his rules (p. 206), thus lending them a scientific air, he relies largely on his own intuitions. As with the judgments of other linguists[2] who have done the same, the reader too often finds that his or her intuitions don't match those of the author's. He does mention that "many speakers" find a sentence acceptable or not (p. 209), but does not show how he verified this. Consequently, we run into the same problem with him as we do with other intuitive linguists. Using myself as a point of reference, I find that some of the sentences he uses as proof for his interpretations don't mean to me what they do to him. Some of those he stars (*) are fine with me, and some which he doesn't star I would. These data cry out for verification by careful investigation like that pioneered by Quirk and Svartvik.

Still, Kuno's work has a great deal of appeal. He is right often enough to be exciting. It certainly makes sense that empathy is a condition on syntax. After all, language did evolve so that we may inform others of our feelings and to express the world from our perspective. Just as concepts like agency and negativity occur in all languages because of the need for all humans to express them, so is empathy a linguistic universal. Recognizing this possibility when interpreting another's speech can enrich understanding. Kuno gives us another place to look, so to speak, in the analysis of discourse making us more sensitive to the possibilities for empathy and perspective. These can be used along with an understanding of semantic feature analysis to enrich our insights.

[4] Subjecthood and Perspective.

Nomi Erteschik-Schir (1981) establishes the pragmatic basis of syntactic transformations. She suggests that a constituent in a sentence is **dominant** if the speaker **intends** to direct the hearers' attention to its **intension**, i.e., its full potential meaning. Dominance of a constituent, then, is what the sentence is about, and has ramifications for what kinds of transformations can apply. For instance, she shows that the kinds of questions that can be formed from a statement depends upon whether or not the NP is the dominant one. Consider the simple statement

3A. Jack eats candy.

One can form a question by using the **wh-word** that stands for *Jack*, which is *who* or the wh-word that stands for *candy*, which is *what.* Two questions, therefore, are possible,

3B. Who eats candy?
3C. What does Jack eat?

In essence, a *wh*-question is a kind of "fill-in-the-blanks" device. The *who* says fill in the blank in "X eats candy." The *what* says fill in the blank in "Jack eats X." In each instance, the X is the constituent the question is about. Therefore, in 3B, the question is about Jack, and in 3C it is about candy (or foodstuffs). One can ask 3B if one assumes that the corresponding declarative sentence would be about Jack. In contrast, one can ask 3C if it can be assumed that the declarative counterpart would be about candy.

Another pair even more graphically illustrates,

4A. I like the gears in that car.
4B. Which car do you like the gears in?
4C. I like the girl in that car.
4D. Which car do you like the girl in?

Erteschek-Schir contends that the unacceptability of 4D arises from the fact that the phrase "in the car" in 4C cannot be dominant in that sentence, therefore it cannot be the topic, but "in that car" in 4A can be dominant, hence 4B can be asked. She demonstrates that the reason that *in the car* in 4A can not be dominant, hence cannot be **extracted** to ask a question about, is that girls are not equipment on cars. She speculates that 4D would be fine in a society in which every car came with a girl so that choice of car also involved choice of girl.

The selection of the subject depends on such things as cultural facts and other pragmatic concerns. This is well illustrated by another fact. For instance, I can think of a setting in which 4D might very well be asked and would not be starred. Many young American males think that they will have an easier time getting a girlfriend if they have the right kind of car (with *right kind* referring to a much admired sports or luxury car). They also assume that different girls will be attracted by different cars. Imagine, then, a typical American high school parking lot with girls sitting in several cars waiting to be driven home by their boyfriends. In that cultural climate, a boy about to buy a new car could properly ask another, "Which car do you like the girl in?", the object being to match a car to the particular girl.

Erteschik-Schir gives another test for determining potential topics of sentences, the *which is a lie* test. In this, the topic of a sentence can be referred to by *which is a lie*. This phrase cannot be applied to an NP which is not dominant. For instance,

5A. Sam said John wrote a book **about Nixon.**
5B. Which is a lie—it was about a rhinoceros.

Here we know that people write about presidents so that focussing on the prepositional phrase "about Nixon" is fine. She opposes 5A and B to

6A. Sam said John destroyed a book about Nixon.
6B. Which is a lie—it was about a rhinoceros.

Here Erteschik-Schir posits that 6B would be possible if we know that John habitually destroyed books. Otherwise one would assume that the focus of 6A is on the act of destruction. If the topic of the discourse had been about Nixon or the Republican party, then John's choice of book to destroy becomes relevant. For instance, as my proof that John is not a loyal Republican, it would be natural for me to produce 6A, and for another person defending John to produce

6C. Which is a lie, it was about Johnson.

6B is odd because we expect the name of another president or of a well-known politician or statesman as a response to 6A. We do not expect another mammal, especially one so far removed from American presidencies. Note the acceptability of 6C as a response to 6A

6C. Which is a lie. It was about his dog.

Here the relevance is twofold. It is primarily signaled by the possessive. Americans do have dogs and they are important to them. The "which is a lie" test is useful for picking out topics, but, still, pragmatic conditions prevail. We can negate a statement but only if our negation is related in some obvious way to the prior statement, the one we are negating. My judgments about negation rest upon the very criteria Erteschek-Schir offers: a given paraphrase of a sentence may be determined as grammatical or not on the basis of pragmatic and discourse possibilities.

Kuno (1987, p. 16) explains that the concept of topichood has ramifications in the syntax, or perhaps more accurately that hearers assume topichood in the presence of certain constructions. For instance, a subject is typically taken to be the topic. If it is not the topic but there is a possessive, the latter is taken to be the topic.

7A. The man bought the woman's portrait of the clowns.

In an "out-of-the-blue" situation, the hearer will assume that this is about the man. Kuno says that this is the "easiest" interpretation. If subsequent conversation shows that the man is not the topic, then it is next taken to be about the woman. It is most difficult, although possible, to take it as being about the clowns.

There are ways to check whether or not a constituent is or can be the topic. Besides the kind of questioning Erteschek-Schir offers, there are regular rules of grammar which can be called upon as well as lexical items which exist specifically to announce a topic, that is to TOPICALIZE constituents, usually nouns. These are called upon when the speaker wishes to ensure that hearers assign topichood to the intended constituent. One syntactic mode of topicalizing is a process called CLEFTING. This puts a dummy subject like *it* or *this* before the noun which is the topic and its puts its verb into a relative clause, as in 7B and C (clefting elements boldfaced):

> 7B. **This is** the man **who** bought the woman's portrait of the clown.
> 7C. **This is** the woman **whose** portrait of the clowns was bought by the man.

In 7B the subject is *the man.* This corresponds to the reading of 7A in which one assumed that the sentence is about *the man.* The second reading of 7A, that *the woman* in the possessive is the subject, is paraphrasable by 7C.[3]

[5] Beyond the Sentence.

We have already seen that both the syntax and meaning of a sentence are dependent upon the discourse or text in which it appears, what VanDijk (1977, 1980, pp. 94–106)) calls MACROSTRUCTURES. He claims (1980 131, 229–242) that these differ from phenomena variously known as FRAMES, SCHEMATA, SCRIPTS and STRUCTURES OF EXPECTATION (Chaika 1989, pp. 11–114). Since they have been variously defined and studied, calling upon those terms can constitute serious ambiguities. For these reasons VanDijk's term is preferable when discussing such matters as relevance and topic. However, it must be borne in mind throughout that we are discussing speech produced in interactions with schizophrenics. We are not discussing problems arising from schizophrenic failure to behave as expected in certain social frames. We are discussing why their discourse fails as discourse linguistically. This may entail the giving of socially inappropriate responses, but it also entails linguistic aberrations definable by linguistic analysis apart from failures in interaction.

Macrostructures are GLOBAL structures to which individual sentences are subordinated. They determine what kinds of sentences are to be produced, what sequencing is allowable, even what kinds of vocabulary may be used. Macrostructures are as various as poems, novels, sermons, classroom lectures, conversations, and dissertations, and even this listing is far from exhaustive. Moreover, all of these can be further subdivided. Conversations, for instance, may range from arguing to kidding to informing, and each of these range from serious to nastiness to frivolity. Although we think of both written and oral communication as ways of communicating ideas, some macrostructures have no such purpose. For instance in conversation of the "shmoozing" or "shooting the breeze" type, the content of what is said is of little or no importance at all. What is important is its having been said. This is phatic communication, which is also seen in such matters as greetings, congratulating, complimenting, and even ritual insulting.[4]

Each kind of macrostructure demands its own forms. The kinds of words and grammatical forms demanded of casual phatic conversation are quite different from those demanded in a sermon. "Hi guys, whatcha doin'" is appropriate for quite different social situations than "Sirs, mesdames, may we proceed to the lecture hall." Similarly, both the syntax and vocabulary of formal written language are different from spoken in many respects. These comments may seem to be so self-evident that they hardly bear mentioning, but they must be kept in mind because breaches in the selection of vocabulary and sentence types are deviations as much as inappropriate neologisms are.

Although each evokes different kinds of speech activities, each with its own particular form, all macrostructures are similar in that they proceed from old to new information. That way the hearer/reader is oriented. The explicitness of the orienting segments ranges from the obligatory review of the literature or a summary of experiments in a scholarly publication to a brief phrase or sentence which plugs a cospeaker into the implicit assumptions of personal mutual knowledge in ordinary conversation. The purpose of the speech act and its locus of delivery also influence its form. A sermon in a cathedral is obligatorily more structured and limited in subject matter and form than is an informal chat in the party room of the same edifice.

The macrostructure itself entails or presupposes certain meanings as well as certain forms, and, by so doing, creates coherence. VanDijk (1980) explicitly argues that coherence is effected simply by producing what belongs in the given macrostructure. It seems to me that this position is an entirely expected result of the fact that all utterances bear meaning in reference to their context. A macrostructure forms a context, just as it itself is formed by the locale and purpose of a speaking activity (Chaika 1989, pp. 182–184).

Brown and Yule (1983, p. 83) advance the interesting concept that the communication source activates a pool of presupposition in the receiver, a pool including both personal and cultural knowledge. As we shall see, there are ways of introducing information which can not be presupposed to be shared.

Constructs like "topic of conversation" or "topic of discourse" refer to semantic properties beyond those of individual sentences within the discourse. Implicata, for instance, are influenced by what we perceive to be the topic of the macrostructure (Chapter 7) strongly influencing our interpretation of what we hear. For instance, consider

8A. Ms. Jones cheats all the time.
8B. She loses all the time anyway.

On the one hand, if we think we are overhearing a conversation about dieting, then 8A gives us no reason to make a negative moral judgment about Ms. Jones. Moreover, in such a context 8B may be an admiring or jealous comment or both. On the other hand, if we think the speaker is talking about an exam, then we do have reason to make such a negative judgment, and 8B becomes a triumphant or vindictive comment. In a sermon, the same sequence would not only be interpreted as a moral discussion, but an example of a greater theological belief, namely that sinners get punished not rewarded for their sins.

Our dependence on perceived topic explains some jokes, like

9A. Z: (coming out of movie): There's nothing better than a good love story.
Too bad this wasn't one of them.

Here, the humor lies in Z's apparently setting up the topic of how good the movie is, so that the negative evaluation contradicts the topic.

[6] The Discourse Topic.

Topics, especially in open-ended oral communications, unfold, with exchanges potentially opening up new topics. Even in volatile conversations with a great many topic switches, comments referring to previous contributions can be charted, just as the topic-producing ones can be. If no such linkages can be ascertained, then we judge the speaker as rambling, drunk, or crazy.

VanDijk (1980, p. 43) contends that we infer a MACROPROPOSITION from the sequence of propositions in discourse. He was actually talking of texts here, but the principle is the same in speech. He offers as a test for macropopositions the fact that they can be summarized. However, in spoken interactions, it is frequently not so easy to find a single global proposition. Typically, there are many topics in a conversation. This is true of extended pieces of writing as in books or even lengthy articles. Therefore, it is usually more accurate to say that one requires a series of summaries which account for changing of topics (Brown and Yule 1983). It must be stressed that these changes are not chaotic. They are introduced in orderly ways.

No one constituent of the discourse or even of a sentence within it need overtly encode what the topic is. A statement of topic should be able to complete the phrase "This is about. . . ." Outside of grammar handbooks, topic sentences are not always overtly encoded in speech or in writing. However, coherent discourse can somehow be summarized as having what Carlson (1983) calls "aboutness."

This does not mean that all parties to an interaction or all readers of a book agree on what the topic is, or, for that matter, what is being said about it. The speaker may think he or she is speaking on one topic, whereas the hearer may perceive it to be on another. This is usually not fatal to the communication process, however, because participants, when made aware of misunderstandings, can say or write, "You misunderstand. By X, I did not mean Y. I meant Z."

[7] Topic and Schizophrenic Speech.

In one way or another, many who would explain schizophrenic speech comment on its lack of topic. Such vague—and traditional—terms as *loose associations* or *flight of ideas* were clearly an attempt to describe such a situation. In order to remedy this imprecision, Andreasen (1979a,b) devised an apparently more precise set of criteria for schizophrenic speech, carefully defining them. Among them, she presents the following as separate diagnostic criteria[5] defining them as follows:

- DISTRACTIBILITY, when a patient breaks off repeatedly "in the middle of a sentence or idea and changes the subject in response to a nearby stimulus."
- TANGENTIALITY, irrelevantly answering a question.
- DERAILMENT, when "ideas slip off the track onto another one" which may be obliquely or completely unrelated.
- INCOHERENCE, incomprehensible speech in which a "series of words or phrases seem to be joined together arbitrarily and at

random,[6] speech lacking "cementing words" such as subordinating and specifically coordinating conjunctions, and "adjectival pronouns" [terminology hers][7] such as *the* and *a(n)*.

Andreasen's careful definitions were an important step towards much needed precision in the psychiatric discussion of language data. However, as she defines them, the above four terms are all actually instances of straying off a topic, whether that topic is introduced by a co-conversationalist who asks a question, or is one brought up by speakers themselves.

Andreasen's definition of incoherence above specifically mentions some of the syntactic categories which are designed to indicate the relationship between phrases and sentences to an overriding topic: the conjunctions and the noun DETERMINERS (articles) *the* and *a(n)*. Determiners have the function of announcing whether or not nouns are encoding NEW INFORMATION or OLD INFORMATION. The latter is called GIVEN INFORMATION by some. By indicating whether or not a noun is one that has been mentioned before, noun determiners tell us whether topic is the same or whether a new one is being introduced. That is how these work as "cementing words."

The indefinite article signals new information, that not previously mentioned, and the definite one signals old information as in the interplay between *a* and *the* below:

10A. **A** dog walked in the room.
10B. **The** dog was carrying **a** bone.
10C. **The** bone was messy.

Names[8] typically do not appear with articles because they are specified by the use of the proper noun itself. Often the name introduces a specific individual or location. Thereafter, pronouns or omissions indicate that the same person is being talked about.

Topicalizers, TOPIC MARKERS, also serve to mark out new information. Typically, they set up the hearer's expectations that a stretch of discourse will be following. Unlike the clefting and passive transformations they usually operate on more than a subject of a sentence. The nominal which comes after expressions like the following are taken as the topic:

- About last night . . .
- As I was saying
- Speaking of [name] . . .
- Do you remember [name] . . .

- You'd never believe it, but . . .
- The subsequent sections deal with . . .
- Today we take as our verse . . .

Some of the most basic rules of grammar have as their *raison d'etre* the signalling of new and old information. The deployment of such simple devices as *the* and *an* in English has such a function. So do such mundane matters as the dummy *it* and *there*, which allow the topic to be thrown to the end of the sentence. This is the part of the sentence which typically takes the strongest stress in English.

11A. It is nice that Bob asked you to the prom.
11B. There's milk in the fridge.

[8] Titles.

Brown and Yule (1983, p. 71–73) discuss the function of a title as a way of announcing topic. In writing and in certain kinds of formal speech these function as topicalizers. People typically assign meaning according to an announced title. Hearers may even complain if they feel that the title did not fairly represent what was actually said. The title functions as a guide to understanding. One of the schizophrenic participants in my study of narration complained that she could not complete the task because she didn't know what the title of the videostory was. This conversation ensued:

12A. I don't know what the title was. [pause] How can I tell you?
(Me: What do you think a good title for it is?)
A pleasant day at the ice cream store. uh [pause] 'n fek [pause].
That's all ike I have to say. [long pause]. A pleasant walk to and from [pause] home to the ice cream store. That still isn't right. I should be . . . It should say that it should say that they went in and bought the ice cream and they came out and that's it.
[to me, clearly ex cathedra] You wait a minute. I ha e to get my lighter . . .]
What? Did they sell everything? I didn't observe because I kept fiddling around.

Actually, the patient did summarize the story correctly if you allow for her use of *they* rather than *she*. The girl did go in and buy ice cream and did come out, and that is the end of the story. The patient became derailed over the question of the title, apparently feeling that a video presentation should have one.

Another patient ascribed a title to the video with quite different results

> 12B. [enunciates clearly with equal stress on each word indicating this is a title] Everyday Life in America.
> Little girl in candy store. Runnin' free.
> Her parents don't really care. So she gets up and takes to the air . . .

This was said as if it was intended to be a poem with regular recurring strong beats and pauses at the end of each rhyming word. Before announcing the title, he had created another rhyme

> 12C. Little girl in candy store. Mommy and Daddy away.
> [pause] That day.

[9] Utterance Pairs.

Across speakers, perhaps the most extreme instance in which topic constrains what may be said is seen in UTTERANCE PAIRS, variably known as ADJACENCY PAIRS (Sacks 1964–1972; Chaika 1989 pp. 119–131). The former term is preferable because such pairs may not always be adjacent in the conversation. Specifically, utterance pairs occur when one utterance elicits another of a specific form and content. These include phenomena like

> greetings → greeting
> questions → answers
> compliments → acknowledgements
> complaints → excuse, apology, or denial
> request/command-acceptance or rejection.

Whoever receives the first part of the utterance pair has to somehow respond with the other. The first part of the utterance pair constrains both the form of the response and the possible subject matter, that is, the topic. If someone says "hello," the other has to give a greeting. The only way to get out of it is to pretend not to see the greeter, or to be drunk, stoned, or otherwise mentally incapacitated.

It is no accident that so many greetings take the form of questions since in mainstream society, at least, the norm is that questions must be answered. Moreover, the question must be answered according to the form used by the questioner. A question preceded by *what* demands a noun, one preceded by a *why* demands a reason, and a *who* demands that a person be designated. A *yes-no* question of the "Are you going?" type must be answered by a *yes, no* or *"I don't know.* The squiggles discribed in Chapter 11 are utterance pairs. Hallowell and Smith (1983), as part of therapy for a schizophrenic patient, offered the patient a line, typically only part of a sentence and the patient completed the sentence. This worked like questions and answers because responses were directly governed by the immediately preceding phrase and left little room for wandering on to other matters.

An answer to a genuine question can often be deferred, as in, "I'm not sure. Let me get back to you later." The degree to which we are constrained by the topic of a question is beautifully illustrated by INSERTION SEQUENCES (Schegloff 1971). In these, a question is asked as a response to another question, as in

12A. Wanna come to a party?
 B. Can I bring a friend?
 A. Male or female?
 B. Female.
 A. Sure.
 B. Yeah, I'd like to come.

The responses are severely constrained here both as to order and to kind of response. B starts the insertion sequence by asking if he can bring a friend. Then A asks about the gender. Then, in the reverse of the order in which they were asked, all three questions get answered. Sometimes when such sequences become derailed, later on in the conversation or even in a subsequent one, one person will answer it, prefacing his or her remarks so that the original question will be recalled or the asker will remind the other to answer:

13A. Oh, gee, I never got around to answering your question . . .
13B. You asked about the party and I meant to tell you . . .
13C. We got so sidetracked that you never told me if you . . .

Such verbal placemarkers seem rarely to be used when psychotics become derailed. Whereas normal conversation loops back to an earlier exchange and then builds on it, schizophrenic ones sometimes just keep going linearly, so to speak (Chapter 8). Normal looping adds new material to the topic. In contrast, schizophrenic perseveration is characterized by not adding new information. Schizophrenics have two difficulties with topic: progression away from it or repetition of phrases without advancing it at all.

[10] Patient X and Utterance Pair Analysis.

Because of the strong constraints on responses, we would not expect such exchanges to be deviant, but in patients who evince a great deal of disintegration this does occur. Even so, Laffal (1965) reports that his patient, Dean, whose speech was so disrupted that he uttered both gibberish and opposite speech, still attempted to answer questions, as did Robertson and Shamsie's (1958) patient who apparently produced copious amounts of gibberish. The following exchange transpired between X, reported on in Chaika (1974), and an unidentified woman poking her head into the room and asking

14. W: Hello. Anybody here want some coffee?
    [pause]
    X: Head, heart, hands, health.

The [h]'s in W's pronunciation of "Hello" and "here" were aspirated with unusual strength and held longer[9] than usually, sounding on the tape almost like slight short-term hissing. What is noteworthy about X's response is that it was clearly motivated by the sound [h], not by the form or content of the question. This, of course, is never normal. One has to respond to both the syntactic form and semantic content of a question.

Sometimes schizophrenics do respond correctly to questions and other utterance pairs. X herself did "answer" the question, bizarrely to be sure, but still recognizably an answer. She just responded to the wrong part of the message. Laffal (1965) reports that his patient, Dean, whose speech was highly disrupted, also attempted to answer questions, as did Robertson and Shamsie's (1958) patient who produced gibberish. They interpreted his gibberish as real language, volitionally produced, explaining that his gibberish responses arose from his not being "prepared" to answer any inquiries about what it meant. The validity of such an assertion aside, even so severely disordered a patient as they describe still attempted to answer questions, that is, to obey this essentially social requirement. It was his linguistic ability which was not up to the task. If people are being uncooperative, they do not answer at all or evade the issue by trying to initiate a new topic.

[11] Theme Versus Subject.

An added complication to the notion of *subject of a sentence* is the relationship between the subject and the THEME of the sentence as opposed to what is being said about it, the RHEME. These are often referred to as the TOPIC versus the COMMENT and coincide with what traditional grammars call the subject and the predicate.

Halliday (1965, p. 37) explains that the first constituent of the sentence is the theme, "...[the] speaker's point of departure for the clause. He believes that the theme and the subject are not necessarily the same constituent of the sentence, a position independently arrived at by Jeng (1982) from his studies of Mandarin Chinese. According to Halliday, in 15A, the theme and the subject do coincide, but in 15B they do not since the theme is *yesterday* but the subject is *they:*

15A. They freed the whales yesterday.
15B. Yesterday, they freed the whales.

There are difficulties with the absoluteness of Halliday's analysis (Lyons 1977, p. 508), not the least of which is that considering the first element as the theme no matter what that element is, is circular. The theme is the first element and the first element is the theme. In addition, the first element in the sentence may be a topicalizer. What follows that is the theme, but the first element is not itself the theme.

The theme in the sense of *aboutness* can be expressed also by such devices as anaphora and deixis. Undoubtedly the reason that it is so common for sentences to start with pronouns is that they signal that the speaker is still talking about the same person or thing. In such a case, the first element is the theme. Another objection to the equation of theme with sentence position is that often, introductory adverbs and adverbial clauses like *yesterday* or *because of you* serve the purpose of orienting one to the discourse following. That is, these provide a context, but the actual theme of the discourse is about someone or something else. Where there is a choice of subject, as in a trivalent verb that allows a subject, object or dative, the particular noun chosen is often the theme, although, as we have seen at other times the choice of subject is dictated by a desire to waffle or to avoid repetition.

Carlson (1983, pp. 242–246) demonstrates that one can make a case for all or at least more than one of the constituents in a sentence being what the sentence is about, showing that

> 16A. Mr. Morgan is a careful researcher and a knowledgeable semiticist, but his originality leaves something to be desired. (Carlson, p. 243)

can be construed as being about Mr. Morgan or about his scholarly abilities. Similarly, in an ordinary spoken sentence like

> 16B. Max gave Griselda a diamond ring.

we can say that the sentence is about Max, Griselda, the diamond ring, or the act of giving which, in itself, implies that Max intended to become engaged to Griselda by his offering.

So long as we are hung up on the notion of the sentence as the bearer of topic and theme, we will continue to face such uncertainty. The problem disappears when we consider that the sentence is part of a larger construct: the discourse and its context of utterance or text. Considered this way, *theme* is what the entire discourse is about, which each constituent in the sentence "may pick out, refer to, or stand for" (Carlson, p. 244). This requires one modification: the theme is what a stretch of discourse is about, for topics do change in discourses.

Lyons neatly explains how the theme may influence at least some passives. He (1977, pp. 510–511) asserts that humans naturally are more interested in humans than in other entities, and that this interest explains which constituent was chosen as the subject. In turn, this can lead to the passive if the object was made subject. For instance, he gives as examples:

> 17A. A man was stung by a bee in the High Street today.
> 17B. A bee stung a man in the High Street today.

Lyons contends that 17A is more usual than 17B because humans are more interested in men than in bees. Hence, in Hallidayan terms, it is more natural to select *man* as the theme as in 17A, than it is to use the active as in 17B. Kuno would say that the perspective is from the human's point of view. In other words, the selection of the object as subject here arises from a natural tendency to thematize human perspectives.

The role that theme, subject, and empathy play in actual narrative is illustrated in the following collected as part of the Ice Cream Stories. Both were produced by patients with the discharge diagnosis of schizophrenia, but the first was not an SD schizophrenic and the second was. The boldface in each indicates each topic and theme encoded:

> 17C. A little **girl** was looking in a window of a Baskin-Robbins ice cream shop 'n **she** wanted some ice cream and uh **she** went home and asked her mother if **she** could have some ice cream and **her mother** said it's too close to supper an' **she** asked her father for some ice cream an' **her father** gave her some money an **she** went down to the ice cream parlor and bought a double scoop of ice cream.

> 17D. One was about I think a little **girl or boy** having a ball and having to be real careful about crossin' the street an' I might be mistaken. I was just thinking of **movies I've watched** . . . It seems like what **children** do in their actions just exemplify what grown-ups are like an' it just gives **grown-ups** a better idea to think that they are necessarily better than children y'know an' I think it's **time to really talk** now approaching 1980's,[10] And peop'—**kids** goin' to college and things like that. I haven't even finished ya know it's ridiculous.

The first is well formed discourse as well as consisting of well formed sentences. The very first sentence thematizes *girl* by mentioning it first. The anaphoric reference *she* ties the next three predicates together to this first mention. Then the anaphoric reference *her* links the mention of her parents to the preceding. The parents are seen only in reference to the girl's wishes, which is as it should be. The anaphoric reference in the last sentence ties it all up. Moreover, it consistently encodes the action from the perspective of the little girl, showing empathy for her.

In contrast, although 17B like 17A shows no disruption in sentential syntax or word choice *per se,* it is deviant. It is only when one examines it from the point of view of the theme and subject of the sentences that we see what is wrong. The sequence opens with a recognized and correctly used topicalizer, "one was about . . ." which introduces the little girl or boy. First the speaker correctly topicalizes with [*was about* + mention of NP], here, the child. Both the facts that the child was "having a ball" and "crossing the street" are possible and logical, and ellipsis is used correctly in not repeating the subject before both verbs.[11] Given the clearly marked topic the next sentence should deal with the child and crossing the street. Instead, a second topic is announced, the movies the narrator had seen. *I think of* is often used as a topicalizer, so is *it seems,* the opener of the very next sentence. The reference to kids' going to college is completely unprepared. Being careful about crossing the street and kids' emulation of adults are tenuous threads to the remark about the 1980s and higher education. So far, we have seen three topicalizers and not one theme. None of the topicalizing sentences are followed by any expansion of the topic, although it is not hard to explain why the speaker introduced these three topics together:

- the video was of a child
- videos remind people of movies
- children do imitate adults

The semantic content of each sentence is fine, but our feeling that the speaker is flitting from topic to topic is explained by the successive topicalizing with no elaboration. The speaker is flitting from topic to topic. At the third, it seems as if the speaker has finally settled on children as his theme, but the conjoined mention of grown-ups' thinking that they are superior to children is a jolt because now the theme has become *grown-ups* just when we thought it was children. There is also no consistency of perspective. It, too, flits from the narrator to the child to the narrator.

[12] Given and New Information.

After its introduction, the theme is given information, referring to something already present in the verbal and nonverbal context (Lyons 1977, p. 508; Halliday 1985, p. 275). The sentence is composed of a theme and a RHEME or COMMENT. Some scholars speak of the *theme* versus *rheme* of the sentence, and other refer to the *topic versus comment* of the sentence. For the most part, these are simply different terms for the same thing, although the pairs are not interchangeable. If one decides upon *theme*, then it must be opposed to *rheme*, and *topic* has to co-occur with *comment.* Often, in fact, usually, these coincide with the traditional *complete subject* and *complete predicate.* All of these actually refer to the flow from old to new information that sentences within a discourse ideally have. Such notational variants using different terms for the same entity and the same terms for different ones afflicts all scholarly fields.

No matter what they call them, discourse analysts agree that many naturally occurring sentences have a given and a new component (Lyons 1977, pp. 508–510; Brown and Yule, 1983 pp. 153–189). Van Dijk (1980, p. 94) elaborates, saying that the subject (a.k.a. *topic, theme*) the part of the sentence is "information that is already *introduced* (. . .) already *supposed*

... to be known . . . , or otherwise *given* or started from" and the predicate (a.k.a. *comment, rheme*) expresses "*new, unknown, unpredictable,* . . . information" about the topic (all italics his).[12] For this reason, such markers of old information as pronouns or deictics usually occur in subject position. As already shown in discussing cohesion, given information can also refer to information known by previous interactions, the physical context or cultural knowledge. This leads to the optimal flow of old to new information with heavily modified constituents at the end of the sentence.

When new information can fill the subject position, there is a very strong tendency to throw it to the end of the sentence leaving a dummy *it* or *there* as the subject, as in

18A. Roses are on the table.
18B. **There** are roses on the table
18C. That you came was nice.
18D. **It** was nice that you came.

As valid as these examples are, and as accurate as the observation is that sentences tend to flow from old to new information, it is still a dubious claim to say that is how all sentences progress. Sentences in isolation do travel from old to new information, as do many sentences in a discourse but, again within the discourse, many sentences in their entirety simply repeat the information or messages given before although not necessarily in the same words and syntax. Culturally known items might be mentioned. This can be done very effectively—or annoyingly—to emphasize a point or to mark out for the hearer that something prior is being brought up again. The flow from old to new information is also a feature of skillful rhetoric, but not all rhetoric is skillful and that which is not is not necessarily psychotic or deranged. In a psychotic population we would expect that flow to be interrupted more than it is in normals since, as a byproduct of psychosis, a speaker may not be in control. The defining difference between normals and psychotics is the way that distinctly psychotic speech does not flow. It is blocked by perseverations of all sorts (Chapters 1 and 2). In contrast, normal speech which is faulty in presentation of new and old information is clumsy or boring (e.g., Williams 1981).

Looking again at the following response to the question about where the patient lived and what it was like living in that place, we see the extent of deviation possible in schizophrenic perseverations.

19. **Mill Avenue is a** house in between avenues U and avenue T I live **on Mill Avenue** for a period of for now a period   of maybe

fifteen year for around approximate fifteen years **I like it the fam—I like every family on Mill Avenue I like every family in the world I like every family in The United State of America I like every family on on Mill Avenue** I like Mill Avenue is a is a block with that is busy **cars** always **pass by** all the time I always look out the window of my front porch front porch at time when I s- **when I'm not sure if it's possible about the way I think I could read people mind about people's society attitude plot and spirit so I think I could read their mind as they drive by in the car** sh- **will I see Paradise will I not see Paradise should I answer should I not answer I not answer w-** their thought of how **I read think I could read their mind about when they pass by in the car** in the house pass by in the car from my house **I just correct for them for having me feel better about myself not answer will I should I answer should I not answer will I see Paradise will I not see Paradise I just correct them to have me feel better about myself about the way I think I can hear their mind** r- **about the way I think I could read their mind as they pass by the house Mill Avenue is also Mill Avenue is also** a place of great event for all **the families** that **live on Mill Avenue** always eht- **receive world wide attention** and I am o- I am just one of **the families** live on Mill Avenue that **always receive world wide attention** so therefore [unintelligible] **to receive world wide attention** is **receive world wide attention** is some some you should be proud of you should be proud of **world wide attention** [unintelligible] there's the family are just too out in the open not to have **world wide attention** so they all have **world wide attention by the cars pa—that pass in the front cars that pass by all the time** so therefore **Mill Avenue is also a a I like a quiet residential n- block like a quiet residential block** with a Italian people talk outside by the fence discuss their feelings their attitudes their opinions opinion about any story feeling concept idea or sentence that they may have and once again when I look outside the window because **I think I could read people's minds about people's society attitude plot and spirit** w-**should I answer should I not answer will I see Paradise will I not see Paradise I not answer** correct them have me feel about better about myself like I said before **I'm not sure if it's possible about the way I think I could read people mind about people's society attitude plot and spirit so I not answer them** I just correct them have me feel better about myself **Mill Avenue is also a place** where **people gather in back yards to have people gather in back yards to have** a barbecue

in the back yard to have relative over to have friend over to talk **in the back yard** to be merry with each other. (data courtesy of Dr. Bonnie Spring)[13]

There is neither a flow from given to new information, nor is there any relevance achieved. Rather the same phrases are repeated cyclically and no connections are made between the problem of seeing Paradise and the street where he lives. Perhaps he is reminded of death, hence Paradise because of the connection between people's plotting and death. It is possible to make some sense of this, at least from the written transcript which gives us the luxury of slowly analyzing what was said. Spoken, as in the original tape recording, one makes no sense out of it at all. The lack of pronouns seriously impedes our understanding. Even in writing, our usual means of comprehending do not work. As with glossomania, we can only seek an explanation of why these phrases are juxtaposed.

[13] New and Brand New Information.

Prince (1981), with much justice, complains that different scholars have used the concept of given versus new information in three somewhat different ways, thus rendering the concept imprecise. Given information has been considered to be information which is predictable, shared, or salient. If the information is predictable, then it is recoverable from the context if it is not fully expressed. We have already seen the importance of anaphora in showing whether or not a constituent has been already introduced.

Prince (1981), discriminates between two kinds of new information: **salient** and **brand new** information. Givenness in the sense of being salient refers to information that the speaker assumes to be in the consciousness of the hearer (Chafe quoted by Prince, p. 228). In this sense, for an NP to be properly signalled as a given entity, it must have been mentioned in the discourse, or be in the same category of something which has been mentioned. A third possibility is that the NP can refer to something in the physical context of the interaction. For instance, in the Ice Cream Stories (Chaika and Alexander 1986; Chapter 8), many people spoke of a little girl asking her mother for ice cream, without introducing the mother as new information. The fact of having mentioned the child was sufficient for the existence of the mother, as in:

20A. A little girl was looking in a window of a Baskin Robins ice cream shop 'n she wanted some ice cream and uh she went home and asked her mother if she could have some ice cream. . . .

20B. Um—in an ice cream store she was lookin' in to see if she could get any she went home her mother said. . . .

In both of these the mention of the mother is the first mention in the discourse. Mothers are salient because children are presumed to have them and it is also presumed that they are the ones to give permission to eat ice cream.

Prince suggests that the term *shared knowledge* be replaced by *assumed familiarity,* since all anyone can do is assume what another knows. She suggests that there are two different kinds of new information. If the hearer already knows about the entity being introduced, it is simply new. In contrast, if the speaker introduces something the hearer doesn't know about, then that entity is brand new. Brand new information has to be created in the hearer's mind. This, of course, puts a greater burden on the speaker in presenting enough information so that the hearer can create what was intended.

To see the difference between these two types of new information, consider the following (examples and analysis mine):

21A. Freud certainly shook up the world of medicine.

21B. Jerry Jones certainly shook up the world of medicine.

21A is fine. I have invoked mention of someone my readers have knowledge of. They know he lived. They know he was a physician, and that he had radical ideas about the human mind. They also know that he has had a great influence on 20th century thought. I am introducing him as new to this discussion, but I don't have to create him in the reader's mind. In fact, I can say many things about him without very much preparation because I assume familiarity. 21A works very well as an utterance bringing up new information.

In contrast, 21B doesn't work well at all for introducing new information, unless fortuitously some reader knows a Jerry Jones who had a strong effect on the world of medicine. Here, Jerry Jones has to be created (in Prince's sense) in the reader's mind by syntactic and lexical choices, as in

21C. I used to know **this guy** who was named Jerry Jones and he sure shook up the world of medicine when he . . .

21D. A man named Jerry Jones had a profound effect on the medical community because he. . . .

Mechanisms for introducing brand new information abound in both speech and writing. In 21C, the expression *this guy* is a colloquialism indicating "I'm going to tell you about someone you don't know of." The indefinite *a* in 21D can be used for salient and brand new information, but the clincher for brand new information in this sentence is the phrase *named Jerry Jones.* This always indicates that nonsalient new information is being introduced. Relative clauses and participles both are frequent markers of brand new information, as in 21C and D respectively. For instance, note the disparity in

21E. *Our *mother* named *Tessie* Dorgan gave you this note, dear.

The distinction between the two kinds of new information appears to be useful in analyzing schizophrenic discourse. When discussing exophora, I noted that using a *she* for first mention of a girl shown in a video was not deviant if the patient had viewed the video with the experimenter. The child in the video was in the patient's consciousness and, presumably, mine since we had both watched the video together. Hence the patient could assume that the reference was salient.

However, in the following, failing to introduce something as brand new information contributes to the deviation of the passages. In 22A, brand new information is presented as if it were simply new salient information. This narrative also contains gibberish, so that the failures in presenting information as brand new or not is matched by a general disruption in linguistic ability.

22A. Okay. I was watching **a film of a girl** and um s bring back memories of things that happened to people around me that affected me during the time when I was living in that area and she just went to the store for a candy bar and by the time oooh of course her brother who was supposed to be watching wasn't paying much attention he was blamed for and I didn't think that was fair the way the way they did that either so that's why I'm just asking yah could we just get together and try to work it out all together for one big party or something ezz it hey if it we'd all in which is in not they've been here. . . .

In 22B, we see typical schizophrenic repetition about his sleeping for 11 weeks. Then the the patient erroneously signals *the man* as if it were given information, but this is the first mention of the man and he is nowhere introduced. Then the narrator fails to tell us why his father told him to call the police. Here, the why is the essential brand new information to ground the events of the narrative. Since she was not dealing with the kinds of data presented here, Ellen Prince (1981) claimed that her formulation of new and brand new information always falls on nouns, but examples like this show that adverbials also may be involved. In the following, an adverbial clause is required in order to explain the reason.

> 22B. I was sleeping in bed on top of my bed from the last time I got out of the hospital which was about 11 weeks that I was released I was lying top of bed for the 11 weeks that I was released and and my father told to call the police car and the police car enter over my house the man stepped out of the police car and he w—entered my house with two patrolmen and they patrolman cherry and patrolman alcolino . . .

One problem in trying to use distinctions such as Prince's in the disordered speech of schizophrenics is that some might say that neologisms and even outright gibberish are brand new information that hasn't been introduced correctly. I would put limits on any analysis of new and old information, such that we presume an error only if we can recognize the words and the markers themselves such as articles, pronouns, adjectives, relative clauses, or any other recognizable construction that is used to identify new information or refer to old.

[14] Empathy and Point of View.

Kuno (1987, p. 17) coins the term HYPER-TOPIC to indicate "a paragraph topic or a conversation topic" as distinct from the subject of a sentence. He offers an important insight, that there is a LATENT TOPIC as well, and this usually is the speaker, the first person, the ego, the *I*. That is, it is assumed that whatever we say we are talking about our own perspective and experiences. He shows how the hyper-topic interacts with the latent first person topic, as in the following example, which for brevity's sake I have here paraphrased.

> 23A. I have been collecting pictures of movie stars, and I can show them to you, but I cannot show you my picture of Marilyn Monroe.

Kuno points out that such a discourse is, indeed, on one level about the first person. This constitutes the latent or hyper-topic, but the picture of Marilyn Monroe is what Kuno terms the PROMINENT topic. Notice here that the actress mentioned can be isolated with clefting,[14]

23B. It is Marilyn Monroe's picture which I cannot show you.

But it is odd to topicalize *I* or even *my*,

23C. ?It is I who cannot show you my picture of Marilyn Monroe.
23D. ?Regarding me, I cannot show you my picture of Marilyn Monroe.
23E. S: I took aerobic dancing until I broke a toe.
       H: Oh, how is it?
       S: I don't know. It wasn't my toe.

I suggest that 23C and D are strange because it is rarely the case that speakers have to emphasize that the discourse is about themselves. That is presumed, hence latent. If it is already presumed to be a topic, then there is no reason for topicalizing it. We topicalize only new or brand-new information. Similarly, the humor of 23E resides in the expectation that S is talking about herself, the latent topic being *I*. Notice that none of these violate syntactic rules. There is no grammar rule which would exclude them. By themselves, they are perfectly good English, questionable only in terms of requirements of discourse.

Notes

[1]Here and elsewhere in actual quotes, this sexist choice of pronoun is Kuno's.

[2]Although they might prefer to have their tongues cut out with burning pincers rather than admit it, the transformationalists did the same thing that traditional grammarians had always done: they invented sentences and rules based upon their own notion of their own speech.

[3]Kuno says that all NP's in a sentence cannot be topicalized. He finds it impossible to topicalize *clowns* as in *These are the clowns who the man bought the woman's portrait of. Kuno claims that the strangeness of this is caused by the possessive. I suspect that another reason this paraphrase seems queer is the very complexity of the sentence which entails one's keeping track both of the noun that goes with the preposition and even the distance of *the clowns* from its preposition.

[4]Typically, these are insults clearly given in jest. Socially, they relieve hostilities safely in tense situations. In some cultures they are readily used to test verbal prowess, as in adolescent male "your mother" jibes. These originated in black male verbal contests called variously *sounding, chopping, cutting, ranking,* and *ragging.*

[5]These are only some of the criteria on which she diagnoses schizophrenia.

[6]Andreasen also includes under this term such phenomena as word salads and schizophasia.

[7]The determiners *the* and *an* are not pronouns. They do not replace nouns or any consitutent of a sentence. Nor do they function as adjectives. Adjectives come between the determiner and the noun; moreover, they can take a word indicating degree as in "very happy" or "most generous." There is no category of "adjective pronouns" in syntax.

[8]Actually, in English, names for animate creatures, most countries, states, cities, and towns do not have articles before them, but rivers, oceans, and mountain ranges do, as in *The Mississippi, The Atlantic,* or *The Rockies.* Lakes and individual mountains do not take the article, but they are typically preceded or followed by the words *Lake* and *Mount(ain),* respectively. Such variation clearly serves the function of building up redundancy in the message, while still specifying exactly.

[9]When speaking about duration and strength of an individual sound, it should be realized that we are talking about milliseconds. The human ear is able to recognize as distinct differences between sounds that are almost imperceptible on a spectograph, and sounds that differ in length so slightly that special equipment is needed to record them.

[10]These data were collected from 1978–1980.

[11]However, it is inaccurate. The video did not show a child having a ball in any sense of those words, nor was there anything about crossing the street. These inaccuracies aren't linguistic ones, just perceptual ones. Additionally, this was elicited one week after viewing the video. He wasn't sure how many videos he had seen; hence, the use of *one* rather than *it.*

[12]Notice that these findings, that the flow of information in the sentence should go from old to new information, therefore the unstressed to the stressed, from short structures to long is diametrically opposed to what students learn in school. They are told to put the important information first. This is always the new information. One of the reasons for the denseness of scholarly and bureaucratic writing is that it violates the flow from old to new information.

[13]Dr. Spring does not necessarily endorse my interpretations of these data, however.

[14]All of these examples and topic tests are mine, not Kuno's

Chapter Eleven

DISCOURSE ANALYSIS: BEYOND FREUD

Ever since Freud, the question has arisen of how a discourse should be understood. How do we interpret discourse? What can be assumed and what are the bounds on derived meaning? The fragmented nature of normal discourse is presented. Then, four modes of interpretation of patients' speech are offered along with a discussion of elicitation and its effect on speech. This includes such matters as resistance to therapy.

[1] Justifiable Interpretation.

The stunning force of Freudian interpretation burst upon the 20th century revolutionizing our perception of human behavior. Ultimately, it affected psychiatry, psychology, literature, the graphic arts, and, eventually, society itself by forcing reexamination of family structure, including the child's obligations to the parent and the blaming of the parent for the child's insecurities, obsessions, and transgressions. All of this occurred because of Freud's mode of interpretation of discourse.

It is not too much to say, for instance, that Bateson's double bind theory could not have been formulated without a prior belief in Freudian analysis, nor, of course, would we have the interpretive methodologies of Harry Stack Sullivan, Harold Searle, Silvano Arieti, Ernest Jones,[1] or the now popular Lacan. All such interpreters depend upon the basic Freudian assumption that language at no level necessarily means what it says. Interpretation derives not from the actual words and grammar as used by nonpsychotic patients, but from reference to beliefs about Oedipal bonds, castration fears, homosexual panic, and even paranoia induced by feelings of inadequacy. Lacan roots his interpretations in the linguistics of de Saussure, but still employs a Freudian model of the unconscious to which the psychiatrist is supposed to be talking. He envisions a dialogue between the Other, the analyst, and the Other, the patient's subconscious (Holloway 1977, 1978; Haskell 1978). Psychosis is believed to stem from avoidance of intolerable feelings.

Analysts differ considerably in their treatment of schizophrenia, ranging from Rosen's belief in uncovering "vivid and shocking interpretations of a primarily oedipal nature, . . . [he] bypass[es] the ego and . . . communicate[s] with the unconscious id material" (pp. 149–150). Analysts were trained by other highly respected senior analysts, so to speak, who offered interpretations of the patient's speech based upon his or her view of what caused the neurotic or psychotic illness. Although all such analysis emanated from Freudian theory, individual analysts departed from this theory to a greater or lesser degree (Hallowell and Smith 1983).

One issue has been the mode of analysis to follow in treating schizophrenics. Analysts perceive themselves as teachers and their mode of analysis is aimed at teaching the patient to cope. Hallowell and Smith (1983, pp. 149–156) summarize some of these methods and the rationale behind them. Some analysts believe that their task is to restore defective ego boundaries. This resulted in an "intrusive, even persecutory style [of analysis] (p. 150). Others believe in entering the patient's psychotic world and then by building trust, help the patients to reintegrate themselves into the world left behind by the psychosis.

The relative validity of any and all of these beliefs about therapy is not the issue here. The issue here is solely the differences in orientation of various analysts and analyzers of discourse, because these lead to very different kinds of interpretations of what a patient has said. It is the relationship between analysis and theoretical positions that have to be examined. We have already seen that interpretation is based upon various strategies, and that these strategies include our ascribing intention to the speaker. We also consider mutual histories of interactors. The influence of theory and of being in a therapeutic setting, then, are important determinants in analysis.

All Freudian or post-Freudian theories rest upon a view of the dynamics of mind and speech that cannot be verified by overt observation or by experimentation. One either believes them or one does not. This doesn't mean that they are valid or not valid. It is just that they are not provable by the usual scientific procedures. There is no way to disprove Freud or his followers, including Lacan, but there is no way to prove that they are correct either. Ultimately, one believes or not according to one's intuitive sense that psychoanalysis strikes a responsive chord. Those who do not intuit this may be, as the analysts claim, simply denying what is true, burying it, even perhaps resisting treatment.

Linguistics itself did not offer many guides to interpreting even normal discourse to Freud or his contemporaries. In fact, psychoanalysis predated linguistics by decades in realizing that language must have some kind of deep structure as well as surface forms. Psychoanalysis also predated linguistics by decades in realizing that the encoding of a message is dictated partly by the speaker's intent, and the meaning a hearer derives depends on the intent that he or she ascribes to the speaker in formulating that message. Until relatively recently, linguists rested semantics upon the flimsy undergirding of sentence grammars and the doctrines of separation of linguistic levels, and that was when meaning was considered at all.

Under the aegis of philosophers of language like Austin and Searle and linguists themselves like Lyons, Fillmore, and Halliday, the context-sensitive view of language finally offered some alternate procedures for analysis. We can make a case nowadays that matters of justifiable interpretation, even of metaphor, seem to be bounded by rules and strategies, so that we are justified in speaking of the grammar of the discourse. It is time to reexamine Freudian inspired modes of psychoanalytic interpretation in the light of our new understandings, not with the view of invalidating psychoanalysis, but to enhance its insights by providing a firmer base upon which to ground interpretations, and, in some cases, to provide alternate interpretations.

[2] Psychology, Psychiatry, and Linguistics.

Psychiatry and its sister disciplines generally downplay the public and social nature of language. Rather, language is treated as a private system which each person can and does use pretty much as he or she wishes. Typically, meaning of a discourse is taken to be holistic with little or no attempt to justify it on the basis of actual syntax or lexicon used. Meaning is assigned to the discourse as a whole according to the analyst's perception of the patient's intent; thus, discourse is taken as a strategy, a cryptic rendering of a person's real, hidden meaning.[2] Imaginative exegesis, as in literary analysis, is admired, and certain analysts, such as Freud or Searles, are often used as guides to interpretation of given utterances because of their acknowledged superior ability to see into the true meaning of discourses. The Seeman and Cole analysis of Carrie's speech, presented below, is an example.

Linguistics also acknowledges that each person's language is, to some degree, unique. It has long been said that, ultimately, we each speak an idiolect, as well as a dialect of a language. However, the idiolect arises because individuals may have learned a few rules of language somewhat differently from others, and because words and even syntax can change over a person's lifetime. Still, idiolectal variation refers to language being used to convey messages to others. For instance, several of my students say and write "concern to" rather than "concern with." This use of *to* seems to be spreading virtually person by person and students even from the same region differ, some keeping the older *with*, and some not. At this point in time, we can only say that there is idiolectal variation of the particle used with the verb *concern*.

We must not assume that the flow of linguistic understanding always proceeds from linguistics to psychiatry. Sometimes the reverse is true. Long after psychiatry, for instance, linguistics has finally begun to consider the roles of motivation and presupposition in meaning, as well as implication derived from both roles.

Still, there are definable differences in orientation between psychoanalytical and linguistic analyses of discourse. It bears repeating that linguistic analyses proceed from actual words combined with actual syntax, and their relation to social context. Implicitly or explicitly, utterances are judged as normal or deviant, idiolectal or dialectal. Linguists are primarily concerned with uncovering regular rules and strategies for conveying meaning; why, for instance, "It's cold in here" may be construed as a command to close a window, or "You live on 56th Street" may be heard as a question (e.g., Ervin-Tripp 1972; Labov and Fanshel 1977; Goody 1978). Such a concern with rules and strategies entails another assumption, that we are all using language, or trying to, in pretty much the same ways (e.g., Searle 1975, pp. 63, 73; Austin 1962; Lyons 1977, p. 735.) Problems naturally arise when language is clearly not being used correctly, when it deviates from linguistic norms. Such speech often cannot be understood by usual decoding strategies. Typically, linguists have treated such error by comparing it to normal production, assuming that the speaker intended to use language so that it could be understood, but that normal production processes have been disrupted (e.g., Fromkin 1973; Clark and Clark, 1977, pp. 211–215; Buckingham and Kertesz 1974; Chaika 1974a, 1977). In such instances, extraordinary measures are employed to gain understanding, but these are based upon normal decoding practices.

Four separate discourses will be presented here, each resulting from data collected in different ways and upon different assumptions, and each interpreting those data according to somewhat different constructs.

The first is based upon poetry as a mode of communication between therapist and patient (Hallowell and Smith 1983). The second, Labov and Fanshel (1977), analyzed five therapeutic episodes between a therapist and her patient in the light of strategies of ordinary conversation, developing what they call a PRINCIPLED ELABORATION of meaning.

In what is perhaps its most shaky premise, classic psychoanalysis guarantees that the analyst can never be successfully proven wrong. According to this theory, the more one denies that one meant what the therapist says one meant, the more one really meant it. For instance, if an analyst tells a woman that she is consumed by penis envy, the more she says she isn't, the stronger her envy is presumed to be. Her denial constitutes proof of her neurosis. The same is true of the man who denies that he is consumed by Oedipal desires. As a concommitant of this premise, analysts speak of the period of resistance, a period of time during which the patient evinces resistance to the therapeutic situation. There is, undeniably, a period that can be called resistance, but I suspect that there are many reasons for resistance, and, in some instances, it is not real resistance at all.

We now examine interpretations of speech data from three patients. These data were elicited in three different ways: squiggles, an ordinary therapeutic interview, and unbounded conversation.

[3] Squiggles and Therapy.

Hallowell and Smith, being highly influenced by Arieti's compassionate view of the psychotic's unbearable sadness and loss, developed a mode of analysis in which they adapted a game of *squiggles* as a way of offering the patient the therapist's ego as a bridge, but one which also allows the therapist to "enter the metaphor of the patient's world." The *squiggles* game consisted of the therapist or patient providing a verbal opener, and the other responding with a short line. Some of these rhymed, some did not, but the result in each instance presented formed a joint dialogue cast into poetic form, as in:

1A. Th.: They said I am a hopeless case
    Pt.: Not I, a member of the human race, in disgrace
    Th.: I wish they wouldn't say that
    Pt.: In a nonjoking way
    Th.: It makes me

Pt.: Suspicious

Th.: And angry and sad

Pt.: Which aren't the strongest emotions I've had

Th.: The strongest are

Pt.: Composed of these

Th.: Combined into

Pt.: Something I don't want to feel

Th.: Something like

Pt.: Rage, but not quite

Th.: Also like

Pt.: An intense feeling

(p. 142)

The patient's rhyming here is controlled, fits the meaning of the entire squiggle. This patient had unusual facility with language, writing superb poetry. He fits the pattern of the negative symptom psychotic, speaking little. He presented poems both on the day of admission and the next day, but did not talk (Edward Hallowell, personal communication). What is noteworthy about these squiggles is that they provide a structured enough frame so that a dialogue can proceed without the patient's becoming derailed. The therapist is able to constrain the topic, and, at the same time, to allow the patient free expression. This constituted an opening for therapy itself " . . . the more personal, affective part of it, especially in the beginning, was contained in the squiggles" (Hallowell and Smith 1983, p. 143). Hallowell's skill in presenting the right kinds of openers for the patient himself must not be overlooked.

Hallowell and Smith do not give any extraordinary interpretations of what the patient has said in these squiggles. They take 1A as a straightforward expression of his feelings. Similarly, he expresses his need to cut off feeling, in

1B. Pt.: Nothing lasts forever

Th.: No one lives that long

Pt.: Not on earth

Th.: Sometimes I want to get away

Pt.: Into the body of a robot

Th.: No feelings there. Just safe steel

Pt.: No way to get hurt or die

Th.: Sometimes I want to die

Pt.: To live in heaven forever

Th.: Where people stay with you
Pt.: And never leave
Th.: Leave, leave, leave
Pt.: I wish my feelings would leave sometimes
Th.: But they stay
Pt.: And haunt

(pp. 143–144)

The degree to which squiggles could be applied to all patients has not been determined, but, given the results in this case, it certainly seems promising.

[4] Schizophrenic Chaining: Three Interpretations.

In Chapter 5 we saw that Forrest interpreted the following as being a metaphorical way to express what it is like to be schizophrenic:

2. Doctor, I have pains in my chest and hope and wonder if my box is broken and heart is beaten ... (Maher 1968 cited in Forrest 1986)

Forrest believes that all language is metaphor (1976, p. 296), that schizophrenic speech is especially poetic and that associational chaining is a way of affirming the "right of choice which exists in thought and language," of "look [ing] for extra connections in words ... to firm up the connection between ideas we feel are related" (Forrest 1965).

Such an explanation ignores the fact that normal speakers do not firm up connections between ideas by uttering glossomanic chains. Rather, the many modes of effecting cohesion firm up those connections as do the ways that sentences are made to fit to a topic.

Another example of chaining, here a response to a question, is here reprised:

3. Looks like clay. Sounds like gray. Take you for a roll in the hay. Hay day. Help! I just can't. Need help. May day. (Cohen 1978, p. 29)

As explained earlier, several patients named the disc in question as being either clay-colored or salmon-colored. Cohen, a psychologist oriented towards behaviorism, explains chaining responses as in 3 as resulting from "anticipation of social punishment contingent upon the emission of a sampled response (1978, p. 21). He says that schizophrenics cannot effectively reject punishable responses to referents, they ... break the perseverative cycle by shifting to different referents. One way to do this is via chaining." He admits that "ultimately" their responses become "remote from the original referents and from the listener's standpoint, seriously tangential to the conversational context." Given such an explanation for the cause of schizophrenic speech, there is, of course, no reason to search for meaning in sequences of chaining, and, indeed, Cohen does not.

In terms of behavioral theory, however, it is puzzling how the chaining can proceed from a need to avoid punishment, since the first sentence is the most correct, and, indeed, the only correct one. It is the phenomenon of chaining itself which is incorrect. Furthermore, as Cohen himself admits, the chaining always moves further away from a correct response. Hence, according to behavioral psychology, no chaining should ever occur because it leads to the very punishment that Cohen says the patient is trying to avoid by chaining.

Also, Cohen's explanation rests upon a belief that the patient has actively chosen this means to avoid punishment. Since other examples of chaining do appear in the literature, and appear as examples of speech especially pathognomic of schizophrenia, his explanation assumes that schizophrenics as a group are very likely to choose this behavior for avoiding punishment.

The problem is that the chaining is bizarre precisely because there seems to be no normal speech behavior like it. Certainly, this is not the kind of speech behavior one calls upon to avoid punishment. Thus there is no possibility it has been learned, except, perhaps those unfortunates who have been hospitalized for long periods with SD schizophrenics. Cohen offers no proof that his patients have "learned" to speak this way. Although I have heard anecdotal evidence that some psychotics have learned to "speak schizophrenic" as a result of hospitalization, I have yet to find hard data to support such a possibility. Even if someone does present such data, it would still beg the question of why only schizophrenics seem to speak this way whether through learning from other schizophrenics or from internal speech difficulties.

If it were an isolated instance, or if it were reported only of members of one social group, however defined, we can explain it as a learned response. Rather, it is reported only of schizophrenics,[4] and of schizophrenics who come from all social classes and nations, and who speak a great many different languages. Since there is no evidence that it is or even can be learned,[5] the natural assumption is that it is caused by the disease. This conclusion is bolstered by the fact that schizophrenics typically create glossomanic chains only when they are being schizophrenic. If they chain deliberately to avoid punishment, why don't they do this when they are in remission? It seems to me that the schizophrenic condition itself is responsible for the chaining.

[5] **Rhoda: The Joint History of the Participants.**

Labov and Fanshel (1977) provide an exceptionally detailed and perceptive analysis of a therapeutic situation involving a girl named Rhoda, an anorexic in conflict with her mother. The mother is a clever manipulator of discourse and Rhoda has to learn to deal with her by some means other than starving herself to death. In the segment described here, the mother has left Rhoda to take care of their shared home while she, the mother, is taking care of Rhoda's sister's children, staying away too long, thus interfering with Rhoda's schooling. Rhoda cannot cope, but to admit this overtly to her mother would be yielding to her mother's opinion that Rhoda is not capable, an opinion fatal to Rhoda's desire to prove her worth by proving she can cope. This power struggle between Rhoda and her mother is complicated by Rhoda's anorexia. It is this last which is being directly treated, with the therapist trying to allow Rhoda to see that her refusal to eat is, indeed, a power play.

Labov and Fanshel (1977, p. 53) demonstrate that one of the specific characteristics of *the* thera*peutic situation* is that both patient and therapist are presumably working towards making explicit *those* propositions which underly the problem *leading to the therapy. As we have seen,* in any situation, part of the meaning derived comes from the personal history of the interactors. Labov and Fanshel, Kreckel (1981), and Sanders (1987) all stress the relationship between the richness and accuracy of interpretations and extensive mutual interaction. Labov and Fanshel (1977, pp. 351–352) stress that one cannot interpret individual texts by themselves, noting that they collected many conversations in which one interpretation seemed correct, but that somebody who knew the interactors better than they was able to show that it was not. For example, a seminar was shown a video of a married couple conversing. At one point, the wife remarked that blood was thicker than water, whereupon the husband turned his head away. The members of the seminar assumed that the husband was angry because the wife had implied that her relatives were more important than he. One viewer knew the parties in question, however; consequently, he was able to give quite a different interpretation of this scene. Knowing the family dynamics, he demonstrated that the wife was complimenting the husband, indicating that he was as much blood to her family as she was because he shared her concern for them. When the husband turned away, far from being in anger, he was being modest, turning aside *when* complimen*ted.*

[6] Rhoda: Propositions as Reference Points.

As a working guide towards establishing what a given patient is referring to, Labov and Fanshel isolated potential conflicts between Rhoda and her mother. They operated under the assumption that anorexics stop eating as a way of defying authority, in this instance, the mother. As they emphasize, nobody knows how to make someone eat if they don't want to. Whether or not all anorexics become that way as a defiance of authority, such as may be embodied in a mother, I do not know, but that Rhoda had a severe problem dealing with her mother is undeniable. As the section shows, one evidence of that is her strategies for mitigating requests to her mother.

Labov and Fanshel isolated several topics that Rhoda refers to which clearly are causing conflict. One way one can tell that these are central to Rhoda's conflict is her direct mention accompanied with the implied request for approval,

> 4. I don't . . . know, whether . . . I—I **think** I did—the right thing, jistalittle situation came up. . . . an' I tried to uhm . . . well, try to . . . use what I—what I've learned here, see if it worked" (p. 363)

She goes on to explain that her mother, as in the past, has gone to her sister Phyllis's house to babysit, leaving Rhoda at home to care for the house, a task which Rhoda finds too difficult as she is also attending school. The opener, "I don't know whether I did the right thing," means "did I do the right thing?" It is a way of asking for confirmation, otherwise why mention it at all, much less mention it with a disclaimer that shows doubt? She does understand clearly that the sessions are to teach her to deal more effectively with her mother.

Labov and Fanshel isolate several recurring propositions in Rhoda's therapeutic session, a partial list of which is (not their words):

- The patient should gain insight into his or her own emotions.
- One should express one's needs and emotions to relevant others.
- Rhoda's[6] obligations are greater than her capacities.
- Rhoda is a student who has a primary responsibility to study.

Labov and Fanshel term these, respectively, the propositions of {INSIGHT},{S}, {STRN}, and {STUD–X} (notation theirs). By isolating these propositions, they often can relate comments in the therapeutic interview to these, showing how frequently they are alluded to as well as justifying their interpretation of what she meant. For instance, 4 above refers to the propositions of {INSIGHT}, {S}, and {STRN} as the situation that came up was her mother's remaining at Phyllis's house too long, leaving Rhoda to cope at home and what Rhoda did was call her mother. She had the dual task of letting her mother know that the mother was shirking her responsibility and that Rhoda herself could not cope. What made this especially difficult is that Rhoda did not want to mention that she couldn't cope because part of the conflict with her mother was that the mother felt that Rhoda was not competent.

Clearly, the propositions become identified through a series of interviews Labov and Fanshel (1977, p. 149) insist that any abstract structures that the therapist claims should be equally available to a native speaker. What they are saying is that the strategies for interpretation in a clinical setting are not different from those in ordinary interactions. The difference is that, in daily interacting, much of what is said is evanescent, simply reacted to. Certainly, interactors do remember prior dealings with each other and judge others' motives or worth on that basis. In the therapeutic situation, participants ruminate on the entire history of the sessions themselves, correlating them with the patient's personal history and present situation as revealed in the course of therapy. Still, normal modes of analyzing speech are not abandoned even in psychotherapy.

These normal modes do include such matters as taking into account the ways that preconditions for making statements lead us to interpret. We have already seen that a statement will evoke a response of an answer to a question if the conditions for questioning are met. Labov and Fanshel demonstrate that elaboration of comments must be principled, verifiable by appeal to ordinary language behaviors. They provide detailed arguments for their interpretations and stress that to expand the full meaning of an utterance, including what was not overtly stated, one must draw upon the whole body of shared knowledge that can be recovered from all the therapeutic interviews. These should include conversations between the therapist and client. This, of course, mirrors the meaning that we get in ordinary daily interactions. If we presume different strategies in the therapeutic situation, we are in the strange position of asserting that once one retreats behind the therapist's door, all normal speech practices are subject to idiosyncratic change.

As we have seen, part of the meaning of any linguistic production is constrained by the intent or motive we attribute to the producer. Truly, the purpose of the therapeutic interview certainly helps determine the topics of conversation and what is made of them, but the strategies for understanding what is meant from what is said are quite ordinary. As we saw in Chapter 6, it is rarely appropriate for somebody to say absolutely everything he or she means. Because so much meaning is hinted at rather than directly encoded we usually have to expand on what is said to get the actual meaning. This expansion constitutes a derivation of meaning. As such, it includes the kinds of "filling-in" of omissions of repetitions already seen, knowledge of utterance pairs and other discourse devices, reference to topic at hand, all of the modes of inference we have seen, references to context, even kinesics and paralinguistics.

Labov and Fanshel maintain that expansion can be open-ended, but their own explanations remain quite close to the bone. If we confine our interpretation to what can be expanded from given utterances, we do find natural bounds. What does happen—and should—is that subsequent interviews might call for reinterpretation of previous ones. The important thing is that expansions derive from the ordinary meanings of what has been said, not from a preexisting theory of what someone must be meaning.

[7] The Many Faces of Resistance.

In traditional psychoanalysis, we frequently saw the antithesis of the the give and take we call conversation. There was no negotiation of meaning. Rather, the therapist told the analysand what the latter meant. If the analysand objected or misunderstood, then he or she was considered to be in a stage of resistance. This ended when the analysand finally accepted the therapist's interpretations and learned to utilize the same terminology as the analyst.

Labov and Fanshel (1977, pp. 34, 306) depict a patient as resisting therapy by denying the strength of her emotions as well as by not following the therapist's advice. Thus, for instance, they assume that when Rhoda says she was bothered she was using a euphemism for the truth, that she was angry. They consider such euphemizing to be a mitigation of her real feelings, hence, to be a way of resisting therapy. This conclusion is reinforced because she precedes bothered by *just,* a further mitigator. The patient, Rhoda is being treated for anorexia, a result apparently of the power play between her and her mother.

They also claim that an even more extreme form of resistance is for a patient to resort to saying nothing at all, something which Rhoda also does at certain times, admitting that in a therapeutic situation, unlike ordinary conversations, the therapist is " . . . sometimes able to say more definitely what another person feels than that person can say himself." This can be extremely threatening of course. Traditionally it has been assumed that the patient cannot yet admit the truth because his or her feelings would be too intolerably intense if he or she did. This is undeniable, but there may be other reasons for such resistance as well. The operative term here is *as well.* It seems to me that there can be several reasons for apparent resistance and that they may operate concurrently, serially, or singly.

It seems to me that an alternate reason that patients may resist is that they do not agree with the analyst's interpretation of their feelings, feelings which patients certainly must know since only they can feel them. Labov and Fanshel (pp. 62–64) term these A-EVENTS, events known to the speaker but not necessarily to another. At times, a patient might refuse to talk because the analyst persists in attributing feelings that are A-events to the analysand. Then, the analysand, not being believed, simply doesn't talk. Notice that this is not necessarily the cause of resistance. It is only possibly the cause. On the one hand, the analysand may be seen as simply not being ready for such truths, thereby resisting the analyst. On the other hand, the analyst may be wrong.

Labov and Fanshel (p. 36) also comment on the fact that psychoanalytic terms like

> "interpretation," "relationship," "guilt," "to present oneself," "working relationship," and so on

are used primarily by the analyst in this situation because the patient they are studying is not as "mature" as many analysands. This lends credence to a suspicion I have long harbored that some of what is called resistance is unfamiliarity with the discourse rules of the therapeutic interview.

Another possibility is that the patient has not yet learned the jargon of analysis. Clearly, one goal of analysis is to teach the analysand to label his or her feelings with the distancing terms of analysis. There is no *a priori* reason to label one's relationship with one's mother as a "working relationship" or to say of one's persona that one "presents oneself as . . ." Language is eminently paraphrasable, as we have seen.

There are other ways that patients have to learn how to have therapy. Wooton (1975, p. 70) cites a good example

5. Patient: I'm a nurse but my husband won't let me work.
Therapist: How old are you?
Patient: Thirty-one this December.
Therapist: What do you mean, he won't let you work?

Here, the patient answers the psychiatrist's first question as if it were bona fide, a real-world question. The psychiatrist was not really asking her age, however. He was trying to lead her to see that she should be making up her own mind, that she is old enough to do so. The patient did not yet realize that the goal of the therapist's questions are rarely factual information. Rather, they are intended to aid in a process of self-discovery.

In sum, resistance — or what appears to be resistance — is not necessarily a unitary phenomenon. The patient may not yet be able to handle the power of emotions that would surface if he or she admitted something, or the patient genuinely does not feel what the analyst says he or she should be feeling, the patient may be uneasy in the situation having been made to feel that he or she is a fool in prior sessions, or that the patient either hasn't yet figured out what the analytic jargon is or has not yet figured out the modus operandi of the therapeutic session.

[8] Mitigating.

The traditional explanation for resistance, that it would prove too painful for the patient if he or she got too close to the truth, is probably also valid. There are truths too painful for many of us to acknowledge even outside of the therapeutic situation. It is well-known that many social routines are couched in a mitigating fashion. For instance, rather than saying, "Shut the door!" to one of our colleagues, we would more likely couch the command as a request, even a pleading one, like "Please shut the door" or, "Would you please shut the door?" Similarly, language abounds in other kinds of mitigating words and phrases commonly used to soften assertions, such as "I may be wrong, but . . . "; "This might sound silly, but . . . "[7]

Labov and Fanshel are very aware of mitigation used both in softening assertions, as above and in reporting one's feelings as well. They give an exceptionally apt example (p. 96) while demonstrating that a rule of interaction could be called the "rule of overdue obligations." This is alluded to whenever one reminds another of something that should or should not have been done. Therefore, Rhoda phones her mother and asks, "When do you **plan** to come home?" rather than, "When are you coming home?" If she had not used the word *plan* (p. 50), her question to her mother could have been taken as a challenge, meaning, in effect, "You belong at home and you've been staying at my sister's long enough." The word *plan* makes it sound as if the mother not only has full authority to do as she wishes, but that it is she, not Rhoda, who is determining the length of the stay (Labov and Fanshel p. 50, 96.) Not only has Rhoda avoided challenging her mother by mitigating with *plan*, but she has also downplayed her own need to have her mother home. That is, Rhoda tries to mitigate the fact that she cannot indeed cope without her mother.

[9] How Shall a Discourse Be Understood: The Case of Carrie.

The therapeutic situation does provide its own special contexts, including an uncovering of personal histories that do impinge on meaning. As we have seen, all utterances are abbreviations for meaning in that they assume certain cultural and personal shared knowledge, as well. The question arises of when extraordinary measures are justified in interpreting a discourse. Remember that only some schizophrenics display structurally abnormal speech, and of those, most use structurally normal speech when not in the throes of a schizophrenic bout. We are entitled to adopt extraordinary measures only when speech is clearly deviant in structure. Then exegesis must proceed on the basis of similarity of sentence structure to normal possible productions and only to the extent that such matchings can be made. If the speech is nondeviant in structure, then, in the absence of strong case history or contextual clues, it should be interpreted in the same way as a nonschizophrenic person's would.

If the context simply does not fit what has been said, then one is justified in searching further for special meanings. If what is said is structurally abnormal, then one must try to compare it with the closest linguistic structure that seems to fit the situation. One can be guided by the voluminous research on the forms of slips of the tongue and speech produced by those with known injuries to the brain. If it still cannot be understood, we must admit simply that we don't know what the subject was trying to say. If the utterance appears to be structurally normal, but is highly obscure, we might still suspect disruption in communicative ability, including such problems as lapses in the ability to monitor another's reactions, to paraphrase what one has just said so that the hearer can understand, or to judge what is necessary to provide in order to allow the co-conversationalist to hone in on what one is trying to communicate. None of these skills in inconsiderable, and all are requisite to successful comprehension.

As an illustration of the above points, it is fruitful to consider a virtually classic case of psychoanalytical interpretation, in this instance guided by the tenets of Harold Searles. This particular case was chosen for illustration because the authors of the study discussed below, Mary Seeman and Howard Cole (1977), were unusually explicit in delineating why they interpreted as they did (Chaika 1981). They presented the discourse of Carrie, a twenty-nine-year-old diagnosed schizophrenic, along with their gloss of that discourse. It must be emphasized that their interpretations are quite solidly in the tradition in which they were trained and, within that tradition, their analysis was both sensitive and sound.

It must be emphasized that, at the time of Seeman and Cole's investigation,[8] there was little reason to delve into the linguistic literature on discourse analysis. With the exception of Labov and Fanshel's groundbreaking study which was published the same year as Seeman and Cole's, the linguistic literature was largely hobbled by sentence grammars. Discourse considerations were still being labeled *pragmatics.* Linguistics at that point was just beginning to show its efficacy and relevance to psychiatric research. There are psychiatrists and clinical psychologists who still doubt the value of an interloping researcher from the field of linguistics. If nothing else, however, the comparison presented here at least shows how far one's assumptions can take one in what one comprehends.

Seeman and Cole's (1977) analysis was chosen because the authors were unusually explicit in showing exactly what they were interpreting, how they interpreted it, and why. Also, felicitously, they provided comparative data which examined the speech of one patient produced under the same conditions within the same experimental context. This provided a sharpness of focus so that the central issue of how a discourse should be interpreted would not be lost.

They used as their authority the analyst Harold Searles, a practice dating from Freud. That is, they applied Harold Searles' guide to what a schizophrenic means given the nature of the illness to what Carrie actually said in the interviews. In contrast, Carrie's utterances are here compared with those gathered from ostensible normals in naturalistic settings. This comparison suggests that Carrie's speech, for the most part, is nondeviant, therefore, in my judgment, not amenable to extraordinary interpretation.

We have already seen that there is high interjudge reliability as to the schizophrenicity of some discourse (Maher, McKeon, and McLaughlin 1966). Nancy Andreasen's widely used diagnostic criteria rest primarily on such shared perceptions of speech.

Seeman and Cole apparently address themselves to the well-known fluctuation of schizophrenic speech disability. They (p. 283) explain that "interpersonal intimacy" is threatening to schizophrenics. The purpose of their study was to "illustrate with verbatim speech samples the daily progression of change" showing that the patient becomes more and more disorganized in her speech as intimacy increases. To this end, they devised an ingenious study in which they had Carrie meet with a first-year medical student, John, for daily discussion of neutral topics such as fashions and learning a foreign language (Seeman and Cole 1977, p. 284). In their article, the authors present excerpted samples from the corpus they obtained. The capital letters represent Seeman and Cole's own numbering of the speech samples.

They judge this monologue as being inscrutable, saying that she [Carrie] switches topic constantly, talks in riddles and ambiguities, abandons the rules of grammar so that it is impossible to know what she is referring to (Seeman and Cole 1977, p. 289).

(A)[*Carrie's discourse*]

You know what the experiment is geared to find is how vulnerable, I guess, and you know, if you get close to this person and how you feel about it and some pretty basic questions like it may have something to do with psychiatry, I don't. I'm beginning to think psychiatry is rather old-fashioned, you know there are young people on Yonge Street selling books about, I don't even how to label them, but there are new ways for man coping with the environment and the

[*Seeman and Cole's commentary*]

The whole segment can be taken to mean: Do you like me, and if you do, that puts me in an intolerable position. And if you don't, that's unbearable. There seems to be no solution.

people in it. And I haven't got into that but, I don't know I, I just, like, you have your set ways of doing things and you're in control. You know and you're talking about yourself personally yesterday, you know, and I walked out of here yesterday and I didn't really have any feeling at all. It was kind of like a release. I like people to confide in me, but, like, where is it going? What, it must serve some purpose, I don't have any theories about it. All I know is what I do get involved with people and it usually ends the same way I, I become very angry and you know something, well not always, but I always get taken, I get sucked in, you know, and I, I was just immobilized last night I didn't accomplish anything and here again today I, I haven't accomplished anything and I thin it's a hang-up I have got with you but I, I don't think I'm alone maybe maybe it's your hang-up too, I, I really don't know. But I do get involved in, with and when someone tells me I want to help out, and I want also to give something of myself like I'm older than you like I would like to give you some of my own insights and I, I don't know if it's appropriate what are we talking about what is it we're talking about? We're just talking about relationships and they're different, you're a man and I'm a woman and I guess I identified a bit with your girlfriend because I've done that with my boyfriend.

(B) Yeah, I don't like this book, uhm, there's a dictionary that I was thinking of buying. It's 75 cents. I might This means: I could be like the dictionary bright, compact and precise, but why should I put out such an buy it just for my own use but it's very compact and it's just it's yellow and red, you know, it's very compact and precise. It's too bad in a way. I was, I was thinking of buying it but you know, I kind of resented having to pay out money you know.

(C) ... time when I first moved into the house, my landlord and landlady had me down to dinner and I was using the living language course which is different and I was using the words of (Italian) and going along with it. But that was when I first moved in. They haven't invited me down for dinner for a while so, and I when I get angry at someone I just shut their language out the way I shut them out, you know, and it's reflected in the way I shut them out, you know, and it's reflected in the way I'm learning it.

(D) I think I became jealous of the relationship the landlady has with the lady on the second floor. They seem to be really good friends, you know, and I feel kind of out of it. Sometimes I get awfully mad in my room listening to them talk, you know, and I was sure she, they were talking about me one day, that much I know, I can pick up when I'm being talked about

effort? I don't know if you're worth it. The displacement and identification with an inanimate object is characteristic of Carrie (cf Searles p. 122) " ... it is nonhuman roles which predominate, more than any ... human ones in the life of the child who eventually develops schizophrenia."

Both passages (C) and (D) seemed out of context to John and he could not comprehend the vehemence with which they were spoken. Carrie seems preoccupied by the question of how important John is to her. As in the dictionary segment she seems to be wondering whether he is worth the effort. This makes the suspiciousness of the last two segments understandable. To quote Searles again (p. 125) "That the paranoid individual experiences the plot ... as centering on himself is in part a reaction to his being most deeply threatened lest he be as insignificant as outside everyone else's awareness, as he himself, with his severe repression of his own dependent feelings, tends to regard other individuals as being (1977, pp. 287–288).

[10] The Bounds of Meaning.

Carrie's words seem to mean something quite different from Seeman and Cole's translation of them. This, in itself, does not necessarily invalidate the interpretations, however. It is well-known that the force or meaning of an utterance may be quite different from the literal meaning of the words used, but when this occurs, we can point to general discourse practices.

In contrast, the Freudian theory of communication assumes that virtually anything a patient says is subject to special interpretation and that this interpretation can be given only by those with specialized training. These interpretations differ greatly from whatever the ordinary meaning would be. Moreover, there is no check on what the analyst says the utterance means. In such a system, *yes* can mean "no," *good* can mean "bad," *boy* can mean "girl," and "there's a dictionary I was thinking of buying..." can mean "I could be like the dictionary...." Certainly, what people say is not always what they mean. Certainly, much of what people say means something quite different from what it literally says. However, the problem still remains of what constitutes a normal and usual decoding of someone else's speech, what constitutes a justifiable construing and what does not. Examination of discourse under a wide variety of conditions has provided us with some guidelines for determining what is and what is not a justifiable rendering of another's meaning. Before considering these, however, let us look at the properties of normal spoken discourse as this impacts on the question of is and what is not deviant.

[11] Deviance in Discourse.

Discourse analysis by linguists or philosophers is based upon the speech of normals. By normal, I mean usual, unremarkable, not apparently deviant because of drugs, illness, injury, or other incapacitation. Notice that *normal* can also refer to the deaf[10] or those who stutter or lisp, as these populations may still both give and get meaning by usual strategies. The question is, what constitutes normal speech? We have already seen that laypersons mistake written language as being real language, not being aware that normal oral language is loaded with hesitations, false starts, and errors. The ear somehow smooths these out in ordinary conversations, so that when written transcripts are produced of actual speech, the effect on many people is that they think the speech is abnormally disjointed or defective.

Seeman and Cole overtly claim (p. 288) that they interpret her speech as they do because she is a schizophrenic. Their reasoning seems to be "Since Carrie is diagnosed as a schizophrenic, her speech is schizophrenic, and should be interpreted according to special rules of schizophrenic discourse as explicated by interpreters like Searles. "Such a belief regards all the speech produced by a diagnosed schizophrenic to be deviant, and, therefore, to necessitate interpretation by other than normal means. The reason for my assumption that Seeman and Cole would consider anything said by a diagnosed schizophrenic to be aberrant, therefore liable to exceptional interpretation, is that all the samples they present of Carrie's speech are quite normal and easily interpreted by normal decoding strategies. That is, there is no other *a priori* reason to assume that Carrie is saying anything more of less or different than what her sentences would mean if produced by a normal.

Compared to spontaneous speech at, say, an academic seminar, Carrie's speech, as reported in Seeman and Cole (1977), is remarkably lucid and well-formed. "Spontaneous speech in the raw can be very raw indeed" (Clark and Clark 1977, p. 260). The more difficult the ideas to encode, the rawer the speech" the more false starts, filled and unfilled pauses, erroneous lexical choices, and assorted slips of the tongue. If each phrase, so far as it goes, is of normal structure, if each slip of the tongue is explicable in terms of that structure, and all is subordinated to an inferable topic appropriate to the occasion, then the speech is most likely normal (Chaika 1974, 1976, 1977; VanDijk, 1977: 121, 134.) Language is so constructed that encoding of ideas need only be exact enough so that hearers can infer what is meant. There are many kinds of difficulty which can lead to raw speech: complex ideas, embarrassing, exciting, or controversial issues.

For instance, consider this passage from a speaker who is embarrassed or uneasy speaking to the police

6. P: Do you know the names of any of these boys?
C: Ahh, gee, I hate—I do? One of them, but I don't like to say anything, you know. (Sharrock & Turner 1978)

C apparently starts to say that he hates to finger any of the boys. Before completing the construction, however, speaker breaks off to ask "I do?" as if he didn't know any of the offenders. Then, apparently realizing that the "I hate" implied an admission of knowledge that could not be counteracted by the innocent sounding "I do?" he answers the policeman's question admitting that he does know one of them, finishing with the statement he started with, that he hates to give evidence.

The pause-laden speech in 7 arises from what appears to be happy excitement from two males talking about an exciting subject, racing cars:

> 7. 'N challenge Voodoo to a race. I mean the hell with drag strips you gotta have ten thous'n bucks ready t'spec—hh I wanna build a street machine . . . It's a 55 Chevy. It's bright orange, and it has—it had hhu lemme tell y'about this car. Hh a three twunny seven Vet in it uhyih an' if wiz, uh, hh dual quads, hh hadda full roller cam [pause] four speeds hydrostick. . . . (Jefferson, 1978, p. 237–238)

In 7, an intrusive thought disrupts the speaker's sentence " . . . ready t'spe—hh I wanna build a street machine." Here the break was right in the middle of a word. Later, he stops after *has,* changes its tense to *had,* then still doesn't tell us what it has or had. Instead he starts all over with "lemme tell y'about this car." The *if* in " . . . an if wuz uh . . . " seems to be a normal slip of the tongue explicable by the phonetic similarity between *it* and *if.*

Raw speech is not hard to find even from brilliant academics who make their living by talking. In 8, we see a sample of spontaneous speech about a complex subject (slashes indicate false starts):

> 8. As far as I know, noone has yet done the/ in a way obvious now and interesting problem of [pause] doing a/in a sense of structural frequency study of the alternative [pause] syntactical uh/ in a given language, say, like English, and how/what their hierarchical [pause] probability of occurrence structure is. (Reported in Clark & Clark 1977, p. 260) (from Maclay & Osgood 1959, p. 25)

Twice here the speaker starts to utter a noun phrase and twice changes his mind after selecting the article, first *the* and then *a.*

The literature on discourse analysis abounds with samples of normal speech like the three above. Here they are discussed only as a yardstick by which to measure Carrie's speech. Unfortunately, Seeman and Cole did not indicate in their data information about pausing or false starts. If that information were deleted from the above segments, or, alternatively, if slashes or [pause] were inserted in Carrie's speeches, then the similarity of her speech to the normal samples would be evident. A closer examination of where these occur in the normal speech, along with a more detailed analysis of Carrie's, might further indicate the essential normalcy of her discourse.

If we assume[11] that Carrie's speech did contain pauses such as those in the three samples of normal discourse above, then we see her speech is quite normal. One reason we might assume this is that the researchers made no reference to her evincing pressured speech, the term used for manic and schizophrenic speech that has no pausing and no false starts, nor is there evidence of glossomania, which is typically produced with no pausing before the chained segments. Since pausing and false starts indicate planning stages in speech, that which does not contain them appears to be essentially unplanned speech, speech on automatic pilot, so to speak.

Pausing during encoding of thoughts (i.e., putting them into words) with or without pause fillers like *uhh, hu, mmm, you know,* and the like is normal as is making false starts and slips of the tongue (Fromkin 1973). Pausing occurs at the beginning of major constituents in sentences (e.g., Boomer 1965; Goldman-Eisler 1958; Rochester, Thurston, and Rupp 1977) and represents a planning of what is to come next. It is easy to see why such pauses might increase as encoding difficulty increases. It is also easy to see why speakers disrupt their own sentences. They start to say one thing, preplanning to the end of, say, a clause, then realize that their wording is not felicitous. Thus they pause, replan, and start over.

Evidence for such planning stages comes from such phenomena as slips of the tongue. These most often are an anticipation of a word selected during the planning stage (Lashley 1951) or selection of another word that belongs in a set with the intended word (Fromkin 1973; Chaika 1977) or a normal intrusion (Dell and Reich 1977) caused by disruption in the context. Like pausing, slips seem related to planning and increase with excitement and embarrassment.

[12] What Does Carrie Mean?

One thing to note in the samples of normal speech above is that each of the fragments can be restored by English speaking hearers. That is, based upon what they know about English and the American culture, hearers can with a good degree of certainty, fill in what has been left out or correct what has been mis-said. No one needs training in this skill (Gleitman, Gleitman, and Shipley 1972). It comes from being a human being who has learned a language. This is what is meant by *normal decoding strategy.* It is the tacit understanding that people can do this which leads to testing procedures such as the Cloze test which has been used to analyze schizophrenic speech (e.g., Salzinger, Portnoy, and Feldman 1978). Being able to decode imperfect speech allows people to understand young children, those with foreign accents or speech impediments, as well as speech produced under noisy conditions. A second thing is that all the speech in the above discourses, including errors and false starts is subordinated to a general topic, an important feature of normal discourse (VanDijk 1977, p. 122; Chaika 1974, p. 275).

Carrie, in common with many younger speakers today, uses "you know" as a pause filler. Goldman-Eisler (1961) says that fillers increase with heightened emotions. We can see why her emotions may be heightened when we consider her situation. Examining Carrie's speech in the light of the well-known fact of the imperfect nature of ordinary conversation, it does not seem so incoherent. Indeed, applying the twin tests of reconstructability and subordination of utterance to topic to Carrie's speech reveals it to be quite normal. Assuming that it is, it is possible to come up with an unstrained gloss of what she meant. Carrie appears excited and embarrassed in (A) above when she says

> You know what the experiment is geared to find is how vulnerable, I guess, and you know, if you get close to this person and how you feel about it and some pretty basic questions like it may have something to do with psychiatry, I don't. I'm beginning to think psychiatry is rather old-fashioned, you know there are young people on Yonge Street selling books about, I don't even how to label them, but there are new ways for man coping with the environment and the people in it . . .

Her embarrassment is quite justified since she is telling a medical student in a psychiatric hospital that she doubts the efficacy of psychiatry. This constitutes a **challenge** (Labov and Fanshel 1977, pp. 96–98), which they define as

> . . . a speech act that asserts or implies a state of affairs that, if true, would weaken a person's claim to be competent in filling the role associated with a valued status.

They stress that this does not necessarily mean that the person challenged will suffer an actual loss of status. The challenge is to the claim alone.[12]

To tell people who have authority by virtue of position and education that they do not know what they are talking about is supremely difficult for those of lower status, normal or not. It seems to me that the operative words in Labov and Fanshel's definition are *valued status.* By virtue of such status, one should be immune from criticism from subordinates. One decides how one fulfills the higher role. That is part of what it means to have valued status. Parents, for instance, are considered to have the right to rear their children as they see fit. The child has no right to tell the parent how the parent should behave. Only "spoiled brats" do that. Often adolescents, as part of their ascent into adulthood, do challenge their parents and other adults in authority. This marks their imminent entry into adulthood, a valued status.

Labov and Fanshel (1977, pp. 124–125) analyze Rhoda's challenge to authority. Like Carrie's challenge, hers was very indirect, but still heard as a challenge. As part of her complaint that her mother has stayed too long at her sister's home, she says "Look—uh—I mean y'been there long enough." Labov and Fanshel interpret the *look* as a way of calling her mother's attention to the fact that Rhoda's needs aren't being met. It seems more overt a challenge to me. Saying "look" warns the other that one's patience has worn thin. This always signals a challenge. The correctness of this interpretation is demonstrated by the especially softened language following the *look*. First there is the weakening pause. This is followed by the hesitation marker *uh*. Then comes the softened phrase "I mean," and then the rest of the challenge. It is a challenge because a child ordinarily has no right to tell her mother how long to stay anywhere. A major goal of Rhoda's therapy has been to teach her to stand up to her mother. Even so, she challenges by indirection.

Comparing Rhoda's challenge with Carrie's, we see a great deal of similarity. Rhoda has been taught through therapy to stand up to her mother. Carrie has not been taught to stand up to her therapist. To the contrary, she is expected to respect his authority. Not surprisingly, her challenge to his superior status, shows even more indirection and hedging than Rhoda's did. There has been a great deal of evidence amassed which demonstrates that women have more difficulty than men in criticizing or challenging, especially in male-female situations; therefore, they hedge their remarks more than men (Lakoff 1975; Eakins and Eakins 1978, pp. 23–52, 66–72). Considering these factors, we are reasonable in expecting Carrie to have many hesitations, false starts, and filled or unfilled pauses in the situation eliciting her speech.

Actually, the comparison of her speech with that of normal males above shows she is no less fluent than they are (as has been already noted).

As with the normal speech presented above, Carrie's false starts are readily retrievable. Although she appears to be switching topics constantly, her adherence to a general topic and the movement within it seem normal in every instance especially when we add dashes to indicate probable false starts, and repunctuating to indicate new sentences whenever they occur, using the usual convention of periods followed by capitals.

...I'm beginning to think psychiatry is rather old-fashioned. You know, there are new—there are young people on Yonge St. selling books about—I don't even know how to label them, but there are new ways for man coping with the environment and the people in it. And I haven't go into that but—I don't know—I- I just like, you have your set ways of doing things and you're in control.

As she starts to explain why psychiatry is old-fashioned, Carrie stops after *new.* Apparently, a word like *ideas* was intended, or, as appears later, *ways.* The reason for the hesitation seems straightforward enough. She is not sure of the label, and, when she does get the notion coded, it is with a whole sentence, "there are new ways for man coping with the environment and the people in it." However, she cannot get all this out until she has invested these ways with the authority of other people, young people and books. In a society which values both youth and newness, to claim that youths have new ways, and in a society which values the printed word over the spoken, to note that youths and books are promulgating new ways, gives the new ways more sanction than if they were something that Carrie, a woman and a mental patient, dreamed up. To have just continued talking about the new ideas or ways would have placed too much of the blame on Carrie herself. Besides, the appeal to authority is always more convincing. Just look at the references in scholarly articles even for quite mundane and self-evident notions. If someone else said it or wrote it, it makes it better than if we have stated it all by ourselves.

Carrie herself explains why she stopped after *about.* She doesn't have a ready label for the concepts which in her opinion are rendering psychiatry old-fashioned. What is important is that the discourse strategy she employs, a false start, followed by "I don't even know how to label them," is entirely usual, one we have all probably used at one time or another. Common paraphrases are "I forget it/his/her/ name." "I don't know the word for it," "you know what I mean," or even "whatchamacallit."

The next set of false starts is especially interesting.

And I haven't got into that but,—I don't know I,—I just,—like, —you have your set ways of doing things and you're in control. You know—and you're talking about yourself personally yesterday,—you know,—and I walked out of here yesterday and I didn't really have any feeling at all. It was kind of like a release. I like people to confide in me,—but,—like,—where is it going?

These, as a set, imply that she disagrees with the student and the psychiatrists that he is representing. Again, this is a normal strategy, a way of letting the other person know that you disagree without your actually doing so in overt words. The passage may look disjointed, appearing as it does in an orthography which normally admits of no false starting, but when read aloud, it does not sound particularly disjointed.

It is significant that the hesitations and false starts cluster at the point at which one would expect Carrie to be stating that she is disillusioned with psychiatry. "I haven't got into that but..." seems like a normal entry into "the new approaches that might be better than psychiatry," or some such paraphrase thereof. Instead, Carrie stops after the *but*, the word which leads one to expect a disclaimer. Then she demurs with the feminine "I don't know" (Lakoff 1975, pp. 15–17) which has the effect of softening any assertion. She starts giving her opinion again, saying "I," then starting all over again with "I just." This *just* is similar in force to the preceding *but* which initiated this string of false starts. It announces that she holds an opinion different from the establishment's as if she were trying to say "I just don't believe in you anymore." This is not to say that those were necessarily the next words she intended, but that the *just* in the given context does have the force of a disclaimer, and she has previously voiced doubt about the efficacy of psychiatry. She stops short of having to put herself overtly on the line, although she has signaled enough for us to infer what she is getting at.

The *like* following the false start "I just" is often used in precisely the way Carrie uses it to mean "what follows is not a direct expression of what I mean, but I'm finding it difficult to say exactly what I mean." In one afternoon's office hours, I collected these samples, all from female students, all in far less socially precarious positions than Carrie.

9. I don't know, but—like, I can't get my act together ever since I got back from Spain.
10. Yeah, like—like—it's interesting, y'know
11. ....-like,—now I got rid of him, like—I dunno I just feel—I found myself.

What Carrie does is most interesting, and most skillful. She has set her hearer up for criticism of psychiatry; then, without really giving that criticism, she tells John, "You have your set ways of doing things." That is, even if other things are better, you'd not be likely to change your mind. "And you're in control" seems to mean just that. He is in control of the situation and himself. Interestingly, the authors themselves stress the businesslike air of the student (p. 284) confirming Carrie's perceptions.

The thesis of the Seeman and Cole paper is to show how Carrie's speech becomes more disorganized as she feels the "intimacy of the daily meetings" (p. 289). In a large sense, this is undoubtedly true. Intimacy makes Carrie dare to question her therapists, but the daring does not extend to her speaking her mind openly. Surely, there is veiled meaning in her words, but the kinds of veiled meaning and the ways she expresses it seem wholly usual and normal, conforming to regular discourse strategies. She is cognizant of social situation, and, contrary to expectation (Rochester and Martin 1977; Rochester, Martin, and Thurston 1977) gives the listener ample information to know what she is referring to.

Unlike the passages just discussed, the rest of Carrie's speech is straightforward if one decodes it as one would normal speech. Her topic at the outset of (A) is the experiment in which she is a participant. She is correct that this experiment is to see if her speech becomes disorganized as the topic become more personal. Seeman and Cole (p. 284) had told her this. In other words, as Carrie says, the experiment is to see how vulnerable she is. She is also correct in assuming the experiment has something to do with psychiatry. This is the lead-in to the indirect, but recoverable critique of psychiatry that we just saw. As part of this critique, she complains that the previous day's session left her devoid of feeling, like a release of tension, a common enough aftermath of a talk session, but she still doesn't see the purpose of the sessions.

She continues the monologue with the unfortunately common human plaint that she is always the loser in human relations. This does not seem to be an inappropriate switch as she is talking about the relations with John. The previous night after the, to her, pointless gab fest, she could not get anything done, nor does she feel that her talking that day has any purpose. She wants to help the experimenters out by participating. Also, being older than John, she feels that she should be giving him insights, but does not know if that would be appropriate, nor, actually, what she and John are talking about. Here I must point out that Carrie is not being particularly obtuse. Nowhere in the transcription is there any indication that John has responded to anything she has said. Apparently, he just lets her rattle on. This constitutes a highly abnormal situation. Normal conversation consists of turn taking (Sacks 1967–71; Jefferson 1978). Even very normal confident people find it upsetting to be in a situation where they are supposed to be carrying on a conversation and the other person doesn't carry the ball. If one adds to this normal discomfort, the social convention that it is up to the female to draw the male out and to keep the ball rolling in social situations, especially in one-on-one occasions like dates, Carries' speech is all the more normal. The situation she finds herself in with John is the same as if she were his girlfriend. In short, John's failure to take his rightful turns in the conversation such as answering Carrie's questions forces her to fill up the silence with a monologue. She is obeying normal everyday conventions of our society[13] when she does so.

Carrie's comments about the dictionary are also amenable to quite ordinary meaning rather ordinarily phrased. These occur in the context of her attempts to teach John a foreign language (Seeman and Cole 1977, p. 287) Many people have ambivalent feelings about buying books and her wording about this ambivalence seems unremarkable.

Carrie's feeling that the landlady and the other tenant are talking about her (passages C and D) may be paranoid, but the structure of the language she uses to express that feeling is perfectly normal. It is puzzling, however, that John could not comprehend the vehemence with which Carrie's complaint was spoken (p. 287). Even normal people get angry if they feel that they are being snubbed for no good reason, and even normals are jealous of friendships between people who exclude them.

Many might object that as a schizophrenic, Carrie's speech must be interpreted differently from that of normals. In other words, the diagnosis determines the meaning. If she had not been diagnosed as schizophrenic, then her words could be taken to mean something entirely different from what they mean in light of a diagnosis. In essence, those who feel that the prior diagnosis determines the mode of interpretation claim that they are among those with a key to it, a key supplied by Freud, Sullivan, Searles, or another analyst.

In contrast, my interpretations of Carrie's speech depend on the assumption that anyone using English is using it in the same way as normals do provided it has normal structure. There may be deviant schizophrenic speech just as there is deviant aphasic speech or heavily accented speech or imperfect toddler speech. However, all such speech, if interpretable at all, is interpretable only if the hearer can match the deviation with the nearest possible rules which produces an utterance appropriate to the given context (Clark and Clark 1977, pp. 211–215).

John Searle (1975, p. 63, 73) says that one assumes that someone speaking to us is cooperating in the conversation so that his/her remarks are intended to be relevant. This does not mean that speakers don't lie, do not use language metaphorically, or do not use one utterance to imply something different from, what is said. Speakers do all of these things but lying, metaphor, and implicature are all rooted in normal uses of language and the shared conventions of speakers of a particular language. For instance, when someone lies, he or she depends on the hearer's understanding of the lie to mean what it normally does. That is, the lie does not consist of unusual uses of the words in the utterance. To the contrary, it depends upon a normal reading of the words. If Max says, "I didn't cut the meat with a cleaver" when in fact he did, the lie is not in the negative *-n't.* The lie works only if the hearer interprets *-n't* as usual, as a denial.

To assume that some conversations must be interpreted by extraordinary means is to assume that the incredibly complex sets of rules which enable us to handle human language, both as a system in itself and as a social system, can be wholly altered by one class of persons, the mentally ill. As John Searle (1975, p. 67) said in a somewhat different content, " . . . an ordinary application of Occam's razor places the onus of proof on those who wish to claim these sentences are ambiguous. One does not multiply meanings beyond necessity." Nor, I hasten to add, does one claim idiosyncratic meaning when conventional meaning is retrievable by conventional means and fits the social context.

Then, too, to assume that schizophrenics abandon the usual meanings of words without clear evidence such as semantic anomaly raises some very sticky questions. If the schizophrenic's meaning can be so very far removed from normals, how does anyone know what the schizophrenic means? At what point in a patient's illness does one suspend the normal rules of decoding and substitute the schizophrenic ones? At what point in remission does one abandon the schizophrenic interpretations and go back to the ones shared by other speakers? Or is the schizophrenic's speech always governed by the rules of schizophrenia? If so, should these rules be applied retroactively, say, perhaps, to five years before the visible onset of illness? Or does one start interpreting differently at the precise moment when schizophrenic illness is diagnosed?

Notes

[1]Jones also had a great impact on literary criticism by psychoanalysis of such figures as Hamlet, claiming, for instance, that Hamlet was suffering from a severe Oedipus complex.

[2]A major problem with this view of language is that it seems improbable that language could have evolved as a means of an intensely personal system of communication to be utilized to express cryptically one's unconscious thoughts. Language had to have been developed as communication in social relations, and there is no actual evidence that it has evolved further to act as Freud and his followers assert.

[3]A major problem with this view of language is that it seems improbable that language could have evolved as a means of an intensely personal system of communication to be utilized to express cryptically one's unconscious thoughts. Language had to have been developed as communication in social relations, and there is no actual evidence that it has evolved further to act as Freud and his followers assert.

[4]The literature on aphasias and normal speech errors report errors made because of intrusions of related words. In normals, however, these never take the form of chaining of related words, and in aphasia, if chaining does happen, it is rare. It is not a usual occurrence as it is in speech disordered schizophrenics.

[5]I am aware of studies by Singer and Wynne and others that tendencies towards glossomania can be found in close relatives of schizophrenics and in those at risk for the disease, but this means that whatever causes schizophrenia causes the glossomania. Not all schizophrenics can be shown to come from such families, however, nor has it been shown that all members of schizogenic families create associational chains. The enormous literature on language acquisition does not offer any parallels to children learning to speak in such a deviant fashion. Rather, it has been shown that they speak like their peers. Children from families of foreign speakers do not themselves speak with a foreign accent.

[6]They actually couch these as "X's obligations..." and use the masculine pronoun as in "his capacities." It is very obvious that they are speaking of Rhoda. In general, however, Labov almost always uses the masculine pronoun as generic to include a female even when he is speaking of a female.

[7]Such mitigators seem to be used more by women than by men, although men in the weaker position in an interaction may use them as much as women (O'Barr 1982; Lakoff 1972, 1975).

[8]Actually, their investigation and subsequent articles about it must have taken place well before the publication date.

[10]The manual languages of the deaf have been shown to be structured remarkably like oral languages and they make slips-of-the-hand in a manner parallel to slips-of-the-tongue. Likewise, the deaf may suffer from aphasia in which case they make analogous errors to the speech errors of hearing aphasics. I know of one bit of anecdotal evidence that schizophrenic deaf patients may produce the counterpart to oral gibberish in their sign language.

[11]Perhaps it should be noted that I have had personal correspondence with Dr. Seeman about her studies of Carrie and she did not contradict my assumption that Carrie's speech had pausing and false starts.

[12]The reader should be aware that Labov and Fanshel provide a detailed and precise anatomy of what constitutes a challenge and why, along with precise mathematically precise rules to characterize challenges and the other speech events that they explain. It must be remembered that their book is not so broad in its presentation as this one is, but their work makes up for breadth in depth. In this work, space does not permit a full a rendering of their rules. Nor would a nonlinguist necessarily find these of practical help. However, and this cannot be stressed enough, their careful attention to proving what something can reasonably be assumed to mean is invaluable, and this can be understood without re-creation of their meticulous set of rules. In this book, I present their methods and conclusions only, but I urge the reader to dip into their work.

[13]Societies vary greatly in this matter. Americans and Canadians typically feel that one must "keep the ball rolling" with chitchat, but in other societies, such as many Native American ones and the working-class Irish in Belfast, long silences are perfectly companionable (Chaika 1989, p. 107).

REFERENCES

Alexander, P., VanKammer, D. and Bunney, W. (1979). Antipsychotic effects of lithium in schizophrenia. *American Journal of Psychiatry,* 136, 283–287.

Allen, H.A. 1985. Can all schizophrenic speech be discriminated from normal speech? *British Journal of Clinical Psychology.* 24:209–210.

Allen, H.A. and D.S. Allen. 1985. Positive symptoms and the organization within and between ideas in schizophrenic speech. *Psychological Medicine.* 15:71–80.

Andreasen, N.C. 1979a. Thought, language and communication disorders: Clinical assessment, definition of terms, and evaluation of their reliability. *Archives of General Psychiatry.* 36:1315–1321.

Andreasen, N.C. 1979b. Thought, language, and communication disorders. II. Diagnostic significance. *Archives of General Psychiatry.* 36:1325–1330.

Andreasen, N.C. 1982a. Should the term "thought disorder" be revised? *Comprehensive Psychiatry.* 23:291–299.

Andreasen, N.C. 1982b. Negative symptoms in schizophrenia: Definition and reliability. *Archives of General Psychiatry.* 39:784–788.

Andreasen, N.C. and S. Olsen. 1982. Negative vs positive schizophrenia: Definition and validation. *Archives of General Psychiatry.* 39:789–794.

Andreasen, N.C. and W.M. Grove. 1986. Thought, language, and communication in schizophrenia: Diagnosis and Prognosis. *Schizophrenia Bulletin.* 12:348–359.

Austin, J.L. 1962. *How to Do Things with Words,* 2d ed., J. Urmson and M. Sbisa, eds. Cambridge, Mass.: Harvard University Press.

Bach, K. and R.M. Harnish. 1979. *Linguistic Communication and Speech Acts.* Cambridge, Mass.: MIT Press.

Bannister, D. 1960. Conceptual structure in thought-disordered schizophrenics. *Journal of Mental Science.* 160:1230–1249.

Bannister, D. 1962. The nature and measurement of schizophrenic thought disorder. *Journal of Mental Science.* 108:825–842.

Bateson, G. 1972. *Steps to an Ecology of the Mind.* San Francisco: Chandler Publishing.

Benson, F. Psychiatric aspects of aphasia. *British Journal of Psychiatry.* 1973, 123:555–566.

Berenbaum, H., T.F. Oltmanns, and I. I. Gottesman. 1985. Formal thought disorder in schizophrenics and their twins. *Journal of Abnormal Psychology.* 94:3–16.

Bernstein, B. 1971. *Class Codes and Control,* vol. 1. London: Routledge & Kegan-Paul.

Berwick, R.C. and A.S. Weinberg. 1984. *The Grammatical Basis of Linguistic Performance.* Cambridge, Mass.: MIT Press.

Bickerton, D. 1981. *The Roots of Language.* Ann Arbor: Karoma.

Bickhard, M. 1987. The social nature of the functional nature of language. In

Hickman, M., ed. 1987. *Social and Functional Approaches to Language and Thought.* New York: Academic Press. pp. 39–65.

Bleuler, E. 1911. J. Zinkin, transl. [reprinted 1950] *Dementia Praecox or the Group of Schizophrenias.* New York: International Universities Press.

Bloom, L. 1970. *Language Development: Form and Function in Emerging Grammars.* Cambridge, Mass.: MIT Press.

Boomer, D.S. 1965. Hesitations and grammatical encoding. In S. Muscovici, ed. *The Psychosociology of Language.* Chicago: Markham Publishing.

Bresnan, J. 1978. A realistic transformational grammar. In M. Halle, J. Bresnan, and G.A. Miller, eds. *Linguistic Theory and Psychological Reality.* Cambridge, Mass.: MIT Press.

Brown, G. and G. Yule. 1983. *Discourse Analysis.* New York: Cambridge University Press.

Brown, J. 1977. *Mind, Brain, and Consciousness.* New York: Academic Press.

Brown, R. 1973. *A First Language: The Early Stages.* Cambridge, Mass.: Harvard University Press.

Brown, R. 1973. Schizophrenia, language, and reality. *American Psychologist.* May, 395–403.

Buckingham, H. A. and Kertesz. 1974. A linguistic analysis of fluent aphasia. *Brain and Language.* I: 43–62.

Buckingham, H., H. Whitaker, and H.A. Whitaker. 1979. On linguistic perseveration. In H. Whitaker and H.A. Whitaker, eds. *Studies in Neurolinguistics,* vol 4.

Caplan, D., ed. 1980. *Biological Studies of Mental Processes.* Cambridge, Mass.: MIT Press.

Carlson, L. 1983. *Dialogue Games: an Approach to Discourse Analysis.* Boston: D. Reidel Publishing Co.

Chafe, W. 1970. *Meaning and the Structure of Language.* Chicago: University of Chicago Press.

Chafe, W., ed. 1980. *The Pear Stories.* Norwood, N.J.: Ablex Publishing.

Chaika, E. 1974. A linguist looks at "schizophrenic" language. *Brain and Language.* 1:257–276.

Chaika, E. 1976. The possibility principle in semantics, *Interfaces.* pp. 9–12.

Chaika, E. 1977. Schizophrenic speech, slips of the tongue, and jargonaphasia: A reply to Fromkin and to Lecours and Vanier-Clement. *Brain and Language.* 4:464–475.

Chaika, E. 1981. How shall a discourse be understood? *Discourse Processes.* 4:71–87.

Chaika, E. 1982a. A unified explanation for the diverse structural deviations reported for adult schizophrenics with disrupted speech. *Journal of Communication Disorders.* 15:167–189.

Chaika, E. 1982b. *Language: The Social Mirror.* Rowley, MA: Newbury House.

Chaika, E. 1982c. Accounting for linguistic data in schizophrenia research. *Brain and Behavior Science.* 5:594–595.

Chaika, E. 1982d. Thought disorder or speech disorder in schizophrenia. *Schizophrenia Bulletin.* 8:587–591.

Chaika, E. 1982e. Normal and psychotic encoding of narrative. Linguistic Society of America. Annual meeting. San Diego, Calif.

Chaika, E. 1983a. Linguistics looks at psychiatry: A Study in the Analysis of Discourse. In R. DiPietro, W. Frawley, and A. Wedel, eds. *The First Delaware Symposium on Language Studies: Selected Papers.* Newark: University of Delaware Press. pp. 106–117.

Chaika, E. 1983b. Cohesion in normal and psychotic narrative. Linguistic Society of America. Annual meeting. Minneapolis, Minn.

Chaika, E. and R. Lambe. 1985. The locus of dysfunction in schizophrenic speech. *Schizophrenia Bulletin.* 11:9–15.

Chaika, E. and R. Lambe. 1986. Is schizophrenia a semiotic disorder? A reply to Lanin-Kettering and Harrow. *Schizophrenia Bulletin.* 9:305–328.

Chaika, E. and P. Alexander. 1986. The ice cream stories: A study in normal and psychotic narrations. *Discourse Processes.* 9:305–328.

Chaika, E. 1989. *Language the Social Mirror,* 2nd ed. New York: Harper and Row, Newbury House Publishers.

Chapman, L., J. Chapman, and G. Miller. 1964. A theory of verbal behavior in schizophrenia. In B. Maher, ed. *Progress in Experimental Personality Research,* vol. 1. New York: Academic Press.

Chapman, L., J. Chapman, and R. Daut. 1976. Schizophrenic inability to disattend from strong aspects of meaning. *Journal of Abnormal Psychology.* 85:35–40.

Chapman, J. 1966. The early symptoms of schizophrenia. *British Journal of Psychiatry.* 112:225–251.

Chomsky, N. and M. Halle. 1968. *The Sound Pattern of English.* New York: Harper & Row.

Clark, E. V. 1971. On the acquisition of the meaning of *before* and *after. Journal of Verbal Learning and Verbal Behavior.* 10:266–274.

Clark, E.V. 1972. On the child's acquisition of antonyms in two semantic fields. *Journal of Verbal Learning and Verbal Behavior.* 11:750–758.

Clark, E.V. 1973. What's in a word? On the child's acquisition of semantics in his first language. In T.E. Moore, ed. *Cognitive Development and the Acquisition of Language.* New York: Academic Press.

Clark, H. and E. Clark. 1977. *Psychology and Language.* New York: Harcourt, Brace, and Jovanovich.

Clark, H. and C. R. Marshall. 1981. Definite reference and mutual knowledge. In: B. Webber, L. Aravind, K. Joshi, and I. A. Sag, eds. 1981. *Elements of Discourse Understanding.* 1981. New York: Cambridge University Press. pp. 11–63

Cohen, B. 1978. Referent communication disturbances in schizophrenia. In S. Schwartz, ed. *Language and Cognition in Schizophrenia.* Hillsdale, N.J.: Lawrence Erlbaum.

Cohen, B. 1978. Referent communication disturbances in schizophrenia. In S. Schwartz, ed. *Language and Cognition in Schizophrenia.* Hillsdale, N.J.: Lawrence Erlbaum.

Cook-Gumperz, J. and J. L. Green. 1984. A sense of story: influences on children's storytelling ability. In Tannen, ed. *Coherence in Spoken and Written Discourse.* Norwood, N.J.: Ablex Publishing.

Cozzolino, L.J. 1983. The oral and written productions of schizophrenic patients. *Progress in Personality Research,* vol. 12. New York: Academic Press. pp. 101–152.

Cromwell, R. 1984. preemtive thinking and schizophrenia research. *Nebraska Sym posium on Motivation 1983.* Lincoln, Neb.: University of Nebraska Press. pp. 1–45.

Cummins, R. 1983. *The Nature of Psychological Explanation.* Cambridge, Mass.: MIT Press.

Curtiss, S. 1977. *Genie: A Psycholinguistic Study of a Modern Day "Wild Child."* New York: Academic Press.

deBeaugrande, R. and W.U. Dressler. 1981. *Introduction to Text Linguistics.* New York: Longmans.

Dell, G. and P. Reich. 1977. To err is (no longer necessarily) human. *Interfaces.* 6:9–12.

DiSimone, F.G., F. Darley, and A. Aronson. Patterns of dysfunction in schizophrenic patients on an aphasia test battery. *Journey of Hearing and Speech Disorder.* 1977, 42, 498–513.

Donaldson, M. and R. Wales. 1970. On the acquisition of some relational terms. In J. Hayes, ed. *Cognition and the Development of Language.* New York: John Wiley & Sons.

Eakins, B.W. and R.G. Eakins. 1978. *Sex Differences in Human Communication.* Boston: Houghton-Mifflin.

Edelson, M. 1978. What is the psychanalyst talking about? In J.H. Smith, ed. *Psychoanalysis and Language,* vol. 3. New Haven, Conn.: Yale University Press.

Ehlich, K. 1982. Anaphor and deixis: same or different. In R.J. Jarvella and W. Klein. *Speech, Place, and Action.* New York: John Wiley & Sons, Ltd. pp. 315–357.

Ervin-Tripp, S. On sociolinguistic rules: alternation and co-occurrence. *In Directions in Sociolinguistics.* Gumperz, J. and Hymes, D. (eds.) New York, Holt Rinehart, and Winston, 1972.

Erteschik-Schir, N. 1981. More on the extractability from quasi-NP's. *Linguistic Inquiry.* 12:665–670.

Ervin, S. 1964. Imitation and structural change. In E. Lenneberg, ed. *New Directions in the Study of Language.* Cambridge, Mass.: MIT Press.

Fauconnier, G. 1985. *Mental Spaces: Aspects of Meaning Construction in Natural Language.* Cambridge, Mass.: MIT Press.

Ferrara, A. 1985. Pragmatics. In T. Van Dijk, ed. *Handbook of Discourse Analysis,* vol 2. New York: Academic Press. pp. 137–157.

Fillmore, C.J. 1966. Toward a modern theory of case. In D.A. Reibel and S.A. Schane, eds. *Modern Studies in English.* Englewood Cliffs, N.J.: Prentice-Hall.

Fillmore, C.J. 1982a. Frame semantics. The Linguistic Society of Korea, ed. *Linguistics in the Morning Sun.* pp. 31–60.

Fillmore, C.J. 1984. Some thoughts on the boundaries and components of linguistics. In T. G. Bever, J. M. Carroll, and L.A. Miller. *Talking Minds: The Study of Language in the Cognitive Sciences.* Cambridge, Mass.: MIT Press., pp. 73–108.

Fillmore, C.J. 1985. Linguistics as a tool for discourse analysis. In T. Van Dijk, ed. *Handbook of Discourse Analysis,* vol. 1. New York: Academic Press. pp. 11–40.

Flor-Henry, P. 1976. Lateralized temporal-limbic function and psychopathology. In S.R. Harnad, H.D. Steklis, and J. Lancaster, eds. *Origins and Evolution of Language and Speech.* New York: New York Academy of Sciences.

Fodor, J.A. and T.G. Bever. 1965. The psychological reality of linguistic segments. *Journal of Verbal Learning and Verbal Behavior.* 4:414–420.

Forrest, D. 1965. Poesis and the language of schizophrenia. *Psychiatry.* 28:1–18.

Forrest, D. 1976. Nonsense and sense in schizophrenic language. *Schizophrenia Bulletin.* 2:286–298.

Forster, K. 1978. Accessing the mental lexicon. In E. Walker, ed. *Explorations in the Biology of Language.* Montgomery, Vt.: Bradford Books.

Foss, D.J. and D. T. Hakes. 1978. *Psycholinguistics: An Introduction to the Psychology of Language.* Englewood Cliffs, N.J.: Prentice-Hall.

Fraser, B. 1979. The interpretation of novel metaphors. In A. Ortony, ed. 1979. *Metaphor and Thought.* New York: Cambridge University Press. pp. 172–185.

Fraser, W.I., K.M. King, P. Thomas, and R.E. Kendell. 1986. The diagnosis of schizophrenia by language analysis. *British Journal of Psychiatry.* 148:275–278.

Fromkin, V. A. 1971. The non-anomalous nature of anomalous utterances. *Language.* 47:27–52.

Fromkin, V.A. 1975. A linguist looks at "A linguist looks at 'schizophrenic language.'" *Brain and Language.* 2:498–503.

Fromkin, V. and R. Rodman. 1983. *An Introduction to Language.* 3d ed. New York: Holt, Rinehart, and Winston.

Fromkin, V., ed. 1973. *Speech Errors as Linguistic Evidence.* The Hague: Mouton.

Gazdar, G. 1978. *Pragmatics.* New York: Academic Press.

Gleason, H.A. 1955. *Workbook in Descriptive Linguistics.* New York: Holt, Rinehart, and Winston.

Gleitman, L., H. Gleitman, and E. Shipley. 1972. The emergence of child as grammarian. *Cognition.* 2/3:137–164.

Gleitman, L. R. and H. Gleitman. 1970. *Phrase and Paraphrase: Some Innovative Uses of Language.* New York: W. W. Norton.

Goffman, E. 1955. On facework. *Psychiatry.* 18:213–231.

Goffman, E. 1981. *Forms of Talk.* Philadelphia: University of Pennsylvania Press.

Goldman-Eisler, F. 1958. The predictability of words in context and the length of pauses in speech. *Language and Speech.* 1:226–231.

Goody, E., ed. 1978. *Questions and Politeness: Strategies in Social Interaction.* New York: Cambridge University Press.

Gordon, D. and G. Lakoff. 1975. Conversational postulates. In P. Cole and J.L. Morgan, eds. *Syntax and Semantics, vol. 3: Speech Acts.* New York: Academic Press.

Green, E. 1985. Interhemispheric coordination and focused attention in chronic and acute schizophrenia. *British Journal of Psychology.* 24, 197–204.

Grice, H.P. 1975. Logic and conversation. In P. Cole and J. Morgan, eds. *Syntax and Semantics: Speech Acts,* vol. 3. New York: Academic Press.

Grice, H. P. 1981. Presupposition and conversational implicature. In P. Cole, ed. *Radical Pragmatics.* New York: Academic Press.

Grice, H. P. 1981. Presupposition and conversational implicature. In P. Cole, ed. *Radical Pragmatics.* New York: Academic Press.

Grimes, J. 1975. *The Thread of Discourse.* The Hague: Mouton.

Grove, W. M. and N. C. Andreasen. 1985. Language and thinking in psychosis. *Archives of General Psychiatry.* 42:26–32.

Grumet, G. W. 1985. On speaking to oneself. *Psychiatry.* 48:180–195.

Halliday, M.A.K. 1985a. *An Introduction to Functional Grammar.* Baltimore: Edward Arnold.

Halliday, M.A.K. 1985b. Dimensions of discourse analysis: grammar. In T. Van Dijk, ed. *Handbook of Discourse Analysis,* vol 2. New York: Academic Press. pp. 29–56.

Halliday, M.A.K. and R. Hasan. 1976. *Cohesion in English.* London: Longmans.

Hallowell, E.M. and H.F. Smith. 1983. Communication through poetry in the therapy of a schizophrenic patient. *Journal of the American Academy of Psychoanalysis.* 11:133–158.

Harrow, M. and D. M. Quinlan. 1985. *Disordered Thinking and Schizophrenic Psychopathology.* New York: Gardner Press.

Harrow, M., I. Lanin-Kettering, M. Prosen, and J.G. Miller. 1983. Disordered thinking in schizophrenia: Intermingling and loss of set. *Schizophrenia Bulletin.* 12:354–367.

Hart, D.S. and R.W. Payne. 1973. Language structure and predictability in over-inclusive patients. *British Journal of Psychiatry.* 123:643–652.

Harvey, P.D. and J. Neale. 1983. The specificity of thought disorder to schizophrenia: research methods in their historical perspective. *Progress in Experimental Personality Research,* vol. 12. pp. 153–180.

Harvey, P.D., E.A. Earle-Boyer, and M.S. Wielgus. 1984. The consistency of thought disorder in mania and schizophrenia. *The Journal of Nervous and Mental Disease.* 172:458–463.

Hasan, R. 1985. *Meaning, Context and Text.* In J.D. Benson and W.S. Greaves, eds. *Systemic Perspectives on Discourse,* vol. 1. Norwood, N.J.: Ablex Publishing. pp. 16–49.

Haskell, R.E. 1978. Lacanian psycholinguistics: The way in. *Interfaces.* 9:15–21.

Herbert, R.K. and K. Z. Waltensperger. 1982. Linguistics, psychology, and psychopathology: The case of schizophrenic language. In L. Obler and L. Menne. *Exceptional Language and Linguistics.* New York: Academic Press.

Hickman, M. 1986. Psychosocial aspects of language acquisition. In P. Fletcher and M. Garman, eds. 1986. *Language Acquisition,* 2nd ed. Cambridge: Cambridge University Press. pp. 9–29.

Holloway, R. 1977. "The unconscious is structured like a language." What does Lacan Mean? *Interfaces.* 7:15–21.

Holloway, R. 1978. Psychoanalysis as linguistic analysis—An examination of the theories of Habermas and Lacan. *Interfaces.* 10:13–14.

Holzman, L. and F. Newman. 1987. Thought and language about history. In Hickman, M., ed. 1987. *Social and Functional Approaches to Language and Thought.* New York: Academic Press. Pp. 105–121.

Holzman, P. 1978. Cognitive impairment and cognitive stability: towards a theory of thought disorder. In G. Serban, ed., *Cognitive Defects in the Development of Mental Illness.* New York: Brunner/Mazel.

Holzman, P., D. Levy, and L. Proctor. 1978. The several qualities of attention in schizophrenia. In L. Wynne et al, eds. *The Nature of Schizophrenia.* New York: John Wiley & Sons.

Holzman, P.S., M.E. Shenton, and M.R. Solovay. 1986. Quality of thought disorder in differential diagnosis. *Schizophrenia Bulletin.* 12:360–371.

Jacobson, P. and G.K. Pullum. 1982. *The Nature of Syntactic Representation.* Boston: D. Reidel Publishing.

Jarrett, D. 1984. Pragmatic coherence in an oral formulaic tradition. In D. Tannen, ed. *Coherence in Spoken and Written Discourse.* Norwood, N.J.: Ablex Publishing.

Jefferson, G. 1978. Sequential aspects of story-telling. In J. Schenkein, ed. *Studies in the Organization of Conversational Interaction.* New York: Academic Press.

Jeng, H. 1982. The development of topic and subject in Chinese and English. Linguistic Society of Korea, ed. *Linguistics in the Morning Calm.* Seoul: Hanshin Publishing.

Johnston, J. R. 1985. The discourse symptoms of developmental disorders. In T. Van Dijk, ed. *Handbook of Discourse Analysis,* vol 3. New York: Academic Press. pp. 79–93.

Julia, P. 1983. *Explanatory Models in Linguistics: A Behavioral Perspective.* Princeton, N.J.: Princeton University Press.

Kaplan, B. 1957. On the phenomena of "opposite speech." *Journal of Abnormal Social Psychology.* 55:389–393.

Kay, P. and W. Kempton. 1984. What is the Sapir-Whorf hypothesis? *American Anthropologist.* 86:65–79.

Kearns, J.T. 1984. *Using Language: The Structures of Speech Acts.* Albany: State University of New York.

Kozulin, A. 1986., Vygotsky in context. In L.S. Vygotsky. *Thought and Language.* Kozulin, ed. and transl. Cambridge, Mass.: MIT Press.

Kreckel, M. 1981. *Communicative Acts and Shared Knowledge in Natural Discourse.* New York: Academic Press.

Kuczaj II, S. 1983. *Crib Speech and Language Play.* New York: Springer Verlag.

Kufferle, B. G. Lenz and H. Schanda. 1985. Clinical evaluation of language and thought disorders in patients with schizophrenic and affective psychoses. *Psychopathology.* 18:126–132.

Kuno, S. 1987. *Functional Syntax: Anaphora, Discourse, and Empathy.* Chicago: University of Chicago Press.

Labov, W. 1969. The logic of nonstandard English. In J. Alatis, ed. 1970. *Bilingualism and Language Contact: Anthropological, Linguistic, Psychological and Sociological Aspects.* Monograph Series on Languages and Linguistics. Washington, D.C.: Georgetown University Press.

Labov, W. 1972. Rules for ritual insults. In W. Labov, ed. *Language in the Inner City.* Philadelphia: University of Pennsylvania Press.

Labov, W. and D. Fanshel. 1977. *Therapeutic Discourse: Psychotherapy as Conversation.* New York: Academic Press.

LaFerriere, D. 1977. The poet's modest madness. *5 Russian Poems.* Englewood Cliffs, N.J.: Transworld.

Laffal,. 1965. *Pathological and Normal Language.* New York: Atherton Press.

Lakoff, G. 1987. *Women, Fire, and Dangerous Things: What Categories Reveal about the Mind.* Chicago: University of Chicago Press.

Lakoff, G. and M. Johnson. 1980. *Metaphors We Live By.* Chicago: University of Chicago Press.

Lakoff, R. 1972. Language in context. *Language.* 48:907–927.

Lakoff, R. 1975. *Language and Woman's Place.* New York: Harper and Row.

Lanin-Kettering, I. and M. Harrow. 1985. The thought behind the words: A view of schizophrenic speech and thinking disorders. *Schizophrenia Bulletin.* 11:1–7.

Lashley, K. A. The problem of serial order in behavior. In L.A. Jeffress, ed. *Cerebral Mechanisms in Behavior.* New York: John Wiley and Sons.

Lecours, A.R. and M. Vanier-Clement. 1976. Schizophasia and jargonaphasia: comparative description with comments on Chaika's and Fromkin's respective looks at "schizophrenic" language. *Brain and Language.* 3:516–565.

Lee, B. 1987. Recontextualizing Vygotsky. In M. Hickman, ed. *Social and Functional Approaches to Language and Thought.* New York: Academic Press., pp. 87–104.

Lee, S–O. 1982. On glossolalia. In *Linguistics in the Morning Calm.* The Linguistic Society of Korea. Seoul: Hanshin Publishing, pp. 551–555.

Lehrer, A. 1983. *The Semantics of Wine Tasting.* Bloomington: Indiana University Press.

Levinson, S. C. 1983. *Pragmatics.* New York: Cambridge University Press.

Levin, S.R. 1977. *The Semantics of Metaphor.* Baltimore: Johns Hopkins University Press.

Lieberman, P. 1984. *The Biology and Evolution of Language.* Cambridge, Mass.: Harvard University Press.

Lorenz, M. 1961. Problems posed by schizophrenic language. *Archives of General Psychiatry.* 4:603–610.

Lucy, J. and J. W. Wertsch. 1987. Vygotsky and Whorf: a comparative analysis. In M. Hickman., ed. 1987. *Social and Functional Approaches to Language and Thought.* New York: Academic Press. Pp. 67–86.

Lyons, J. 1977. *Semantics.* vols. 1, 2. Cambridge: Cambridge University Press.

Mac Cormac, E.R. 1985. *A Cognitive Theory of Metaphor.* Cambridge, Massachusetts: A Bradford Book: MIT Press.

Maclay, H. & C. Osgood. 1959. Hesitation phenomena in spontaneous English speech. *Word.* 15:19–44.

Macnamara, J. 1977. On the relation between language learning and thought. In J. Macnamara, ed. *Language Learning and Thought.* New York: Academic Press. pp. 1–9.

Maher, B. 1968. The shattered language of schizophrenia. *Psychology Today.*

Maher, B. 1972. The language of schizophrenia: A review and an interpretation. *British Journal of Psychiatry.* 120:4–17.

Maher, B.A. 1983. A tentative theory of schizophrenic utterance. *Progress in Experimental Personality Research,* vol. 12. New York: Academic Press.

Maher, B., K. McKeon, and B. McLaughlin. 1966. Studies in psychotic language. In P. Stone, D. Dunphy, and D. Ogilvie, eds. *General Inquirer.* Cambridge, Mass.: MIT Press. pp. 469–501.

Manschreck, T.C., B. A. Maher, T. M. Hoover, and D. Ames. 1985. Repetition in schizophrenic speech. *Language and Speech.* 28:255–267.

Martin, R.M. 1987. *The Meaning of Language.* Cambridge, Mass.: MIT Press.

McCawley, J.D. 1986. What linguists might contribute to dictionary making if they could get their act together. In P. C. Bjarkman and V. Raskin. 1986. *The Real World Linguist: Linguistic Applications in the 1980s.* Norwood, N.J.: Ablex Publishing, pp. 1–18.

McNeill, D. 1979. *The Conceptual Basis of Language.* Hillsdale, N.J.: Lawrence Erlbaum Associates.

McNeill, D. and E. Levy. 1982. Conceptual representations in language activity and gesture. In R. J. Jarvella, and W. Klein. 1982. *Speech, Place, and Action.* New York: John Wiley & Sons, pp. 271–295.

Menyuk, P. 1969. *Sentences Children Use.* Cambridge, Mass.: MIT Press.

Menyuk, P. 1971. *The Acquisition and Development of Language.* Englewood Cliffs, N.J.: Prentice-Hall.

Miller, G.A. 1978. Semantic relations among words. In M. Halle, J. Bresnan, and G.A. Miller, eds. *Linguistic Theory and Psychological Reality.* Cambridge, Mass.: MIT Press. pp. 60–118.

Miller, G.A. 1982. Some problems in the theory of demonstrative reference. In R.J. Jarvella and W. Klein. 1982. *Speech, Place, and Action.* New York: John Wiley & Sons, pp. 61–72.

Montague, R. 1973. On the proper treatment of quantification in ordinary English. In K. J. Hintikka, J. M. E. Moravcsik, and P. Suppes eds. *Approaches to Natural Language: Proceedings of the 1970 Stanford Workshop on Grammar and Semantics.* Dordrecht: D. Reidel Publishing.

Morton, J. 1979. Word recognition. In J. Morton and J. Marshall, eds. *Psycholinguistics 2: Structures and Processes.* Cambridge, Mass.: MIT Press.

Mowrer, O. H. 1980. *Psychology of Language and Learning.* New York: Plenum Press

Neale, J. M., T. F. Oltmanns, and P. D. Harvey. 1985. The need to relate cognitive deficits to specific behavioral referents of schizophrenia. *Schizophrenia Bulletin.* 11:286–291.

Neisser, U. 1976. *Cognition and Reality.* San Francisco: W.H. Freeman.

O'Barr, W. M. 1982. *Linguistic Evidence: Language, Power, and Strategy in the Courtroom.* New York: Academic Press.

Ochs, E. 1987. Input: a socio-cultural perspective. In M. Hickman, ed. 1987. *Social and Functional Approaches to Language and Thought.* New York: Academic Press. pp. 305–319.

Ortony, A. 1979. The role of similarity in similes and metaphors. In A. Ortony, ed. *Metaphor and Thought.* Norwood, N.J.: Ablex Publishing, pp. 186–201.

Paprotte, W. and C. Sinha. 1987. A functional perspective on early language development. In M. Hickman, ed. 1987. *Social and Functional Approaches to Language and Thought.* New York: Academic Press. Pp. 203–222.

Polyani, L. 1985. *Telling the American Story: A Structural and Cultural Analysis of Conversational Storytelling.* Norwood, N.J.: Ablex Publishing.

Prince, E. 1981. Towards a taxonomy of given-new information. In P. Cole, ed. *Radical Pragmatics*. New York: Academic Press, pp. 223–255.

Prince, G. 1982. *Narratology: The Form and Functioning of Narrative*. New York: Mouton Publishers.

Quirk, R. and J. Svartvik. 1966. *Investigating Linguistic Acceptability*. The Hague: Mouton.

Ragin, A.B. and T.F. Oltmanns. 1986. Lexical cohesion and formal thought disorder during and after psychotic episodes. *Journal of Abnormal Psychology*. 95:181–183.

Reilly, F., M. Harrow, and G. Tucker. 1973. Language and thought content in acute psychosis. *American Journal of Psychiatry*. 130:411–417.

Reilly, F., M. Harrow, G. Tucker, D. Quinlan, and A. Siegel. 1975. Looseness of associations in acute schizophrenia. *British Journal of Psychiatry*. 127:240–246.

Robertson, J. and S. Shamsie. 1958. A systematic examination of gibberish in a multilingual schizophrenic patient. In H. Vetter, ed. 1968. *Language Behavior in Schizophrenia*.

Rochester, S. and Martin J. The art of referring: the speaker's use of noun phrases to instruct the listener. In *Discourse Production and Comprehension*. Freedle, R. (ed.) Norwood, N.J.: Ablex Publishing, 1977.

Rochester, S., J. Martin, and S. Thurston. 1977. Thought process disorder in schizophrenia: The listener's task. *Brain and Language*, 4, 95–114.

Rochester, S., S. Thurston, and J. Rupp. 1977. Hesitations as clues to failures in coherence: a study of the thought disordered speaker. In S. Rosenberg, ed. *Sentence Production: Developments in Research and Theory*. New Jersey: Lawrence Erlbaum Associates.

Rosch, E. 1973. Natural categories. *Cognitive Psychology*. 4:328–350.

Rosch, E. 1975. Cognitive representations of semantic categories. *Journal of Experimental Psychology: General* 104:192–233.

Rosch, E. 1977. Linguistic relativity. In P.N. Johnson and P.C. Wason, eds. *Thinking: Readings in Cognitive Science*. New York: Cambridge University Press. pp. 501–519.

Rosch, E. 1981. Principles and categorization. In E. Rosch and B.B. Lloyd, eds. 1978. *Cognition and Categorization*. Hillsdale, N.J.: Lawrence Erlbaum Associates. pp. 27–48.

Rumelhart, D.E. 1979. Some problems with the notion of nonliteral meanings. A. Ortony, ed. 1979. *Metaphor and Thought*. New York: Cambridge University Press. pp. 78–91.

Rutter, D.R. 1985. Language in schizophrenia: The structure of monologues and conversations. *British Journal of Psychiatry*. 146:399–404.

Sacks, H. 1964–1972. Lecture notes. Mimeo (unpublished). University of California.

Salzinger, K., S. Portnoy, and R. Feldman. 1978. Communicability deficit in schizophrenics resulting from a more general disability. In S. Schwartz, ed. *Language and Cognition in Schizophrenia*. New York: Academic Press.

Sanders, G. and J. Wirth. 1985. Discourse, pragmatics, and linguistic form. In J. Wirth, ed., *Beyond the sentence: Discourse and Sentential form*. Ann Arbor: Karoma Press. 1985:1–19

Sanders, R.E. 1987. *Cognitive Foundations of Calculated Speech: Controlling Understand-*

ings in Conversation and Persuasion. Albany, N.Y.: State University of New York Press.

Schatzman, L. and A. Strauss. 1972. Social class and modes of communication. In S. Muscovici, ed. *The Psychosociology of Language.* Chicago: Markham. pp. 206–221.

Schegloff, E. A. 1971. Notes on a conversational practise: formulating place. In D. Sudnow, ed. *Studies in Social Interaction.* New York: Free Press.

Scollon, R. and S. Scollon. 1981. *Narrative, Literacy and Face in Interethnic Communication.* Norwood, N.J.: Ablex Publishing.

Scribner, S. 1977. Modes of thinking and ways of speaking: Culture and logic reconsidered. In P.N. Johnson and P. C. Wason, eds. *Thinking: Readings in Cognitive Science.* New York: Cambridge University Press. pp. 483–500.

Searle, J. R. 1969. *Speech Acts: An Essay in the Philosophy of Language.* New York: Academic Press.

Searle, J. R. 1975. Indirect speech acts. *In Syntax and Semantics,* vol 3. P. Cole, and J. Morgan, ed. New York: Academic Press.

Searle, J. R. 1983. *Intentionality: An Essay in the Philosophy of Mind.* New York: Cambridge University Press.

Seeman, M. and H. Cole. 1977. The effect of increasing personal contact in schizophrenia. *Comprehensive Psychiatry.* 18:283–292.

Seuren, P. A. M. 1985. *Discourse Semantics.* New York: Basil Blackwell.

Sharrock, W. W. & R. Turner. 1978. On a conversational environment for equivocality. In J. Schenkein, ed. *Studies in Organizational Interaction.* New York: Academic Press.

Shimkunas, A. 1978. Hemispheric asymmetry and schizophrenic thought disorder. In S. Schwartz, ed. *Language and Cognition in Schizophrenia.* New York: Lawrence Erlbaum Associates.

Silverstein, M. 1987. The three faces of "function": Preliminaries to a psychology of language. In M. Hickman, ed. *Social and Functional Approaches to Language and Thought.* New York: Academic Press. pp. 17–38.

Simpson, D.M. and G. C. Davis. 1985. Measuring thought disorder with clinical rating scales in schizophrenic and nonschizophrenic patients. *Psychiatry Research.* 15:313–318.

Slobin, D. 1982. Universal and particular in the acquisition of language. In E. Wanner and L.R. Gleitman, eds. *Language Acquisition: The State of the Art.* New York: Cambridge University Press.

Sternberg, R.J., Torangeau, and G. Nigro. 1979. The convergence of macroscopic and microscopic views. In A. Ortony, ed. *Metaphor and Thought.* Norwood, N.J.: Ablex Publishing. pp. 325–353.

Stillings, N. Feinstein, M., Garfield, J., Rissland, E., Rosenbaum, D. Weisler, S. and Baker-Ward, L. 1987. *Cognitive Science: An Introduction.* 1987. Cambridge, Mass.: Bradford Books.

Stubbs, M. 1983. *Discourse Analysis: The Sociolinguistic Analysis of Natural Language.* Chicago: University of Chicago Press.

Svartvik, J. 1966. *On Voice in the English Verb.* The Hague: Mouton.

Sweetser, E. E. 1987. The definition of *lie:* An examination of the folk models underlying a semantic prototype. In D. Holland and N. Quinn, eds. 1987. *Cultural Models in Language and Thought.* New York: Cambridge University Press. pp. 43–66.

Szasz, T. 1976. *Schizophrenia.* New York: Basic Books.

Tannen, D. 1984. *Conversational Style: Analyzing Talk Among Friends.* Norwood, N.J.: Ablex Publishing.

Vachek, J., ed. 1964. *A Prague School Reader in Linguistics.* Bloomington, Ind. Indiana University Press.

VanDijk, T.A. 1977. *Text and Context: Explorations in the Semantics and Pragmatics of Discourse.* London: Longmans.

Van Dijk, T.A. 1980. *Macrostructures: An Interdisciplinary Study of Global Structures in Discourse, Interaction, and Cognition.* Hillsdale, N.J.: Lawrence Erlbaum Associates.

Vonnegut, M. 1976. *The Eden Express.* New York: Ballantine Books.

Vygotsky, L.S. 1934a. E. Hanfmann and G. Vakar, eds., transl. *Thought and Language.* 1962. Cambridge, Mass.: MIT Press.

Vygotsky, L.S. 1934b. A. Kozulin, ed., transl. *Thought and Language.* Cambridge, Mass.: MIT Press.

Wanner, E. and L. R. Gleitman. 1982. *Language Acquisition: The State of the Art.* New York: Cambridge University Press.

Werner, O., G. Lewis-Matichek, M. Evans, and B. Litowitz. 1975. An ethnoscience view of schizophrenic speech. In M. Sanches and B. Blount, eds. *Sociocultural Dimensions of Language Use.* New York: Academic Press.

Williams, J. M. 1981. *Style: Ten Lessons in Clarity and Grace.* Oakland, N.J.: Scott, Foresman.

Zimmerman, D.H. and C. West. 1975. Sex roles, interruptions, and silences in conversation. In B. Thorne and N. Henley, eds. *Language and Sex: Difference and Dominance.* Rowley, Mass.: Newbury House Publishers. pp. 105–129.

NAME INDEX

SUBJECT INDEX

subject vs predicate 255
  complete 258
subordinating structures 38
surprise 85
synecdoche 108
synonyms 13, 24
  as cause of glossomania 13
  non-substitutability between 13
synonymy 174
  and meaning networks 174
synonymy of *have* and *be* 21
syntactic boundaries 76
syntactic construction
  leaving out element in 127
syntactic error 202, 205, 207
syntactic form,
  overriding of 160
  as rule-governed 152
syntactic gapping 199, 204, 210
syntactico-semantic rules 103
syntactic structures 79
  complexity in psychotics 132
  processing of 77
  punctuation in 77
syntagmatic associations 34
syntax 78, 84, 214, 269
  correct, incomprehensible 219
  discourse-based 100 (*also see* context-free)
  explanatory power of 98, 100
  interpretation of 152
  and lexical choice 83
  and thoughts 54, 255
systematic delusions 46

tangentiality 147, 214
targets 151
TD vs NTD schizophrenics 132, 137
temporal misordering 86, 204, 210, 234
terminology 123, 254
  aphasia 52
  description vs explanation 147
  non-speech disordered (NSD) 4
  psychoanalytic 279
  speech disordered (SD) 4
terminology (*see* thought disordered or non-thought disordered 53)
testing 34, 289
text-as-product 125

texts
  many topics in 249
theme 255, 256, 257
  and discourse deviance 257
  and given information 258
  and human interest 256
  vs rheme 255, 258
theories
  accounting for data 28, 131, 140, 100, 103
  and interpretations 268
The Prague School 83
therapeutic interview 271, 275, 278
  avoidance of 19
  as context 281
therapist 277, 278
therapy, goal of 276
thought 31, 50, 56–57, 62, 251, 259
  intrusive in normals 288
  as non-visible process 60–62
  without verbalizing 60
  relative to syntax 54, 255 (*see also* speech, equivalence to thought)
thought disorder (TD) 31, 53–54, 56, 59, 251, 253, 255, 256, 260, 266
  correlation with speech (*see* speech, equivalence to thought)
  in manics 53
  non-specificity in diagnosis 54
  thoughts, kinds of 60
title
  and ICS task 252
  and meaning 251
TLC 54
topic 16, 17, 133, 138, 168, 214, 217, 221, 223, 237, 239, 245, 249, 240, 290, 294
  advancement of 130, 136, 222
  agreement on 249
  changing of 18, 223, 225, 228, 239, 248, 291
  constraining of 272
  as determinant of meaning 39, 239
  discourse and sentence 248
  expansion of 258
  extraneous matters 39
  global 239
  identifying conflict 277
  and new information 239
  and point of view 240